PENGUIN BOOKS
INDIA:
THE SIEGE WITHIN

M. J. Akbar, an Indian Muslim, was born in January 1951. His maternal grandfather, Mir Habibullah, was a Kashmiri who took his shawl business to Amritsar. In the chaos of 1947, Amritsar was emptied of Muslims and the family went as penniless refugees to Pakistan. His paternal grandfather was orphaned early in life, and ran away from the poverty of his village in Bihar to the industrial outskirts of Calcutta. A Hindu called Prayaag, he later converted to Islam and took the name Sheikh Rahamatullah. He remained in India because of his commitment to the Congress Party.

M. J. Akbar was educated at the Calcutta Boys' School and graduated with honours in English from Presidency College, Calcutta, in 1970. He then became a trainee sub-editor with the *Times of India* organization and was posted to the *Illustrated Weekly of India* under Khushwant Singh. He was given the job of editing the fortnightly magazine *Onlooker* of the Free Press Journal group in 1974 and joined the Ananda Bazar Group of Publications in Calcutta in 1976. Here he reshaped and edited the successful weekly magazine *Sunday*. In 1982, he conceived, designed and edited the new daily English newspaper of the group, *The Telegraph*, which soon achieved great success. Apart from editing these two publications, the author has also undertaken a great many on-the-spot reports and interviews.

M. J. AKBAR

INDIA:
THE SIEGE WITHIN

Penguin Books

Penguin Books Ltd, Harmondsworth, Middlesex, England
Viking Penguin Inc., 40 West 23rd Street, New York, New York 10010, U.S.A.
Penguin Books Australia Ltd, Ringwood, Victoria, Australia
Penguin Books Canada Ltd, 2801 John Street, Markham, Ontario, Canada L3R 1B4
Penguin Books (N.Z.) Ltd, 182–190 Wairau Road, Auckland 10, New Zealand

First published 1985

Made and printed in Great Britain by
Richard Clay (The Chaucer Press) Ltd,
Bungay, Suffolk
Filmset in 9/12pt Monophoto Photina by
Northumberland Press Ltd, Gateshead,
Tyne and Wear

Contents

III · KASHMIR

For Ammiji and Abbaji
with love and gratitude

Introduction

'To endeavour to understand the India of today would be the task of a brave man. To describe tomorrow's India would verge on madness.' – So said Jawaharlal Nehru, in the Maulana Azad Memorial Lecture, 1959.

There could hardly be a better judge of the problem than the first Prime Minister of free India. Historian, orator, man of letters, master of politics, visionary, head of government, often a victor, often a failure, democrat, dreamer, Nehru could not, in the end, win the independence of his country without seeing it partitioned. Mahatma Gandhi and his disciples, among them Nehru, were passionately committed to the unity of an India stretching from the Khyber Pass to Assam, and from Kashmir to Kerala. As Nehru wrote in his autobiography in 1936, perhaps no country in the world had been as truly made, geographically, for unity as India. What he also realized was that no country had as much potential for disunity – thanks partly to its misinterpreted history – as India. And between the reality of a well-defined, culturally interlinked land mass and the birth of a modern nation state would lie many pitfalls.

The very word 'partition' implies the division of a whole. The partition in 1947 was a defeat for Gandhi, Nehru and Maulana Azad, the Muslim leader who stayed with Gandhi rather than support Jinnah's two-nation theory. However, while Pakistan was conceded, a substantial part of multireligious, multiracial and multilingual India remained committed to one flag and a secular, democratic Constitution. But the ideas and forces which had divided the country once were not satiated; they would try again. In truth, only one of the two arguments – Gandhi's or Jinnah's – could be proved right by history: it was difficult to see how both could survive. What happened in 1947 was only a semicolon in the evolution of the subcontinent, not a full stop. Muslim communalism took the river Indus away from India and put it in Pakistan. Now, in the mid eighties, Sikh communalists are determined to create Khalistan. But the emerging question is: will the communalism of a section of the Hindu elite now divide the Ganga and destroy India? There was a shiver of dread on Wednesday 31 October 1984 when, at 9.38 in the morning, two Sikh guards satisfied their community's appetite for revenge by gunning down Mrs Indira Gandhi, and Hindus unleashed nationwide violence against the Sikhs. Had the oft-postponed nightmare finally begun? Mrs Gandhi had become a martyr, had given the ultimate sacrifice, but was there still a further price to pay?

'Long years ago,' said Nehru at the stroke of midnight on 15 August 1947, 'we made a tryst with destiny, and now the time comes when we shall redeem our pledge, not wholly or in full measure, but very substantially ... At the dawn of history India started on her unending quest, and trackless centuries are filled with her striving and the grandeur of her success and her failures ... Before the birth of freedom we have endured all the pains of labour and our hearts are heavy with the memory of this sorrow. Some of these pains continue even now ...' These pains have acquired a dangerous strength in the eighties.

But whose vision was correct in 1947, Gandhi's or Jinnah's? For the author the search for the answer had a personal dimension. I am an Indian Muslim; my maternal grandfather, Mir Habibullah, was a Kashmiri who took his shawl business to Amritsar. In the chaos of 1947, Amritsar was emptied of Muslims and my mother's side of the family went as penniless refugees to Pakistan. My paternal grandfather was orphaned early in life, and ran away from the poverty of his village in Bihar to seek sustenance in the industrial outskirts of Calcutta. He was a Hindu called Prayaag, but later, after he had managed to settle down, he converted to Islam and took the name Sheikh Rahamatullah. My parents were married before the partition which sent the two sections of the family into two countries; my father was urged to go to Pakistan but he remained loyal to the movement he belonged to, the Congress, and stayed in India despite the inevitable sorrow and suffering that he underwent during the riots. In a sense, 1947 was the crucial centre of their lives. I was a child born more than three years after that August midnight of 1947, and it was still vital to know – in the interests of my present as much as my future – where the truth lay. As a guide I took a couplet from that master Urdu poet Faiz Ahmed Faiz, which he wrote about August 1947:

> *Ye daagh daagh ujala, ye shab gazeeda sahar*
> *Woh intezaar tha jiska, ye woh sahar nahin hai*

– 'This stained dawn is not the one we waited for.'

This effort to learn would have been impossible without the extraordinary help and affection I received from friends and colleagues. I wish this did not sound so predictable, but I really do not know how else to put it. I first came to know Aveek and Arup Sarkar when they hired me to edit the weekly *Sunday*. Today they are also friends, but no person could expect or get as much help as they have given me. I do not know how to describe my gratitude. Three men have, in the last two decades, given me the education which has made my work possible: Professor Arun Kumar Dasgupta, my tutor at Presidency College, Calcutta; my affectionate editor at the *Illustrated Weekly of India*, Khushwant Singh; and the admirable Kuldip Nayar. To Khushwant Singh I am also grateful for his critical examination of the Punjab section, and to Kuldip for the documents which were in his possession and which he lent me.

To my colleague Shubhabrata Bhattacharya I owe a special debt of gratitude, not only for his help in the Kashmir section but also for the great consideration he showed. Manini Chatterjee was a gem; her enormous help in research and correction and her ungrudging generosity of time cannot be repaid. To my friends Zamir Ansari and Sonny Mehta I am thankful for advice about the difficult first section. Shekhar Bhatia (and, of course, Pakhi), Subir Roy, Tooshar Pandit, Ashis Ray and all my friends and colleagues in *The Telegraph* and *Sunday* gave enormous sustenance during these trying months when I was concentrating far more on the book than on my journalism. A special word of thanks to Farooq Abdullah and Vijay Dhar for their generous contribution of information about a past they were uniquely placed to know. Many thanks to Biswaranjan Sarkar and Tarun Karmakar for secretarial help, and to Tushar Sanyal and others in the Ananda Bazar library for unstinted co-operation.

The idea of this book owes much to Peter Mayer, a friend who showed faith when not a word had been written. And Peter Carson's guiding hand helped craft and shape the argument in a manner which taught me many lessons in editing.

There is one extraordinary person in my life to whom I can never be thankful enough. Mallika, my wife, has given me more love than I deserve, and built with love and care a home that has cocooned and nourished a difficult husband. In addition, her advice regarding the book was sharp and important. There has been no greater joy in my life than the love and company of my children, my daughter Mukulika and my son Prayaag, and this joy has become a unique rationale for life and work. The book is also a father's attempt to tell his children what he has learnt.

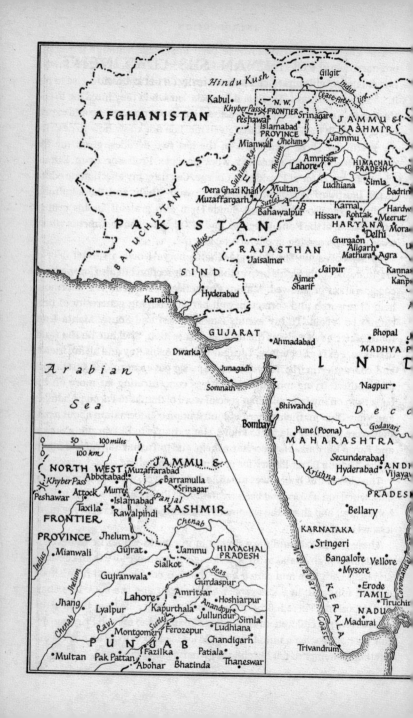

THE INDIAN SUB-CONTINENT
showing places mentioned in the text

```
          0     100      200      300 miles
          0   100  200  300  400  500 km
```

C H I N A

T I B E T

Brahmaputra

Kathmandu •
Darjeeling •

BHUTAN

A S S A M

Gauhati •

Patna •

H A R

BANGLADESH

Ganges

Dhaka
(Dacca) •

Hooghly

WEST

•mshedpur

Calcutta •
B E N G A L

Chittagong •

B U R M A

A

S S A

•neswar

Puri •

Bay of

Bengal

Rangoon •

PART I

THE BIRTH OF PAKISTAN
AND
THE SURVIVAL OF INDIA

1
The Rationale of 1947

The name India derives from Indus, the great river born in the Himalayas which sweeps down the north-west on its way to the Arabian Sea. 'Indus' itself is a variation of the Sanskrit word *sindhu*, meaning river. *The Oxford English Dictionary*, pointing out that King Alfred mentioned India in his manuscripts, notes that the name has, from before the birth of Christ, defined 'a large country or territory of southern Asia, lying east of the river Indus and south of the Himalaya mountains'. In 1947, the British left this large country free but divided. And the Indus which gave this land its name was now in the new nation of Pakistan.

Some historians have felt obliged to sell the thesis that the concept of India as one nation is a gift of British imperial power. The implication is that it is merely a matter of time before the unifying effects of the British empire wear off and the different lingual groups go back to the destructive warfare of the past. Among the recent theorists is David Page who writes in *Prelude to Partition* (Oxford University Press, 1982): 'Long before the foundation of the Indian National Congress or the All-India Muslim League, there existed in India a "national" organization whose ramifications extended into the remotest village – the Imperial power itself.'

The British took Delhi in 1857; the Indian National Congress was born in 1885. It must have been an extraordinary rule which in just three decades managed to integrate a territory as large as this subcontinent whose parts had, it seems, 'nothing in common' for thousands of years. Two hundred and fifty years before Christ, Ashoka's administration took Buddhism into every corner of India, but apparently did not leave any sense of common identity. Brihaspati's principles of natural justice have been a part of popular faith for centuries, but it is the British courts which allegedly gave India a sense of law. The Mughal emperor Akbar's administrative structures held together his vast empire in the sixteenth century, but we must believe that it is the British Collector in the district who taught Indians how to rule themselves. Shankara walked from Kerala to Kashmir to preach Hinduism before William of Normandy reached Britain, but it is the British railways which united India through a communications network! The argument of unity by courtesy of the British empire falls on many counts, but the simplest is that even in 1947 nearly half of this country was not ruled by the British but by their native allies, who employed Indian administrators. School maps did show the whole of India painted red, but the princely states were not technically a part of British India. A separate accession treaty had to be obtained from each one of the 565 princely states on this subcontinent at the time of independence.

India has, of course, been divided into an assortment of feudal kingdoms, their maps changing with the success or failure of different rulers. But it hardly behoves the European who knows anything about Germany or Italy to say that feudal divisions signify separate countries. Even across the barriers of language, there was a geographical and cultural sense of a single entity from the Sulaiman Range and the Hindu Kush in the north-west, to the Himalayas across the north, to the seas in the west, south and east. Irrespective of the number of kingdoms along the way, the Hindu did not need permission to go to Hardwar or to Banaras; nor the Muslim in later times to the shrine of Khwaja Moinuddin Chishti at Ajmer Sharif. Currents of faith and challenge flowed through this land independent of passing dynasties. The difference between the railways and the roads was simply a difference of pace, the difference between a new technology and an old one, not the difference between a new country and an old chaos.

What the British did bring were the latest ideas in political systems, jurisprudence and science. But the most important asset India got from the British was not so much something that the British offered as something that the Indians took: a democratic polity. It was in this idea and this structure that Mahatma Gandhi and the Congress found the solution to a modern India, one which could combine old heritage and modern aspiration and be strong enough to resist the extraordinary conflicts which human beings manage to devise for themselves. It was co-operative achievement, Gandhi believed, rather than class-based violent revolution or feudal-theocratic fascism, which could power a united India to prosperity. This, broadly, was the philosophy of the Congress nationalists.

Against this doctrine was ranged what has come to be known as the ideology of communalism. Simply put, its basic plank was that the different communities in India could not coexist to their mutual benefit, that the minorities would become victims of Hindu subjugation, and that neither history nor culture would allow co-operation. There were communalist parties representing all three major religions, Hindu, Muslim and Sikh. Democracy, instead of being seen as an asset, was called a liability. The Muslim League argued that in a one-man–one-vote system the minorities could never enter the ruling class since the overwhelming Hindu majority would successfully shut them out. Any examination of the population mix in united India would have exposed this argument as bogus, but it was simple enough to become useful propaganda. The very first demand of the Muslim League politicians, therefore, in the first decade of this century, was for separate electorates where Muslims could vote for Muslims and Hindus for Hindus. The British granted this demand very easily, which was not in the least surprising since it fitted well with their policy to keep Hindu and Muslim at each other's throats so they would not join hands and turn against the British. As the Muslim leader Mohammad Ali told Lord Sankey, presiding over the first round-table conference in November 1930: 'My Lord, divide and rule is the order of the day. But in India, we divide and you rule.' Hindu fanatics with their extravagant talk of Hindu domination reinforced minority fears and prejudices. Such Hindus wanted their own theocratic state where they could take 'revenge' on the Muslims and Christians for a curious anomaly of history: for seven hundred and fifty years no Hindu had held power in Delhi. From 1192 to 1857 Muslim kings, despite enormous fluctuations in the true extent of their control, had sat on the throne of Delhi. And in 1857 British Christians had replaced them.

But feudalism was a dead concept by the twentieth century. The nature of power and the terms of its acquisition in post-colonial India would be radically different. The legitimacy of the ruler would now be decided by the strength of the vote, not genetics or the sword. By the turn of the century the battle between the nationalists and the communalists began to control the mind of India. There were clashing dreams about the kind of nation the new India would be. In 1947 the British granted partial victories to both. The Muslims who said they could not live with Hindus were given Pakistan; the nationalists who wanted a united, democratic India were given the rest of the country. But the struggle is not over. In Pakistan, those who want a restoration of democracy and the creation of a secular state continue to protest and hope. In India, those who would divide the country once more, such as the propagators of a Sikh nation, have carried their war against the democratic state to extraordinary levels of sophistication and violence.

The historian Bipin Chandra, in a well-timed book, *Communalism in Modern India* (Vikas Publishing House, 1984), describes the evolution of the two main political inspirations thus: 'In India, both nationalism and communalism were recent, that is, modern historical processes – the transformation of India under the impact of colonialism. They were reflections of a new widening reality that was being born out of the ashes of the pre-colonial social structure. This also followed from the very newness of the modern politics that arose in India in the nineteenth century. Modern politics were the politics of mass participation, of the emergence of public opinion and of the revolutionary and unprecedented notion of popular sovereignty. The new political life and loyalties had to be based on new uniting principles, new political identities.'

'It is a dream that the Hindus and Muslims can ever evolve a common nationality,' said Mahomed Ali Jinnah, in his speech in 1940 supporting the Lahore resolution of the Muslim League which became the charter of the demand for Pakistan. The nationalist point of view was best presented by Mahatma Gandhi, in an article published in January 1942: 'I hold it to be utterly wrong to divide man from man by reason of religion. What conflict of interest can there be between Hindus and Muslims in the matter of revenue, sanitation, police, justice or the use of public conveniences? The difference can only be in religious usage and observances with which a secular state has no concern.' Gandhi's ideology was not only a public posture: he also displayed it in his personal life. It is not commonly known that Gandhi's eldest son converted to Islam. When taunted about this, Gandhi replied that if on becoming a Muslim his son had stopped drinking (which Islam forbids), then he welcomed the conversion! And he said to those who believed Muslims to be a separate nation: 'My eldest son embraced Islam a few years back. What would his homeland be – Porbandar [where he was born] or Punjab [where the idea of Pakistan was being formed]? I ask the Mussalmans [Muslims]: If India be not your homeland, what other country do you belong to? In what separate homeland would you put my son who embraced Islam?' (Quoted from Gandhi's speech at the historic Congress session at Bombay in August 1942 where the 'Quit India' resolution was passed.) Contrast this with Jinnah, who renounced his daughter when she wanted to – and did – marry a Parsi. Jinnah went to Pakistan. His daughter remained in India.

It took more than five decades of struggle, sacrifice and determination to persuade the British to grant Indians their freedom. It took just seven years to create the country called Pakistan. Before 1940, even the hard-liners in the Muslim leadership used to stress that all they wanted was coexistence with honour, not a separate country. The idea that Muslims were a separate nation was dismissed as absurd over and over again by Muslim leaders of all shades of opinion. In December 1915 the man who presided over the Muslim League session, Mazharul Huq, put it succinctly: 'We are Indian Muslims. These words, "Indian Muslims", convey the ideas of our nationality and of our religion ... When a question concerning the welfare of India and of justice to Indians arises, I am not only an Indian, but an Indian first, an Indian next and an Indian last, an Indian and an Indian alone ...' The famous Mohammad Ali told the first round-table conference, 'Where God commands I am a Muslim first, a Muslim second and a Muslim last, and nothing but a Muslim ... But where India is concerned, where India's freedom is concerned ... I am an Indian first, an Indian second, and an Indian last.' Or to quote the President of the Muslim League in 1931, Khan Sahib Mohammad Abdulla, addressing the 22nd session which commenced on 26 December: 'At the outset I must frankly state that we claim to be and are as much Indians as any other community in India and are as keen to see our country achieve freedom ... Troubles really begin when we are accused of Pan Islamism or for planning Muslim rule in India merely because we demand certain safeguards ... I take this opportunity to assure my Hindu brethren that we the Mussalmans belong to Indian soil and that our outlook is essentially Indian ... We must strive in unity to develop a common Indian culture and build a happy and progressive Indian nation, which should be composed of all that is best in the varied cultures that have found their way into India. But so long as one community strives for domination over the other and dreams of Hindu or Moslem Raj ... there is little hope for speedy realization of our legitimate aspirations to become a great and free nation.' Pakistan was the dream of but a handful of committed theocrats.

A strong section of the Muslims remained, in fact, with Gandhi and the nationalist mainstream till the bitter end. The greatest of them was Abul Kalam, whose scholarship in theology enabled him to use the title 'Maulana' and whose spirit was such that he took on the honorific 'Azad' (meaning 'free'). The quintessence of his philosophy was summed up in the moving speech he gave to the Ramgarh session of the Congress in 1940, where he was elected president of the party in the same week that the Muslim League passed its Pakistan resolution in Lahore: 'I cannot quarrel with my own convictions; I cannot stifle my own conscience ... I am a Mussalman and am proud of the fact. Islam's splendid tradition of 1,300 years is my inheritance. The spirit of Islam guides and helps me forward. I am proud of being an Indian. I am part of that indivisible unity that is the Indian nationality. I am indispensable to this noble edifice and without me this splendid structure of India is incomplete. I am an essential element which has gone to build India. I can never surrender this claim.'

If India's unity is destroyed once again, it will be for the same reasons this time as last – because the leadership of a minority managed, in the midst of deliberately provoked violence, to sell the thesis that a Hindu majority would either subjugate them or swallow them. The Muslims were told that the Hindu's secularism was a pretence, his democracy a trick to disguise a sinister ambition – to turn the Muslims into slaves. The Sikh is being told today that the faith cannot survive the Hindu effort to absorb it unless the Sikhs get their own country.

Even a casual look at the map of India makes it very clear where the vulnerable points are: the Sikh state of Punjab and the Muslim state of Jammu and Kashmir, contiguous to each other and to Pakistan. If the theocrats win the renewed battle for the mind, then Punjab and Kashmir cannot be kept inside India. If the democrats can prove that coexistence is not only possible but beneficial, then the map of India could in fact change in a different way. If we want to examine the possibilities that lie in the future, then it is vital to understand the partition of 1947. For in the rationale of that decision lies the ideology of the state, and in the truth or fraud of the ideology will lie the success or failure of a nation.

The birth of the Congress in 1885, thanks in part to a self-effacing Britisher, Allan Octavian Hume, was the seminal event on the journey to 1947. Constantly adjusting to the tides of history, the Congress kept afloat long enough to find the leader who could convert the party of lawyers into a mass organization and show the way to independence, Mohandas Karamchand Gandhi. Even in its pre-Gandhi phase, the Congress was clear on the vital question of the relationship between the various religious communities. If the first President was a Christian from Britain, then the third was a Muslim from Bombay, Sir Badruddin Tyabji. Sir Badruddin stressed the principle in his presidential address: 'I, at least, do not consider that there can be anything whatsoever in the position in the relations of the different communities of India – be they Hindus, Mussalmans [Muslims], Parsees [Parsis] or Christians – which should induce the leaders of one community to stand aloof from the others in their efforts to obtain those great general reforms, those general rights which are for the common benefit of us all.'

The second half of the nineteenth century was a period of search and revaluation in India. The old order, the feudal power structure, had collapsed, and the various interest groups were searching for ways to retain their niches in a changing world. Simultaneously, a new educated Indian elite began to give voice to ideas and sentiments in an effort first to discover the true India and then to place it in the modern context. Reformers like Keshub Chandra Sen wanted a 'Young India' freed of caste and united in 'one mighty federation'. Others with different aspirations began to search for an official language which might reflect the Hindu ethos of North India better than English or Persian: Hindi was a child of this need. Literature and history were written to explain the past and chart the future. There was a sense that the white man's rule was a temporary phenomenon – but who would take over power when the British had tired? Conflicting answers were offered. While the liberal elite wanted rule by the law of a great and wise Constitution, others had more dangerous ambitions. One of the most prominent Hindu communalists of this century, M. S. Golwalkar, set down his vision very clearly in his book *We*, published in 1939: minorities must live by the grace of the majority; only a Hindu could be a true Indian; those whose faith did not originate on this subcontinent were 'foreigners'. Muslims, Christians, Jews and Parsis would have to 'adopt the Hindu culture and language, must learn to respect and hold in reverence Hindu religion, must entertain no idea but the glorification of the Hindu race and culture ... [they] may stay in the country, wholly subordinated to the Hindu nation, claiming nothing, deserving no privileges, far less any preferential treatment – not even citizen's rights ... In this country Hindus alone are the nation and the Muslims and others, if not actually anti-national, are at least outside the body of the nation.' The organization which Golwalkar led for many years, the Rashtriya Swayamsevak Sangh, was the one which inspired the assassination of Mahatma Gandhi. However, such Hindu fundamentalism, long the thirst of a section of the middle class, has never got much response in an India whose population is 80 per cent Hindu. It needs to be pointed out that India remains a secular state not because one-fifth of its population is Muslim, Sikh or Christian, and therefore obviously has a vested interest in a secular Constitution, but because nine out of ten Hindus do not believe in violence against the minorities. If all the Hindus had been zealots, no law-and-order machinery in the world could have prevented the massacre of Muslims who are scattered in villages and towns all across the country.

The old Muslim elite, created out of centuries of feudal rule, had two broad components: the landlords and the *ulema*, or clergy. Neither was comfortable with the concept of a democracy, in which, inevitably, there would be land reform and a common law. In no major religion are the word and the deed so closely connected as in Islam: the Quran and the Hadis (the sayings of the Prophet) are respectively the word of God and the basis for social law. Hence the power of the mullah, who is the interpreter and teacher. The clergy had influence not only in the Muslim court but also in the daily life of the community through its control over the educational system. The mullah had no wish to relinquish his hold over the law and education which would guide and shape the Muslim community; he could never want a society in which law and education became the function of the state. And so a section of the priesthood took the lead in the effort to create the cultural and emotional separation between Hindus and Muslims as the prelude to the geographical separation. Its primary target was the urban or semi-urban middle class, whose voice was much stronger than its numbers. Its principal weapon was fear – and here it got invaluable help from Hindu fanatics whose excesses were propagated as the reality of Hindu mass opinion and whose fantasies were repeated as a foretaste of things to come if the Hindus ever acquired power. The war-cry was that the Muslim was in danger. The first solution proposed constitutional 'guarantees' of security. Later, no 'guarantees' were found sufficient and the demand was changed to that for a separate country, where the clergy could protect itself with a theocratic Constitution. It was a difficult task and took a long while. As long ago as the last century, administrative reforms like the decision to allow the use of Hindi in the governments of the Central Provinces in 1872, Bihar in 1881 and the United Provinces in 1891, were skilfully used to spread the fear that this was only the beginning of the effort to deprive the Muslims (who knew Urdu, not Hindi) of government jobs. It is easy to see how a middle class might respond to such propaganda. But despite all this, the Muslim masses never showed any support for the Muslim League until madness seized the subcontinent in 1946 and 1947.

The landlords, the Nawabs and the Khan Bahadurs, gladly joined hands with the clergy. It was a classic combination of two traditional forces, one desperate to preserve its economic power and the other determined to continue its social domination. The All-India Muslim League, formed in

1906, was the product of this alliance. It was started in Dacca (Dhaka), at the initiative of the Nawab of Dacca. The efforts to inject hatred into the sensitive province of Bengal, where the Muslims were in a majority but Hindu landlords held the economic power, had already begun. One of the constant sources of tension used to be cow-slaughter, with the mullahs claiming beef as a right and their Hindu equivalents demanding that the community protect the holy cow by killing Muslims. In such an atmosphere the nationalist was most often drowned out. Says Rafiuddin Ahmed in *The Bengal Muslims: 1871–1906* (Oxford University Press, 1981): 'Mir Musharraf Husain, a leading Bengali Muslim writer of the period, thus found himself in the centre of a heated controversy when he advocated the voluntary abolition of cow slaughter by the Muslims for the sake of amity with the Hindus ... [he] pleaded that the Hindus and Muslims were so interdependent on each other that "even if they profess differing religions, in heart and action they are identical". Musharraf's rationalism was hardly shared by many others, either in his own community or among the Hindus.'

In 1905 Lord Curzon partitioned the province of Bengal to create Muslim-majority and Hindu-majority sections. Both communities had protested vehemently when it became known that such a decision was being mooted. Lord Curzon won the Muslims over by offering rewards: in a speech at Dacca (Dhaka) on 18 February 1904 he told the Muslims that he would help them create a centre of Muslim power in Dacca 'which would invest the Mahomedans in eastern Bengal with a unity which they have not enjoyed since the days of the old Mussalman viceroys and kings'.

The Muslim League displayed no embarrassment about its feudal–theocratic nature. Its Constitution of December 1907 restricted membership to four hundred 'men of property and influence'. The first demand it made was for those guarantees: it asked for separate electorates for the Muslims. Within just three years of the birth of the League, the Indian Councils Act of 1909 (better known as the Morley–Minto Reforms) gave statutory recognition to separate electorates and a weightage to Muslims in the legislatures. But the Muslim League was to suffer a serious setback soon after, when King George V at the Delhi Durbar of 1911 gave a 'boon' to India by removing the 'partition ulcer' of Bengal and reunifying the province.

A depressed Nawab Salimullah withdrew from active politics in 1912. The Muslim League had, so far, supported British rule as a safeguard against Hindu domination. In 1913 it accepted the Congress demand for self-government. By 1916, M. A. Jinnah and Sir Wazir Hasan, on behalf of the Muslim League, and Motilal Nehru and Sir Tej Bahadur Sapru for the Congress, had worked out the famous Lucknow pact between the two parties. The implications of that agreement are best summed up in the statement made by the Muslim League leader, the Raja of Mahmudabad, welcoming the pact: 'We are Indians first and Mahomedans afterwards.' (There was an interesting echo of this statement during a conversation this author had with General Zia of Pakistan, in 1982. Said the General: 'I wish that Indian Muslims establish their own identity, as Indians and as Muslims. It would be a matter of great pride for me to see that the Indian Muslims take pride in calling themselves Indians first and Muslims next. I would be a very proud man listening to that.' Excellent. But if it is possible for Muslims to be Indians, and proud ones at that, why then was Pakistan torn out of the country?)

The most serious problem that the Muslim League faced was that the party created in the name of the Muslims was not getting their support. If anything, Muslims seemed more attracted to the Congress platform. It needs to be mentioned here that neither the Congress nor the Muslim League were parties in the formal sense; they were movements, one for the independence of the country and the other for the protection of Muslims. Senior leaders like M. A. Jinnah held important positions in both organizations in the twenties without feeling any sense of confusion. It was only when Gandhi began shaping a firm ideological base for the Congress that both Hindu and Muslim communalists moved away from it, much to the relief of Gandhi and the new lieutenants, like Jawaharlal Nehru, Subhas Bose, Maulana Azad and Acharya Kripalani, whom he was grooming. By the thirties the Muslim League had split and become moribund. Three men who could have still rescued it died: the fiery leader of the Khilafat movement, Maulana Mohammad Ali, died of diabetes on 4 January 1931 in London and was buried in Jerusalem; on 31 May of the same year the old Raja of Mahmudabad died after a stroke; and on 6 January 1932 they were followed by the Punjab leader, Sir Mohammad Shafi. A disgusted Jinnah decided to give up politics and in 1931 stayed behind in London, after the second round-table conference, to renew his law practice.

This is how Choudhry Khaliquzzaman, one of the key figures in the pre-independence Muslim League, describes his own party (*Pathway to Pakistan*, Longmans, 1961): 'The Muslim League ... was dominated by the titled gentry, Nawabs, landlords and *Jee Huzoors* [yes men] ... Since its very birth in 1906, the Muslim League's activities had always been confined to indoor political shows. Even its annual sessions were held either in well-decorated *pandals* or in big halls where a few honourable visitors were allowed by special cards. Mass public meetings were unknown to the Muslim League organization. From 1906 when it was founded in Dacca [Dhaka], its central office remained in Aligarh till 1910 ... The income from membership and annual subscriptions was not sufficient even to maintain a decent office, much less to work among the masses. It began to live on a grant from the Raja of Mahmudabad of three thousand rupees annually. This was its main fixed income.'

Jinnah was eventually persuaded to return and rescue the Muslim League in 1934. In February of that year, the Raja of Salempur organized a dinner for him at the Cecil Hotel in Delhi where he was reintroduced to the Muslim leaders of the country. On 2 July 1935 the Government of India Act received the royal assent and the stage was set for the 1937 elections, through which power would for the first time be transferred in the provinces to Indian parties. This was the opportunity for both the Congress and the Muslim League to display how much support they had from the masses they claimed to represent. Jinnah did his best. Backed by the mullahs who went to canvass from door to door, he made 'Hindu tyranny' the hub of his campaign. The 230 million Hindus were going to wipe out the 70 million Muslims, he said, and the Congress was the cunning instrument of annihilation that the Hindus had found. In his 1937 presidential address to the Muslim League he told the Muslims that there were forces which would 'bully you, tyrannize over you and intimidate you'. In his 1938 address he said the Congress wanted the Muslims to 'submit unconditionally to the Hindu raj ... the high command of the Congress is determined, absolutely determined, to crush all other communities and culture in this country and to establish [Hindu] raj ... [Gandhi's] ideal is to revive Hindu religion and establish Hindu raj in this country'. Indian nationalism was defined as slavery of the Muslims, and therefore the worst enemies were those Muslims who remained in the Congress, like Maulana Azad and Rafi Ahmed Kidwai.

But Jinnah and the Muslim League discovered that the Muslim masses did not share this view at all. The Muslim League was decisively rejected in the 1937 elections. (It is ironical that the only elections that the Muslim League has won were those held in 1946, on the eve of partition. The League could not win an election even in the country it had created, Pakistan.) Choudhry Khaliquzzaman, leader of the League in its stronghold, the United Provinces, admits that it was a Muslim party without Muslim support. He writes in his autobiography: 'We invited Mr Jinnah in December 1936 to address a meeting for raising funds for the election. The meeting, held in Ganga Parshad Memorial Hall, was a very poor show, which speaks of the interest of the Muslims in the Muslim League at that time.' By the conditions of the Communal Award of 1932, the Muslims had been given 485 seats in the provinces. The party which was allegedly going to save the Muslims from annihilation won only 108 of those seats! And this was the party which the British kept calling 'the voice of Indian Muslims'. In fact, not even the clergy were completely with the League. In 1938, for instance, Maulana Madani of the Jamaat-e-Ulema-e-Hind was telling Muslims, 'Nowadays nations are determined by their homelands. Race or religion does not make a nation.' Maulana Azad had managed to persuade the Jamaat-e-Ulema the previous year to leave the Muslim League and go over to the Congress unconditionally, and on 17 May at a conference in Allahabad the Jamaat passed a resolution to this effect. (The fundamentalist clergy then broke away to form its separate organization, the Jamaat-e-Islami, in August 1941 at Lahore.)

Most of the important Muslim leaders refused to respond to this communal view espoused by Jinnah in 1937. If anything, they had begun to feel that the relevance of the Muslim League was over, now that the 'guarantees' had been provided to the Muslims. They fought the 1937 elections very successfully on the basis of political rather than communal manifestos. In Punjab, leaders like Sir Sikandar Hayat Khan and Sir Fazl-e-Hasan created the Unionist Party in partnership with the peasant leader Sir Chotu Ram, and swept the polls. Despite the efforts of the poet–philosopher Sir Muhammad Iqbal, who campaigned hard for the League, it could win only 2 out of the 86 Muslim seats in Punjab (and one of these two victors, Raja Ghazanfar Ali Khan, went over to the Unionists after the elections). In Bengal, Fazlul Haq's Krishak Praja Samiti, or Peasants and Tenants Party, championing the cause of the poor peasant and demanding agrarian reform, emerged the victor: in fact, Fazlul Haq showed where the Muslim vote stood by defeating the Muslim League leader Khwaja Nazimuddin in the latter's home constituency. In Sind, there were 35 Muslim seats out of a total of 60: the League got nothing. The Sind United Party won 18 seats; the Muslim Party won 3; the Sind Muslim Azad Party got 2, while independents won 12. Sir Hidayatullah formed the government with support from across the House. In the North-West Frontier Province, the results were equally embarrassing for the Muslim League.

So this was the extent of the mass support for the Muslim League in those areas which were to become the land of Pakistan.

In fact, it may sound astounding but the Muslim League never got much support in the Muslim-majority provinces where it might have been expected to be king. There were no elections in Kashmir since it was a princely state, but there, too, the Muslim masses preferred the National Conference of Sheikh Abdullah to the Muslim League, despite Jinnah's unflagging efforts to woo them. Even in the United Provinces, where the League had its hard core, the party could not win more than 29 of the 66 Muslim seats. And yet the myth is given currency – that the Muslim masses wanted Pakistan. The Muslim League did win Muslim support in 1946, but only after the country had begun spinning in the vortex of a great storm. Such a storm comes but rarely in human affairs, and its force can blind everyone.

Nor can it be argued that the 1937 elections were not truly indicative of the popular mood. The franchise, which had been very selective in the 1923 elections, had been expanded, and for the first time the peasantry got a chance to vote. In the very same elections, the Congress, contesting from its nationalist platform, pleading for unity, democracy, secularism and by now also, under the presidentship of Jawaharlal Nehru, socialism, showed how deep was its support base: it won handsomely. It even did comparatively better than the Muslim League in the Muslim seats, winning 26 of the 58 it contested. (The Hindu communal party, the Hindu Mahasabha, created as a reaction to the Muslim League, was, incidentally, also thoroughly demolished in these elections.) The 1937 elections were considered crucial because they were the first testing-ground for the League's claim to represent all the Muslims of the country; and the results were keenly awaited. Which philosophy, Gandhi's or Jinnah's, had caught the imagination of the people? Gandhi offered a simple slogan: in his quaint English he called it 'heart unity between Hindu and Muslim', and proposed 'Hindu–Mussalman ki jai' ('Victory to Hindu–Muslim unity'). Non-violence was a cardinal element of this ideology. Since Gandhi had taken charge of the Congress after its 1920 session at Calcutta, that had been his message to the masses, whom he loved and who loved him. He associated the Congress with peasant concerns and took up their causes – the indigo movement in Bihar or the Bardoli struggle in Gujarat. He had contempt for the traditional upper-class Hindu and Muslim powerbrokers; the millions ('Surely the millions do not want to become legislators and politicians') were his concern. He had the courage to distance the Congress from those who wanted to convert it into the Hindu version of the Muslim League. 'Those Hindus who, like Dr Moonje and Sri Savarkar, believe in the doctrine of the sword may seek to keep the Mussalmans under the Hindu domination. I do not represent that section. I represent the Congress,' he explained in his speech to the Congress session of 1942. And just as he would not allow the Congress to become a 'Hindu' party, he would not recognize the 'right' of the Muslim League to treat all Muslims as the private property of the League. This was what Jinnah wanted the Congress to concede. And this, of course, was something the Congress could not do, without destroying its very ideology. It was this conflict which was at the root of a problem in 1937 which many consider to be the decisive element in the creation of Pakistan – the abortive bid to form a Congress–League coalition in the United Provinces after the 1937 elections.

Defeat at the polls did not dampen the Muslim League's desire for power. It had to sustain the fiction that only the League could protect the Muslim interest. If the Congress Muslim ministers showed during their term in office that they could be of benefit to the community despite being part of a Congress government, what little was left of the Muslim League would also collapse. Jinnah was most anxious to get into power in the crucial United Provinces, and he asked the Congress to form a coalition with the League despite the fact that the Congress had won a majority on its own. Predictably, the only demand that Jinnah made was that the Congress should not appoint any Muslim ministers from its side, but behave in practice like a Hindu party. The Muslim League had won only 29 seats in a House of 228, but it insisted on having two ministers in the Cabinet – Choudhry Khaliquzzaman, who had been appointed leader of the Muslim League legislature party, and Nawab Ismail Khan.

The League proposed that if its demands were accepted, this could become the basis on which the Hindu–Muslim conflict could end, and a common front be built against the British. But it was impossible to see how the Congress could accept the League's terms which would, in effect, destroy the legitimacy of its claim to represent every Indian irrespective of religion, caste or creed in the common struggle for freedom from colonial rule. The Congress could not become *de facto* a Hindu party. The fight against the proposed coalition was taken up most actively by Congress Socialists and Muslim Congressmen who felt that any deal with the League would be a betrayal of all that they had stood for. Khaliquzzaman records that on 12 May 1937 he went to discuss the proposed coalition with Nehru, who was in bed at Anand Bhavan in Allahabad that day: 'Quite contrary to my views he [Nehru] believed that really the Hindu–Muslim question was confined to a few Muslim intellectual landlords and capitalists who were cooking up a problem which did not in fact exist in the minds of the masses. He ridiculed the idea of Muslims having any separate organization within the precincts of the Legislature.'

The man in charge of negotiations with the League was Maulana Azad, with help from Rafi Ahmed Kidwai and G. B. Pant. The Maulana objected to the idea of keeping Nawab Ismail Khan in the Cabinet since he represented those feudal interests which were so contrary to the Congress economic philosophy, but the League would not relent. By 15 July Maulana Azad had offered the minimum line of the Congress. He handed a two-page typed note to Khaliquzzaman which the latter would have to sign in return for a coalition. 'The Muslim League group in the United Provinces shall cease to function as a separate group. The existing members of the Muslim League Party in the United Provinces Assembly shall become part of the Congress Party and will fully share with other members of the Party their privileges and obligations as members of the Congress Party,' began the note. The League protested that this was too harsh. The Maulana modified the agreement. However, the League would not surrender its right to vote separately from the Congress when it came to problems concerning the Muslims. This, in fact, was precisely what the Congress feared and could not accept. On 27 July 1937, when the Assembly session started, the Muslim League legislators were sitting on the opposition benches. Beside them but not with them was Nawabzada Liaquat Ali Khan, who was to become Jinnah's successor in Pakistan; as late as 1937, Liaquat Ali Khan had not joined the Muslim League. Even the Raja of Salempur, the man who had been among those who brought Jinnah back from London, had left the Muslim League. He, too, was sitting as an independent member in that House.

Who was right? Was Nehru correct in describing the Muslim League as only the creation of the elite, with no relationship to the needs of the masses? The proof can only be found in the practice, in the fundamental nature of the Pakistan that was created. It is quite clear now how the landlord–clergy alliance shared out Pakistan. While the landlords and capitalists allowed the clergy to make Pakistan a religious state, the clergy allowed the landlords guaranteed property rights and the capitalists unbridled control over the economy. Theocracy and landlordism/capitalism are the two pillars of Pakistan and Bangladesh. No matter who comes to power, whether the leader be in uniform or not, these two things will never be tampered with. Anyone making even a mild effort to challenge these two 'rights' will be removed from power. Jinnah's belief that he had created Pakistan was an illusion which everyone encouraged because they needed a leader of his extraordinary determination, talent and sophistication. And it is true that without such qualities as Jinnah had, Pakistan might never have become a reality.

The man who eventually destroyed Gandhi's dream of a free and united India was also a Gujarati, whose parents came from a village about thirty miles south of Gandhi's ancestral home. Mahomed Ali Jinnah was born on Christmas Day 1876 and spent his childhood in Karachi where his father had established his business.

At sixteen Jinnah was sent to England for further studies so that he might be better qualified to inherit his father's firm. There was one precondition, though, which his mother insisted on – that he would be married before he went. She did not want her son to be lured by an English Miss. The dutiful son married a fourteen-year-old girl he never saw. In London, business studies bored him. At one point he even thought of joining the stage, and he actually signed a three-month contract with a theatre group. But then he decided to concentrate on a degree in law, entering Lincoln's Inn; it was a wise decision since Jinnah was to become one of the best lawyers of his generation. While Jinnah was abroad, his father's health began to fail and he started to plead with his son to return and take over the business. Jinnah stayed in London till he finished his legal studies. By the time he could return, both his mother and his wife had died. Instead of staying with his unwell father, Jinnah decided to come to Bombay to start his law practice. With him came his sister Fatima, who was devoted to him. (In his will, he left all his fabulous wealth to her, earmarking only nominal sums for other relatives.)

Jinnah was the archetypal 'confirmed bachelor', with the habits characteristic of an Indian gentleman returned from England. His portraits dominate the offices of the Islamic government of Pakistan, but General Mohammad Zia-ul-Huq must be a very relieved man that Mr Jinnah, the 'father' of Pakistan, is not alive today – or he would have to be flogged publicly for his personal habits. Mr Jinnah not only chain-smoked Craven-A cigarettes but also liked his whisky and was not averse to pork. His was the life of an upper-class liberal – which indeed Jinnah was for most of his life, both private and public.

In 1916 Jinnah went for a holiday to the hill resort of Darjeeling with a Parsi friend, Sir Dinshaw Manockjee Petit. There, at the age of thirty-

Liaquat Ali Khan, Jinnah's lieutenant and successor, echoed the liberal sentiments of the *Quaid-e-Azam* ('the great leader') when he explained to the Constituent Assembly at Karachi on 11 August what the Pakistani flag that he was about to unfurl stood for. He said: 'This flag is not the flag of any one particular party or community. This flag will stand for freedom, liberty and equality of all those who owe allegiance to the flag of Pakistan ... As I visualize the state of Pakistan, there will be no special privileges, no special rights for any particular community or individual.' But then – why create Pakistan?

The contradictions between the people and those who had created Pakistan were visible even in Jinnah's lifetime. Jinnah himself knew no Urdu, Gujarati being his mother tongue and English the language of his survival. The whole of Bengali Pakistan did not know Urdu. But, under pressure from the United Provinces lobby, Urdu became the national language of Pakistan. When Jinnah went to address the students of Dhaka University on 24 March 1948, he warned them, 'Make no mistake about it. There can only be one state language ... and that can only be Urdu.' Herbert Feldman (*The End and the Beginning: Pakistan 1969–1971*, Oxford University Press) puts it a little more bluntly: 'It is doubtful whether Mahomed Ali Jinnah himself understood the political implications inherent in the Pakistan he eventually accepted.'

Pakistan was conceived in the thirties, launched in the forties, distorted in the fifties, choked in the sixties and decimated in the seventies. With yet another gun-and-moustache man at the helm in the eighties, the future looks as tenuous as the past.

The subcontinent is becoming fluid again. If Jinnah was right, then 1947 was only the beginning of a process towards a 'moth-eaten' subcontinent (to use the word Jinnah chose when describing post-partition Pakistan). After thirty-five years of self-rule the time has come to examine the evidence and try to find out which has been, despite all the enormous problems, more successful: the democratic federal entity Mahatma Gandhi wanted, or the theocratic state Jinnah left behind. Was partition the reality or only a rude pause in the evolution of the subcontinent? The last viceroy, Lord Louis Francis Albert Victor Nicholas Mountbatten, gave his answer to this question. He wrote down privately just after he had obtained agreement on the partition of India: 'The responsibility for this mad decision [must lie] squarely on Indian shoulders in the eyes of the world, for one day they will bitterly regret the decision they are about to make.'

2
Mullah Power in Pakistan

On 20 February 1947, Prime Minister Clement Attlee finally declared the end of British resolve, removed the last imperialist, Lord Wavell, and announced that by June 1948 Lord Mountbatten would preside over the closing ceremonies. There was more than a year still left to the deadline; if anything, given the complications, Lord Mountbatten might have feasibly asked for a small extension. Instead, he got into a hurry which has still not been rationally explained. Lord Mountbatten's excuse has been that if he had not handed over power as quickly as he did, the price would have been much higher. But that is only an assumption. In any case it is difficult to see how it could have been worse: not only was the country divided but partition cost hundreds of thousands of lives in a matter of weeks, and launched a series of wars which has not yet ended. It has been suggested that the British hurried the transfer of power because they were aware of something which no one else, apart from Jinnah, knew – that the 'father' of Pakistan had terminal tuberculosis, and if he died before the plans for Pakistan could be announced the whole campaign for the separate country might collapse. There was reason behind such thinking. As we have seen, the Muslim voters had never supported the Muslim League, and the move for Pakistan acquired momentum only in the mid forties thanks to the fear psychosis which Jinnah so successfully unleashed.

Pakistan was not created by the Muslim masses; it owed its birth to a handful of 'leaders' who were not content with separate beliefs – they wanted separate electorates, separate languages, separate dress, separate identities and, finally, separate homes. The only time since its inception in 1906 that the Muslim League has got some votes is in the 1946 elections; not before and, indeed, not after. The League could not survive in the country it created! Even commentators sympathetic to Pakistan have noted the absence of mass support for the Muslim League. Ian Stephens, for instance, who as the British editor of the very British newspaper *The*

Statesman (which was also British-owned) had, as it were, a ringside seat and an insider's view of events, and was warm enough to the new country to go and work for the Karachi government, says in *Pakistan, Old Country/ New Nation* (Penguin Books, p. 90): 'In 1934 Mr Jinnah came back to India from a spell of law practice in London, and he soon found himself the leader of the Muslim League. Like the Indian Liberal Party but unlike the Congress, it had as yet scarcely attempted "mass contacts", and remained little more than a discussion society for upper-class persons interested in a particular brand of politics.' The poet–philosopher Sir Muhammad Iqbal made the same point in a letter to Jinnah sent on 28 May 1937 (which Tariq Ali quoted in *Can Pakistan Survive?*). Said the poet to the politician: 'The League will finally have to decide whether it will remain a body representing the upper classes of Indian Muslims or the Muslim masses, who have so far, with good reason, taken no interest in it. Personally, I believe that a political organization which gives no promise of improving the lot of the average Muslim cannot attract our masses.' So once again we return to the basic question: in whose interest was Pakistan created? Certainly not that of the Muslim masses.

Jinnah was able to 'represent' the Indian Muslims thanks solely to the British. When the Second World War broke out in Europe, the Congress refused to support the British effort and asked all its provincial governments (elected in 1937) to resign. For Jinnah, who could not hope to come to power through elections, this was an Allah-sent opportunity. The Muslim League had decided that the only way it could get Pakistan was through the grace of the British, and so in the decade between 1937 and 1947 it played an active pro-British role. In those ten years it did not launch or participate in a single movement against the British, reserving all its anger only for the Congress, which continued to challenge the colonizers; Jinnah, on the other hand, time and again co-operated with the British. And so when the Congress ministries resigned, Jinnah announced that a 'Deliverance Day' would be celebrated on 22 November 1939. During the war, in a crucial province like Bengal, the Muslim League tasted the power it had been denied in 1937. Jinnah got the chance to use the state machinery to spread his propaganda. In 1937 the Muslim League had made 'danger to Islam' from the 'Hindu Congress' its campaign theme, only to be rejected by the Muslims. Now the British decided – most crucially – to grant this same Jinnah, defeated at the polls, the right to be the sole voice of Indian Muslims. By early 1946, when a war-weary Britain began searching for an Indian solution, Jinnah was confident enough to threaten civil war in India if the subcontinent was not divided. On 16 August 1946, 'Direct Action Day', the Muslim League government of Shahid Suhrawardy in Bengal showed what the League in power could do: Calcutta was plunged into terrifying riots as the League's armed hoodlums began large-scale attacks on Hindus, who answered with equal brutality. This was the warning of civil war come true. Murder and arson raged, fear entered the heart; and only in this unnatural atmosphere could the Muslim League finally manage to increase its vote. In February 1947, freedom was announced. In March came Mountbatten. In early April, Mountbatten held six meetings with Jinnah. On 10 April, the British accepted partition. On 1 May, the Congress surrendered, when its high command authorized Nehru to accept the freedom of a divided India. Gandhi pathetically tried to make some sense of what was happening all around him, and could not. He even appealed to the Congress to let Jinnah assume power in a united India. But who would listen to the voice of understanding in the midst of butchery and mayhem that must rank among the most cruel ever seen?

Partition was formally ratified at a round-table conference on 2 June: Nehru, Sardar Patel, and Acharya Kripalani came from the Congress; Jinnah, Liaquat Ali Khan and Sardar Abdur Rab Nashtar came from the Muslim League; Mountbatten with Lord Ismay and Sir Eric Mieville represented the imperial interest. On 4 June Mountbatten held only the second press conference addressed by a viceroy of India, and announced that power would be transferred by 15 August. There were just two months left, and the most difficult task had not even begun – the drawing of boundaries. The lawyer Sir Cyril Radcliffe was summoned from his chambers in London to run a scalpel through the heart of a subcontinent he had never seen. The mullahs had won their country.

Jinnah lived under the illusion that since he had made the 'impossible dream' of 1933 come true, he could also give it an ideology. But Pakistan was not created to express the liberal principles Jinnah himself had held till an obsession conquered him. Jinnah was only the last and most effective weapon of the mullahs who had begun their task many decades before. History has now confirmed who really conceived Pakistan and who was going to rule this country built in the name of religion. In less than five years after 1947, Jinnah's secularism was dead, with the assassination of Liaquat Ali Khan; in a decade Jinnah's democracy had been buried, by Ayub Khan; and within twenty-five years Jinnah's Pakistan was destroyed. So what then did Jinnah prove on 14 August

1947 except that he never really understood what he had done in the last decade of his life? The mullah had to struggle for a while after 1947 to establish his dominance in Pakistan, but that was what finally happened. How long this phase will last, however, is another story.

Why does one presume that the mullah raj cannot last? Primarily because the subcontinental experience shows that religious extremism, with its oppressive economic ideas, may hold temporary sway in a climate of fear but cannot ever sustain the support of the majority. The mullahs in Pakistan want nothing more dearly than to get democratic legitimacy for their theocracy, but time and again, whenever the opportunity has been given in any way, major or minor, the religious parties have been drubbed in Pakistani elections. Why does that happen if, as the army–bureaucracy–clergy elite in Pakistan insists, everyone in Pakistan is deeply committed to the creation of an Islamic state? The classic example of the clergy's inherent unpopularity came in 1977, paradoxically at the very height of the anti-Bhutto movement. That was the moment, thanks to the arrogance and mistakes of Bhutto, when the right wing and the clergy were riding the crest of the highest wave generated in their favour. But when, after deposing Bhutto, General Zia offered elections and meant it, it was the clergy who persuaded him to postpone a vote since they were certain of being demolished at the polls. The only elections the clergy can win are those in which the secular, popular parties are debarred from contesting. Such false legitimacy can only be a temporary phase.

Currency is still given to the notion that if Jinnah had lived he would, by the sheer force of his personality, have set his nation on the correct democratic path, and you might have had today the Pakistan of Ruttie Jinnah and not of Begum Zia. *'Dil ke behalane ke liye, Ghalib, khayal accha hai'* (a famous line from a great Urdu poet, which means, 'That is a good thought, Ghalib, to idle away the time'). Jinnah died on 11 September 1948, when his lungs, two-thirds of one and a quarter of the other eaten by tuberculosis, finally gave up. Jinnah's doctor in Bombay, J. A. L. Patel, had diagnosed the problem in June 1946, say Collins and Lapierre in *Freedom at Midnight*, but this was perhaps the best-kept secret of partition. Jinnah gave no public indication of this reality, continuing to smoke his usual ration of cigarettes, and attributing his cough to bronchitis. Speaking to Ian Stephens as late as February 1948, Jinnah said, 'Yes, Mr Stephens, I am better. They said I have been ill; I have not'; Stephens quotes him in *Pakistan, Old Country/New Nation* (p. 281). Certainly the

British knew that Jinnah was ill. Lord Wavell has recorded in his diary that Jinnah was a sick man.

It is a very fragile country which can be distorted by the tuberculosis of one old man. An individual, by his presence and genius, may hasten the pace of progress or delay it, but there is nothing much he can do if the very foundation is built on an untenable ideology. Jinnah could have given Pakistan a different direction if he had, like Gandhi, authored a new ideology – but he had nothing to offer his country apart from what he had accepted from the clergy. The state was created in the name of the crescent and the Quran; there was no way now that Islam's self-appointed cadre would allow a lawyer educated in England to experiment with fancy ideas.

There has been too much obsession with the idea of a personality making the vital difference between India and Pakistan. In this same vein, Jawaharlal Nehru's survival has been called the reason for the success of democracy in India. Nehru played a great role, perhaps a unique one, in stabilizing his nation, but to say that he alone established democracy is patently untrue. It was such an attitude that sponsored the question which dominated reportage about India in the fifties: after Nehru, who? Well, after Nehru, the next person to be elected. In 1964 the question had to be answered. Nehru died, and a successor took office through the democratic system. That was what the book said would happen, and that was precisely what did happen. India may progress faster because of the brilliance of one Prime Minister, or stagnate because of the indifferent quality of another. But the nation will collapse only if its fundamental ideology, its democratic secular base, is eroded – nothing else. The most brilliant dictator will not be able to keep India together. And the shoddiest democrat will find it difficult to break the country.

The only interest group which really knew its agenda for Pakistan was the clergy. The bureaucracy, children of English education, thought that they could ask Frankenstein to go back to the closet now that they had got their places in a Muslim government. They thought wrong. The clergy knew better than they where to attack and how to work towards the seizure of power. The crucial battle would, of course, be over the Constitution. Writes Ian Stephens (*Pakistan, Old Country/New Nation*, pp. 286–7): 'We have on the one hand in Pakistan the typical product of the Aligarh movement, culturally very much a Muslim but lax in religious observance, English-speaking, an eager participant in the world of the present. On the other, there is the mullah, the theologian, steeped in Arabic and the past, brought up from boyhood at seminaries such as in Deoband near Saharanpur, or the Nadvat-ul-Ulema at Lucknow ... Incomprehension between the two types can be almost complete ... it was inevitable that spokesmen of the two types, nurtured almost in different worlds, should to their surprise and distress at times find themselves in total, blank disagreement about the form the country's Constitution should take.'

Prime Minister Liaquat Ali Khan, now burdened with greater responsibility after Jinnah's death, went about the business of preparing a Constitution with some diligence. A report of the Basic Principles Committee was submitted on 7 March 1949 to the Pakistan Constituent Assembly. It could not survive since the mullahs did not find any commitment in it to a theocratic state. Instead it promised democracy and, worse, said that 'adequate provision shall be made for the minorities freely to profess and practise their religions and develop their cultures'. By November 1950, it was withdrawn. It is obvious that even if Jinnah had submitted such a concept for the future of Pakistan, he too would have faced the wrath of the clergy; after all, their loyalty was to their version of 'Allah's will' and not to Jinnah. (Stephens, ever sympathetic to Pakistan, admits with a hint of embarrassment that the mullahs succeeded in scuttling the effort to create a democratic Constitution.)

On 16 October 1951, Liaquat Ali Khan, Jinnah's chosen heir, was assassinated by a gunman whose identity and motive still have not been officially established. The ruling elite has always dismissed it as the work of an individual, but the conspiracy theory has taken root in the popular mind, and this points the finger towards the clergy. Liaquat Ali Khan could, with the help of the bureaucracy, have created the structures for a responsible government. The chances diminished after his death. Now the political merry-go-round began to whirl crazily; cause, action, reaction, instigation, footless floundering, some craziness – all combined in the end to bring every institution down to its knees.

Liaquat Ali Khan's place was taken by Khwaja Nazimuddin who stepped down from the ceremonial office of Governor-General to become Prime Minister. The pattern of totally arbitrary succession had begun. It is important to understand that the *only* time power has changed hands in Pakistan on the strength of popular will has been when the humiliated army handed over the government to Zulfiqar Ali Bhutto in 1971 because Bhutto had won the majority of the seats in West Pakistan in the fateful elections of 1970 and had the people's sentiment behind him at that nervous hour. Otherwise, every shift of authority has been a drawing-room decision made by whichever was the most powerful section of the ruling elite. Pakistan was run just as Muslim League politics had been conducted before 1947: by a small coterie, always acting in the name of the manipulated masses, without any reference to their true will. This is not surprising since it was the same elite. Such convenient habits die very, very hard; and they are still flourishing in Pakistan. There was no reason why Khwaja Nazimuddin should become Prime Minister, or why, out of the blue, the Finance Minister, Ghulam Mohammad, not very long ago just another Punjabi bureaucrat, should worm his way up the ladder to become the Governor-General of the country, except that a handful of persons sat in some drawing-room and decided that this should be so. There was no system or political ideology governing the acquisition, and therefore the exercise, of power. It was open house for schemers. The politics of the first decade, perhaps more than anything else, exposed Pakistan as a gift made out to an elite for services rendered – and showed how an elite with little ideology and less morality could destroy a munificent inheritance.

The clergy decided to show very early who was going to be in charge of the new country. It first sabotaged the proposed Constitution. Then it began to demonstrate what it meant by Pakistan, the 'land of the pure'. Not a trace of adulteration would be allowed. The Ahmadiyas, or the Qadianis, are one of the sects that have arisen out of the main body of Islam; they are a small, well-knit and highly able community (Professor Abdul Salam, the Nobel prizewinner for physics in 1979, belongs to this sect). The best-known Pakistani Ahmadiya in the forties and fifties was Sir Zafrullah Khan, the Foreign Minister who argued the Pakistani case on Kashmir at the United Nations and became a minor hero. But in 1952 he in particular, and his community in general, were made the target of the wrath of the mullahs on the familiar charge of heresy, even while the Ahmadiyas bent over backwards to show that they were good Muslims. For nearly a year the clergy, led by the fanatical Maulana Maudoodi, head of the Jamaat-e-Islami, took to the streets to demand the expulsion of the Ahmadiyas from the land of the 'pure' Muslims. (This, incidentally, was happening less than five years after Jinnah dismissed the thought that Pakistan would become a theocratic state in the hands of the clergy.) The movement reached such a pitch that between 3 and 7 March 1953, mullah-led mobs took over Lahore, and Khwaja Nazimuddin, who had been afraid to move against the clergy so far, was forced to introduce martial law, arrest the mullah leadership, including Maudoodi, dismiss the provincial Punjab government of Daultana and replace him with Feroz Khan Noon. The anti-clergy forces tried to make full use of this chance to crush the mullahs. Maulanas Maudoodi and Niazi were not only jailed but were given death sentences for their murderous role in the riots. But who in Pakistan was going to hang a maulana? A Bhutto could be hanged, but not a Maudoodi. The death sentences were quietly remitted and the maulanas released.

In the meanwhile, within the very first five years of its existence, the idea of Pakistan had begun wearing thin in the east of the country. (Time and again we see how shallow the roots of Pakistan were in the people's consciousness – and, conversely, how deep they were in the minds of the committed elite.) By early 1949, Maulana Abdul Hamid Khan Bhashani had founded the Awami Muslim League at Narayanganj in East Pakistan, with Sheikh Mujibur Rahman as one of its three assistant general secretaries. A parallel gesture was visible at the other extreme of Pakistan, across the subcontinent, when a party with the same name was announced by Pir Manki Shariff in the North-West Frontier Province (the NWFP, it might be recalled, had always been a Congress stronghold, despite being fully Muslim, and to the west of Muslim Punjab). In February 1950, the two Awami Muslim Leagues came together under the presidentship of Shahid Suhrawardy. As Herbert Feldman explains (*The End and the Beginning*, Oxford University Press): 'It is known that [only] after [communal] massacres in Bihar, in 1946, Jinnah took the view that Muslims must be masters in their own house in all respects ... On the whole, it seems fair to say that the kind of Pakistan which emerged in 1947, notwithstanding all the many unanswered questions, was acceptable to the provinces astride the Indus. For East Bengal, at that euphoric moment, acceptable likewise, but many people had doubts and reservations. It was also said that unpublished documents existed showing that Jinnah expressed readiness for East Bengal to form its own independent government but, not surprisingly, very little has ever been remarked on this, much less disclosed. What we do know for certain is that within three years of Pakistan's emergence, signs of discontent in the eastern wing were plain, and that within five years lives were being lost in the course of political controversy.'

The lives were lost thanks to a fellow Bengali, Khwaja Nazimuddin. Jinnah and Liaquat Ali Khan had made it clear that the Bengalis would have to learn the national language, Urdu. On 26 January 1952 (while India, after accepting its Constitution two years earlier, was conducting its first, and mammoth, general elections on the basis of complete adult franchise), the Basic Principles Committee of the Constituent Assembly of Pakistan announced, in its recommendations, that Urdu should be the only state language of Pakistan – a country in which Bengalis were a majority. By the end of February, serious strikes, demonstrations, and consequent police action had taken the lives of students and children. Eventually Bengali was given equal status, in the 1956 Constitution, but by that time the Martyrs' Memorial had become a place of pilgrimage in Dhaka and the seeds of East Pakistan's independence had been fertilized.

On 17 April 1953, Pakistan again went through the drawing-room syndrome. That day Pakistan witnessed its first coup; it was also perhaps the first coup in history organized and executed solely by the bureaucracy. It was extraordinary both for its suddenness and for its complete absence of any of the values and norms that guide a system. Governor-General Ghulam Mohammad simply sacked the government of Khwaja Nazimuddin, without allowing the Prime Minister the option of facing the Legislature. At a stroke the balance of power changed: the legislator no longer had the decisive authority. The ceremonial head of state had used his technical rights to abrogate power; it was a coup from above.

The replacement for Prime Minister Khwaja Nazimuddin was another instance of completely arbitrary decision-making. An obscure ex-politician, Mohammad Ali of Bogra, who had been living the comparatively good life of an ambassador since 1948, was summoned to take over as Prime Minister. As simple as that. His only qualifications, to the extent that anyone could make them out, were two: first, he was considered too unknown to be anything but pliant; and second, he was from East Pakistan and therefore his appointment could be presented as a sop to those Bengalis who might feel that the dismissal of Khwaja Nazimuddin was another insult from the Punjabi to the Bengali. But hardly had Mohammad Ali of Bogra become Prime Minister than the politician in him came out. He began trying to create a power base to challenge his mentor.

The charge of Punjabi contempt for the Bengali was valid as early as this. Enough has been written about this relationship, in the aftermath of Bangladesh, and need not be repeated here. Just one quotation will convey the flavour of what the Punjabi felt for the Bengali. It is from a fine book by Siddiq Salik, attached to the public relations department of the Pakistani army in Dhaka in 1971, and consequently a man who saw the war from the defeated side. In *Witness to Surrender* (Oxford University Press, Karachi, p. 94) Salik describes the methods that the Punjabi and

Pathan army officers used to tackle the Bengalis before the 1971 war actually broke out: 'Instead of eradicating those germs of independence, the authorities thought it wise to perpetuate the reign of terror "to keep the Bingos under control".' Bingos: a typical Sandhurst–Sialkot term of contempt for the Bengalis. The problem that the 'Bingos' of East Pakistan posed in terms of the Constitutional power equation was simply this: they outnumbered the non-Bingos of West Pakistan. And given the fact that the western side of Pakistan was divided into four competitive provinces, there was no way anyone could theoretically stop a Bengali from becoming the chief executive of the country in a one-man–one-vote election. Rather than surrender their control, the Punjabis preferred to allow the weeds of disintegration to flourish.

By 1953, the Bengalis were openly sceptical about the ideology that had created Pakistan. The Awami Muslim League deliberately dropped the word 'Muslim' from its name. This was not a mere gesture. Despite the huge population transfers at the time of partition, a substantial portion of the 30 million Hindus who lived in pre-partition East Bengal had remained in East Pakistan. The Awami League now consciously began wooing this Hindu support. Meanwhile Fazlul Haq created his Krishak Sramik Party, or Peasants and Workers Party, in September 1953. These were deliberate efforts to provide an alternative to the clergy–feudal politics of the Muslim League. The people fully endorsed this in the East Pakistan provincial elections of 1954. The Muslim League (the pro-Pakistan party) got a foretaste of what was to come in 1970 when it managed to win just 10 seats in a House of 309, in March 1954. The United Front of the Awami League, the Krishak Sramik Party and smaller allies swept the polls.

But the Punjabi civilian dictator, Governor-General Ghulam Moham-mad, was not going to allow a silly thing like the will of the people to come in the way of his plans. What he would not tolerate would not be. And he would not accept the United Front government of East Pakistan. Chief Minister Fazlul Haq visited Calcutta in May and made a few remarks which touched on his disillusionment with the Pakistan he had helped create. Ghulam Mohammad used that as the excuse to sack the Huq government. Once again, the message was that he was the boss. He decided to divide the United Front, and rule. The legislators soon became willing preys to Karachi's machinations. Such were the depths which the degenerate factionalism reached that the Awami League conspired to get the Speaker declared insane. In retaliation, members of the Krishak Sramik Party threw pieces of furniture at their foe, the Deputy

Speaker, Shahid Ali, and killed him. From insanity to death: that seems an appropriate image not only for the Legislature but also for the country.

The collapse was becoming evident in the west too. On 24 October 1954, Ghulam Mohammad, once again acting arbitrarily, dismissed the entire Constituent Assembly, citing his 'regret that the Constitutional machinery' had broken down. He authorized himself to announce the new Prime Minister and Cabinet, which was, to say the least, convenient. However, there were signs that the armed forces would soon have to step in. Field Marshal Ayub Khan told Pakistan in his first broadcast after he seized power in 1958, 'You may not know, but I refused on many occasions Mr Ghulam Mohammad's offer to take over the country.' It seems certain that Ghulam Mohammad, now ill enough to be near death, preferred handing over power to the generals rather than the politicians. He had begun grooming the army in the practice of civilian administration. General Ayub Khan was made Defence Minister in Ghulam Mohammad's nominated Cabinet of 1954. Also inducted was Major-General Iskander Mirza, a bureaucrat who had left the army but been allowed to keep his military rank, as Minister of the Interior. Another effort was now made to give Pakistan a Constitution. A second Constituent Assembly was formed in April 1955. Before it met in July, the politicians of the two wings agreed on a compromise formula (the 'Murree pact'): Bengalis surrendered the advantage of their numerical majority and got recognition of the Bengali language and a promise of autonomy in return.

In August 1955, a dying Ghulam Mohammad finally quit; Iskander Mirza took over and appointed a new Prime Minister, Chaudhury Mohammad Ali. It was largely through the latter's efforts that the 1956 Constitution became law. Pakistan was formally named an Islamic nation in which only a Muslim could be the head of state. (General Zia, in an interview with the author in 1982, carried the idea a bit further by saying that since Islam did not make any provision for a woman to be the head of a Muslim state, no woman could become the head of the Islamic Republic of Pakistan.) Neither of these two conditions existed in the basic principles of the first draft Constitution which the mullahs sabotaged. However, the Constitution of 1956 could go down in the *Guinness Book of Records* as the Constitution with the shortest life in the world. In less than two years it would be scrapped.

Mirza appointed three more prime ministers, including Shahid Suhrawardy, but nothing worked. On 7 October 1958, he finally asked General Ayub Khan to take over the government, abrogating the 1956 Constitution and dismissing the central and provincial cabinets. By 27 October President Iskander Mirza himself was eased out by a newly blooded army, Ayub Khan using the poor excuse (according to his memoirs) that Mirza's wife would not allow him to stop 'conspiring'. Like all generals on the morrow of a coup, Ayub Khan promised, 'Let me announce in unequivocal terms that our ultimate aim is to restore democracy, but of the type people can understand.' The people, of course, would never 'understand'. The army had not 'forsaken democracy', said Ayub. Actually, neither had democracy forsaken the army. It was simply that the two were never quite made for each other.

Army rule was inevitable. The army had one crucial thing in its favour. While every other institution was busy committing suicide in the very first decade of Pakistan's existence, the army had been consolidating its strength, power and prestige. It is interesting that in India precisely the opposite was happening. While the judiciary, the legislatures, and the other vital organs of a democratic society, such as the media, were learning the difficult lesson of how to manage the coexistence of freedom with responsibility, the Indian armed forces were neglected – as was all too evident during the China war of 1962. This neglect of the Indian army may have been unintentional, but it was not accidental: it was simply due to the fact that the energies and the interests of the men who took charge of India were concentrated either on economic development or on the growth of democratic institutions. The task was not easy, and it required all the genius of a Jawaharlal Nehru to protect the values enshrined in the Indian Constitution while trying to solve the enormous problems that stood in the way. India and Pakistan inherited many similar problems: refugees, regionalism, the threat inherent in a national language unacceptable to large sections of the people, religious conflict (far more dangerous, now, in India than in Pakistan) and, worst of all, poverty and hunger. But the two nations went about trying to find answers in completely different ways. While Pakistan indulged in a harlequin era, India went through hardship with a belief in itself that has been only grudgingly recorded, when it has been mentioned at all. While India defied the world's worst predictions, Pakistan had to experience the rule of generals (which was never on Jinnah's agenda) to find out about itself. And after its first decade of army rule, now described as the Golden Era, Pakistan discovered that it was not a country at all.

3
Masters, Not Friends

In January 1948, General Ayub Khan (later, impressed by his own success, he was to appoint himself Field Marshal) was transferred from the command of the Gardai Brigade in Waziristan to take over as General Officer Commanding, East Pakistan. Let us take a look at the general's career from a most sympathetic account: his autobiography, written when the author was at the very height of his power in Pakistan, in June 1964, during a convalescence in the hill resort of Murree. (By the time the Pakistan branch of Oxford University Press had published the book, in 1967, the situation was far less comfortable for the dictator.)

The autobiography has a defensive title, *Friends, Not Masters*, which is understandable enough, given what the people have always believed about the army. It opens with the ritual benediction: 'In the name of Allah the Beneficent, the Merciful.' The quotation below this line, from the Quran, is an attempt to justify why Ayub Khan seized power in 1958: 'Surely Allah changes not the condition of a people, until they change their own condition.' Ayub Khan decided to change the condition of the people of Pakistan since all Allah seemed to be doing up till 1958 was changing it for the worse. The autobiography is an easy read, if you overlook the terrifying use of cliché ('The hour had struck', etc.), and provides an insight into the attitudes that shaped the history of Pakistan through the crucial sixties.

Ayub Khan makes no attempt to disguise his unhappiness over his early East Pakistan posting. 'I could not say that I was excited at the prospect,' the general recalls. It was an 'abroad' assignment of the worst kind. (Conversely the Bengali bureaucrat or officer took pride in being transferred to West Pakistan; it was a privileged–underprivileged relationship.) Certainly the general did not take his wife and children to the hardship posting, and spent most of his time in the east trying to get back to the west. His contempt for the Bengali was obvious in both deed and word. He narrates the story of how he asked Mohammad Ali of Bogra, later to become Prime Minister but then a small-time leader in the East Pakistan Assembly, during a demonstration in July 1948, 'Are you looking for a bullet?' Bhutto, who worked with Ayub Khan, has recorded that his mentor bore an 'intense prejudice' against the Bengali. It was not just a matter of individual whim. Ayub Khan symbolized the Pathan–Punjabi arrogance which would catalyse the destruction of Pakistan. When the army came to power, it transferred these prejudices into policies, both economic and cultural. As scathing to the Bengali heart was the oft-expressed belief that the Bengali language and culture was inferior/Hindu/non-martial/feminine and therefore contemptible (the woman is very much a third-class human being in the machismo of the 'virile' Pathan or Punjabi of Pakistan). It is astonishing to the observer that the Punjabis and the Pathans, given the state of their own achievements in this field, should consider anyone actually inferior to them culturally, but who can argue with such a marriage of arrogance and ignorance? The only thing one can say about the army in Pakistan is that it is consistent: the first time it came to power, it helped create Bangladesh, and in its second spell, it is doing its level best to make Sind an independent country.

Army rule is only another manifestation of all that is wrong with the idea and state of Pakistan. Being non-ideological by training and ability, it was inevitable that the military would one day seize power in a nation without an ideology. Pakistan was a geographical area turned into a country, without a controlling cohesive idea which could generate a genuine nationalism among the masses or the leaders. The civilian politicians tried their best to disguise this fact, but they floundered and failed because their minds were not rooted at some point in political faith. You cannot rule an artificial creation; you can only provide temporary order. And it was only logical, therefore, that the uniformed guardians of order, the armed forces, would one day seize power. But the essential problem remained, of course: behind the order, there was no law, there was nothing to believe in, nothing to respect, nothing to unify the people. You cannot create a country simply to express faith in Allah; the Muslim who believes in Allah will do so anywhere – in Africa or America or China or India. It is not surprising, therefore, that notwithstanding three attempts (all endorsed by the legislatures), Pakistan still does not have a Constitution upon which the country is agreed. A Constitution is an expression of faith, not an exercise in semantics.

The only faith that the soldiers had was in themselves, and that was good enough to provide the veneer of success in the midst of collapsing confidence. Ayub Khan did not organize a coup until he had built the army's ability and confidence. That was his foresight; otherwise the only institution to acquire some strength in Pakistan might have ended up as brittle as the country. In 1971, of course, even the army could not save the nation; but then no army can defend a country from itself.

The first attempt at a coup by the armed forces was not led by Ayub Khan, nor did it come in 1958. When General Ayub Khan, the first Pakistani to head his country's army, took charge from General Sir Douglas Gracey (who had refused to accept Jinnah's order to send Pakistani troops to Kashmir in the 1947 war, since he said he still took his orders from the Governor-General of India, Lord Mountbatten), on 17 January 1951, the very first thing he learnt from his British predecessor was that there was a group of 'young Turks' in the army which could cause both the country and the new Commander-in-Chief concern. All that Gracey would say in addition was that officers like Major-General Akbar Khan were 'peculiar'.

Ayub Khan writes that Prime Minister Liaquat Ali Khan confirmed the suspicion at a lunch with him and Iskander Mirza at Sargodha railway station. A restless Prime Minister is quoted as saying, 'Gentlemen, I have some bad news for you. It has come to my knowledge that a military coup to overthrow the government has been planned by certain army officers and it is going to be put into effect very soon.' Ayub Khan suspected an officer known for having troublesome ideas, Brigadier Siddique Khan. The interrogation was brief: 'Siddique, you tell me the truth or I shall string you upside-down,' said the Commander-in-Chief. In the event, Siddique told a lie and remained upright. He denied flatly that there was any such conspiracy and was allowed to return to his command at Bannu. But Siddique forgot that his telephone was tapped. The intelligence services exposed him when he phoned a fellow-conspirator, Colonel Arbab, at Thal to tell him, presumably in a Sandhurst accent, 'The cat is out of the bag.' Inspector-General of Police Qurban Ali Khan led the raids that rounded up the military and civilian conspirators in one night.

An in-camera trial was held, and the man the conspirators chose to conduct their defence was none other than Shahid Suhrawardy. The proceedings are still secret, but it is known that the conspiracy was not the work simply of a small handful, and that support for a coup was widespread among the officers. One can hardly blame the officers for having such ideas as early as 1951, even though this was at a time when the civilian government had not yet been discredited in the public eye.

They saw, as much as anyone else, that the civilian elite was feasting on this sudden gift of a country, and they thought they were as deserving as anyone else of the loot. All you had to do was pay a bit of lip-service to Allah, and that did not sound very difficult.

Later, Ayub Khan was to justify his own 'revolution' (the official term for the coup) in 1958 by saying that Karachi, the capital, was 'a hotbed of intrigue ... Why were people not attending to their work with some honesty of purpose and why could they not evolve some team spirit? Why all these factions, dissensions and disputes? And why all this malice and distrust? They were all busy destroying one another. It used to take me three or four days to recover from [the depression of] a Karachi visit. Whatever institutions we had inherited at the time of Independence, or had set up since then, were crumbling one by one ... Everyone had joined the political vaudeville. There was no organ of administration which was not pressed into service to promote individual political interests.'

On 9 June 1958, Prime Minister Feroz Khan Noon gave General Ayub Khan an extension of two years as Commander-in-Chief. On 8 October, General Ayub Khan decided to give himself a slightly longer extension. But he had been actively working for at least six months towards the October coup. The diary he kept during the period, and which he quotes in his autobiography, records that on 13 May 1958 he visited Begum Liaquat Ali Khan at The Hague, and she thought the only solution was 'tight rule for about ten years' (actually, that was about how long it lasted, before unravelling into the confusion that broke the country). The entry of 30 June shows that the general was preparing himself; the book he was reading was *The Men Who Ruled India*.

On 4 October, Ayub Khan left Rawalpindi, in his special railway saloon coach, for Karachi where Generals Hamid and Yahya Khan were waiting for him. By 7.00 p.m. on 7 October Prime Minister Noon had finally worked out yet another compromise between his squabbling coalition colleagues, but at 8.00 p.m. all the compromise was over. Aided by President Iskander Mirza, General Ayub Khan ended the first phase of Pakistan's history.

Pakistan's history can be divided into four distinct parts, two in the old Pakistan, and two in the new: from 1947 to 1958, a progressively deteriorating civilian rule; from 1958 to 1971, a progressively destructive military dictatorship; from 1971 to 1977 in present-day Pakistan, an increasingly non-representative democracy; and from 1977 onwards, as we are witnessing, a military dictatorship working towards making this the permanent form of government. They are parallel eras, the future a mirror-image of the past – except that the second time around both civilian and military rule were far more dangerous and destructive than in the first spell.

Pakistan's initial experience with democracy ended in despair thanks to the hollow pettiness of the men at the helm; the second ended in blood thanks to the decline of one man from brilliance to megalomania. If the line of leaders from Ghulam Mohammad to Iskander Mirza destroyed themselves by presiding each morning in front of the mirror over the argument between their face and their nose, then Zulfiqar Ali Bhutto began fantasizing in front of *his* mirror about becoming an emperor. Neither the stupidities of the former nor the ego of the latter could be controlled by institutions having faith in something more important than the transient leaders. Ghulam Mohammad died unmourned; Iskander Mirza was sent by Ayub Khan to exile in London; Bhutto had to be hanged. That symbolized the deterioration in the system better than anything else.

Bhutto was a product of Thomas Babington Macaulay's educational system and an unbroken feudal tradition stretching back centuries. In the club he was a liberal with interesting ideas and captivating conversation; at home he would make the peasants wait for days outside his residence before he, the prince and landlord, granted them an audience – humiliation was good for the riff-raff and taught them their place in life. On the streets and at election meetings he was the destroyer of the conservatism of the mullahs, the man who could take on the clergy and the military, the people's hero, intoxicated by the cheers of millions and in turn intoxicating them with his finely tuned oratory. He understood need and response, mood and wavelength. There is the famous story about a speech he made in front of a massive and roaring Lahore audience. It was well-known even then in the Islamic Republic of Pakistan that Zulfiqar Ali Bhutto was not terribly Islamic in his personal habits, and liked a bit of good Scotch to keep the spirit going. The mullahs knew this too and were determined to embarrass him. And so they began to heckle Bhutto at this meeting, calling him a drunkard, assuming that the Muslim crowd would not quite approve of such anti-Islamic tastes. Bhutto took this for a while, and then turned to the crowd and said: 'They say that I drink liquor. Yes, I do. I drink liquor but, unlike the mullahs, I do not drink the people's blood.' The crowd roared in approval, and a slogan resulted from the incident: *'Peewey, peewey, Bhutto peewey; jeewey, jeewey, Bhutto jeewey'* ('Drink, drink, Bhutto drink; live, live, Bhutto live'). A new and liberal mood was beginning to seep through Pakistan in the aftermath of the 1971 war, with both the army and the clergy being held responsible by the people for the decimation of the country. Bhutto rode that mood, carrying his war against the clergy to cruder but more powerful levels when on the streets of Lahore he made public fun of the clergy's notorious predilection for homosexuality. (Jokes about the bearded, pompously pious mullah and the little boy are common throughout the Muslim world, and the clergy, irrespective of culture and nationality, do seem to share this particular taste. There are jokes, for instance, in Iran about how exceptionally warm the brotherly Islamic hug gets when the mullahs go through the accepted greeting with young revolutionary guards.)

A different facet of Bhutto's personality is revealed by an experience narrated to this author by Bhutto's press adviser, Khalid Hassan. Once Bhutto wanted to send a personal, and therefore not very formal, letter to the Russians, and the Foreign Ministry was duly instructed to prepare such a letter. After much effort, Bhutto got the Foreign Office version of an 'informal' letter. Bhutto read it and called Khalid Hassan in. With a resigned look on his face, Bhutto asked his aide, 'You know what was the biggest failure of the British on our subcontinent?' It was now the turn of Khalid Hassan to look resigned, since he thought that the boss was going to go off into one of his long, rambling monologues. But Bhutto, for a change, answered his own question crisply: 'Their biggest failure was that after ruling here for two hundred years, they still couldn't manage to teach anyone English.'

Between the rousing orator and the sophisticated wit existed a Bonaparte with an ego larger, and an ability considerably smaller, than Napoleon's. Even his loyalists would not go to the extent of calling Bhutto a democrat. Perhaps in his fantasy he was to be crowned by the popular will; in any case, he quickly organized a title for himself which was in direct association with and succession to the one the country had given to its father figure, Jinnah. Jinnah was the *Quaid-e-Azam*, 'the great leader'; Bhutto nominated himself the *Quaid-e-Awam*, 'the leader of the people'. (This is the kind of absurdity Mrs Indira Gandhi would never have dreamt of perpetrating: nobody would know when to stop laughing.) If Pakistan had had institutions nurtured by democracy, Bhutto might have been saved from his excesses. But it was a confused Pakistan which was given to him, eager but unsure of the way to return to stability; and there were no reference points which might have kept it on course, within the confines of legitimacy. Bhutto got the chance to create a democratic

Pakistan, but either he did not know how, or it was simply not possible. If 1971 had ensured a return to civilian power, then 1977 equally ensured the return of a new rehabilitated army.

It did not need any exceptional insight to work out what Bhutto's immediate priorities should be when power was handed over to him after the fall of East Pakistan to Jagjit Singh Aurora's armies in December 1971. The country was physically and morally shattered but, interestingly, even then the military had to be pushed out. Dhaka fell on 17 December, and Yahya Khan's name disappeared from the Radio Pakistan news bulletins for twenty-four hours; then it reappeared. There was great apprehension about the future; for instance, the State Bank of Pakistan had to deny rumours that large-denomination currency was being demonetized. Bhutto was in New York, trying to lead the battle in the United Nations, as he had done in 1965. He was recalled, but the word was put about that Nurul Amin, the Bengali collaborator with Islamabad, might become the Prime Minister and Bhutto his deputy. There was no categorical statement that Yahya would step down. Air Marshal Asghar Khan met Yahya Khan and bluntly told him to get out before he was lynched. Said Asghar Khan, 'Yahya humiliated the army ... [unfortunately] we do not have the Japanese tradition [of hara-kiri] ... I don't give a damn who replaces him.'

By the time Bhutto reached London for a meeting with Sir Alec Douglas-Home, on his way back from New York, he was on top of the world. 'The people have confidence in me,' he told the Press. And then he began visualizing his role in the future· 'We are going to have to build a new country again. Many problems face us. It is almost like the first chapter of Genesis.'

In Bhutto's mind, it was Genesis and he was playing God.

Certainly the first address to the nation was dominated by the pronoun 'I'. Yahya Khan had sworn-in Bhutto in the same way as power had been transferred between Ayub Khan and himself – to one man's regret and the other's delight, but peacefully done. Bhutto went on the air and spoke to the waiting nation. Apart from the jarring refrain of 'I', it was good populism: 'I wish I were not alive today ... I want to speak to you from my heart [referring to the absence of a formal text for the speech] ... Military victory is no victory ... [The new Constitution] will not be my Constitution. I am a servant of the people ... I need your co-operation; I need your support ... I will not move one step without your approval ... I have been five and a half years in the struggle for democracy. It has not been an ordinary struggle.'

Earlier, speaking to newsmen in London, Bhutto had said that a 'loose federation of provinces is the only solution'. There was at least public recognition then by Bhutto that the two things that could still hold Pakistan together were democracy and greater regional autonomy. Bhutto was talking in the context of Bangladesh, bolstering the myth that Pakistan had not yet broken, but he surely knew that Baluchistan and Sind too were simmering under what they felt to be Punjab's yoke. However, instead of doing anything to create and strengthen those institutions which might ensure present and future freedom, Bhutto began using them for the promotion of his personal power.

The signs were visible early. For instance, within months of taking office Bhutto had made it clear that only those journals and journalists would survive who saw the truth through Bhutto's eyes. Three Lahore periodicals were banned and their editors and publishers arrested: *Zindagi*, *Urdu Digest* and *Punjab Panch*. *Dawn*, the newspaper which was once the voice of the Muslim League, called it the severest attack on the Pakistani press since independence.

It soon became clear what kind of democracy Mr Bhutto had in mind. The White Papers published by the Zia government are obviously biased; many of the quotations are from political and personal opponents of Mr Bhutto, and therefore stained with doubt. But even if we restrict our evidence to what is quoted from the official government documents of the Bhutto period, it is quite clear that the only thing that Bhutto really respected was himself. Anyone who dared challenge him, for whatever reason, serious or trivial, became not only his but also the state's enemy. Bhutto did make one mistake which less arrogant or more careful people might have avoided – he put down quite a bit on paper, including govern- ment files. Or he spoke out on record. Two incidents relating to the passage of the 5th Constitutional Amendment in 1976, concerning the judiciary, will provide the flavour of what the Bhutto government thought about this vital institution. 'On March 2, 1976 [according to Volume 2 of the White Paper on the performance of the Bhutto regime, "Treatment of Fundamental State Institutions"] an officer on special duty, Malik Fazal Karim, addressed a note to the Prime Minister in which he blamed the defeat of the pro-Bhutto candidate for the presidentship of the Lahore High Court Bar Association on the then Chief Justice of the High Court, and recommended, "Now that the judiciary has come out in the form of a parallel government, the stage has come that the 5th Constitutional Amendment be made bringing the judiciary under the control of

Parliament instead of Supreme Judiciary Council, as is the case in America.'''

Mr Bhutto was apparently pleased and noted in the margin, 'Most Important'. And during the debate on the Fifth Amendment Bill, Mr Bhutto and his colleagues launched a vicious attack on the higher judiciary. Bhutto declared on 4 September, 'The judiciary cannot become a parallel executive by wholesale misapplication, misrepresentation and misinterpretation of laws. This must be clearly understood . . . and anyone who does not understand it does so at his own peril.'

The amendment had been introduced to protect the right of the executive to detain a person and be the sole arbiter of detention. Arguing in favour of the executive, Bhutto told the Assembly: 'This must be clearly understood, Mr Speaker, Sir, preventive detention is synonymous with the Emergency. It is part and parcel of it. The Emergency has been upheld and it has to be upheld because the executive alone has the authority to declare and determine whether an Emergency exists.' Incidentally, the Emergency that Mr Bhutto was referring to had been imposed in Pakistan before the 1971 war, on 23 November; Bhutto went through his whole term of more than six years without lifting it.

The judiciary was emasculated, the bureaucracy was turned into a fiefdom. There is instance after instance of arbitrary dismissal and punishment, all noted on the file, for the crime of being less than loyal to the imperious Bhutto.

In the end, the very institutions Bhutto used turned against him, and when he also insulted the people by rigging the 1977 elections they turned against him too – violently. Bhutto, however, was always convinced that he had taken out an insurance policy with the army by appointing loyal generals to the senior posts. This, coupled with his own assessment of his genius (Machiavelli – Cicero – Talleyrand – Plato – as and when he wanted to be any one of these), made him infallible in his own eyes. His pathetic disbelief at his wretched state in jail, waiting for the noose, makes sad reading. Nothing saved him, not even his foreign policy, of which he was legitimately proud, and of course there was no question of his escaping the consequences of either his character or his domestic policy.

But why did the army, which Bhutto had done so much to restore to respectability, turn against him? And how did Zia, Bhutto's chosen general, send him first to jail and then the gallows?

In 1969, after Bhutto had broken with Ayub, he became convinced that the only way he could come to power was through democracy, since

obviously the army would not let him take the top job with their support.
He then began a major political movement against army rule. In 1969 he
told Tariq Ali (*Can Pakistan Survive?* Penguin Books), while requesting the
firebrand student leader to join his party: 'You are too much of a purist.
This is Pakistan and we cannot ignore Islam. There are only two ways to
get rid of those bastards [the army]. Mine or that of Che Guevara. It's either
me or the Baluchis in the mountains with their guns.'

In the end, as Tariq Ali has so convincingly demonstrated in his book,
the class character of Bhutto and his regime drew him into a confrontation
with those 'Baluchis in the mountains'. Bhutto, forgetting all his ideas
about granting more autonomy to the regional nationalities, set in motion
an operation to crush them. Sind did not revolt because Bhutto himself
was a Sindhi and the area had some emotional stake in his government
even if it did not benefit to any great extent economically. Power remained
in the Punjab, and Bhutto throughout his tenure always made sure that
Punjab got its expected share (a huge one) of the pie.

The Baluchis had been dragged into Pakistan; before partition, theirs
was a feudal state, and they wanted to retain that status after 1947.
Pakistan sent its army to ensure accession in 1948, and the first Pakistani
army campaign against the Baluchis was conducted by Ayub Khan in
1949. Baluchi leaders were hanged; the movement subsided, only to
revive with the new currents flowing in the post-Bangladesh era. A civil
war ensued, in which up to four Pakistani divisions were engaged. In
August–September 1974, the Pakistani army and air force launched a
massive aerial–ground operation which once again brought the Baluchis
into submission.

Tariq Ali sums up the consequences in his book: 'The Pak army,
discredited after the debacle of Bangladesh, was now given a new
opportunity to reoccupy the country's political stage. It is worth stressing
that the longest military campaigns conducted by Pakistani generals since
1947 have been directed against the Bengalis and the Baluchis inside
Pakistan. One led to the disintegration of the state, the second paved the
way for the post-1977 military dictatorship ... Bhutto's downfall and the
end of civilian rule can be traced directly to the PPP's [People's Party of
Pakistan] refusal to tolerate a meaningful regional autonomy. Bhutto's
Baluch adventure was a disaster on every count. It poisoned the political
atmosphere of Pakistan and the country is still suffering from the
pollution. It thus laid the base for the military coup of July 1977. When
Bhutto and his Defence Minister General Tikka Khan ordered four army

divisions to crush the Baluch, they sealed the fate of their own regime.'
(When in 1983 Sind asked the Baluchis to join the movement it had
launched against Zia and the Pakistani army, the Baluchis, remembering
the Sindhi leader Bhutto and what he did in 1974, refused.)

Bhutto was also plagued by one of Pakistan's oldest problems – the
foreign, and more specifically the American, arm twist. The military
governments, unsure about support at home, had always needed the
crutch of foreign arms, money and sustenance. When the army re-
emerged in 1977, it needed some prodding from the Americans. Bhutto,
through his friend and ally Colonel Gaddafi, was effecting a slow turn in
Pakistan's foreign policy. His distrust of Washington had deep roots; he
believed that the USA had bailed India out in the 1965 war (Bhutto's book
The Myth of Independence covers this in Chapter 5, 'America aids India and
ignores Pakistan', and Chapter 6, 'American policy to bring Pakistan
under Indian hegemony').

It was, interestingly, General Zia who confirmed this, in an interview to
the Indian Member of Parliament, Subramaniam Swamy, published in
Sunday (13–19 November 1983). General Zia told Swamy: 'It may interest
you that American refusal to ditto what Bhutto wanted nearly landed
Pakistan in the Soviet camp in 1977 ... Bhutto had approached
Muammar Gaddafi for a proper introduction to the Russians because he
was not getting anything from the Americans. He told Gaddafi that he
would go a long way to accommodate Soviet interests. Gaddafi then con-
tacted Marshal Tito who was going to Moscow, and apprised him of this
Bhutto offer and urged him to plead Bhutto's case. Tito told me later that
in fact he did persuade the Soviets for a price that Pakistan would have to
pay. But it came too late, because soon after Bhutto fell from power.' Fell
– or was pushed out, jailed and then hanged, marking the end of
Pakistan's second and more tragic experiment in democracy.

4
The Believer

Every popular movement is a pile of many layers; people of bitterly conflicting ideologies, interests and motives come together against the common target. The movement launched in Pakistan after the rigged elections of 1977 had wide support, stretching from the mullahs in the PNA (Pakistan National Alliance), via the secular National Democratic Alliance, to leftist independents who had come into their own in the years of civilian rule after 1971. But the movement to remove Bhutto acquired strength and steel mainly because of the unprecedented participation of the people, who could accept dictatorship with a straight face but were furious at being cheated by a turncoat democrat. From the moment that Bhutto announced general elections, he also began a sustained effort to ensure that he could not lose. The media, always pliant, were converted into a propaganda vehicle; traditional powerbrokers, like the landlords, were quietly wooed, while Bhutto tried to win the masses with populist rhetoric. He had reason to be confident of victory. But in the elections Bhutto, obviously paranoid about defeat, indulged in blatant rigging. Commentators say that Bhutto would have won even if he had allowed the election to be free and fair; perhaps, but nobody in Pakistan was going to believe it after the experience at the polls. Pakistani anger was heightened by the fact that democratic India in March 1977 not only sent Mrs Gandhi out of power, but did it completely peacefully. Nor did Mrs Gandhi try to rig the polls, or attempt to remain in office after her defeat.

Normally when a popular movement against a ruler nears success, the dominant group within it takes on the responsibility of replacing the incumbent. There will be a period of confusion and conflict among those who once fought on the streets together, but obviously the most powerful element will triumph. It was the right wing, particularly the fundamentalists, who had provided the rallying core of the anti-Bhutto movement. But no sooner had they neared success than their essential weakness was also exposed. They realized that while they might have been able to bring out the crowds for the limited purpose of destroying Bhutto, they did not have the support of the people in sufficient strength to create a new government. If at the very height of the anti-Bhutto wave the mullahs could not bank on the people's support, what hope of their winning popularity at any other time?

It is not an assessment that this author makes arbitrarily: the point was also made by none other than General Zia during an interview in May 1982, when he said frankly that he did not hold the promised elections in 1977 because the right-wing parties were certain that they would be demolished and that the PPP (People's Party of Pakistan), under Bhutto, would come back to power. General Zia said: 'The PPP would have won [in 1977]. The PPP was the party we had thrown out. And they [the non-PPP politicians] said, "What is the good of this? You might as well hand over power to them. We forced the army to take this initiative not only to overthrow the regime but also to take measures so that Islamic laws were brought in, Nizam-e-Mustafa is established, and a regime comes to power which has the mandate from the people of Pakistan."' I pointed out that there was a contradiction in saying that such a regime would have the 'mandate' if it could not even face an election, and General Zia answered very simply: 'Yes, there is a contradiction.'

There is also the interesting use of the word 'forced'. The mullahs 'forced' the army to take over, according to General Zia. The reason is very simple – because there was no other way that their extremist ideology would ever become the law of the land. Since the mullahs could not rule in a democracy, the army was made their instrument. The mullahs had, by now, found the fundamentalist generals. This was their chance; to seize power in this confusion, with Bhutto momentarily in disarray. And the generals got a great alibi: Allah. In July 1977, General Mohammad Zia-ul-Huq walked into Bhutto's office and told him that his time had come.

General Zia told this author that he had in fact given Bhutto fifteen days' notice of the coup. This crept into the reply when I asked whether he had ever felt that the hanging of Bhutto was wrong, and he had said, 'No, no, never.' I followed up with a question as to how exactly he felt personally at the moment that Bhutto was being hanged. General Zia gave a lengthy reply: 'Again I felt the same: he was destined to be hanged, because he committed so many murders. His own five years' record, when you look back – perhaps this was the punishment which was destined by God. I have no regrets or second thoughts because a man of his intelligence and talent, and so much education ... if he was only loyal and sincere and would not have indulged in the atrocities and in the inhuman behaviour which he allowed under his rule, he would have ruled this country for the rest of his life. Why then was he thrown out? There must be something. That something was his atrocities. Under his own regime, and perhaps with his knowledge, the daughters of respected people were lifted off the street and raped, people were subjected to acts of sodomy, just to take out the venom of political enmity. Is this human? There are a hundred and one things ... And I was surprised, honestly [when I learnt all this]. I went to him [Bhutto] and I said, "Mr Bhutto, please hold the election. I assure you, you will win a thundering victory." Then a second time I went to him and said, "Please, Mr Prime Minister, this is a critical problem, solve it politically before the army breaks, because then you will not be able to solve it." And on 20 June 1977, I went to him alone and told him, "Sir, there have been 400 casualties. I am standing on dynamite in the sense that if the army starts getting cracks, then we have had it. If you do not solve the problem politically then I will have to use the military option" ... [Bhutto's] reaction was, "Please give me some more time. Please do not do anything rashly." I said, "I assure you of my loyalty. But if I have to stay, I cannot face the public any longer. You have to resolve this issue politically or I will use the military option."' I suggested to General Zia that he must be the only person in the world who had given advance notice of a coup, and General Zia replied, 'Fifteen days, and it is on record. Of course it was only he and me, my word against his. But this was the reality.'

What happened in those fifteen days, and what were the 'cracks' in the army that General Zia spoke about? He must have been referring to the debate in the military about whether a coup was necessary and what should be the rationale for it. In the end, the fundamentalist generals carried the day, and Bhutto had to pay the ultimate price. The generals knew exactly what they were going to do – perhaps that is why they have lasted so long.

General Zia came with a gun in his right hand and a speech promising the restoration of democracy in his left. In a very short while, the left hand was not being told what the right hand was doing. Elections would be allowed only if and when the PPP was safely put out of the way. General Zia said as much to this author: 'Yes, there is no doubt about that. I said, "Election is not an end in itself; it is a means to an end."' The end, of course, was the creation of a Nizam-e-Mustafa in Pakistan, an undiluted theocracy.

But it would be foolish to imagine that Islam alone is going to bale out a Pakistan run by the generals. After Ayub Khan's spell in power, the East Pakistanis used the search for democracy as an outlet for many frustrations. General Yahya Khan's sole contribution to his country was that, thanks to a miscalculation, he held the only genuine elections Pakistan has known. The results of the 1970 elections indicated that the legacy of 1947 was now exhausted.

5
'Is the Weather Freezing?'

If a dictatorship had the imagination to absorb popular sentiment and respond to it, it would not long remain a dictatorship. The only option that it has is to use repression and try to control the consequences for as long as it can. This was precisely what General Zia did in the last quarter of 1983.

When he first assumed power, General Zia was generally dismissed as being of passing importance, chosen by accident, a man who would not survive the flood of ideas and emotion released by the elections and the mass movement of 1977. But he survived because he was the first ruler Pakistan had who not only understood why and by whom Pakistan had been created, but was totally unembarrassed by the truth. He realized that the country had been created in the name of faith, not in the name of the people – and therefore if the country had to survive, then it would only do so by the logic of faith, not the logic of popular will. Democracy was contrary to the birth of Pakistan, and therefore any permission to allow it would lead to confusion, and eventually to a requestioning of the idea that had in 1947 created the country. As General Zia told this author: 'It was accepted, even at the conceptual stage before Pakistan was born, that not all the Muslims would be able to be housed in this homeland of Pakistan though it would be open to everybody. But a large minority would be left in India, and it was expected that they would grow as Indian nationals having the Islamic faith. Bangladesh, of course, is a creation of different circumstances, but even there you find a sizeable minority of Hindus, so the question is not as clearly defined as in Pakistan. But this country was created in the name of Islam. And the moment that sight was lost, what remained? You take away the ideology of an ideological state, nothing is left. And this is why Pakistan faced hurdle after hurdle: the identity was not established. The basic philosophy was lost and people were groping in the dark, whether it is the 1956 Constitution, the 1963 Constitution, martial law or no martial law, People's Party, socialist regime, and back to martial law. That is why we have been unfortunate. You had your goal set, and went off on that way. This is why we find that India is well set while Pakistan is still groping.'

A fine assessment, only flawed at the nodal point by one reality – that the people want democracy and not an ideological state which will define their lives according to the notions of the mullahs and their latest friends in the army. The people do not believe that to be a good Muslim you have to live according to the intellectual wasteland of the mullah's mind; the people do not feel that a permanent confrontation with 'Hindu' India is a necessary concomitant to their existence. Instead, they envy the breeze of democracy and freedom that blows through their neighbour's large and varied territories, and want such a wind to set them free too. So the confrontation between the people and the elite will take many, and sometimes even distorted, forms, while the continued efforts of the elite to retain their power will draw it towards policies which, in the short term, will create imbalances within the country, and so lead eventually to dismemberment, as the internal colonization becomes unbearable. Israel is the other important theocratic state, but it can afford to hold elections because majority commitment to its ideology was born out of centuries of suffering, culminating in the holocaust unleashed in Christian Germany. Such a motivation does not exist in Pakistan for the very simple reason that while Islam may have had its ups and downs on this subcontinent, which is as large as Europe, it has never been in danger of extinction – not before partition and not after. Commitment to personal faith is not the same thing as commitment to a religious state; the first can exist without the second, as indeed it does for by far the majority of the world's Muslim population. The tragedy is that the 'Islam in danger' slogan was such an easy blindfold.

Unable to get the genuine support of the masses, the current military–mullah raj has embarked on the same strategic policy which Ayub Khan's military–bureaucracy raj tried unsuccessfully: make Punjab the well-nourished fort, with an independent army, from which you can rule the hinterland. Pakistan has become not the first country of the Indian Muslim, but the first empire of the Punjabi Muslim. Rarely was this more evident than during the upsurge of 1983.

On Pakistan's Independence Day in 1983, the Movement for the Restoration of Democracy (MRD) launched yet another effort to make the soldiers hold the elections they had been promising ever since they had come to power. It was a brave attempt to end more than six years of vacillation and false promises. On 14 August, according to a Reuters report, two bombs were thrown at a government office, seriously hurting one person. Within days the whole of Sind was on fire, with villagers in the interior challenging – often violently – any image of martial authority they could find. Policemen were lynched, soldiers attacked; in one symbolic gesture, dogs were let loose with 'Zia' painted on their bodies. It was a spontaneous and even inspiring display of the people's disgust. But in the end it failed, because it remained confined to Sind. Punjab refused to join the movement to any significant extent. Mary Anne Weaver, the Delhi-based correspondent of the *Christian Science Monitor*, in an excellent series of reports on the situation in Sind, quoted Iqbal Haider, the joint secretary-general of the MRD, as saying, 'In the long term, if the Punjab does not come in, it will be even more damaging for the future of Pakistan ... only a democracy based on some autonomy for the provinces will keep this country integrated.' Note that autonomous democracy was precisely the idea offered by the Congress against the Muslim League's demand for Pakistan.

Punjab's attitude, far from creating any depression, delighted G. M. Sayed, the grand old man who has been under house arrest for more than twenty years in his village, Sann, for demanding a separate Sindhu Desh. It confirmed what he had begun to feel about this patched-up job called Pakistan, much earlier – that given the system, there was no alternative to disintegration. The eighty-year-old who had seen so much told Mary Anne Weaver: 'There is no longer room for compromise ... Sind must become an independent state.' He quoted figures to prove why he felt discriminated against: 'Only 2 per cent of the armed forces now come from Sind. Sindhis comprise only 5 per cent of the federal civil service. Of 2,000 industrial units now operating in the province, only 500 are controlled by Sindhis.'

General Zia, of course, used the two easily available weapons: repression, and promoting the fear that 'Hindu' India was once again destroying 'Islamic' Pakistan. A mild statement by Mrs Indira Gandhi supporting, in principle, democratic forces anywhere, including in Pakistan, was converted into the 'proof' that Mrs Gandhi wanted to repeat in Sind what she had done in Bangladesh, that she was behind it all. But this was a tired argument. The Sindhis either ignored it or, indeed, welcomed the thought. Mary Anne Weaver reported G. M. Sayed's reaction: 'He would even prefer that Sind be part of India, he told me, exuding unabashed delight now that

Indian Prime Minister Indira Gandhi had given tacit approval to the present protest and to Pakistan's ground-swell now demanding its political rights.' Perhaps this might be considered an extreme Sindhi reaction. But even PPP leader Ghulam Mustafa Khar told journalists, 'No patriotic Pakistani would tolerate interference by another country ... [But] in fact her [Mrs Gandhi's] statement has been welcomed by the people of Pakistan fighting for their democratic rights ... a new and harmonious relationship would emerge between the people of Pakistan and India after democracy is restored in Pakistan.'

Inevitably.

Bhutto had won the people's support both in his native Sind and in Punjab, but his daughter, Benazir, sounded more bitter than her father when she was able to talk to the world after she had been expelled from Pakistan in January 1984. Speaking to Tariq Ali, who was reporting for *The Telegraph*, Calcutta (15 January 1984), she said, 'The condition of our people, especially in Sind, is terrible. My condition is nothing compared to what men and women have suffered under this dictatorship ... I am delighted to be free but sad that I cannot be free in my own country.'

And in a long interview given to Ramesh Chandran of *India Today* (15 February 1984), she said: 'There are widespread allegations about army atrocities in Sind. Because I was under detention I do not have access to these sources. None the less there were amazing stories of crops being burned, bodies being discovered in the sugar-cane fields, of men, women and children being machine-gunned. One of our people told me that an officer who had served in Bangladesh said the situation was worse than it had been in Bangladesh. Massive force has been used ... The army does not realize the depth of the people's resentment. The whole of rural Sind has become revolutionized.'

And in reply to the question about whether Zia's Islamization was working, Benazir answered: 'What Islamization? When anybody says it's winter, you don't take him at his word. You look around to see if the accompaniments are there. Are people wearing overcoats? Have the trees shed their leaves? Is the weather freezing?'

In 1947 Jinnah got his 'moth-eaten' Pakistan. In 1971 Mujib took half of it away. What is left is shivering, as the early tremors of another earthquake are beginning to be felt.

But according to all the conventional wisdom, it was India, not Pakistan, which was scheduled to splinter within a quarter-century of its freedom. There was, in fact, in 1947 a formal, powerful and growing secessionist political party in the Indian state of Madras, which loudly proclaimed from every platform that it wanted independence. What happened along the way to 1985 that India remained united?

6
A Home for Gandhi's Soul

On Independence Day, 1947, Pakistan was in an euphoria. The long caravans of unutterable sorrow were still making their bloodstained way across the subcontinent, but at least for the Muslims there was some balm in the fact that they were going to what they thought was their promised land, a country washed clean of the dread that had stifled them these last awful months. The Hindus and Sikhs crossing over to India were not even allowed the psychological satisfaction of hate. Mohandas Karamchand Gandhi insisted that they learn to live in peace and friendship with the community which in the name of religion had killed their children and destroyed their women. And Gandhi's disciples, Rajendra Prasad, Jawaharlal Nehru, Vallabhbhai Patel, Abul Kalam Azad, no matter what their personal prejudices, were soon to enshrine Gandhi's message that Hindu and Muslim could live together, in a document that would become the heartbeat of the country: the Constitution of India. India would not be a Hindu state.

There was dancing on the streets of India after Jawaharlal Nehru, banking only on the memory of the scribble he had jotted down earlier, but speaking truly from the centre of a long dream, made a unique promise: 'Long years ago we made a tryst with destiny, and now the time comes when we shall redeem our pledge, not wholly or in full measure, but very substantially. At the stroke of midnight, while the world sleeps, India will wake to life and freedom ... A moment comes which comes but rarely in history, when we step out from the old to the new, when an age ends, and when the soul of a nation, long suppressed, finds utterance ... We have to build the noble mansion of free India where all her children may dwell.'

But it was equally impossible on the day India became free to hide the sadness. This was not the freedom they had really dreamed of; it was a freedom reduced by division and hate, and wrought in the midst of the most appalling civil war in history, a brutal war which was to take an estimated 500,000 lives before the fires lit by the communalists finally turned to smouldering ashes. Till this day that fire has not yet died, and there are enough people who spend their time trying to provoke the embers into another conflagration. And who else but Gandhi could best symbolize the tragedy behind the freedom?

On 15 August 1947 he did not participate in the joy because he had nothing to celebrate. He was in Calcutta at Hydari House, 151 Beliaghata Road, performing the last miracle of his life. When Nehru announced freedom at the stroke of midnight, Gandhi was asleep on a mat, with a handful of disciples, in the ruined house of a Muslim, in the same room as the others, his *Gita*, steel-rimmed spectacles and dentures beside him. The previous evening he had asked a friend 'Have I led the country astray?' He woke up an hour earlier than normal, at two o'clock, and began the day as usual with prayer and a recitation of the *Gita*. It was a day of mourning for the father of the nation. He was sitting in Calcutta instead of participating in the tumult of Delhi because he had promised himself that he would not allow a holocaust between Hindus and Muslims in the most explosive city in the country, Calcutta. If Calcutta had become a battleground on that day, the death and destruction would have surmounted even the wretched, barbaric heights of Punjab. Gandhi kept Calcutta peaceful: he told the Hindus and Muslims that he would fast to death if they did not stop killing one another. In an unbelievable display of faith, the whole of Calcutta surrendered to this prophet of courage and peace. The same Calcutta which had unleashed this terrible national havoc one year ago, on 16 August 1946, remained calm. But the rest of the north was engaged in carnage.

Those were bitter times for the man who gave the subcontinent its freedom. Increasingly, even his most sacred moment of the day, the public prayer meeting, was being disturbed by Hindus who were angry that he continued to read from the Quran, too, at these meetings. Gandhi did not waver; in the midst of the chaos, his vision remained steady. In January 1948 he was planning a visit to Pakistan; he would walk across the boundary of communalism. On 30 January he was stopped, not by any government, but by the bullet of a communal Hindu Brahmin, Nathuram Godse, at seventeen minutes past five in the evening. The first question on everyone's lips was: who had done this? Everyone knew that if the assassin had been a Muslim, the ensuing violence would destroy the new nation. All-India Radio did not interrupt its broadcast to announce the death of

India's greatest citizen when it got the news. Its scheduled programme continued. The police ultimately calmed the tense nerves of the government by identifying the assassin. At six o'clock All-India Radio finally broadcast a message whose every word had been carefully vetted: 'Mahatma Gandhi was assassinated in New Delhi at twenty minutes past five this afternoon. His assassin was a Hindu.'

Gandhi's death shocked the country out of its communal madness. The greatest immediate problem had been solved by this sacrifice, but there were others. All the potential tensions that existed in Pakistan were present in India too, and in far greater depth and dimension: language, race, regionalism, poverty, 70 million untouchables, 40 million Muslims, refugees, tribals, princes who were struggling to keep their feudal power, and on and on and on. Nothing could have been more difficult for the government in Delhi than those first two years of tension and uncertainty. Lord Mountbatten, many years later, told the admiring authors Dominique Lapierre and Larry Collins that at one point Prime Minister Nehru had actually asked him to take charge of the administration of free India. This is disputed, of course, and may be a result of the exaggeration that age brings to memory, but that there was a touch of desperation in the early days can hardly be denied. Almost any excuse could have been used, and with rational justification, to postpone the exercise of democracy, particularly since no one quite knew what forces it might unleash. Would there be a resurgence of communal riots? Would the demand for lingual states become violent during elections? Would secessionists get fresh legitimacy through a victory in the popular vote, as had happened in 1946? Would communalists win? In hindsight it is easy to say that Nehru expected the landslide Congress victory, but before the elections that looked far from inevitable. Not only was Nehru threatened by obscurantist and divisive forces, but some of the most talented leaders of the Congress independence movement, a group of men in whom Gandhi himself had shown great faith, had left the Congress Party to form the Socialist Party and the Krishak Mazdoor Praja Parishad, or Peasants, Workers and Tenants Party. The Socialists, in particular, with their radical slogans, bubbling conviction and energetic leadership, had convinced themselves that they were actually going to win the first elections to be held in free India. But Nehru and the Congress used no excuse to stall democracy and postpone elections. It was a display of faith which saved India.

By 26 January 1950, while Liaquat Ali Khan in Pakistan was still struggling with his basic principles, the Constituent Assembly of India had done its work, and India had become a secular republic. The date was chosen because it was on 26 January 1930 that the Congress took its first pledge to free the country. Among the first three military heroes honoured by the President of the new Republic of India was a Muslim, Brigadier Usman, who had died fighting against the Pakistanis in the Kashmir war of 1948; he was awarded the high military honour of Maha Vir Chakra. The other two honoured were Lieutenant-Colonel Dewan Ranjit Lal and Major Som Nath Sharma. The national anthem was also given to the nation on this day, the piano score of 'Jana-gana-mana' being written by the 'well-known composer Herbert Murrill'.

The first general elections, which had to be conducted in the desolate villages at the edge of Tibet as well as in the teeming slums of Calcutta, were spread over a period of six months. On 25 October 1951, in the remote villages of Chini and Pangil high in the mountains of Himachal Pradesh, the first of the 175 million voters of 1951–2 cast their votes. It was only on 13 May 1952 that Jawaharlal Nehru was sworn in.

The elections were as Indian as India could be, and the incidents narrated below are taken from the sole study done on the 1952 polls, *Indian General Elections, 1951–52*, by a group of academicians (edited by S. V. Kogekar and Richard L. Park, Popular Book Depot, 1956). There is no better way to begin than to mention what some Orissa Congressmen did to win votes. They spread the word among the villagers that Gandhiji's soul had taken residence in the ballot boxes, and the Mahatma would be watching to see whether the voter cast his ballot for the Congress or not. Some voters took this so seriously that they fell prostrate before the ballot box in homage to the Mahatma before voting for his party.

In those very first elections the theory of the 'Hindu backlash' was bandied about. According to this, the Hindus would, particularly after the violence of the partition riots, return only those candidates who specifically represented the Hindu interest. Both the Hindu Mahasabha and the newly created Jana Sangh, under the leadership of Dr Syama Prasad Mookerjee, fought the elections on this platform. Both were demolished so convincingly that they could never recover. Dr N. B. Khare, President of the Hindu Mahasabha, was a parliamentary candidate from his home town, Nagpur, still the citadel of the Rashtriya Swayamsevak Sangh movement (the RSS) which had inspired the assassination of Gandhi: he lost his security deposit. But obviously what the Hindu fanatics most dearly wanted was the defeat of Nehru himself in his Phulpur constituency.

Nehru's sole opponent was a sadhu, Prabhudutt Brahmachari, who had taken a vow not to speak. The issue around which he concentrated his non-verbal campaign was the Hindu Code Bill which liberalized the social law for Hindus. Nehru himself would not deign to campaign against such an opponent, but there was a time when his Congress Party began to worry about Phulpur sending an upset result. They need not have: the silent sadhu got only 56,718 votes against Nehru's 233,571. After losing, the sadhu sent a message to Nehru expressing delight at the latter's victory and adding, a bit unnecessarily, that he would have resigned his seat in favour of Nehru had he won.

Even the Communists learnt that an Indian's vote was not wooed by Marx alone. In Bengal, the Congress was making heavy play of the fact that its party symbol was a pair of bullocks on a yoke, which represented the peasantry. The Communist Party of India countered this by saying that its own election symbol, the ear of corn and a sickle, was an image of the Goddess Lakshmi, the goddess of prosperity. In Delhi, an astrologer did nothing to help the reputation of his tribe. In the Nanakapura constituency of the capital, he issued a poster prophesying that the Congress would win this seat. In an election in which the Congress swept the polls in most of the country, including Delhi, this was one seat that they lost, to the Socialists. On a more serious level, the mood of the moment was evident in the Sitaram Bazar constituency of Delhi, which was a known RSS and communal Hindu stronghold. The Congress made a gesture of its faith by putting up a Muslim candidate in this predominantly Hindu constituency; the Congress Muslim defeated his Hindu rival by more than 3,000 votes. The Muslims voted overwhelmingly for the Congress. Out of the 37 Muslim MLAs in Uttar Pradesh, 36 won on the Congress ticket, while 1 was an independent.

The Congress in Tamil Nadu displayed a touch of sophistication; its research section got in touch with Britain and asked both the Labour and the Conservative Parties for help in the designing of posters. But this unusual form of British aid did not prove very helpful as the party did much worse than expected. Perhaps the British design could not quite convey the message of one poster: 'Why hesitate, come along, let us vote for Congress which abolished drink.' In Punjab the voter proved that he was more than a match for the wiles of politicians. Reports Bodh Raj Sharma in *Indian General Elections, 1951–52*: 'A voter in the Hoshiarpur district related the following anecdote. He said, "One candidate offered me Rs 3 for the vote and the other offered Rs 2 and I accepted both thankfully."

When asked the name of the person for whom he had voted, he said that he had voted for the latter. The reason given was that he offered less, and so was considered less dishonest and would prove to be a better legislator.'

One member of the Nehru family always seems to rebel. In 1952 it was Krishna Hutheesingh, Nehru's sister, who said that the Congress was leading the country to disaster. This was duly quoted by the Socialists in an election poster. The main Socialist slogan was *'Kaam do, makan do, varna gaddi chor do'* ('Give us work, give us a house, or leave office') but this proved no match for the Congress theme, which was 'For a Stable, Secular and Progressive State, Vote Congress.' After they had been defeated, the Socialists began to complain that the election had been rigged. Dr Ram Manohar Lohia, the charismatic Socialist leader, said that 'a conspiracy was hatched in Lucknow to distort the electoral verdict in Uttar Pradesh'. No one took the charge seriously. The Socialists had suffered a legitimate defeat. There were aberrations, of course; in Bihar, for instance, there was repolling in 60 of the 19,427 polling booths. But the people were convinced that the elections had been as fair as was possible. Indian democracy had got off to a most satisfying start. On 13 May, Jawaharlal Nehru was sworn in as the first elected Prime Minister of free India. Now would come the task of delivering his promise of freedom, stability and progress.

7
The Rise of the Jailbird

All that the Bengalis of Pakistan wanted was respect and equality. Instead they got a country. What the Tamils of the South India state of Madras wanted was a country; they were content to settle for respect and democracy. The comparison best illustrates the unifying quality of a democracy against the destructive capacity of a dictatorship. India's Tamil problem was, in fact, much more serious than Pakistan's Bengali dilemma. To begin with, it was perfectly legal in India to advocate secession. Till 1963 the Indian Constitution granted any political party the right to preach separation.

Related to this situation were the demands of regionalism and language. Hindi, being the tongue of the largest segment of the country, was made the national language in the Constitution, but there was no way that the southern states or Bengal would accept its unbridled use. Language has always been an explosive issue anywhere in the world, for good reason, and India, too, often tumbled dangerously over this problem. There are nearly 900 identified dialects in India; Kashmiri, Punjabi, Rajasthani, Gujarati, Marathi, Kannada, Malayalam, Tamil, Telugu, Bengali, Assamese and Urdu each claim enough adherents to populate a larger than average European country; Hindi could claim a continent by itself.

Hardly had freedom come than the demand was raised that the internal map, which till 1947 had been based on British political and administrative convenience, should be redrawn to create states on the linguistic principle. Having, through their difficult lives, seen where such an idea could lead, both Nehru and Patel, the Home Minister, were horrified, and did their best to promote the theory of a strong Centre, and divisions made on administrative principles. But the people came out on the streets, and when they spoke their voice was heard, not suppressed. They were not called traitors or spies; instead, they were allowed to have the kind of nation they wanted. That was how India survived.

The story of Tamil separatism is closely linked with the life of a remarkable man who started the movement for a separate nation. After the obligatory education in England, this son of a wealthy landlord entered politics, the traditional nesting place of the nascent Indian elite. But the story of E. V. Ramaswamy Naicker (or 'EVR' as he is known), despite its prosaic start, would turn out to be one of the most fascinating of an era crowded with heroes.

EVR began traditionally enough, joining the Congress Party and by virtue of his social status soon becoming one of the general secretaries of the Madras Congress. He was still in the Congress when Dr C. Nadesan Mudaliar began, in 1914, the Dravida Association. Its aim was to help the development of the Dravidian peoples of South India (as opposed to the Aryans in the North). The special enemy of this movement was the Brahmin caste, a small minority dominating the South thanks to the oppressive caste system. For instance, till the twenties no untouchable could walk on the streets in the kingdom of Travancore, much less raise his or her eyes in front of a person of a higher caste. The Dravida Association evolved into the South Indian Liberal Federation, which started a daily called *Justice*. The paper gave its name to a political party called the Justice Party. In the mean while, EVR was fighting a parallel war to free the Congress from the hold of the Brahmins. This brought him into inevitable conflict with the doyen of the Brahmins, the Congress stalwart, C. Rajagopalachari; eventually EVR joined the Justice Party.

EVR was ferocious in his opposition to the iniquitous caste system. His philosophy was simple and practical. He likened a religion which allowed caste to malaria, and used to say that his search was not for the medicine but for the mosquitoes who spread the disease. The caste system was based on the Purana which, said its devotees, had been uttered by the gods, so he became an atheist. The Brahmins were the agents of those gods, so he would war with them. Till the day he died at the age of ninety-four, EVR was unrelenting both in his atheism and in his war against Brahmins.

In the twenties he launched the Vaikom agitation in the kingdom of Travancore for the uplift of the untouchables. The Maharaja was a personal friend of EVR, and often used to stop over in Erode, where EVR lived, to dine with him, but that made no difference to the crusader. EVR was imprisoned, but the agitation succeeded and special legislation was enacted to make the life of the untouchable just a little more bearable. It was after this that EVR was given the title of 'Vaikom Warrior'. One of the more amusing stories about this agitation is that the Brahmins, worried at this threat to their domination, organized a *yagna*, a massive offering of gifts and prayers to propitiate the gods and ward off evil (a *Vhataru Samagara Yagnam*, to use the local term), and to ask the gods to kill the atheist agitator. But something obviously went wrong with the prayers. While atheist EVR survived, it was the Maharaja who died.

In 1935 EVR started the aptly named Self-Respect Movement: there is till this day a Periyar Self-Respect Propaganda Institution at 50 Sampath Road in Madras which publishes EVR's work. Sample: 'The Aryans who came to India to eke out their existence concocted absurd stories in keeping with their barbarian status ... The blabberings of the intoxicated Brahmins in those old days are still faithfully observed in this modern world as the religious rituals, morals, stories, festivals, fasts, vows and beliefs.' For EVR, the Hinduism of caste and Brahmins was a result of the northern Aryan colonization of the country – the same Aryans who had driven the Dravida communities away from the Gangetic plains by conquest and subjugation, and then maintained their power by religious and cultural domination. Inherent in his doctrine was the separation of the Aryan North and the Dravidian South; and the destruction of the southern Brahmins was necessary because they were the true agents of the Aryan North. In Tamil Nadu is seen as Ravana a South Indian prince and his defeat by Rama is interpreted by the Tamils as the subjugation of a nationalist, not the downfall of a demon. The main reason for the powerful sentiment against Hindi in the state is because the language is seen as only the latest instrument of the northern Aryan imperialism against which EVR warned his fellow men.

However, in the crucial elections of 1937 the Congress, led by a Brahmin, C. Rajagopalachari, smashed the Justice Party, then led by Bobli Raja, winning every seat but one. The Congress had ably exploited the one serious contradiction in the Justice Party: its leadership was dominated by the landlord. Against this, the Congress identified itself as Gandhi's party of the peasantry. The untouchables, of course, did not have a vote then. The Congress formed a government and C. Rajagopalachari became the Prime Minister (as the regional designation was then known) of Madras province. But no sooner had he assumed power than he did something which resurrected EVR, who had in the wake of the defeat been named chief of the Justice Party. Rajagopalachari, in pursuance of the national Congress policy, made Hindi compulsory in the schools. It was a weapon made for EVR: once again a Brahmin was becoming a 'tool' of North Indian imperialism, 'destroying' the Tamil language and culture.

EVR launched an anti-Hindi agitation; this was to flower into the movement which would, by 1967, bring his successors to power in Madras. The Congress government sent EVR to prison (and deliberately put him in one of the hottest places in the region, Bellary). For two years EVR was behind bars; in fifteen years he went to jail twenty-three times and got the nickname 'jailbird'. But during those two years in Bellary, the anti-Hindi movement caught the imagination of the people. Since he could not be physically present, EVR's picture or statue would be placed on the dais at public meetings. After he was released, EVR was formally honoured by his party with the title of 'Periyar', or the man of genius, at the Madras conference of 28–30 December 1938. Such was his popularity that the Congress now tried to buy him over. In 1939, his old foe Rajagopalachari offered EVR a place in his government.

Periyar refused. He had other plans. He could see the shifts taking place in the Muslim League. And he began to argue that if the North Indian Muslim could not live with the North Indian Hindu, when the two had so much in common (origins, language, food), how could the Dravida, and in particular the Tamil, be expected to coexist with the North? Their language, script, food, features – everything was different. EVR now articulated his cry for 'Dravida Nadu', a Dravida nation. In its fuller concept, it would be a separate federation of the four southern lingual blocks – the Malayalis, the Kannadigas, the Telugus and the Tamils. But even if this was not possible, there was no question but that there should be a separate Tamil country, 'Tamil Nadu'. (The name is today a reality, but the area remains within the Indian Union, of course.) 'Secession began as a genuine effort,' recalled S. Rajaram, who worked with EVR and later became Speaker in the Tamil Nadu Legislature, when discussing the past with the author.

There was also the realization that the Congress allegation of a landlord-dominated leadership had truth in it, and if the movement wanted mass support it would have to attract the bulk of the middle peasantry. In 1944, the man who had already risen to become EVR's deputy, a brilliant orator called C. N. Annadurai, moved at the Salem conference the resolution changing the name of the Justice Party to Dravida Kazhagam (DK) and asked all the party's leaders to relinquish the titles that the British had given them. However, the DK did not feel confident enough to contest the 1946 elections, leaving the field free for the Congress. An added problem had arisen. Annadurai had begun chafing at the eccentricities of the Periyar, and his view was shared by the bulk of the party, which went with him in the split of 17 September 1949. But such was the respect that the new party, the Dravida Munnetra Kazhagam (DMK), had for EVR, the man who had shaped their ideology, that they did not name a president of the DMK; there would only be general secretaries. The physical presence of EVR had been rejected, not his ideas. The presidential chair was kept vacant for the 'soul of Periyar'.

But before the Tamils could give teeth to their demand for separation by marching on the streets, an enormous conflagration burst out in their neighbourhood.

8
The Man Who Changed the Map of India

While the Tamils were the principal inhabitants of the Madras Presidency, they were not the only ones. Spread across eleven of the districts of the British-created Presidency were the Telugus, the people of Andhra (the rest of the Telugu population and its land were ruled by the Nizam of Hyderabad). They had raised the demand for a division of the Madras Presidency and the creation of their own state. There was nothing new in this. In both its 1916 and 1920 sessions the Congress Party had accepted the principle of linguistic states after independence. The Motilal Nehru report of 1928 reaffirmed this assurance. In the Calcutta session of 1937 the Congress specifically approved the idea of the formation of the Andhra and Karnataka states, and in Wardha, 1938, also agreed on the creation of a Kerala state for the Malayalis within the free federation of India.

But in the aftermath of partition, Nehru's commitment to linguistic states began wavering, as did Home Minister Patel's. Responding to a discussion on the subject in the Constituent Assembly on 27 November 1947, Nehru said coolly, 'First things come first, and the first thing is the security and stability of India.' Rather than implement the Congress promise, the government appointed the Dar Commission to re-examine the concept of linguistic states. The Dar Commission dutifully reflected the new thinking of Nehru and Patel, and in the strongest terms recommended that any change at that moment would be dangerous. It added that administrative convenience and not language should become the basis for the reorganization of India. In other words, the British principle should stay, and Nehru should be allowed to create just four administrative zones rather than a number of linguistic states.

The British had divided the country 'by the military, political or administrative exigencies or conveniences of the moment' (Report on Indian Constitutional Reforms, 1918). By 1801 and 1827 respectively, the Madras and Bombay Presidencies had reached their full size, though

Bengal, which had become the centre of British power by then, had not. With time and success, both on the battlefield and in the conspiracy-laden courts of the Indian princes, the British empire continued to grow, and in 1833 the Agra Presidency came into existence. With the defeat of the Sikh armies by 1848–9, Punjab came into the fold and was made a separate province. Awadh fell into the British grasp by 1856. In 1861 the Central Provinces were formed. Assam, annexed and made a part of Bengal in 1826, was separated in 1874. In 1905, the east, from Chota Nagpur to Assam, was divided into Curzon's two Bengals. In 1912 Bengal was merged again, Assam was separated, and Bihar and Orissa were joined to form another province. In April 1936, the last province that the British created, Orissa, was born.

In 1947, India inherited 565 kingdoms of varying sizes and importance, constituting more than two-fifths of the subcontinent. Of these, 215 small princely states, with a total population of a little more than 19 millions, were married to the existing provinces; 61 states, with 7 million people, were given to the central administration; and 275 states, with 35 millions, were converted into the provinces of Rajasthan, Madhya Bharat, Travancore–Cochin, Saurashtra, and the Patiala and East Punjab States Union (PEPSU). The three major kingdoms, Hyderabad, Mysore, and Jammu and Kashmir were left as they were. The determined Sardar Patel made his last great contribution to his country by effecting this integration, but this was not quite what the people wanted. They wanted to live within the boundaries of their languages and cultures, not by the needs of administration.

At 6.30 a.m. on the morning of 12 March 1931, Mahatma Gandhi, his walking-stick keeping the pace, set off on a march that would take him to Dandi, 241 miles away at the edge of the Indian Ocean, where in the dawn of 6 April the Mahatma would scoop a handful of salt and once again launch a national upsurge that would electrify the world. One of the seventy-nine disciples who accompanied Mahatma Gandhi all the way on the Salt March was Potti Sriramalu. The Mahatma himself often praised this disciple for his total dedication and commitment. On 20 October 1952, this Gandhian decided to do to the Indians what his master had done to the British – test the strength of a mighty government against one man's faith. He began a fast which, he said, would end either in his death or in the creation of a separate Andhra state. Prime Minister Nehru, who had perhaps forgotten in the worry of governing his free India what a Gandhian could do, issued a few appeals to Sriramalu to end his fast, then ignored him. At 8.40 p.m. on 15 December 1952, Potti Sriramalu, lying on a bed at the house of Bulusu Sambamurthy in the Mylapore area of Madras, lost consciousness. By 11.20 that night, on the fifty-eighth day of his indefinite fast, Potti Sriramalu had died of hunger.

Jawaharlal Nehru was busy building his new India in the House of the People all that day. He had presented the preamble to his first Five-Year Plan to Parliament. It was a great day, he said, for the nation; the Plan was the first attempt to create 'national awareness of the unity of the country', and he spoke of this as the first step in the march towards a 'classless society'. The emotions of unity were going to be tested severely on a different plane the next day.

As the news of Sriramalu's death spread, a roar rose in all eleven Telugu districts of the Madras Presidency; spontaneous demonstrations broke out. In Vijayawada, the mob took over the railway station for five hours. (Not wanting to put too holy a face on their anger, the crowd used the trains at their temporary command to carry home the goods they were looting.) Violence was widespread and the police had to open fire. Newspapers estimated the damage at more than Rs 20 million (and those were days when the rupee had far more value). Within twenty-four hours Nehru's carefully orchestrated concept of a strong Centre and four administrative zones had collapsed. On 18 December, the Indian Cabinet decided that the state of Andhra Pradesh would be formed. The other states, up till the formation of Punjab in 1966, followed in logical sequence to that decision. A three-member States Reorganization Commission, headed by Saiyid Fazl Ali, with H. N. Hunzru and K. M. Panikkar, was set up on 29 December 1953. After studying 2,000 'well-considered memoranda', travelling 38,000 miles and visiting 104 places, and interviewing over 9,000 persons, it presented, on 30 September 1955, the basis of the linguistic division of India.

9
The Roll-Call of Honour

Having replaced his old political party with a new wife, Periyar E. V. Ramaswamy Naicker was reduced to indulging in dramatics. But they were powerful dramatics, none the less, and kept the spirit of the movement alive. In 1952, the old man announced that he would publicly burn the Hindu epic, the *Ramayana*, which told of the war between Rama and Ravana, and had the pleasure of receiving hundreds of telegrams from outraged Brahmins pleading with him not to desecrate their holy book. In 1958, he organized a programme to burn the Indian Constitution to symbolize the Tamil demand for secession. But while the old man concentrated on the newspaper headlines, his followers in the DMK were hard at work.

They had not been ready for the first general elections in 1951–2. But at the Tiruchirapalli conference in 1956 the DMK decided that it would contest the general elections of 1957 under the leadership of C. N. Annadurai. Party members had been encouraged by the popular response to some of their action programmes, as for instance the walk led by Annadurai in 1954 from the offices of the Simpson Company in Madras to Napier Park, to the sands of the famous Marina beach. Partisans say half a million people participated; even if one allows for the notorious exaggeration characteristic of politicians' memories, the response was obviously good enough to enthuse the DMK. The party won 15 seats in the State Legislature in 1957 and the secessionist Annadurai became a member of the legislative system. This enabled the party to get recognition from the Election Commission, and its rising sun became one of the official, reserved symbols. Secession, as we have noted, was perfectly legitimate in India till then.

By 1959, the DMK had won the elections to the Madras Corporation, and got its first elected official, the Mayor. In the 1962 elections, it continued its improvement, winning 50 of the 173 seats in the State

Legislature. But in an ironic twist of fate which was to have remarkable consequences, Annadurai himself lost, thanks largely to the personal interest the Congress Chief Minister Kamaraj Nadar took in getting the secessionist leader defeated. The DMK decided to send Annadurai to the Rajya Sabha (the Upper House) in Delhi, where elections are indirect. Annadurai duly became a Member of Parliament. And this not only brought the DMK movement into the national limelight, but it also brought the national ethos to the DMK movement: 1962 was to be a crucial year in the history of the country.

In April 1962, when Conjeevaram Natarajan Annadurai rose to speak for the first time in the Rajya Sabha, on the Motion of Thanks to the President's Address, he brought all his oratorical skills to plead for his Dravida Nadu. He asked the members to 'bestow deep and sympathetic thought' on his people's need to be separate from 'northern imperialism'. 'I am pleading for separation of Dravida Nadu not because of any antagonism, but because, if it is separated, it will become a small nation, compact, homogeneous and united ... Then we can make economic regeneration more effective and social regeneration more fruitful.' His other target, of course, was Hindi.

In June 1962, the tone was similar during the debate on the Finance Minister's speech (the best of Annadurai's speeches in the Rajya Sabha have been collected in *Anna Speaks*, edited by S. Ramachandran, Orient Longman, 1975): 'I must say categorically that neither cannons nor contempt is going to deter me from the mission to which I am wedded. About that there can be no compromise.' But by October that year, something radical had happened: Chinese cannon had opened up in the north, and the Indian mind, so far completely involved with peace and the '*bhai-bhai*' slogan, suddenly had to tackle not only the war with China but also the humiliation of defeat. Brigadier J. Dalvi, who commanded a brigade and ended up as a prisoner of the Chinese for seven months, describes the war thus in his famous book, *Himalayan Blunder* (Orient Paperbacks): 'The Sino-Indian conflict of 1962 was restricted to a small fraction of the opposing armies; was fought in a small, remote corner of the border and lasted a mere month – with only ten actual days of fighting – and yet it is a fact that it did initiate profound changes in our international standing, domestic politics and economic progress.'

The war deeply affected the Indian psyche. It was as if suddenly the adolescence was over and the country had to mature through a most painful crisis. The protective figure of Nehru collapsed. There was pain felt at this, but in that pain was also the recognition that the time of holding on to anyone's hand was over. A shattered Nehru aged quickly and in twenty months he was dead. In those ten days when it seemed as if the Chinese would march across the Himalayas or seep through into Assam, capturing Gauhati, there was the realization that freedom and nationhood could not be taken as casually as the country had tended to do. That hour of defeat became the country's most regenerative; one emotion swept the nation as nothing before had done. There were many fortunate outcomes of that humiliating defeat in 1962 – for instance, if the country had not been shocked into remedial action, the Indian army would not have been able to meet the Pakistani challenge in 1965 and Kashmir would have been lost, leading in turn to a downspin of despair. But one of the most unexpected benefits was the surge of patriotism and the collapse of secessionist feeling.

Annadurai first read the news of the Chinese invasion in a jail in Vellore; he was serving yet another minor spell of political imprisonment. Madras, or the future Tamil Nadu, was at the other end of India from where the war was taking place; in fact, the North which they hated was under attack, the South being completely unaffected. But the first thing that Annadurai did on being released on 2 October was to place a 'moratorium on all DMK activities, agitational or otherwise, and direct its entire energy and place its entire apparatus at the disposal of the Government of India to thwart the ambitions of the aggressor'. As Annadurai told Parliament: 'I enter the name of the DMK in the roll-call of honour that is being now formulated for the safety, for the dignity and future of this country, this nation.' As the editor of Annadurai's speeches, S. Ramachandran, says in his introduction to *Anna Speaks*: 'In a sense, 1962 was also the finest hour for India, because the misfortune brought the Indian people together, made them forget their differences and take a united stand against the aggressor.' In September 1965, Annadurai confirmed in an interview with the *Illustrated Weekly of India* (26 September issue) that 'we have since withdrawn the demand for Dravida Nadu. We first realized its dangerous potentialities at the time of the Chinese aggression.'

The government of India did not sit on the opportunity. In 1963, with support from all sides of the House, it excised the clause in the Constitution of India which had been an obvious loophole. Law Minister A. K. Sen tabled the 16th Amendment Bill, 1963, to change Article 19 of the Constitution to make any secessionist party ineligible to contest the elections. The DMK, despite its changing heart, still found itself unable to support a Bill which challenged so much of what it had stood for. However, the Bill was passed with an overwhelming majority. Soon the DMK formally gave up its call for secession, and began preparations to become instead the ruling party of its state. This was the key. The very fact that it was able to rule in Madras made the DMK call for secession largely redundant. But there was one more major battle left for the DMK to fight before the party and the movement were integrated fully into India.

10
The Great River

Europeans who have seen the Ottoman and the Austro-Hungarian empires collapse into small countries reborn on the basis of language find it particularly difficult to understand why the South Asia regions of the British empire did not suffer a similar destiny. By the eighties, at the latest, India also should have splintered into a mess. The Indian experience has not been without its moments of danger. If there was one Potti Sriramalu to give his life to establish linguistic states, there were many in India who gave their lives to prevent the national language of the country, Hindi, from becoming an instrument of subjugation.

On 12 September 1949, the Constituent Assembly of India gathered to debate what would be one of the most crucial decisions they would take, the resolution on the national language of free India. On one side were those who wanted the soonest possible end to the use of English and the soonest possible conversion of Hindi into the official working language of the country, on the principle that Hindi was understood by 140 million out of the 330 million who populated India in the forties. The other side saw in this the end of coexistence. Many members were to warn the Constituent Assembly that if Hindi became the language of economic or cultural domination, the country would break. The moderates wanted the continuation of English as the official language until an acceptable version of Hindi could be evolved. The Congress Party had committed itself to Hindi twenty-five years before, when the Congress Working Committee had agreed on Hindi as the national language of free India (it was a one-vote majority, incidentally), but the scheme was to allow two concurrent scripts for Hindi, both Devanagari and Urdu. But that was 1924. India had not been divided; the Congress claimed to represent both Hindus and Muslims, and had to satisfy the sentiments of both in its resolutions. Mahatma Gandhi, however, had always pleaded for the acceptance of a merged Hindi–Urdu tongue, Hindustani, as the national language, rather than a Sanskritized Hindi with its overtones of communal fervour. The language he envisaged would be an open one, absorbing words and influences from Urdu and other Indian languages to make it a symbol and definition of an Indian culture rather than the preserve of Banaras. But by 1949 Urdu had become the national language of Pakistan. In the backlash of the terrible partition riots, the Indian Muslim's voice was muted; not even a Maulana Azad could do more than talk about his 'heavy heart', his sadness that it was Hindi and not Hindustani which was becoming the national language. Only a Jawaharlal Nehru could stress the need to maintain a relationship between Hindi and its 'sister Urdu'. Other ideas had been thrown up, too: for instance, the use of the Roman script instead of the Devanagari script for Hindi. (This is not as difficult as it might seem; Hindi journalists using the English telex communication system regularly send their stories in the Roman script.) The most famous advocate of this idea was the great and completely secular nationalist Subhas Chandra Bose; it was India's loss that he died too soon.

However, there was broad consensus that if there had to be a national language, it could only be Hindi. There was also strong argument over how to go about it. The dangers of a mistake in the language policy could be traumatic; everyone realized that. The President of the Constituent Assembly, Dr Rajendra Prasad, warned before allowing the debate to open: 'If it does not meet with the approval of any considerable section of the people in the country, whether in the North or the South, the implementation of the Constitution would become a most difficult problem. The question of language is to be carried out by the country as a whole. Let us not forget [that] there is no other item in the whole Constitution of the country which may be required to be implemented from day to day, from hour to hour, almost from minute to minute in actual practice.'

Jawaharlal Nehru was equally specific: 'We are on the threshold of a linguistic revolution in India and we have to be careful that we give it the right direction, the right shape, the right mould, lest it go wrongly and betray us in the wrong direction.' He reminded the Assembly of Gandhi's views when he said that Hindi should be 'inclusive' and, second, that it 'should not be forced down on anyone'. Some idea of how passionate reactions could get was available in the august Assembly itself. Sardar Hukum Singh, from East Punjab, a prominent Sikh leader, had originally supported the idea of Hindi as the national language in the Devanagari script. During the three-day debate he shifted his position. Speaking on the last day, he said: 'I have now changed my mind. The enthusiastic supporters of Hindi have alienated my sympathy and now I agree with Mr Anthony [Frank Anthony, the Anglo-Indian leader who was pleading for the retention of English in many spheres]. I am one of those who have withdrawn their support from Hindi in the Devanagari script simply because of the fanaticism and intolerance of those who support it.'

It was not only the Muslims, with their weakness for Urdu, who were scared by Hindi. The whole of the South, which did not know Hindi, was against it. The Tamils were the most virulent. Naturally, the government of the Union of India asked a Tamilian Brahmin to draft the resolution making Hindi the lingua franca. On 12 September, N. Gopalaswami Ayyangar moved the draft resolution asking the Constituent Assembly to agree on Hindi as the national language of the country and, to quote the speech he made that day, 'bidding goodbye to the language by which, I think, we have fought and achieved independence'. That goodbye was going to linger a bit.

Resolution 301A, in the name of Ayyangar, Dr B. R. Ambedkar and K. M. Munshi, began: 'The official language of the Union shall be Hindi in the Devanagari script and the form of numerals to be used for the official purposes of the Union shall be the international form of Indian numerals.' English would stay for another fifteen years from the moment the Constitution of India was accepted, and then Hindi would take over as the national language. But good lawyer that he was, Ayyangar had left an escape provision: 'Notwithstanding anything contained in this Article, Parliament may by law provide for the use of the English language after the said period of 15 years for such purposes as may be specified in such law.' The Hindi lobby was happy enough to get away with such a compromise: what is fifteen years in the life of a dream? Seth Govind Das, President of the Hindi Sahitya Sammelan and a member of the Constituent Assembly, told the House that '95 per cent of the language question had been solved'. The 5 per cent that remained unsolved in his account, was probably the use of Roman numerals instead of Devanagari numerals. Rabindranath Tagore had described the many languages of India as its rivers, and Hindi as the Mahanadi, the great river. The Mahanadi was finally assigned its role in the country's affairs. But it remained to be seen whether the country was fully ready to employ productively the currents of that large river, or not.

By 1963 it was obvious that large sections of the country still found 'the great river' threatening; its waters had not yet been dammed to satisfy the country's needs. And within less than two years, by January 1965, according to the Constitution, all official communication in English must cease and be replaced by Hindi. The government of India, still under Jawaharlal Nehru, did the only sensible thing – used the escape clause. The Official Languages Bill of 1963 was introduced in Parliament. The debate that followed was another good example of how solutions can be found if grievances get an opportunity to be ventilated. As C. N. Annadurai put it: 'Apart from political arithmetic, this august House will pay some attention to political ethics and democratic liberalism, for democracy does not mean merely majority rule. It means, fundamentally, also recognizing, sanctifying and safeguarding minority rights and even minority sentiments.'

Predictably, Annadurai's speech was the centrepiece of the debate, and he exposed the difference between a professed position and the reality in an excellent way. Bhupesh Gupta, the Bengali Communist leader, had been advocating the cause of Hindi, and when Annadurai's turn came to speak, he took up Bhupesh Gupta. 'Let not my friend, Mr Bhupesh Gupta, feel that we are acting like some toadies and therefore we want English. No. He has stated that he pleads for Hindi and he wants Hindi to become the national language and official language; yet he did not attempt to learn Hindi and speak in Hindi.'

Bhupesh Gupta, a very able Parliamentarian himself, was quick to interrupt. 'I did not have time,' he said.

Annadurai was not one to let this pass. His answer came immediately: 'But he [Bhupesh Gupta] had the time to learn *Das Kapital*; he had time to learn the underlying difference between Russian Communism and Chinese Communism. He has had time to read everything except Hindi.'

Annadurai also answered the argument that Hindi's claim to its status lay in the fact that 42 per cent of the country recognized the language. The fact that this 42 per cent lay within one compact geographical area was what made the idea dangerous, he argued; had it been scattered throughout the country, use of the language might have been more acceptable. 'Therefore, the 42 per cent, entrusted in a compact area, cannot be taken as an index of ethical majority. It is merely an arithmetical majority.' What was then the solution to the problem? 'Keep the status quo by amending the Constitution. Let there be a solution not necessarily by us. We are not the last scions of India. Perhaps we are more confused. We have more political rancour. In future times a proper solution may be arrived at . . . if this imposition of Hindi were to become a fact . . . the entire South will revolt against this.'

An approximation of what that revolt might look like was soon visible. The Home Minister who had piloted the Official Languages Act through Parliament in 1963 was Lal Bahadur Shastri; after the death of Jawaharlal Nehru in May 1964 he became Prime Minister. And he was still in the initial uneasy months of office when his first major crisis erupted. The Constitution of India had become law on 26 January 1950, the day India became a Republic, and on 26 January 1965, the fifteen-year grace period for the use of English was over. Of course, the 1963 Act had removed the worry that the English language would actually be sent packing, but the South had its doubts. The DMK in Madras decided to spend the fifteenth Republic Day of free India as a 'day of mourning'.

On Sunday, 24 January 1965, Sir Winston Churchill died. The Indian papers splashed the news in banner headlines. Long stories occupied most of the front pages and everyone politely refused to mention that if the great Sir Winston had had his way, the sun would have never set on the British empire. However, the 'end of an era' headlines pushed onto the inside pages a news item which would normally have been on page one – the Union government's concern at what might happen on and after 26 January. Even if English was not going to be killed, certainly Hindi was going to become the official language of the country. English would be relegated to the status of an associate official language. The Hindi-speaking states were elated; the non-Hindi states were nervous and apprehensive – to them the day of 'imposition' had come.

Home Ministry officials in Delhi briefed special correspondents in the capital to file stories explaining that the nation would not suddenly become a one-language state. An official told the special correspondent of the Calcutta newspaper *Hindusthan Standard* that the process of making Hindi the only official language would take a 'very, very long time. I cannot specify any time limit.' The practical implications would be as follows, the official said:

a) letters received by the Central government, written in Hindi, would be replied to in Hindi 'as far as possible' (previously only 1 per cent of the letters going out were in Hindi); any letters sent in English would be replied to in English; important letters and standing orders would be sent in both Hindi and English

b) Hindi equivalents of English terms would be evolved

c) the official gazette would appear in both English and Hindi

d) notings on files could be in either English or Hindi

e) Hindi states would have to send English translations of their communications to non-Hindi states

f) English would remain the sole language of the Supreme Court, though states could apply to introduce their state language into the High Courts.

On 25 January, the first Hindi notification appeared from the government of India, a Gazette Extraordinary called *Bharat Ka Rajpatra* announcing the traditional presidential awards to Indians who had achieved distinction in their professions. And thus the first official use of Hindi was made to honour, among others, the Bengali film-maker Satyajit Ray and the brilliant Maharashtrian scientist Jayant Narlikar with Padma Bhushans. London had announced a new High Commissioner for India, John Freeman, and he loyally told Aley Hassan of the BBC's Hindi Service that he would do his best to learn free India's new national language: 'I don't speak a word of Hindi at the moment, and I think I must warn any Indian listeners, who may be listening now, that I am remarkably untalented at learning tongues. Nevertheless it will be my endeavour when I get to Delhi to take lessons in Hindi and do all I can to familiarize myself with at least the simpler elements of the language.'

But in Madras they were in a far less charitable mood. Apprehending trouble, the Congress Chief Minister, Bhaktavatsalam, had arrested Annadurai and the top leadership of the DMK at the midnight on the cusp of 25–26 January. But this did not prevent 20,000 students from taking out a procession with a 'Hindi demon' at the head, garlanded with shoes and slippers. In Madurai, Congress flags were pulled down and replaced by black flags; at other places the national flag was desecrated. And this was only the prelude. Over the next twenty-four hours, two young men killed themselves to save Tamil. In Virugambakkam, a postal employee, Rangarajan, aged thirty-two, burnt himself to death in a public square and kept shouting as the flames engulfed him, 'Long Live Tamil.' At Kodambakkam, Sivaliangam, twenty-two years old, did the same.

The demonstrations turned violent. The Madras Chief Minister (standing 'hard as a rock', in Union Home Minister Gulzari Lal Nanda's description) decided to treat this as just another law-and-order problem and sent in the police. Now demonstrators began dying in police firing, and the anger began to touch the rest of the country. On 28 January, Home Minister Nanda told reporters during a scheduled visit to Calcutta, 'I have given positive assurance that Hindi will not be imposed,' and his colleague in the top echelons of the Congress, Atulya Ghosh, warned Hindi zealots to 'make haste slowly'. In Delhi, Prime Minister Shastri offered, 'We can always sit together and iron out differences.' (Shastri spoke in English when making the statement.)

But the top leadership of the DMK was still in jail, and the people were on the streets; no one was in any mood to 'sit together'. On 29 January, a twenty-year-old waiter in a hotel in Keeranur wrote two letters, one to his father and the other to the DMK leader, Annadurai, saying that he was sacrificing his life for Tamil; then he drank 'bug poison' and died. The rest of the country inevitably was drawn into taking sides, and the cleavage was on the traditional Hindi/non-Hindi lines. In Bombay, the brilliant cartoonist, Laxman (a southerner, from Karnataka), published a cartoon in the *Times of India* (for which Laxman still works) showing the ship of the Indian state being battered by the huge waves of communalism, poverty, graft and weak defence, while the captain and the oblivious crew were busy trying to replace English with Hindi. In Calcutta, the poet and teacher of English literature, P. Lal, published a blistering defence of the place of English in India, ending with, 'Few things are shoddier than the hawking of language in the Temple of Demos.'

On 30 January, the anniversary of Gandhiji's assassination by Hindu communalists, Shastri told the country formally, 'English will continue to be the associate language and will be freely used in Madras, as envisaged in the Act of Parliament.' The next day the Central government offered to provide statewise quotas in government jobs to allay the fear that non-Hindi-speaking youth would suffer discrimination with Hindi becoming the national language. On 3 February, students came out in Calcutta carrying banners which read, 'We'll speak no Hindi, read no Hindi and hear no Hindi music.' (Of the three, the last was probably the most difficult sacrifice since popular Hindi film music is a rage all over the country.)

On 10 February, the violence in simmering Madras reached a new peak. There were two dozen deaths in one day, with the police opening fire at six places; eventually the army had to be called out in Salem which saw the worst disturbances. At Tiruppur an angry mob lynched and burnt to death two police sub-inspectors, Ramaswamy and N. K. Venkatesan. Such was the reaction to the violence that the two most important Union ministers from Madras, C. Subramaniam (the minister who later pioneered India's green revolution) and O. V. Alagesan, resigned from the Congress Central government after they could not persuade Shastri to settle with the Madras demand. By 12 February, the police had begun using light machine-guns against the people in Pollachi. And another Tamil, this time the headmaster of an elementary school in Tiruchi, Veerappan, burnt himself to death. (Later, when the DMK government came to power, it wanted to honour the martyrs of this movement with financial awards to their descendants, but the Supreme Court ruled this to be unconstitutional since the Constitution enjoins all state governments to help promote the cause of Hindi.)

The resignation of the Central government ministers created a sensation; after all, Indian politicians have generally to be asked to go, they do not quite like resigning. But it had its desired effect. The movement made them champions. Prime Minister Shastri, a quiet supporter of the Hindi lobby, did not want them back in his Cabinet, but President S. Radhakrishnan warned him that the consequences of obstinacy would threaten national unity. Only now was there some serious thinking as to how to meet the demands.

What were the demands? The Tamils did not want Hindi to be abolished as the national language; they knew this was impossible. What they wanted was to give legal shape to what became termed the 'Nehru assurance' – that Hindi would not be imposed on those who did not want it. It was Nehru's vision which was again coming to the rescue of this country. The philosophy of the 'Nehru assurance' can be best summed up by a quotation from his speech to the Constituent Assembly on 13 September 1949: 'We must have our own language. But English in India ... Are we to make a democratic or authoritarian approach? I venture to put these questions to the enthusiasts of Hindi because in some of the speeches I have listened to here and elsewhere, there has been very much the tone of authoritarianism. That is not only a fundamentally incorrect approach but also it is a dangerous approach. If you consider the question from wisdom, it is not helpful to the development of Hindi if you force down any language upon a people or a group who resist that. Certainly in the democratic context of India it is an impossibility. Therefore you will have to win the goodwill of those groups of Indians whose mother-tongue is not Hindi. You will have to win the goodwill of those who speak a variation of Hindi called Hindustani, or Urdu. If you do something which will appear to others as an authoritarian approach it will fail.'

On 17 February 1965, the Budget session of the Indian Parliament was inaugurated by the President's address to the joint sitting of the two Houses, and President Radhakrishnan assured the members that English would stay in India. On 24 February, the Congress Working Committee decided to ask the government to bring an amendment to the Official Languages Act to give legal shape to Nehru's promise. The crisis was defused.

In the 1967 elections, thanks particularly to their leadership of the language movement, DMK broke the psychological barrier and swept the polls in Madras. Till the time of writing, the movement has not been defeated. Today, Hindi and Tamil Nadu are still not on talking terms; Hindi simply does not figure in the official or non-official business of the state government. However, Hindi is gradually playing a greater role in the national consciousness – but no one is going out on to the streets crying 'language imperialism'. Twenty years after 1965, people have forgotten that once, not very long ago, the country's survival was threatened by the debate over language.

11
Past and Future

In the fifties and the sixties, reporting about India was full of metaphors of the region-of-uncertainty or the area-of-darkness kind. There was a great deal of superior moaning about how awful, poor, divisive, filthy and, on top of everything else, how pompous India was; there were sniggers that the hand which seemed permanently stretched out to beg should be used to better purpose – to close the mouth. And of course democracy simply did not have a chance in this illiterate and hungry land; at best it would be a farce, at worst a chaotic Babel which would encourage all the latent, fissiparous forces, ensuring the quick destruction of the country. The hurt of lost empire added to the jaundice in the British eye; and in the American, Indian foreign policy distorted the vision. That was an age of simpler perceptions, and Pakistan, member of SEATO and of the Baghdad Pact, was on the side of the good guys. It is remarkable that while there was no shortage of books predicting the imminent demise of India, there was hardly a 'scholar' who foresaw the death of Pakistan.

India was caught in the pincer of predetermined attitudes. And these attitudes still affect minds. It is still 'Beggar India' both for the Washington official and the American tourist, although the country has been able to end starvation (but, of course, poverty remains its greatest problem), has acquired an impressive industrial base, promises to become an oil giant, and is confident enough already to refuse the final instalment of an IMF loan in 1984. But say that in Washington and you would probably raise a laugh. All they want to know about is the dead in Calcutta, the Taj Mahal in Agra and the snake-charmers on the road to Jaipur. (Well, they are not dying in Calcutta any more; a massive oil refinery has been commissioned near the Taj Mahal; and the snake-charmers seem to have joined the Ministry of Tourism.)

We need not dwell too much on books like V. S. Naipaul's *An Area of Darkness*: that was only prejudice disguised in elegant English. More relevant would be to re-examine a work like *The Most Dangerous Decades* by Selig Harrison, who was a respected Delhi correspondent of Associated Press, covering India, Pakistan, Nepal, Sri Lanka and Afghanistan (there was no Bangladesh, of course, in his time). The reason for choosing his book is not only for the powerful influence it had on the political elite, but also because it is informed with an essential sympathy for this region. Harrison uses research and argument to present the doubts which were very alive in the fifties, and which are still being misused by a range of vested interests to cloud the world's perception of this country. Lastly, Harrison's book was published by Princeton University Press in 1960, and obviously the 'most dangerous decades' of the title were the sixties, seventies and eighties. The time, then, has come to compare yesterday's prediction with today's reality.

The major threat that Harrison saw was from lingual nationalism. He begins his book with a quotation from an eminent Bengali, Professor Suniti Kumar Chatterjee, a great Sanskrit scholar and a Bengali nationalist, who in 1957 was not convinced about the permanence of Indian unity: 'India stands the risk of being split up into a number of totalitarian small nationalities,' he said. The sentiment expressed was that the nine prominent lingual groups that made up the non-Hindi India would be unable to live with the dominant heartland, that political anarchy would ensue, racial politics would lead to secession which would bring tinpot dictators into the capitals of Punjab, Rajasthan, Gujarat, Maharashtra, Karnataka, Kerala, Tamil Nadu, Andhra, Orissa, Bengal, Assam and Kashmir. Nor would this necessarily be the end of the matter since subgroups would begin claiming their independence – and so on and so forth.

Harrison had seen the India of the early fifties, and he wrote his book in the second half of the decade. He had witnessed the passions generated by Potti Sriramalu's sacrifice, the still unresolved secessionist demand of E. V. Ramaswamy Naicker, the doubt and cynicism of the Bengali, and the new doubt in the Kashmiri commitment. He had heard Nehru himself warn over and over again that linguistic states might open the 'Pandora's box' that would fragment the land. (Nehru had accused the British, who lived by 'divide and rule', of wanting to 'fragment and leave'.) Harrison had seen Jinnah's successful bluff give rise to hope in a hundred breasts. Many were convinced that they too could become prime ministers and governor-generals in their own backyards. When he was writing his book, Maharashtra and Gujarat were still part of the merged

Bombay State; it would require another spell of public violence to achieve their separation by 1960. And Harrison had seen the inability of the Congress government to give the one minority in the country with a geographical base, the Sikhs, a state for themselves, for fear that they might use that to declare their own Sikhistan. Kashmir's Sheikh Abdullah, the man who had kept his Muslim followers away from theocratic Pakistan, was languishing in jail. Selig S. Harrison looked at this Indian potpourri and had a great deal to be despondent about in the late fifties. But one by one, these problems were almost imperceptibly solved – with time and democracy. The other Asian giant, China, shut off the world and began mixing totalitarianism with compassionate economics. India continued her experiment in full public view, leaving all her doors open for anyone to come and examine her warts, even if the visitor wanted to concentrate on the warts to such an extent that he didn't notice the face at all.

'India's struggle for national survival is a struggle against herself. As a civilization and as an integrated cultural whole, India has shown a power of survival rivalled only by China. But multilingual India's separate territories have failed as consistently as Europe's to hold together as a political unity . . . India is a whole world placed at close quarters. Nowhere do so many linguistically differentiated peoples, all of them so self-aware, all numbered in millions and tens of millions, confront each other within a single national body politic. The prospect that "anarchy", "fascism", and "totalitarian small nationalities" will each torture this body politic, at one time or another in the decades ahead, is a measure not of some endemic Indian incapacity but of the challenge built into Indian nationalism,' wrote Selig Harrison in 1960. And this was not the most pessimistic part of his conclusions.

But multilingual India's separate territories have failed to disintegrate, a quarter of a century after 1960. Anarchy is a word that has been sometimes used to describe Indian politics, but no one now uses it to define the polity. And the flirtation with Fascism did not come from Mr Harrison's dreaded Communists, but from a democrat who chose wisely to return to democracy and did so very successfully: Mrs Indira Gandhi. Instead of the emergence of totalitarians in the nationalities of the South, the only unusual ripple India has had, after Mr Harrison's time, is a couple of film stars who transcended the dividing line between two kinds of drama, to become elected chief ministers of their states.

The only real danger that India still faces comes from the same theocratic interests which created Pakistan in 1947; the other dangers have been or are being resolved. In the 1940s the Muslim priests played the divisive game, with help from many quarters, since they knew that their future was bleak in a democratic and secular society. In the 1980s the Sikh priesthood has intensified a similar battle. The Muslim mullah succeeded partly because the secular politician did not know how to confront him; the Sikh sant is hoping for the pattern to repeat itself. All the priest hopes for is a temporary anger to sway his community; this anger can be used to destroy unity and transfer yet another region into theocracy's hands. For the politician on the other side, the challenge is extraordinary: the balance has to be found between serving a minority's economic needs and its emotional and religious fears, and maintaining the democratic environment where the majority may, in fact, resent any particular attention being paid to the minority. We will examine the complicated interweave of a multitude of strands in the section on Punjab.

Relations between Pakistan, Bangladesh and Nepal on one side and India on the other will always reflect the mix of hope and fear that is the legacy of 1947. Delhi keeps getting accused of 'Big Brotherhood', not only by Islamic Islamabad and Dhaka, but also by the very Hindu Kathmandu and Buddhist Colombo. It is not, therefore, merely a question of 'Hindu' India versus 'Muslim' Pakistan. The Republic of India is bordered, apart from China and Burma, by the Islamic Republic of Pakistan, the People's Islamic Republic of Bangladesh, the Hindu Kingdom of Nepal and the smaller Kingdom of Bhutan. There is one thing which all these nations have in common – none of them is a democracy. While Bhutan largely lives in its own world, the others are part of the international order. The nations or subnations of the subcontinent itself are linked not only by history, religion, language and culture, but also by economic determinants which flow through international affairs like rivers, the control of whose waters are a constant source of friction.

Pakistan, Bangladesh and Nepal take what might be called a 'negative sustenance' from India. To maintain their separate identities they have constantly to keep stressing, both to themselves and to the world, how different they are from India – ethnically, culturally and, therefore, politically too. The effort takes many forms. On one level, for instance, is the Bangladeshi's effort to retain the 'Islamic' tinge to the Bengali language he speaks. On a par are the efforts of the Pakistani elite to search for culture associations to their west, in the deserts of Arabia or the fields of Iran, rather than in the lanes of Lucknow. All this might be transient and harmless were it not that the constant effort to distance oneself from 'hostile India' can lead to dangerous geopolitics.

It is not just India's size that creates insecurity among neighbours; it is also the paranoia of their rulers, fearing that the lure of democracy and friendship might prove too tempting for their people, particularly when amalgamated to the truth of a common culture. That is why these regimes need barriers. Democratic urges wafting across the borders could fuel movements to overthrow the vested interests who have seized power in both Pakistan and Bangladesh. If India, with its immensely greater problems, can afford democracy, why cannot Pakistan or Bangladesh? This is the question which terrifies the mullah–military combination both to the east and the west of India. Similarly, if India destroyed its feudalism, why should Nepal continue to live in the nineteenth century? There are, therefore, enough powerful interests on the subcontinent who would be delighted to witness the collapse of Indian democracy, and the disintegration of its unity. The battle for the heart and mind of the subcontinent is far from over.

PART II

PUNJAB

1
The State of a Problem

There were more advertisements for television sets and video-cassette-recorders in the Punjab of 1984 than in any other state of India. Hoardings and banners in profusion sold every consumer product on the Indian market; it was startling visual confirmation of the fact that the state of Punjab no longer belonged to the Third World, where most of the rest of India still was. There were no mud huts in the villages; it was all brick and stone. The people worked hard; the fields were rich; water came streaming down from the nearby Himalayas; new strains of seed and fertilizers had turned this into the granary of India. If any one part of the country could be called a success story, this was it.

The paradox was that Punjab was also the one state in the Union of India where the country's survival was being tested by extremists' guns. A well-equipped, well-organized group had come on the scene whose ambition was simple: an independent country for the Sikhs, provisionally named Khalistan ('the land of the pure'; Pakistan, incidentally, means the same). If East Punjab could manage to convert itself into the theocratic state of Khalistan, as West Punjab had become Pakistan in 1947, then the whole federal experiment of a united India would receive a blow from which it would probably never recover. If Punjab went, so would Kashmir: even the most casual glance at the map will confirm this. Not only were the two states contiguous to Pakistan, but Hindu-majority India ended south of Punjab. Punjab was a Sikh-majority state, Jammu and Kashmir a Muslim-majority state. The close Sikh–Hindu relationship had tended to disguise this reality. The Hindus saw Sikhism as a variation of Hinduism, and not as a separate religion: Muslim Kashmir was perceived as a threat to the unity of India, not Sikh–Hindu Punjab.

The debate about how 'Hindu' was Sikhism is an old one. The Sikhs had never accepted the Hindu interpretation of their faith, but the problem did not reach the dimensions of a conflict until the Sikhs discovered,

towards the turn of the twentieth century, that not only had they lost
control of their places of worship to non-Sikhs but that the very existence
of their faith was in danger. Sikhs were returning to Hinduism, as the
Jains and Buddhists had once done. This fear of reabsorption was
heightened by sermons from proselytizers insisting that the Sikhs were
only Hindus by another name. But saying a Sikh is a Hindu is a bit
like calling every Muslim a Jew: Muslims and Jews, and indeed Christians,
have as much in common with one another as Hindus have with the
Sikhs. The three 'Judaic' religions believe in one God and the same lineage
of prophets; their dispute centres on who was the messenger of God.

As the distance between the Sikh and the Hindu began to grow, so
did the idea that the survival of Sikhism was not possible except under
the umbrella of a separate country. At the forefront of this campaign
were inevitably the clergy, who had clearly the most to lose if the flock
lost its faith, and the most to gain by the creation of a religious state.

To Delhi, a hostile Punjab was unacceptable. If India were to survive,
Punjab had to stay within the Union, by persuasion if possible, by force
if necessary. Delhi, once at the heart of an India stretching from the
mountains around the Khyber Pass to the jungles of Burma, would end
up as a border city if Punjab, too, broke away. After this, which ruler
could be strong enough to control and canalize in one productive direction the many forces that course through the subcontinent? India has
seen the disastrous consequences of an impotent Delhi, the last time during
the decline of the Mughal empire when the country was at the mercy
of any freebooter, local or foreign. India has seen progress when the Centre
has held firm without becoming either tyrannical or profligate.

Obviously each age has its own fund of ideas, new patterns of relationships, fresh urges to improve the quality of life, which in turn inspire
attempts to create different structures of governance, and change social
relationships. But the present often mirrors the past in many essential
ways; and some needs are older than the politics of democracy, or
colonialism, or feudalism. Man needs identity and belief as much as bread.
The Punjab crisis is an intricate kaleidoscope of urges, fears and needs;
the slightest shift of the hand creates a new combination. To understand
the problem it is vital to understand the parts so that one may see the
whole in a better perspective. Punjab can be healed, but not through
prejudiced or ill-informed diagnosis.

In the years since partition in 1947, has the country preserved by
the Constitution of India grown strong enough to absorb the challenge

from efficient fanatics without becoming tyrannical in its response? Is India larger and stronger than both the Punjab problem and the Punjab extremist? Is the Sikh truly fighting for a new nation, or is he asking for a solution which could stop far short of secession? Does the current frustration of the Sikh leadership lie in its relationship with the Hindus, or in the new trends visible within the Sikh community, or both? Where does Hinduism end and Sikhism begin? What has been the impact of the education and the new prosperity of the sixties and the seventies? Has the very enterprise of the Sikh changed him? Short questions. The answers are a bit longer.

A perceptive light on this medley of questions was thrown by the Sikh historian and journalist, Khushwant Singh, in *A History of the Sikhs* (Oxford University Press, Vol. 2, p. 302): 'A student of Sikh affairs may indulge in speculation on the future course of the two movements – Sikh resistance to being reabsorbed by Hinduism, and the movement for a Sikh state. The two are more intimately related to each other than is generally realized or admitted.'

2
An Old Fear

For more than a thousand years, from about the fifth century BC to the fifth century AD, the religion established by the Aryans, later to be known as Hinduism, was under serious threat. The Aryans are believed by rational historians to have come to this subcontinent around 1500 BC, when the migration of the Russian tribes, which was to take them to Greece, Asia Minor and Iran, brought them through the passes of the Hindu Kush mountains across Afghanistan to enter the land that is now known as Punjab.

The name means 'land of the five rivers'. It comes from *panj*, 'five', and *ab*, 'water'. The five rivers are the Jhelum, Chenab, Ravi, Beas and Sutlej. A more correct name would have been Sat-ab, or 'the land of seven rivers', which was the number when the Aryans came, but the Indus, which marked the western border, was deleted from the count, and the seventh river, the Saraswati, dried up. (Saraswati is also the name of the Hindu goddess of learning, and some cynics consider the drying up of her namesake an appropriate symbol of what is going on in Punjab in the 1980s.)

The Aryans did not come upon a land of barbarians. They arrived during the dying throes of a great civilization, now called after the Indus Valley, with a range of cities extending from the famous Harappa and Mohenjodaro to Kot Diji in Sind, Kalibangan in Rajasthan, Lothal in Gujarat and Ropar in Punjab. It was in Punjab that the Aryans first settled, and their priests composed and collected the 1,028 hymns of the Rig-Veda which form the first records of life in the early Aryan period. North of Delhi was fought the famous war which became the subject of the longest poem in the world, the *Mahabharata*. The two epics, the *Mahabharata* and the *Ramayana*, attributed to Vyasa and Valmiki respectively, are believed to describe events between 1000 and 700 BC. They are central texts in the Hindu scriptures, providing a great deal of the symbolism that sustains the Hindu imagination. For instance, the rule of King Rama, who is the hero of the second and later epic, is considered the ultimate in the fair and just exercise of power, and it was Mahatma Gandhi's dream to usher in a *Ramrajya*, or 'Rule of Rama', after the British left. However, it was not an image which could hope to find favour with the Muslim leadership of the twentieth century; they called it putting an 'acceptable face' on Hindu domination, and finally cut Punjab and Bengal in half to create their Pakistan in 1947.

The technological breakthrough wrought by the coming of the Iron Age, around 800 BC, enabled the Aryans to clear their way to the east and the south of the subcontinent faster. The kingdom of Rama, called Kosala, was in the area of eastern Uttar Pradesh and western Bihar, in the Gangetic belt of eastern India, and in the epic King Rama goes south to fight his great war with Ravana, the King of Sri Lanka (or Ceylon), over the abduction of Rama's wife, Sita. Obviously the Aryans had also begun to conquer the South by this time. As we saw earlier (p. 76), in the revised pantheon of the southern state of Tamil Nadu Ravana is the local Dravidian hero battling against the Aryan colonizer, represented by Rama. But while the South may have rationalized and partly rejected this epic, it could not always challenge the other traditions and beliefs that the Aryans took with them across the subcontinent.

One tradition, born out of the early Aryan experience in India (and therefore out of Punjab), was the respect and protection accorded to the cow. The Aryans came as wandering pastoralists, living off the produce of cattle, and the cow was both the chief source of their comfort and the best measure of their wealth. The animal was considered so auspicious that its meat was banned in normal fare, and eaten only on very special occasions. The priests soon made the cow sacred, and beef disappeared completely from the diet. The sanctity of the cow established deep roots and was not challenged even by those who questioned Vedantism, like Buddha or Mahavira.

The cow became a political problem only with the arrival of the Muslims, who did not consider beef to be any more holy than mutton or chicken. No single issue has led to more bloodshed in modern India between Hindus and Muslims than the conversion of a cow into beef. At the moment of writing, slaughter of kine in secular India survives, legally, thanks largely to the Marxists who share power in West Bengal and Kerala, and have refused to fall in line with the rest of the country where cow-slaughter has been banned. Even the Muslim-majority state of Kashmir does not permit the slaughter of cows, asking the Muslims to remain content with lamb. The Kashmiri Brahmins reciprocate the gesture by maintaining a distance from pork, which the Muslims, like the Jews, consider unclean. (Unlike the majority of their caste brethren, the Kashmiri Brahmins are not vegetarians.) The Sikhs, during the period of their struggle against the Muslim rulers of Delhi and Punjab, also made great play of their desire to protect the cow, but in the changing equation of the eighties Sikh extremists had begun to provoke Hindus by placing the severed heads of cows in Hindu temples.

The unique caste system of India also owes much to the Aryans of Punjab. Historians like Romila Thapar (*A History of India*, Penguin Books, 1966) have called this institutionalized intolerance a direct result of the Aryan prejudice against the darker races they encountered and subjugated on the subcontinent. The three upper Aryan castes were the Brahmins, or priests, the Kshatriyas, or warriors, and the Vaishyas, or traders and peasants. At the bottom of the heap were the Shudras, the dark, original inhabitants of the land, who were first made landless agricultural labourers and later condemned to the worst physical and moral humiliation possible. Soon the lowest caste was deemed untouchable and subjected to cruelty beyond belief. No later ideology could eradicate caste prejudice, though some succeeded in reducing it. Buddhism, with its anti-Brahminical and anti-caste thrust, won a large number of converts from the Shudras, but the religion itself did not survive in India when the upper-caste converts eventually went back to Hinduism. Islam, despite its egalitarian message and obvious display of equality in front of Allah, also fell prey to the insidious temptations of the caste system. While Indian Muslims never made their caste prejudice as brutal or vicious as the Hindus did, neither was there the true brotherhood envisaged in the faith. Guru Nanak's faith, Sikhism, banned caste too, but the converts to Sikhism from the untouchables are still looked down upon by their upper-caste co-religionists.

The Aryan priesthood was quick to calculate the benefits and immediately appointed itself the highest of the high by arguing that only the Brahmin could bestow divine sanction on the insecure kings. The Brahmin became the mind and the mouth of the community; the warrior, the arm; and the peasant, the thigh; while the untouchable was trampled underfoot. The mind produced the doctrines of *karma* and *dharma*: the former attempted to justify the injustice of caste by the convenient explanation of reward and punishment for deeds in a past life; the latter provided the theological cover of a 'natural order' in which everything had its place, including caste.

Obviously, the caste system has lasted till this century; but not for lack of challenge. And it is necessary to look briefly into the action and reaction of the last three thousand years, because they play a recurring part in the drama of the politics of post-British Indian democracy. Punjab, in particular, thanks to its geography, has had a unique place in the nurturing and cross-fertilizing of ideas. Every invader, apart from the British, entered India through its lands – the ones who came to stay, like the Aryans, the Scythians, the Turks, the Afghans or the Mughals, and the ones who went back, like the Greeks, the Huns or the Persians (the latter came in the time of Darius, 521–485 BC, and ruled for a hundred years over the area which includes Peshawar, Taxila and Rawalpindi, all now in Pakistan). If Vedantic Hinduism matured in Punjab, then more than two thousand years later Islam, too, was to take root here and make its own contribution to the culture and mind of the people. And perhaps only in a land like Punjab could the marriage of emotions and ideas lead to a child in the form of a new religion, Sikhism.

The first major threats to Hinduism came as early as the fifth century before Christ, and were led by two great contemporaries, Mahavira and Gautama Buddha. Mahavira gave this subcontinent the doctrine of *ahimsa*, or non-violence, central to Jainism. There are still 2 million believers. But it was Buddhism, with its great warrior kings and missionaries, which not only quickly spread through the subcontinent but became the major religion of Asia, finding converts from Iran to Japan. Both religions got the majority of their Indian converts from the third and fourth castes, who were chafing under the warrior–priest alliance of the upper two. The emerging trading classes saw in Jainism a chance to obtain a new status; and the untouchables were desperate for any alternative to the cruelty of the Brahmins. Buddhism did better, largely because of vital feudal support, particularly from the great Maurya emperor Ashoka, a Bihari who extended his reign throughout the subcontinent, and for a time Brahminism and Vedantism were on the verge of disappearance.

The response of the Brahmins was to change and survive. Romila Thapar describes the evolution (*A History of India*, Penguin Books, 1966, p. 131): 'Brahminism did not remain unchanged through all these centuries, nor was it impervious to the effects of Buddhism and Jainism. Some of the Vedic gods had quietly passed into oblivion and some were being reborn as new gods with additional attributes. This was the time when the Brahminical religion assumed features which today are recognized as Hinduism. To call it Hinduism at this stage is perhaps an anachronism, since the term was given currency by the Arabs in the eighth century A D when referring to those following the prevailing religion of India, the worship of Shiva and Vishnu ... Hinduism was not founded by a historical personage as a result of revelation. It is not a revealed religion but grew and evolved from a variety of cults and beliefs, of which some had their foundations in Vedic religion, and others were popular cults which became associated with the more sophisticated religion, a concession which the priests had to make to popular worship.'

Hinduism evolved from the myriad to the specific. A trinity of three dominant gods became the fulcrum: Brahma, the Creator; Vishnu, the Preserver; and Shiva, the Destroyer. Vishnu and Shiva, with their direct appeal to the imagination of the people, acquired huge and separate followings, and around them grew the two main Hindu sects. The religion was, in fact, tending towards monotheism, with faith concentrated around one deity. And the dislike which the people felt for the oppressive intermediary between God and worshipper, the Brahmin, led to an idea which was to have a dominant influence on the country – the concept of a personal relationship between the individual and the god, the concept of devotion, or *bhakti*. Having reduced the importance of the Brahmin and the rituals, Hinduism could survive the Buddhist challenge. The final triumph of Hinduism was to announce, after Buddhism had been defeated, that Buddha was the ninth reincarnation of the god Vishnu, who comes down periodically from the heavens in the shape of man to rescue the world from evil. It was a small price to pay for the defeat of the greatest threat Hinduism has faced.

It is the conquest of Buddhism which still lurks within the psyche of the minorities of India who have to live in the lap of this loosely defined culture called Hinduism. It is this which makes minority leaderships overprotective of identity, symbols and social laws. They are frightened of the power of absorption and assimilation, a gradual process which works on the principle of erosion, not subjugation, therefore making the battle far more subtle, far more difficult. This, as we shall see later, is at the root of the Sikh crisis of the 1980s.

3
A Faith and Two Religions

It took time, medicine and effort, but the revelation in the deer park at Sarnath, and the first sermon, on the Turning of the Wheel of Law, which Buddha preached to just five disciples, were eventually digested by Hinduism. A revelation in the deserts of Arabia to Muhammad, son of Bibi Amina and Abdullah, proved harder to digest. The message of Islam came in AD 610, and by 622 the Prophet had to flee from his birthplace, Mecca, to Medina, to escape the anger of the vested interests. Two years later came victory in the crucial battle for survival, near the wells of Badr, but it was only in 630 that the city of Mecca finally surrendered to the new belief, Islam. And in 632 the Prophet was dead.

But his message took on the force of a hurricane. With nothing faster than camels and horses, within a hundred years the armies of Islam were on the road to Paris in the west and at the gates of China in the east. Arab traders brought the idea to the Malabar coast, and the first Indian Muslims were converted here and at scattered points along the western coast within a decade of the Prophet's death. The term for the Malabar Muslim is still 'Moplah' (*Maha Pillai*), an Arab derivative which can be loosely translated as the 'great child'. (In the ninth century, according to popular belief, the King of Malabar himself was converted. There were no Muslim armies there, incidentally, so there was no question of any forced conversion.) By AD 712 the Arabs had won their first Indian possession when the armies of Muhammad Bin Qasim marched through Baluchistan and seized Sind. But the Arab effort stopped at the deserts bordering Sind, and the Muslim invasions that left their indelible imprint on the population, culture, politics and administration of North India were only to start two hundred and fifty years later, with the raids of a man whose name still arouses strong passions. Time does not necessarily heal in India.

This man was Mahmud of Ghazna, a Turk whose father had established a kingdom in what is now called Afghanistan. His hopes of empire were concentrated on central Asia, but since Afghanistan was too barren to finance his dreams he had to turn to a country whose wealth was already the envy of her neighbours. From the year AD 1000 onwards, he crossed Punjab almost annually with a highly trained and mobile army, went as far south as he could ride, looted as much as he could take, and turned around with bewildering speed to continue his efforts to conquer territory in Afghanistan, Turkestan or central Asia. In his first decade of plunder in India he concentrated on the strategic Punjab towns like Multan, and on the rich peasantry along the way. By 1010 he finally tumbled to the fact that the truly fabulous wealth was in the temple towns, and more particularly in the temples themselves, which received the people's rich offerings of gold and cash. Till 1026, Mahmud plundered the temples and temple towns of Mathura, Kannauj, Thaneswar and, eventually, the richest of them all, Somnath, on the Gujarat coast. Since Mahmud of Ghazna could not make simple greed a formal excuse for his uninhibited looting, he disguised his temple campaigns as religious fervour – he was the 'Believer' smashing the idols of infidels. Revenge for his looting and desecration of the temple of Somnath remains a war-cry of fanatic Hindus till today.

However, it was another clan which was to make a lasting impression on India. This was the Afghan tribe of Ghoris. Muhammad Ghori came at the end of the twelfth century, defeated and slew the romantic hero Prithviraj at the second battle of Tarain in 1192, and established what was to be known as the Sultanate, in Delhi. Muslim rule from Delhi was to last for the next seven hundred and fifty years.

This absence of feudal heroes at the accepted political centre of the country has been a source of some frustration to the communal Hindu elite, and its reaction has been to report the history of this subcontinent in terms of foreign Muslim invaders versus Hindu nationalists, rather than as the rise and decline of different sets of feudal forces who used whatever weapons, including religion, they could exploit. The fair-skinned Aryans, who used the same routes others would take later on, are not called outsiders, but those who followed them are.

Obviously the Turk, Afghan and Turk–Mughal invaders first came to raid, and then to rule. They ended up by staying. They created local alliances and won the allegiances which enabled them to build empires and set up administrative structures that have left their impact on modern India. The crucial point, however, is that even after defeat, they stayed on in India. The difference between the invader and the settler is best illustrated by the behaviour of Timur and Babar. In 1398, Timur destroyed the existing feudal power across the north of India, his victories and plunder culminating in death and destruction at Delhi. Having ravaged the country, he went back. His descendant Babar followed a century and a quarter later, and persuaded his troops that India was to be their new home. Delhi has never been sacked and destroyed by the settler, only by the invader – Timur, Nadir Shah, Ahmed Shah Abdali, and the British in 1857. Each time it was a Muslim aristocracy which suffered the most; logically enough, since they had the larger share of the power and wealth. Timur denuded the Turkish sultanate; Nadir Shah, Abdali and the British finished off the tottering Mughals. The British went home in 1947, whereas previous empire-builders – the Turks, Afghans or Mughals – never returned to their countries of origin. They had, in fact, lost the concept of 'home' just like the Aryans in 1500 BC. Fanatic Hindus have tried to go to absurd lengths to 'prove' that the Aryans did not come, like the Muslims, across the Hindu Kush mountains; one of them has seriously suggested that the Arctic polar region from which the Aryans set out on the first of their migrations was once in the heart of India before the world turned upside-down! The theory of the 'foreign' and the 'local' faith has a bearing on the Punjab situation. Since the Sikhs cannot be accused of being 'foreign', their faith, by reverse logic, is called a part of Hinduism.

Timur left the north without a strong ruler. The centre had collapsed, and the ensuing confusion brought out the worst in the Muslim and the Hindu. Commenting on the relationship between the two antagonistic religions, scholar–diplomat K. R. Narayanan writes in *Essays in Understanding*, a Government of India publication (p. 73): 'The story of Islam in India has not been one of a new militant force overwhelming an old civilization nor of the latter swallowing and digesting the former. It has been what one might call, a prolonged process of mutual accommodation and adjustment, interspersed with stormy periods of antagonism and conflict.' The fifteenth century was an age of storms, similar to the eighteenth, with the conflicts beginning at the level of the elite and then seeping down to the people as the feudal protectors poisoned their minds. The Muslim ruling class, anxious to fill the coffers depleted by Timur, attacked the 'infidel' Hindu trader in the name of religion. Naturally, the Hindus reacted. Khushwant Singh quotes a moving passage from Guru Nanak in *A History of the Sikhs* (Oxford University Press, vol. 1,

p. 29): 'The age is like a knife. Kings are butchers. Religion hath taken wing and flown. In the dark night of falsehood I cannot see where the moon of truth is rising ...' It would be seers like Nanak and Kabir who would begin to restore light after the dark night of falsehood.

Parallel to the clash of Muslim and Hindu swords, there was also the intermix of ideas. And just as the invader's sword eventually became no longer a foreign but an Indian sword, so Islam too both influenced and was influenced by its experience of the Hindu mind and practice. The turn of the millennium had seen a great Hindu revival, led principally by the Kerala Brahmin, Shankara, who travelled through the land, establishing institutions in Dwarka on the western coast, Badrinath in the Himalayas, Puri on the eastern coast of Orissa, and Sringeri in the south. He challenged the ritual of the Brahmins, and repudiated the duality of divinity, using the Upanishads to back his arguments but perhaps influenced by the ideas of Islam as well. It was Shankara who helped in the final defeat of Buddhism (and for his pains was excommunicated by the Brahmins). The concept of the devotee's personal relationship with his god was now carried forward into a great flowering called the Bhakti movement.

The fifteenth century was a political swamp from which India was rescued by a truly astounding intellectual renaissance, bringing to the fore a group of men and women who have left an indelible mark on the Indian consciousness, whose hymns are part of people's lives, whose message, though it may now have merged into dogma, still acts as a great dam, preventing the Hindu ethos from plunging into the torrents of fanaticism. The Bhakti movement may not have finished the Brahmin, but it certainly rescued the Hindu from Brahminism. The movement had its counterpart in Islam in the message of the Sufis, who were the true mass leaders as opposed to the priesthood, the *ulema* (whose Hindu equivalent, of course, would be the Brahmins). The shrines of Sufi saints like Khwaja Moinuddin Chishti, Qutubuddin Bakhitiyar Kaki, Fareed Shakarganj, Nizamuddin Auliya and Ali Makhdum in Ajmer, Delhi, Lahore and Pak Pattan are still places of pilgrimage both for Muslims and Hindus. As distinct from the efforts of the priesthood, these religious leaders preached and attempted a social harmony between Hindu and Muslim, by stressing what was common rather than promoting what was different.

In Assam there was Shankaradeva; in Bengal and Orissa, Chaitanya Mahaprabhu; in the north, Ramananda; Mira Bai in Rajasthan; Sadhana in Sind; Tukaram, Nam Dev and Parmanand in Maharashtra; Vallabha

Swami in the Deccan. But the greatest of them were two near-contemporaries (as close in time as Mahavira and Gautama Buddha), who fostered, in the bitterness of that post-Timur century, religions based on the unity of God, the complete devotion of the worshipper, and the paramount role of the *guru*, or teacher. The two were Kabir (1440–1518) and Nanak (1469–1539). They preached that the conflict between the Hindu and Muslim was false because God was one. 'Falsehood reigns supreme ... The Muslim mullah and the Hindu pandit have resigned their duties, the devil reads the marriage vows,' said Nanak. Kabir called himself the 'child of Allah and of Ram', and more than four centuries later Gandhi would use the same images and sing Kabir's hymns in his efforts to create Hindu–Muslim unity.

Kabir was an illegitimate child whose foster-father was a weaver. According to one tradition he was born a Muslim; in any case, Kabir remains a prevalent Muslim name in India. However, Kabir was not simply a reformist. He started an order, the Kabirpanthis, which had the parameters of a new religion, borrowing from both the older ones but adding many new aspects, particularly in the realm of social behaviour. Kabir won an impressive following largely from the artisans and the peasantry, but his religion had a short life even if his ideas did not die. Hinduism had managed to assimilate yet another threat.

Nanak was born in 1469, in the village of Talwandi Rai Bhoe, forty miles from Lahore, now in Pakistan. He was the son of Mehta Kalian Das Bedi, a village accountant. He learnt the alphabet from a pandit, and Persian and Arabic from a mullah. He was married at twelve; began living with his wife at the age of nineteen; and had two sons (Sri Chand, born in 1494, and Lakhmi Das, in 1497), before he announced in 1499 his mission: 'There is no Hindu, there is no Mussalman.' He composed hymns in the Bhakti tradition, and some of the terminology of that movement can be heard in today's Sikhism – for example, the word 'Sant', still applied to a Sikh religious leader. Male leaders of the Bhakti movement, like Tukaram, were called *Sant*, meaning a 'worthy and virtuous one' (today some of the names to which the title is attached are not necessarily carried by the worthy or the particularly virtuous).

There were differences, of course, in the philosophies of Nanak and Kabir. Both called God by a wide variety of traditional names, both Hindu and Muslim (the Golden Temple of the Sikhs, for instance, is called the Temple of Hari, which is a Hindu name of God), but Nanak was a strict, uncompromising monotheist. He defined God, calling Him the *Sat Kartar* (meaning the 'True Creator'); Truth was Godhood. In addition, and of vital importance, was the fact that he gave his followers a specific tenet which could be converted into daily practice by the Sikh: *nam* (the Word), *dan* (charity), *isnan* (cleanliness), *seva* (service) and *simran* (worship). He created institutions through which his followers could practise what he preached. He challenged caste by the concept of *Guru ka langar*, meaning 'the food in the name of the Guru', which is cooked at every Sikh temple and distributed to everyone without questioning his caste. Once you got the separate castes to eat together, caste was automatically broken. As we have noted before, caste is still prevalent in Sikhism, but this does not extend to the prejudice of eating separately, or to untouchability; it is limited to intermarriage.

But all this most probably would have not been sufficient to save the Nanakpanthis from the fate of the Kabirpanthis were it not for the fact that Sikhism was soon to find its St Paul.

4

Punjab versus Delhi:
The First Sikh Homeland

Guru Nanak announced his mission in 1499; a quarter of a century later the Mughal Babar attacked the decaying Afghan Lodi dynasty in Delhi. The smaller, better-led, better-motivated Mughal army defeated the much larger Muslim force under the Afghan king Ibrahim Lodi in what is famous as the first battle of Panipat (fifty-six miles to the north of Delhi) on 21 April 1526. Next year, in the less famous but equally decisive battle of Kanwaha, on 16 March 1527, Babar defeated the army, over 100,000 strong, of a Rajput–Afghan alliance led by Rana Sangha of Mewar, and effectively laid the base for a great empire before he died in 1530. There was a hiccup along the way, thanks to the unpredictable abilities of his beloved son Humayun, but Akbar gave life to his grandfather's dreams.

In other words, the Sikh religion and Mughal power developed simultaneously, and in close geographical proximity. Nanak's Punjab was just north of imperial Delhi. The two were bound to come into contact with each other, either peaceful or violent. The initial relationship was totally harmonious, but as the Sikhs grew more powerful, the friendliness soured. As it happened, the first long war which the Sikhs fought was not with Hinduism, which had swallowed the Kabirpanthis, but with those Muslims who were defending their empire. It did not, of course, begin as a war of survival, but a combination of mischief, regional ambitions and the dynamics of feudal behaviour ensured that it ended up as such. As long as the relationship between the Sikh and the Mughal empire was one of a new religion with a new power, it was remarkably friendly. It was when the Sikhs began seeking a geographical base where their new religion could flourish in security that war took on life-and-death dimensions. The old empire was not willing to allow a new one to arise without a fight, and the new religion was just as certain that without a protected home it could never survive.

There were nine Gurus after Nanak. The last, Guru Gobind Singh, rescued his religion from becoming a victim of feudalism, which is what the Guru system had degenerated into, by ending it. The Guru had the right to nominate his successor, but as the Sikhs acquired territory, the power of the Guru became as much temporal as spiritual, and bitter, divisive quarrels about hereditary succession resulted. By then, however, a good deal had been achieved. It was Guru Nanak's immediate successor, Guru Angad, for example, who made a vital contribution to a separate Sikh identity by introducing a different script, into which he put the hymns of Nanak: the Gurumukhi script.

That Delhi and the new religion were friendly was evident when the Emperor Akbar visited the third Guru, Amar Das, and to show his respect for Sikhism, ordered that the revenues of several villages be given to the Guru's daughter Bhani as a marriage gift. To the next Guru, Ram Das, the Emperor Akbar gave a grant of 500 bighas of land on which the present Sikh holy city of Amritsar is situated. It was here that Arjun, the fifth Guru, built the sacred Harimandir, or the Golden Temple. There was obviously great friendship between Sikhs and Muslims then; the foundation stone of the Golden Temple was laid by a Muslim divine invited from Lahore, Mian Mir. It was during the twenty-five years of Arjun's ministry that the compilation of the Granth Sahib was completed, and the Sikh church truly established. The number of conversions increased rapidly, much to the anger of the Brahmins and the mullahs; four new towns were built, and the people began to refer to Arjun as the *Sacha Padshah* (the 'True Emperor').

But here the problems began, particularly since Guru Arjun could not resist the temptation of playing power politics. With his influence on the increase, Guru Arjun entered that vicious whirlpool of Mughal succession wars. He supported the revolt of Jehangir's son Khusrau. If Khusrau had succeeded, Guru Arjun would surely have been a star in the court of Delhi, ensuring recognition, reward and even perhaps a Sikh–Mughal coalition on the Rajput–Mughal pattern. Instead, he earned the anger of Jehangir, whose fits of virulence and cruelty have been recorded by every historian. The enemies of Guru Arjun, particularly the priests, found this an excellent opportunity to destroy the 'upstart'; Sikh tradition names one of Arjun's tormentors as the banker Chandu Shah who had been rebuffed when he proposed a marriage between his daughter and Guru Arjun's son. Guru Arjun was arrested and tortured, and he died in captivity on 30 May 1606. The martyrdom of Arjun, and later, during the reign of Aurangzeb, the execution of the ninth Guru, Tegh Bahadur (who had begun exacting tribute from the people, along with an ally, a Muslim fakir, Hafiz Adam), and of the two young sons of the tenth Guru, Gobind Singh, have become symbols of a Sikh hatred for Muslims that has lasted more than three centuries.

Religion was only another weapon in the extensive armoury of the feudal class; one king might use it to a greater or lesser degree as his perception of his needs determined his decisions. The trouble with history is not the fact but the memory. A selection of incidents is funnelled into the popular imagination to serve the interests of a political elite; the most successful in this game are those who have an educated middle class in the vanguard to carry on the necessary propaganda. Such partial history was drummed into the Sikh psyche, particularly in the second half of the nineteenth century when the Hindu revivalists were anxious to ensure a united front against the Muslims. Till the creation of Pakistan, this suited the Sikh leadership very well too, and so the mental landscape of the community was crowded with calendar art showing blood spurting from the severed head of Guru Tegh Bahadur or, more evocatively, the death of the minor sons of Guru Gobind Singh. After the massacre at Jallianwala Bagh in 1919, white men joined the gallery of rogues, all past collaboration being conveniently pushed into the background. The news of the 1980s is a little different: the Hindu is the latest villain.

The early Sikh leaders clearly distinguished between the Muslim and the Muslim feudal interest. The great warrior–hero of the Sikhs was Guru Gobind Singh, who lost his father and four of his sons to Mughal tyranny, but the nucleus of his army consisted of 500 Muslim Pathans. His life was saved on one occasion, when he was surrounded by Mughal troops at Machiwara, by two faithful Pathans who took him away in a curtained palanquin, explaining to the Mughal besiegers that they were carrying away their *pir*, or holy teacher. It was rarely a straight question of Sikh army versus Muslim army. The forces sent to crush the Sikhs by Aurangzeb, although led by the subahdar of Sirhind, Wazir Khan, also included Rajputs, for instance those led by the Raja of Bilaspur. The same Wazir Khan's closest adviser was his Hindu Prime Minister, or *Dewan*, Sucha Nand who pressurized Wazir Khan to kill Guru Gobind's sons after they were captured. (Sucha Nand was therefore a special target of Banda Bahadur, Gobind's successor as leader of the Sikhs, when Banda captured Sirhind on 24 May 1710.) Guru Gobind was a friend of Aurangzeb's son Bahadur Shah, and helped him in the succession war; he was honoured in Bahadur Shah's court, and marched together with the imperial army till his assassination at the hands of his Pathan retainer. It was, incidentally, the first time that the Sikhs had made the right choice in the Mughal succession wars, having earlier supported Dara Shikoh, Aurangzeb's brother, thus earning the Alamgir's wrath. History just might have been different if Guru Gobind had not been assassinated by killers hired by a jealous Wazir Khan who was fearful of the influence the Guru had on the Mughal emperor.

Among the first talents hired by the great Sikh emperor Ranjit Singh were the three Bokhari brothers, Azizuddin, Imamuddin and Nuruddin. The last became Ranjit Singh's personal physician (a most trusted post, obviously), while Azizuddin became Prime Minister and, more important, one of the Maharaja's closest friends, eventually outliving both Ranjit Singh and his successor Kharak Singh. Ranjit Singh's artillery was manned by Muslim gunners, led by Ghaus Mohammad Khan and Shaikh Elahi Baksh; the former was to become the legendary Mian Ghausa. Even during the decisive Anglo-Sikh wars of 1849, which finally ended the Sikh empire, it was not a purely Sikh army which fought the British officers, with their sepoys of the Bengal Company, but as the British themselves put it, a 'Sikh–Moslem army'. Lieutenant-General Sir George MacMunn may not necessarily be trustworthy about historical detail, but there can be no question of the accuracy of regimental memories. As he puts it, when describing the British victory at Chillianwala in *The Martial Races of India* (Mittal Publications, New Delhi, 1979, p. 214): 'This last spectacular scene of surrender, when the undaunted Sikhs and Moslems of the Sikh Army threw down their weapons, before the long scarlet line that presented arms to them, *salaamed* to the Commander-in-Chief, and stalked off the field sadder and wiser, beaten but not disgraced ...' Apart from the Punjabi Muslims, the Afghans had come to fight alongside the Sikh army against the British. Sardar Akram Khan, son of Amir Dost Muhammad, brought a contingent of 5,000 Afghans to the battle for Gujrat (in the north Punjab). Instances of this sort can be multiplied, not only in the Sikh–Muslim relationship but also in the Hindu–Muslim nexus. Unfortunately, history at the popular level is often distorted by those who want to destroy rather than build India. Shivaji, the great Maratha empire-builder, is projected as the Hindu leader who spent all his time fighting the Muslim foreign invaders to save his motherland. But it was not a Muslim commander who captured Shivaji and brought him as a prisoner to Aurangzeb's court; it was Raja Jai Singh, a Rajput chief proud of belonging to the Hindu warrior class. If India learnt more of the truth of its own past, it would perhaps have fewer problems today.

Guru Gobind Singh was killed on 7 October 1708; it was his legacy that ensured as much as anything else that Sikhism would survive as a separate religion. It was a simple but resoundingly effective technique: he externalized the Sikh identity. Where Guru Nanak had given the content, Guru Gobind gave the form. In 1699, on the day of Baisakhi, the spring festival, the followers of Nanak were summoned to the city of Anandpur by Guru Gobind. He asked that day for five volunteers ready to die by his sword in the name of the faith, at that very moment, and by his own hand. The five who eventually stood up were not killed, but named the 'Beloved Five' (*Panj Pyare*). The Guru's wife had sweetened some water by stirring it with a double-edged dagger; the five were baptized by a drink of this 'nectar'. They were given the new surname of *Singh* (meaning 'lion') and called the *Khalsa* (the 'Pure'); they were the first of the clan which was given the task of defending the Sikh faith, and of ensuring its survival by the creation of a country over which the Sikh would rule. (The inevitable intelligence agent sent by Delhi reported to the Mughal court that 20,000 men joined the Khalsa that day.) The Khalsa would be identified by five marks: *kes* (uncut hair), *kangha* (a comb), *kacha* (the military underwear), *kara* (a steel bracelet) and *kirpan* (a sabre), which they would always carry. The Sikh that we recognize so easily today was, in fact, created precisely two hundred years after Guru Nanak began preaching his message. And from that year, a cry went up which is still heard at every time of prayer: '*Raj karega Khalsa*' ('The Khalsa shall rule'). The full form leaves no doubts about the intention:

> *Dilli takht par bahegi, aap Guru ki fauj*
> *Chatter phirega sis paar, barhi karegi mauj.*
> *Raj karega Khalsa, baaqi rahe na koe*
> *Khwar hoye sab milenge, bache saran jo hoye.*

Simply translated, this means that the armies of the Guru will rule Delhi, and only those will survive who seek the protection of the Khalsa; the frustrated shall submit, and enemies be vanquished. After the British conquered Punjab, they did not quite like the idea of anyone ruling Delhi but themselves, and so they banned this verse. The Sikh leaders compromised by removing the first two lines from the popular recitation, and then rationalized the last two by explaining that the pure would rule only in the spiritual, not the temporal, sense. It was an old trick: to preserve a dream by calling it an illusion. The British let it pass. The slogan can still be found daubed on the walls of Delhi and Amritsar, and is part of the Sikh's prayer.

The Khalsa found a leader in a fanatic Rajput convert disciple of Guru Gobind, Lachman Das, who took on the name of Banda Bahadur, meaning the 'Brave Slave'. By the time he was arrested and executed on 19 June 1716, Banda had taken the Khalsa banner into virtually every corner of Punjab, even if he could not hold what he subjugated. His main targets were those he perceived as the special enemies of Sikhism, with Muslims at the top of his list. But in the process he indulged in wanton destruction and alienated the masses, particularly the large Muslim population.

The eighteenth century was an unruly and unruled period in Indian history. Any authority other than the Mughal would have collapsed much faster, but even the extraordinary decadence of the successors could not easily destroy the empire that six kings, from Babar to Aurangzeb, had built. It took a full century and more for the great Mughal empire to wither. But in that time Delhi became vulnerable, not only to regional ambitions from the west and the north, but also to plunderers from abroad. Nadir Shah came from Persia, and returned with an enormous booty including the Peacock Throne and the Koh-i-noor diamond (which was to undergo a strange journey before ending up in the hands of Queen Victoria, and becoming a part of the Crown Jewels, now on display at the Tower of London). Incidentally, those who might wonder at the frequency of Persian, Turk and Afghan raids might care to remember that Iran is much closer to Delhi than Delhi is to the southern Indian state of Kerala.

The country was to face worse trouble with the invasions of Nadir Shah's ablest general, Ahmed Shah Abdali, the Afghan ruler who styled his clan the Durrani. Abdali came, saw, looted and came again. Nine times between 1747 and 1769 the Afghan invaded India, plundering at will while playing political games with the local pawns. The one force which could have challenged Abdali, the Marathas, were defeated at the third battle of Panipat in 1761, and after that the Durranis had only the Sikhs who had grouped themselves under *misls* (a word meaning both 'example' and 'equal') to challenge him. Sikhs remember with horror the massacre Abdali ordered at Amritsar during his sixth invasion, and the blowing up of the Golden Temple to take revenge for the successful counter-attack by the Sikhs looting the wealth-laden caravans returning to Kabul. The gross national product of Afghanistan in that era seemed to consist totally of booty from India.

The Khalsa was a movement searching for a leader, a man who could convert Guru Gobind's idea into the reality of a homeland and an empire. This man, Ranjit Singh, was born on 13 November 1780, in Gujranwala, west of Lahore, now in Pakistan. His father died when he was twelve, leaving him, in Khushwant Singh's words, 'a large district in the heart of Punjab and an ambition that knew no bounds'. The times were right for such a spirit.

In 1761, the Mughal emperor had asked the ascendant Marathas to save Delhi from the marauding Afghan, Abdali; if they had managed to do so, rule from Delhi would have been the logical next step, and we could well have seen a Maratha dynasty on the throne of Delhi. But Abdali crushed not only the Maratha army at Panipat but also the Maratha ambition, and from a Peshwa-led confederacy the Marathas became five autonomous kingdoms (the Peshwa, Gaekwad, Bhonsle, Scindia and Holkar). Divided, they fell. And the condition of the Mughal empire in this period is best illustrated by the fate of Shah Alam, who was blinded by an Afghan chief in 1788 and became a pensionary of first the Scindias and then the British. But if Delhi was weak, so were the contenders for power, none of whom had sufficient strength to displace the Mughal. For a brief while the Jats surrounding Delhi, under the charismatic leadership of Suraj Mal (1707–63), behaved as if they might fill the vacuum, but the Rajput, Jat, Maratha and Muslim aspirants (like the Rohillas) preferred the long sunset of the Mughal to a new dawn. It was left to the British to infiltrate from Bengal and settle the issue by 1857. But before the British came, a star shone in the north; its arrival was sudden, its glory lit the sky, and then it disappeared as suddenly as it came. The Peshwa had boasted before meeting Abdali at Panipat that the Maratha would leap across the walls of Attock, the point on the Indus, on the road from the Khyber Pass, through which the Afghans marched. But it would be the Sikh armies of Ranjit Singh who would claim the honour of carrying the Khalsa banner across the walls of Attock, and into Afghanistan and Kabul.

The first – and, indeed, only – Sikh kingdom once again proved that growth, development, expansion and stability come only in those periods when the ruler's policy shifts away from fanaticism and towards co-operation. Given the bitterness and violence which had characterized Sikh–Muslim relations, it would not have been in the least surprising if Maharaja Ranjit Singh had indulged in the luxury of revenge against the Muslims. But he would never have then achieved the unique integration of Punjab, from the Indus river in the west to the Jumna in the east.

Ranjit Singh made a conscious effort to win the friendship of both Muslims and Hindus, sharing power with them while making full use of the gestures which go such a long way to reassure people. The extraordinary authority given to Fakir Azizuddin has been mentioned. Ranjit Singh's Prime Minister was Dhian Singh, a Dogra Hindu from Jammu, while his Finance Minister was Dina Nath, a Hindu Brahmin. His artillery commander Mian Ghausa was given the title of 'Commander and Faithful Friend', and other senior Muslim officers included General Elahi Baksh, Khuda Yar and Sultan Mohammad. There were Muslims among his twenty-two wives, Bibi Gulbahar Begum being a favourite. The first thing that Maharaja Ranjit Singh did upon conquering Lahore was to pay his respects at the famous Badshahi mosque, at the tomb of Wazir Khan, and at the mausoleum of Data Ganj Baksh, later rebuilt, mainly by his Sikh wives. When Ranjit Singh reorganized his army, Muslims and Hindus were co-opted in the ranks. When the Sikh army entered Srinagar, the standard was carried by General Zorawar Singh, a Dogra Hindu, and when Sikh troops made their triumphant entry into Kabul in 1839 (just after Ranjit Singh's death) the Khalsa colours were carried by the Muslim troops led by Colonel Shaikh Bassawan. Muslims were allowed their *qazis*, or judges, to administer justice by the Quranic law, while the state treated every Punjabi as an equal.

And Ranjit Singh did all this without indulging in any humbug. His was a proclaimed Sikh kingdom. The title of Maharaja was given not by Delhi or Kabul but by the Khalsa Panth (the Sikh religious leadership). The first Sikh coins did not carry a portrait of the Maharaja but were in the name of Sarkar Khalsaji. But Ranjit Singh's political philosophy was non-partisan, as he would tell his friend Fakir Azizuddin. An early attack of smallpox had left his face ugly and scarred, in addition to destroying one eye. Ranjit Singh once explained to Azizuddin why this had happened: 'God wanted me to look upon all religions with one eye, that is why he took away the light from the other.'

The Sikh empire touched the borders of Tibet in the north, went across to Afghanistan in the west, and reached beyond the Sutlej to the southeast. Its quick disintegration after Ranjit Singh's death in 1839 had a profound impact on the Sikh psyche. Ranjit Singh's seven sons by different mothers degraded their inheritance; it did not need the British to question their legitimacy, they did it themselves, accusing one another of being bastards. From a healthy ripeness, the empire quickly turned rotten. The British, despite their promise by treaty not to interfere in the affairs of the Sikh kingdom, could hardly resist the temptation. Using a few poor pretexts, they started the wars of the 1840s which brought the vast Punjab into their hands. Perhaps the worst psychological blow to the Sikhs was the conversion of Maharaja Dalip Singh, son of the great Ranjit Singh, to Christianity and his reduction to the status of a fancied toy in the court of Queen Victoria. (It was Dalip Singh who was forced to 'present' the Koh-i-noor diamond to Queen Victoria; his father had restored it to India, after recovering it from the Afghans. Victoria immediately had the 'mountain of light' cut to one-third of its size.)

The Sikh homeland, which had become a reality, was now once again a dream. The faith itself was under threat. The Maharaja had become a Christian and missionaries were now flooding the Punjab, offering the conversion of Dalip Singh as an example of their moral superiority, with worldly benefit as a more practical inducement. Soon Hindu preachers also came, asking the Sikhs to return to the 'purity' of the 'mother religion', arguing that the Khalsa was only a variant of the Hindu faith and part of the Arya Samaj (the 'Aryan Society'). The leader of the organization by that name, Dayanand Saraswati, was willing to make the necessary concessions to the ideas of Nanak, and to Islam too (rejecting the caste system and idol worship, and accepting monotheism instead), to win reconversions. The Muslims did not have much problem resisting the Arya Samaj, but the Sikhs, confused and depressed, were caught in what was their first identity crisis. Were the followers of Nanak going to disappear, as had the followers of Mahavira, Siddhartha and Kabir?

In 1499 Guru Nanak had proclaimed his mission; in 1699 Guru Gobind gave the Sikh the Khalsa identity; in 1799 the first independent Sikh kingdom was set up; and within precisely fifty years, by 1848, the one-generation empire had dissipated in waste of spirit. The Sikhs had survived their terrible battle against Muslim arms. Could they survive the war with the Hindu mind?

5
The Identity Crisis

Rarely in history has the fall from the sublime to the ridiculous been as astonishing. Maharaja Ranjit Singh preferred to be called 'Singh Sahib' though he was truly an emperor. Kharak Singh, his eldest son, wanted desperately to be a Maharaja and was, to put it mildly, a goof whose limited wits were further dulled by an addiction to opium. One of the main arguments he used to win the throne was that his six brothers, Sher Singh, Tara Singh, Kashmira Singh, Peshawara Singh, Multana Singh and Dalip Singh, were bastards. Given the reputation of their mothers, the Sikh nobility was probably ready to believe this; as eldest son, his claim was anyway strongest. Kharak Singh's son, Nao Nihal Singh, soon took charge, after personally disembowelling his father's favourite, the power behind the throne, Chet Singh Bajwa, while his father spent his time trying to convince everyone that he was not an idiot. Kharak Singh's death, on 5 November 1840, from alcohol, dysentery, opium and high fever (in which order, who knows) was an occasion for relief rather than sorrow. There was hope that Nao Nihal Singh might be able to pull things together. But a stone fell on Nao Nihal Singh's head and he died on the very day that his father was cremated. Sher Singh, Kharak Singh's brother, succeeded, with British approval. Already the British had begun to play a part in the palace politics of Lahore, which was not much of a surprise since the various factions had begun seeking their help in the succession battles.

One of Kharak Singh's wives, Bibi Chand Kaur, did not allow whatever affection she might have had for her late husband to induce her to commit sati (a practice which had been forbidden in Sikhism, but which had returned). She revived the old allegation, calling Sher Singh the bastard son of a dyer (*sheroo coba*) rather than of the blood of Maharaja Ranjit Singh. So she put in her claim for the throne. By 2 December 1840 she had usurped power and was proclaimed *Malika Mukaddas*, the 'Revered

Empress'. That was enough to make the fortune-tellers prophesy doom; and they were right too, since soon there would be neither reverence nor an empire left. Sher Singh (perhaps the first of the Sikh anglophiles, a tribe which was to flourish later) took the help of the British, and marched on Lahore. Both sides wooed the soldiers by promises of pay hikes; Sher Singh was believed, the Empress was not since the army's pay was already heavily in arrears. She tried to salvage matters by seeking the help of the Jammu Hindus, and appointed their leader, Gulab Singh Dogra, her Commander-in-Chief. But Sher Singh won the battle and on 17 January 1841 she was forced to surrender. The previous midnight the Dogra chief had crept away from the Lahore fort, taking with him all the gold and jewellery of the Sikhs, which made him one of the most successful jewel thieves of all time. (Part of that hoard still exists in the government treasury in Srinagar, and is claimed by some Sikhs as their, rather than Kashmiri, treasure. If these things matter at all, they have a point.)

From here to British rule in Punjab was a short step. In 1843 Sir Charles Napier took Sind without giving any formal reason. In September that year, Ajit Singh Sandhawalia, once supporter of the Revered Empress and now in the pay of the British, in a singular display of treachery, killed Sher Singh and his elder son Pratap Singh, hacked off their heads, stuck them on to spears, and paraded them on the streets of Lahore, before occupying the fort. Loyal Sikh troops reacted by storming the fort and putting the rebels to the sword. The only one lucky enough to escape was Ajit Singh Sandhawalia, who was immediately given protection by his puppeteers, the British. Seven-year-old Dalip Singh, the youngest son of Ranjit Singh, was placed on the throne, with his mother, the winsome Jindan Kaur, now taking the decisions.

The story till the British annexed Punjab is one of unbelievable pettiness and intrigue, and a fine explanation of why exactly the British managed first to conquer India and then to hold it. The Indian feudals, now in a state of mental and physical debauchery, simply gave the country to them (later, the Indian middle class helped the British hold their empire). To narrate the complexities of the Lahore Durbar in this period would, apart from serving no purpose except that of prurience, take the rest of the book, but once again an illustration could serve as a symbol. Matters were now so out of hand that one of the most powerful persons in the palace was a pretty thirty-year-old maidservant, Mangla, the mistress of Dalip Singh's uncle. Mangla was the daughter of a water-carrier, and one of the accusations against Dalip Singh was that he was not the true son of Ranjit

Singh but the product of the liaison between Bibi Jindan Kaur and a water-carrier.

In early 1845 the British established an alliance with the Dogra chief Gulab Singh, and by autumn began assembling their forces for the Punjab offensive. The traditional feudal Indian art form, treachery, helped the British once again to win, when the Sikh chief Tej Singh, who had arrived with reinforcements, withdrew rather than help finish off Lord Gough's nearly defeated army at the battle of Ferozeshah on 21–22 December 1845. The British rewarded Gulab Singh's alliance by allowing him to 'purchase' the territory which today constitutes the state of Jammu and Kashmir, and which was ruled by his successors till Hari Singh ran off in fright in 1947.

On 29 March 1849, after a futile Sikh uprising, the British formally announced the end of the Sikh empire, and Maharaja Dalip Singh handed over the Koh-i-noor. 'Today Ranjit Singh has died,' said the older Sikhs. He had; and along with him had died a part of the spirit of the new faith.

In the mean while, in Delhi the charade of empire was being conducted in ludicrous detail; the reality of the last days of the Mughals defies the imagination. The last emperor, Bahadur Shah Zafar, crowned in 1837, still called himself the 'Ruler of the Universe' and believed, according to Sir Syed Ahmed's *The Cause of the Indian Revolt*, that he could transform himself into a fly or a gnat. Freud should have an explanation for that; if there was any opposite to delusions of grandeur, this was it. But four times a year, on the Muslim festivals of Id and Bakr-Id, on New Year's Day, and on the birthday of the Queen of England, representatives of the British would stand barefoot in front of this ruler of a ghost empire, and present the *nazar*, or tribute. Actually, the British cheated. Unable to bring themselves to come barefoot, a sign of inferiority, they wore socks over their shoes. As for the Emperor, when he was not writing self-pitying poetry he was appealing to the British for a larger pension.

But the Emperor's mystique was not dead. The throne of Delhi, once held by Babar, and Akbar, and Shah Jehan, and Aurangzeb, was still the symbol of true power, even if the man sitting on it was worthless. The Holkar coins continued to bear the Mughal emperor's name till the reign of Tukaji Rao (1844–86). The British had, by this time, defeated and exiled all the important feudal families who could possibly have threatened their supremacy in India. The Maratha Peshwa had been banished to a North Indian village; the heirs of Tipu Sultan to the outskirts of Calcutta; the rulers of Awadh, also to Calcutta; and Ranjit Singh's converted son to a country house in England. The only one left in the way of the British was the doddering relic in Delhi.

On the morning of 11 May 1857, the sepoys of the Black Platoon (*Kali Paltan*) of Meerut, spurred by the success of a day earlier, crossed the Jumna on a bridge of boats to enter Delhi between the Calcutta Gate and the royal palace. As is generally known, the mutiny was officially sparked off by the anger of Hindus and Muslims against the animal fat used to grease cartridges which had to be bitten open when loading the new Enfield rifle. But the mutiny had been simmering for a long while. The peasantry of the area surrounding Delhi (who had never been asked by the British to taste any grease) joined the revolt, and it became a unique ground-level upsurge in which Hindus and Muslims forgot their differences and made common cause against the white man. The upheaval won the support of a wide spectrum across North India, including the Santhals and the Bhils – tribes which recognized no caste, but did recognize a foreigner. The problem of the mutineers, in the end, was that too many myriad forces were fighting for too many different things, and some may not have been quite sure of what victory would mean. Added to this was the incompetence of most of the feudal leadership.

When the sepoys first reached Bahadur Shah's palace and demanded that he lead them, he asked his resident British agent, Captain Douglas, to shoo them away. When they insisted, he pleaded with them that he was a mere pensioner, and he could not pay them. They did not want any pay, the sepoys said. Some people clearly have to have greatness thrust upon them; the last scion of the Mughal dynasty was one such. But the spirit of the moment was strong enough to catch the imagination even of a Bahadur Shah Zafar. He agreed to lead. The sepoys took over Delhi.

The British waited for religious differences to destroy the new sepoy unity, and in particular for the day of Bakr-Id, on which Muslims sacrifice animals to God. They expected the traditional hostility between Hindus and Muslims over the killing of a cow to break the alliance. Instead, the Muslim leaders prohibited cow slaughter and Bahadur Shah Zafar himself showed the way by publicly sacrificing a goat. In the battles to raise the British siege there was much bravado on the Indian side, including a fascinating Muslim woman who declared herself a *jehadeen*, or martyr, and, wearing a green turban, led a cavalry charge. She was made prisoner by the British but not before she had killed two Britishers with her own hand. However, on 14 August John Nicholson's column arrived in support of the British; by 13 September the walls of the Delhi fort had been

breached; and by 20 September the British had saved their empire, though
at a cost of 3,837 officers and men dead, missing or injured. Twenty-one
Mughal princes were hanged; as many Delhites as the marauding troops
wanted they shot; the capital was plundered and looted by the British, as
had been done by previous conquerors. According to British records, every
officer could have retired at once after the loot, and an 'unusual number'
immediately bought their discharge. Ghalib, the famous Urdu poet, wrote
about the 'vast ocean of blood before me'; and the British began a rule from
Delhi which would end precisely ninety years later with another blood-
bath, though this time in a war between Hindus and Muslims.

It was during this mutiny that the Sikhs showed that, as a community,
they had interests and motives of their own which differed from those of
the Hindus and the Muslims.

At midnight on 11–12 May, the sepoys and the younger princes had
finally forced our reluctant hero, Bahadur Shah Zafar, to assume
command of the mutiny, and 21 salvoes of the royal cannon dutifully
announced the temporary end of impotence. The Punjab garrisons then
had 60,000 troops, of which only 10,000 were British. On 13 May the
Indian regiments were asked to pile arms. The empire was at stake; even
the Gurkhas stationed in the Simla hill cantonments had begun murmur-
ing, and those at Kasauli looted the treasury and won concessions before
returning to the barracks. It was at this point that the Sikhs, Kashmiri
Dogras and Punjabi Muslims came to the rescue of the British. They had
their reasons. First, the newly mutinous sepoys were the very troops who,
as soldiers of the East India Company, had destroyed the Sikh–Punjabi–
Dogra empire only a decade ago. The crucial elements in this alliance, the
Sikhs, could not become enthusiastic about either the Hindu aspiration of
a Maratha emperor in Delhi or the Muslim hope of the restoration of
Mughal glory. Apart from stray cases of Sikhs joining the sepoys, as in
Banaras or nearby Jaunpur, Sikh soldiers fought to save the British in the
principal centres of the revolt across North India. The British helped this
by encouraging the idea of an Anglo-Sikh seizure of Delhi. In fact, this did
happen, but the British got the power and the Sikhs a pat on the back –
plus some of the satisfaction and the loot that followed the capture of Delhi
in September.

Sikh princes got part of the land seized from the anti-British feudals.
For instance, the Nawab of Jhajjar, a Muslim, was hanged and his property
divided between the Sikh estates of Patiala and Nabha (the former also got
a house belonging to Begum Zeenat Mahal, Bahadur Shah's wife, in

Delhi). And the Khalsa became the new darlings of the army. So far, Sikhs had been restricted to a maximum of 100 men per regiment (there were 74 regiments in the British army). After the reorganization in the wake of the mutiny, the theory of 'martial races' was propounded: Sikhs, Punjabi Muslims, Rajputs, Jats, Dogras and Marathas would now be hired, on the interesting principle that they were Aryan or sub-Aryan races, and thereby essentially European. The Biharis, who had in fact given the British their previous victories, but who mutinied in 1857, were now converted into a non-martial race, and the Sikhs, Gurkhas and Dogras became the martial soldiers. A further reward for the Sikhs came in the programme to build canals in Punjab.

In an interesting twist, it was this that helped the Sikhs surmount their first great crisis. As Khushwant Singh notes: 'The prosperity ushered in by the development to the Imperial army had an important bearing on the feature and caste complex of the community. *The economic advantages of being Sikh checked the disintegration of Sikhism and its lapse into Hinduism* [author's italics]. On the contrary, the last decade of the nineteenth century and the first decade of the twentieth saw a phenomenal rise in the number of Sikhs ... Thus the gloomy foreboding of Lord Dalhousie of the possibility of the disappearance of the Sikhs was staved off by policies initiated by Dalhousie himself and supplemented by army commanders and administrators of the Punjab.'

The British simply made it profitable to be a Sikh. The network of canals turned waste stretches into golden fields; the deliberate offer of the best plots to Sikh farmers was to have far-reaching consequences. The Chenab canal alone made 2.25 million acres of land cultivable and brought in a yearly revenue of more than Rs 78 million, or three times the cost of the canal. The poorest Sikh settlers were given from 14 to 16 acres of land free; the middle category got from 111 to 139 acres, on a payment of between Rs 6 and Rs 9 an acre; and the rich got from 167 to 556 acres, on a payment of between Rs 10 and Rs 20 an acre. Land which had been only Rs 10 an acre before the canalization programme now brought Rs 400 an acre. The export of wheat rose to more than a million tons a year. And though Sikhs formed only 12 per cent of Punjab's population, they constituted more than 20 per cent of India's imperial army. It was good to be a Sikh after the mutiny.

But the question to ponder is why Lord Dalhousie had prophesied that the Sikhs would disappear, and why historians have reported that the journey back to Hinduism had begun. There is no question that the relationship between the Hindus and the Sikhs was very close, and has remained close till recently. This amity was sharpened by the common enmity against Muslims, and in its day-to-day manifestations took the shape of, for instance, the Sikh reverence for the cow (although there is nothing in the Sikh religion which would call for more than the normal respect for a revenue-earning animal). Hindus began worshipping in the Sikh temples, and this quickly led to the introduction of idols, strictly forbidden by Guru Nanak. In the nineteenth and early twentieth centuries it became the practice among Hindus to let the eldest son become a Sikh. Cynics have suggested that this generosity was a direct consequence of the benefits that the British were handing out to the Sikhs, which the Hindus did not want to lose out on. Whatever may have been the reasons, the interrelationship was close enough for observers to predict that the Nanakpanthis would soon return to Hinduism. In this flux, religious movements of many kinds started. Various sects appeared, midway between the Sikhism of Nanak and Guru Gobind, and the Hinduism of the Brahmins; one was the sect of the Nirankaris, led by Dyal Das, a Peshawar merchant. Similarly, a Hindu banker, Shiv Dayal, established the sect of Radha Soamis.

But however much the British inducements may have helped the Sikhs, this alone could never have been enough to meet the challenge of Hinduism, or the lure of the Christian missionaries. Christian proselytizing had begun with the establishment of an American Presbyterian mission in Ludhiana in 1835, and then spread out. The Christians won their first converts from the untouchables, but later scored a few successes from the elite too, the most notable being Raja Harnam Singh, whose daughter Rajkumari Amrit Kaur was to become a minister in free India.

The Arya Samaj (the 'Aryan Society') was founded by Swami Dayanand Saraswati, a Gujarati Brahmin who preached a return to Vedantism and obviously had a special interest in the land where the Vedas were composed. He came to Punjab in 1877, six years before he died, and made a substantial impact, with many Sikhs undergoing the *shudhi*, or purification, to return to Hinduism. Dayanand left no one in any doubt about his views; his book *Satyarth Prakas*, published in 1874, abused the prophets Muhammad and Christ and Guru Nanak with equal force. For Nanak, who could not be accused of being a 'foreigner', he had a particular venom, calling him a hypocrite. Sikh intellectuals tried to answer, and *Ham Hindu Nahin Hain* (which means 'We Are Not Hindus') was written by Kahan Singh of Nabha state, in response to the Arya Samaj.

What made the Sikhs truly vulnerable was not the assault from outsiders but their own weaknesses, which had so quickly crept in. Just fifty years earlier, the numbers of Khalsa were increasing; now they had begun falling at a rapid rate. The census of 1881 reported, 'Sikhism is on the decline', although the overall population had grown by a huge 20 per cent since the last count. All the evils that Guru Nanak had fought against were rampant, particularly casteism. In the temple of equality, the sacred Harimandir at Amritsar, 'low-caste' Sikhs were allowed in only at special times, and were not allowed to touch the *karha prasad*, the food offered from the common kitchen to every devotee, a practice started specifically to challenge the taboos of casteism. But the state of the religion was best illustrated by the condition of the Sikh temples. It was a level of degeneration which would kill the community unless checked.

6

'Pagri Samhal, Jatta'

By the turn of the century, one of the places in the Punjab where you might fancy your chances of buying pornographic literature, or bedding a prostitute, or perhaps gambling, depending on the entrepreneurial abilities of the man in charge, was the Sikh temple, the *gurdwara*. This was not an isolated scourge. And this astonishing decadence had touched even the holiest of places, the Golden Temple at Amritsar. Innocent women coming to pray in the temples were not safe; and the *mahants*, or priests, used to boast about this, rather than feel embarrassed, announcing that those who felt too concerned about the morality of their women should avoid sending them to gurdwaras. Women from the 'best' families often got pregnant after a bout of 'worship'. The mahant at Guru ka Bagh, for instance, used to keep two mistresses, Isro and Jagdei, in addition to a regular harem of prostitutes. Theft and drunkenness were clearly only minor crimes.

But the most interesting aspect was that the mahants of the Sikh gurdwaras were not necessarily Sikhs. Many of them were Hindus who had introduced idol worship, along with debauchery, in the temples of a religion which expressly forbade idol worship. In fact, idols were removed from the most sacred Golden Temple only after intense Sikh pressure in 1905. Such was the reputation of the mahants that the Nizam of Hyderabad passed a law stating that only a 'celibate of good character' could become the priest of the gurdwara built at Nanded (which fell in his domain) to mark the place where the great Guru Gobind had been murdered. Obviously, both celibacy and good character had been noticeable by their absence. The reason for Hindu, or non-Sikh, mahants lay in history.

The first half of the eighteenth century had seen the peak of repression against the Sikhs by the Muslim governors of Punjab, like Zakaria Khan, Yahya Khan and Mir Mannu, and the Khalsa had often to retreat from the cities. At this point, a sect begun by Guru Nanak's eldest son, Baba Sri Chand, the Udasis (a name derived from the long journeys which Guru Nanak undertook, called *Udasian*) stepped in to help protect the gurdwaras. The Udasis did not wear long hair or carry any of the revealing signs of the Khalsa identity, and so escaped persecution. However, when the danger from the Muslims was over they showed no signs of handing back the temples to the Sikhs. With the coming of the Sikh empire, the gurdwaras were given extensive lands, from whose income the priests were expected to help the community and maintain the temple. In course of time, all they did with the money was help themselves and use it to maintain their fiefdoms. And when the British began to write fresh settlement records after they had annexed Punjab, the mahants declared the temple lands to be their personal hereditary property.

The Sikhs had clearly lost control of their independence, their symbols, their temples, their destiny. The return to Hinduism was accelerating, with the gurdwaras becoming either Hindu temples or dens of vice, or both. The Sikh leadership diagnosed the malady as lack of education, both secular and religious, and a consequent absence of pride in Sikh faith and identity. If the Sikh were to survive as an independent religious entity, he had to know what his religion meant. On 1 October 1873, at Amritsar, the Sri Guru Singh Sabha was born, first to restore the Sikh confidence, and then to defend the faith against the Arya Samaj and the Christian missionaries. The Sabha resolved to publish historical and religious books; to spread modern education in Punjabi; and to bring apostates back into the fold. The movement soon built a network of Khalsa schools and colleges. The biggest dream was realized when Sir James Lyall laid the foundation stone of the Khalsa College in Amritsar, on 5 March 1892. Teaching started on 22 October 1893. By 1908 the Sikh Educational Conference had been established to spread much-needed western education and to promote knowledge of Punjabi literature and the Sikh faith. The year 1873, which saw the birth of the Singh Sabha, is a crucial date in Sikh history.

The political wing, the Chief Khalsa Dewan, was set up in 1887. However, it soon came under the control of those who felt that Sikhs could only prosper through political subservience to the British. But education inspired new ideas, and the younger generation began associating with the freedom movement. As the famous British CID (Central Investigation Department) informed the Punjab government, the Khalsa College by 1907 had become an 'important centre for inculcating national feelings among the students'. When Gopal Krishna Gokhale visited Khalsa College in 1907, the Sikh students got so carried away that they unhitched the horses from his carriage and pulled it themselves from the railway station to the campus.

The resentment of an already burdened peasantry, in the meanwhile, had come to a boil with the Colonization Bill of 1907 which raised land revenues. Figures reflect the growing impoverishment. Moneylenders had risen from 52,263 in the 1868 census to 193,890 in the 1911 census; land sales had gone up from an average of 88,000 acres annually in the 1870s, to 338,000 acres in 1910–20; mortgages showed a similar pattern. It was during this period that Banke Dayal's now famous song became a rallying cry: *'Pagri samhal, jatta'* ('Save your turban, Jat'). The Colonization Bill was eventually vetoed by the Viceroy. By this time the intrepid Sikhs who had left India to settle in other parts of the British empire and in the USA in search of employment had begun to feel the heat of colour prejudice. Their anger against the whites took the shape of the futile *Ghadr*, or rebellion, during the First World War. The Sikhs living in Punjab may not have supported this rebellion, but they were beginning to understand the relationship with a colonial master. However, they did their duty in the First World War, fighting in Europe, Africa and Turkey, and winning fourteen of the twenty-two Military Crosses awarded to Indians for gallantry. But soon things were to change, as the British were to find out, particularly in the Second World War when the 'loyal' Sikhs crossed over in droves to Subhas Bose's rebel Indian National Army.

The turning point, of course, is 13 April 1919. Brigadier-General R. E. H. Dyer was born in India, at Murree, on 9 October 1864. He was the scion of a well-known family of North Indian brewers, Dyer Meakin and Company (the firm is now in the control of Indians and is called Mohan Meakin). He studied at Bishop Cotton's School in Simla and grew up on a diet of scare stories about the mutiny of 1857. In 1919 he ordered the massacre of a largely Sikh assemblage of unarmed men, women and children at Jallianwala Bagh, which left, by the official count, 379 dead and over 2,000 wounded. (Even the imperialist Winston Churchill was horrified.) At Jallianwala, Dyer was not only being more loyal than the King, but also expressing the complete disdain of the master for the slave. Given the behaviour of the official Sikh leadership of the period, it is easy to understand why Sikhs like Arur Singh, the chief of the Golden Temple at Amritsar, actually *honoured* General Dyer after the massacre at Jallianwala Bagh. In fact, General Dyer was given the ultimate accolade of a *siropa*, or turban and sword, and proclaimed an honorary Sikh. The dialogue that is quoted in Mohinder Singh's *The Akali Movement* (Macmillan, 1978) is a classic example of a conversation between the fawning sycophant, for whom no humiliation is enough, and the master who, with an ironic smile, toys with the toady. This is the record of the dialogue:

'"Sahib," they said, "you must become a Sikh even as Nikalseyan [a corruption of John Nicholson, the British hero of 1857] Sahib became a Sikh." The General [Dyer] thanked them for the honour, but he objected that he could not, as a British Officer, let his hair grow long. Arur Singh laughed. "We will let you off the long hair," he said. General Dyer offered another objection. "But I cannot give up smoking." "That you must do," said Arur Singh. "No," said the General, "I am very sorry, but I cannot give up smoking." The priest conceded, "We will let you give it up gradually." "That I promise you," said the General, "at the rate of one cigarette a year."'

But now the Sikhs and their new leaders were at the beginning of a new age, in which they would relearn the meaning of self-respect. Punjab rose against the British after Jallianwala Bagh. Mahatma Gandhi visited Punjab and with his encouragement the Central Sikh League was formed in the winter of 1919 as counterpoint to the pro-British Chief Khalsa Dewan. The League worked closely with the Congress, and in 1921 declared that freedom from the British was its true objective. It demanded the resignation of Arur Singh; when he refused, the Sikhs made their intentions clear by organizing his mock funeral. Arur Singh got the message and resigned by 29 August 1920. And now this new Sikh leadership turned its attention to the debauched mahants. A movement was launched that was not only to create and shape the Sikh political institutions that exist to this day but also, in a crucial sense, finally to roll back the tide of apostasy. This was the Gurdwara Reform Movement, between 1920 and 1925.

The British, recognizing the larger threat that the Sikh reformers posed to imperial rule, decided to support openly the corrupt and therefore pliable mahants. General Dyer and Sir Michael O'Dwyer, the Lieutenant-Governor of Punjab, had blooded the Sikhs not only on the day of the massacre but during the seven weeks of agitation that followed, when many hundreds died on the streets, fifty-one were hanged by the decision of summary courts, the jails were filled, and thousands were flogged, made to crawl on their bellies or subjected to an assortment of indignities. The

Sikhs were now ready to respond to Gandhi's call of 'Nirbhay' (fearlessness). The Central Gurdwara Management Committee (or, as it is commonly known today, the SGPC, standing for the Shiromani Gurdwara Prabandhak Committee) was formed to take over the Sikh temples from the mahants. On 15 November 1920, the first elections to the 175-member SGPC took place. (The SGPC has remained a kind of Sikh Parliament, with elections to the committee hotly contested.) A corps of volunteers was formed on 14 December: the Shiromani Akali Dal, which eventually became the formal political party we know today. Akali means 'immortal'; the term was first used by Guru Gobind Singh to define those willing to sacrifice their lives to defend Sikhism. Their turbans were of steel-blue colour which became a badge of the Akali party. The Akalis should not be confused with the Nihangs, whose name comes from the Persian word for crocodile. Nihangs are an anachronistic remnant of the old warriors, while Akalis are a political party and have controlled the SGPC since its inception.

The mahants were not ready to surrender; the powerful ones decided to fight. The story of two confrontations will indicate the character and success of this unique movement. Such was the influence that Gandhi had already begun to exercise on the Indian mind that the Gurdwara movement, over a spread of more than four years, and despite suffering the worst excesses, remained totally non-violent; the Sikhs, in fact, gave heroic displays of non-violence.

Nankana is the name of the village where Guru Nanak was born. Along with the main gurdwara at the Janam Ashthan (the birthplace), there are other gurdwaras, like Mal Sahib, where a snake is believed to have spread its hood to protect a sleeping Nanak from the sun, Patti Sahib, where Nanak is said to have written his first words on a wooden slate, or Kiara Sahib where Nanak compensated for his loss a farmer whose fields had been ruined by the Guru's buffaloes. The main gurdwara at the Janam Ashthan was, at the turn of the century, under the control of Mahant Sadhu Ram, who divided his time between drinking and womanizing, and died of venereal disease. His successor, Mahant Narain Das, began by promising the Sikhs at his predecessor's cremation that the evil was also being burnt on the pyre, but this was obviously nothing more than an election promise. Drinking and adultery returned to the gurdwara (the favourite mistress of Narain Das was a Muslim drummer's wife), and he earned the added distinction of organizing nautch dances on the holy premises. Molestation was common; there is a record of a thirteen-year-old daughter of a retired senior government officer from Sind being raped by a sadhu in 1918, and the record probably exists only because the father was more angry than embarrassed and went to the authorities. While the mahant enjoyed himself, the Sikhs passed resolutions. The British were quite ready to support Mahant Narain Das, as the behaviour of C. M. King, the commissioner of the Lahore division, shows. In February 1921, the Akali Dal decided to confront Mahant Narain Das, seize the gurdwara and hand it over to the newly created SGPC.

Narain Das was prepared. He collected four hundred mercenaries, led by brigands like Ranjha and Rehana, and armed with pistols, swords and hatchets. On 20 February the Akalis, led by Bhai Lachman Singh, reached the shrine. Only a handful had started out but the group had grown as peasants spontaneously joined them on the way. The police inspector at the local station was conveniently absent that day. The mahant had already transferred his family and his valuables to Lahore, just in case his plans went wrong. The Akalis gathered at the gate and, singing hymns, entered; the mahant's mercenaries replied by opening fire from the rooftop. About twenty-five Akalis were shot dead inside the compound; sixty who shut themselves in a nearby room were pursued and hacked and speared to death; another twenty-five were sniffed out from other hiding-places and butchered. The bodies of the dead and dying were then chopped up, piled on to a stack of logs and burnt.

The outrage shocked the country almost as much as the Jallianwala Bagh tragedy had. Mahatma Gandhi visited Nankana and said, 'Everything points to a second edition of Dyerism [the word is obviously from Dyer], more barbarous and more fiendish than the barbarism at Jallianwala Bagh.' Eminent Muslims and Hindus rallied to the Sikh cause. Maulana Shaukat Ali made fiery speeches, as did Lala Lajpat Rai. Mahant Narain Das was arrested and sentenced to deportation, and the shrine went under the control of the SGPC. But there were more battles ahead. The British were not yet willing to grant the SGPC the right to control all the gurdwaras. They decided to fudge and, if required, to face the Akalis rather than submit to the demand for a new Gurdwara Act, since they were afraid that an Akali victory might give a fillip to the freedom movement. The CID had told the government that a 'strong national spirit and contempt for authority pervaded the assembly' which had gathered at Nankana to mourn the tragedy. On 11 May 1921, the Akali leadership formally committed itself to the cause of freedom by passing a resolution supporting Gandhi's call for non-cooperation with the British.

In 1921 the British sponsored a compromise bill giving a board of commissioners the authority to arbitrate over the gurdwaras. A large number of mahants immediately declared that their shrines were not Sikh but Hindu temples. The British winked at this subterfuge. The Sikhs were appalled and the Hindus quietly pleased. The Akali agitation continued, but, as before, peacefully. When the British seized the keys of the Golden Temple from the new President of the SGPC, the fiery Baba Kharak Singh (known as the *Betaj Badshah*, the 'Uncrowned King'), the Akalis offered themselves for arrest, and their continuous agitation finally forced the British to return the keys. Gandhi called this the first victory of the national movement. But the truly great achievement was the agitation for the control of Guru ka Bagh, in August 1922.

This site, thirteen miles from Amritsar, commemorates a visit made to the spot by the fifth Guru, Arjun. Its mahant, Sundar Das, had habits which should be familiar to readers by now. However, in January 1921 he had come to terms with the SGPC; he had agreed to become a Khalsa Sikh and, to provide some legitimacy to his proclivities, to marry one of his mistresses, Ishro. But when he saw the support the British gave to Narain Das he broke the agreement. On 9 August the Akalis began their non-violent agitation at Guru ka Bagh. Ranged against them this time were not the mahant's toughs but the forces of the British empire.

The Sikhs organized themselves into groups called *jathas*, each with a maximum of a hundred members. Each jatha would take a vow of non-violence at the Golden Temple in the morning and then begin the march towards the gurdwara to offer themselves for arrest. The police first took them into custody but then, as the waves of jathas kept coming, the irritated authorities began resorting to lathis and jackboots. The Sikhs simply stood there and allowed themselves to be beaten, many until they fell unconscious, before being carted off to jail. This extraordinary display of peaceful resistance caught the imagination not only of India but of the world. The inevitable American film-maker turned up, a Captain A. L. Verges, and produced a documentary called 'Exclusive Picture of India's Martyrdom'. (The British authorities tried, unsuccessfully, to have this film banned.) Nationalist Hindu and Muslim leaders, like Swami Shradhanand and Hakim Ajmal Khan, once again rallied to the Sikh cause, making speeches at the site of the confrontation. The Congress set up a committee of inquiry which concluded that the 'force was excessive on all occasions and on some cruelly excessive'. (The committee included the American missionary, the Reverend S. E. Stokes.) Pandit Madan

Mohan Malaviya said that after this it was the duty of every Indian to 'express hatred and contempt for the actions of this government'. Gandhi's friend the Reverend C. F. Andrews, who had come to India to convert the heathen and stayed to fight for their independence from his own countrymen (he died on 5 April 1940 in Calcutta, at the age of sixty-nine), visited Guru ka Bagh and described what he saw as 'inhuman, brutal, foul, cowardly and incredible to an Englishman, and a moral defeat of England'. He protested to the Lieutenant-Governor of Punjab, Edward Maclagan, who was persuaded to stop the beatings; four days later, on 17 September, the police were removed. The toll: 5,605 Akalis arrested; 936 hospitalized. But they had won another vital battle. By 1925, the war was also won. The Sikh Gurdwaras Act, providing that elected bodies would replace mahants, became law.

The gurdwara agitation established the pattern that Sikh movements would follow in the future: the same strategy of offering peaceful arrest in jathas proved an extremely effective weapon during the Emergency between 1975 and 1977 when each day a jatha left the Golden Temple to protest against Mrs Gandhi's government. There is even a parallel to the violent extremist fringe, which has always been an aspect of Sikh politics. During the gurdwara agitation a group which called itself the Babbar Akali, led by Havildar Major Kishen Singh Bidang and Master Mota Singh, chose the option of violence. But the Babbar was never more than a fringe force, though it specialized (as extremists do today) in taking 'revenge' on real or imagined enemies and 'traitors' to the Sikh cause. The British arrested sixty-two Babbars; twenty-two turned witness for the Crown; six were sentenced to death, thanks to the testimony of their erstwhile comrades; and the rest were either acquitted or given varying terms in prison.

The key consequence of the movement was the gulf that now became firmly established between the Sikh and the Hindu of Punjab. The tension which had started in the last quarter of the nineteenth century was accentuated. Despite the support of Punjabi Hindu leaders, like Lala Lajpat Rai, in specific instances such as the Guru ka Bagh episode, the large mass of Hindus had their sympathies with the mahants, who were only too keen to declare the gurdwaras Hindu shrines in order to retain their control. Local Hindu leaders, like Sir Gokul Chand Narang, insisted that Sikhs were only a branch of Hinduism. Others, like Raja Narendra Nath, speaking in the Punjab Legislative Council (5 April 1921) referred to the Privy Council ruling of 1903 which held that the Sikhs were Hindus, and added, 'I look upon Sikhism as higher Hinduism ... The Granth Sahib is nothing more nor less than the higher teachings of the Vedas and the Upanishads in popular language ... It is well known that of two brothers one may be a Hindu and the other a Sikh ...' Unfortunately for Raja Narendra Nath, the Sikhs did not want to be any form of Hindu, either higher or lower; they were quite content, in fact anxious, to remain Sikhs, without getting into qualitative arguments about their place in the Hindu hierarchy. They saw the Hindu effort as yet another attempt at reabsorption. The Sikhs wanted to maintain their identity; and this, it cannot be stressed enough, remains a prime motivator even in the 1980s.

Mehtab Singh, one of the Sikh leaders of the gurdwara movement, put it quite bluntly in the Punjab Legislative Council on 8 April 1921, during the debate referred to above: 'I, for one, say that if the Sikhs do not wish to remain in the fold of Hinduism, why should the Hindus seek to force them to do so? What benefit can they obtain by keeping an unwilling people as partners in their community? That, Sir, is at the bottom of the whole excitement. The Hindus may say, we will manage your affairs for you as your gurdwaras are partly yours and partly ours, we say that we wish to manage our own affairs and look after our gurdwaras and are determined to do so.'

That, Sir, was indeed at the bottom of the excitement in the 1920s, and remains at the bottom of the excitement of the 1980s. And Mehtab Singh was a moderate. The resurgence of Sikh consciousness had had a major impact on the community and its following. The Akalis had, in fact, saved Sikhism. In the census of 1881, 43.84 per cent of the population of Punjab (excluding the princely states) had described itself as Hindu; 47.56 per cent as Muslim; and just 8.22 per cent as Sikh. And the Sikhs had declined further. In 1891, the Hindus were 44.08 per cent, against 8.09 per cent Sikhs; this was the high point of Hinduism after the impact of the Arya Samaj. Even the Muslims declined in that decade, from 47.56 to 47.39 per cent. But in 1901 the efforts of the Singh Sabha had already begun to show results: the Sikhs were now 8.63 per cent. In 1911 they were 12.11 per cent, in 1921, 12.38 per cent; by 1931, 14.29 per cent; and by 1941, they had risen to 14.62 per cent. Even the Muslims increased (without help from sword-wielding Muslim kings) from 47.39 per cent in 1891 to 52.88 per cent in 1941. The Hindus were only 29.79 per cent of the population in Punjab in 1941, and were concentrated mainly in the cities. Only 8.36 per cent of the Sikhs lived in urban areas. By now not more than 6 per cent of the Hindus were describing themselves as Arya Samajis.

After this narrow escape, Akali politics would hinge primarily on the protection of the faith, particularly from Hinduism. At the back of the Akali mind, whether put into words or not, would be the belief, first expressed by Guru Gobind, that it was not possible to protect the faith without the control of political power. Since such power would never be possible without an area in which the Sikhs were a majority, it was imperative to get a Sikh 'homeland'. The question, both in the days of the British Raj and later, was whether this home would lie within the boundaries of a Hindu-majority India, or outside. A section of the Akalis have always chosen to answer the question with varying degrees of ambiguity. Their first leader was Master Tara Singh.

7
The Complex Minority

The Sikhs had a problem in the forties; there were not enough of them. Barely 1 per cent of the population of undivided India, and only a scattered 14 per cent of undivided Punjab, they found themselves on the sidelines of the great debate of the decade – to divide or not. Even when, in the last stage of their rule, the British were willing to hear out any talk about new homes, the Akalis realized that while in theory they might have a historical claim, they had no geographical location in which to place that dream. There was, in fact, no Sikh-majority area in Punjab province. The Congress, the Muslim League and the British knew this too.

The experience of the second half of the nineteenth century, and then the long struggle back to the healthy figure of 14 per cent in the 1941 census, had made the doctors (that is, the Akali leaders) only too conscious of how vulnerable the patient really was. Moreover, it was not just the Vedic revivalism of the Arya Samaj which could kill Sikhism, but the simple realities of post-colonial life. The days of the British Raj were at an end; job reservations on the basis of the Khalsa identity would soon be over. Urban jobs would be available on competence and a secular education. A new generation might not have sufficient faith to avoid the razor blade, or calmly carry the kirpan. (As time would prove, the sword became a most impracticable object to carry in the hijacking era.) And then where would the Sikh be? Nowhere. Without the identity that Guru Gobind Singh had given him, how would anyone differentiate the Sikh from a Hindu?

Add to this the equally simple fact that if Sikhism disappeared from Punjab, it would also disappear from the earth. If the Indian Muslim was destroyed, Islam would still survive, whether in south-east Asia, central and west Asia, or Africa. But Sikhism had no geographical base apart from the Punjab, and even in this land of 29 districts, stretching from the Sulaiman Range to the river Jumna, which the Sikh had so proudly ruled only a century ago, there was not one district which the Sikh could call his own. It was a unique and complex minority problem, which in the view of a section of the Akali leadership could never be solved without the creation of a theocratic Sikh state. And it was this dilemma that made the Akali leadership, from its very inception in the twenties, always maintain a lifeline to the idea of an independent Sikh country. Akalis have lived in a demographic and political environment in which they have not been able to express this sentiment openly, but that takes away nothing from its reality.

The Sikh problem in the forties was that the only real choice they had was between the devil of the Muslim League and the very deep and very blue sea of Hindu-majority India. That was not much of a choice. In a memorandum submitted to Sir Stafford Cripps in 1942, the SGPC had approvingly quoted the Simon Commission's analysis: 'Sikhism remained a pacific cult until the political tyranny of the Mussalmans and the social tyranny of the Hindus converted it into a military creed.' Between the two 'tyrannies', the Hindu option was clearly preferable. Punjab before partition was a clear Muslim-majority state (53 per cent). That advantage was reinforced by a substantial Muslim majority over a large contiguous land area in the west: the districts of Dera Ghazi Khan, Muzaffargarh, Mianwali, Attock, Jhelum, Rawalpindi, Shahpur, Gujrat, Jhang, Multan, Bahawalpur, Lyalpur, Montgomery, Lahore and Gujranwala. Similarly, the Hindus (30 per cent) dominated the districts of Hissar, Rohtak, Gurgaon, Karnal, Hoshiarpur and the hill areas in the east. The Sikhs were in a minority everywhere, including the central districts where they had their largest concentrations – between 20 and 43 per cent in Amritsar, Ferozepur, Gurdaspur, Ludhiana and Patiala. (Gurdaspur had a bare Muslim majority of 50.4 per cent but the district was awarded to India to ensure a road link to Jammu and Kashmir; this is the road Pakistan attempts to cut off, unsuccessfully, in each war with India.) Worse, the Sikhs were equally divided, 2 million each, between the two sections of Punjab, one scheduled to go to India and the other to Pakistan. And their richest lands were in the 'canalized' zones of the west, which they would have to leave if Pakistan became a reality.

The Sikhs were few, but they were prosperous. They were the biggest landowners in the central districts, thanks to British gratitude in the post-mutiny phase. In the Lahore division, for instance, they paid as much as 46 per cent of the land revenue. The Hindus, with their strength in trade and moneylending (the Sikhs also had moneylending castes, like the

Aroras) came a close second. Out of the total capital of Rs 6.29 crores invested in pre-partition Lahore, the Hindus and Sikhs controlled Rs 5.12 crores; of the ninety branches of the banking system, the Muslims owned only three; of ninety branches of insurance companies, only two. Kirpal Singh points out in *The Partition of Punjab* (Punjab University, Patiala): 'Next to agriculture, moneylending was the most important commercial activity. The Muslim peasants of the Western Punjab were, as a body, heavily indebted to the Hindu and Sikh moneylenders of the Multan and Rawalpindi divisions. This economic domination lent colour to the Muslim contention that they were in danger of economic exploitation by the Hindus and the Sikhs.' According to government statistics, 4.35 million Muslims went to Pakistan from East Punjab, leaving 47 lakh acres of land; and 4.29 million Sikhs and Hindus came to India, leaving behind 67 lakh acres – this itself indicates the disparity, even ignoring the fact that the land of West Punjab was qualitatively superior. In the end, as in Bengal, the Muslim League used the prospect of rich land released from Hindu and Sikh ownership, to lure the Muslim peasantry in East Punjab towards Pakistan; nobody told them, of course, that it would be replaced by a new domination.

Efforts to find a resolution to Punjab's tripartite tangle had been in the air for a long time. At the round-table conference of 1932, the Sikhs offered a simplistic solution: remove the 12 districts of the Rawalpindi and Multan divisions, with over 80 per cent Muslim population, from Punjab, and the demographic balance would be more evenly poised between Muslim and non-Muslim. The Muslim League was in no mood to listen to such ideas. In fact, the optimists among the Muslim League were fantasizing about a Pakistan stretching from the borders of Afghanistan in the west to Aligarh east of Delhi, from Kashmir and the borders of China and Tibet in the north to Jaisalmer in Rajasthan in the south – which is why Jinnah described the Pakistan that he got as 'moth-eaten'.

By 1940, four options were being mooted for Punjab. The Congress wanted an undivided India, but had accepted the Sikh rider that Punjab be partitioned, in any case, with both parts in the Indian federation. The Muslim League wanted Pakistan. The third and fourth options were related – an undivided, autonomous Punjab either within or without the Indian Union, depending on what was possible. The last was being canvassed by the indomitable Sir Sikandar Hayat Khan of the Unionist Party, just as his counterpart in Bengal, Fazlul Haq, was trying for a middle, independent option between the League and the Congress. The

Unionists were an anti-urban, peasant party; their appeal was to the tiller of the land, irrespective of religion. Sir Sikandar had, in partnership with Sir Chotu Ram, very successfully built up a Muslim–Hindu peasant alliance which kept both the Muslim League and the Congress out of rural Punjab. Sir Sikandar was active in the Muslim League till his disillusion-ment with the League's separatist ambitions saw him drift away. Jinnah, very deliberately, made him a co-sponsor of what became known as the Pakistan resolution, passed by the League at its Lahore session in 1940. But it is important to note that Pakistan itself was never mentioned in that resolution. Sir Sikandar, in his famous and much-quoted speech to the Punjab Legislative Assembly on 4 March 1941, made this point over and over again: 'When that resolution was passed it was termed the Lahore resolution, the word Pakistan was not used ...' Sir Sikandar had absolutely no sympathy with the idea of Pakistan, which was 'undesirable even from the Muslim point of view', and warned the Punjab peasantry of the dangers of division. As Sir Sikandar said, 'We do not ask for freedom that there may be Muslim Raj here and Hindu Raj elsewhere. If that is what Pakistan means I will have nothing to do with it ... If you want real freedom for the Punjab, that is to say a Punjab in which every community will have its due share in the economic and administrative fields as partners in a common concern, then that Punjab will not be Pakistan, but just Punjab, land of five rivers; Punjab is Punjab and will always remain Punjab whatever anybody may say. This, then, briefly, is the political future which I visualize for my province and for my country under any new Constitution.'

You cannot get more categorical than that. Sir Sikandar proposed a united India divided into seven zones, each with a powerful, semi-autonomous regional assembly, with the Centre having limited powers of defence, foreign affairs, communications and currency. He tried his best to persuade the Muslim League to accept this idea; when they refused he resigned from the League in 1942. He could still have given a dramatic turn to Punjab's, and thereby India's, future by his role in the crucial 1946 elections, but that was never to be: he died in December 1942. His successor as Premier of Punjab, Sir Khizr Hayat Khan, was unable to challenge the turbulence let loose by Jinnah and his feudal–mullah vanguard.

The Sikhs were, unfortunately, always sceptical of Sir Sikandar; they could not overcome their historical distrust of Muslims. They could understand the modern Aurangzeb, Jinnah; not the modern Akbar or

Ranjit Singh, Sir Sikandar. With freedom in the air, they tried to bargain with, of all people, Jinnah. Sardar Baldev Singh, a wealthy Akali financier who had become chief negotiator for the Sikhs by then, and was soon to join Nehru's first Cabinet as Defence Minister, and the Maharaja of Patiala (who, as head of a princely state, had the technical right to opt for Pakistan), discussed with Jinnah and Liaquat Ali Khan the feasibility of a Sikh state within the boundaries of Pakistan. Jinnah and Liaquat Ali accepted the Sikh proposal even to the extent of allowing the Sikhs their own military establishments within a Muslim–Sikh Pakistan. But the Sikhs insisted on the right to secede and the constitutionalist in Jinnah simply would not allow that. (If Jinnah had been more flexible, either Pakistan would never have been born, or it would have been much larger than it was. India, after all, did allow political parties to canvass their right to secede.'

The Akali leadership by this time was firmly in the hands of Master Tara Singh, who had displaced the venerable Baba Kharak Singh in 1935. Tara Chand was born a Hindu of the Malhotra caste on 24 June 1885, in the village of Harial in Rawalpindi district. He only became a Sikh, and thereby a Singh, when at school. He created a flutter as a student in Khalsa College by helping organize a demonstration against the Governor of Punjab, Sir Charles Rivaz, in 1907. He took a diploma in teaching, and was a popular master – hence the honorific which stuck to him through his life. State-level prominence came with his role in the Gurdwara Reform Movement, and by 1935 he had reached the top. He was the most powerful Akali politician through the difficult days of partition and re-settlement, till 1961 when a 'fast unto death' ended in a meal rather than martyrdom, and he was disgraced.

As we have noted, Master Tara Singh was ambiguous about the nature of the Sikh homeland that the Akalis were demanding – and he was consistent in his ambiguity. In fact, the first breach between the Akalis and the revered Mahatma Gandhi came precisely on this issue, as early as in the twenties, when Gandhi wanted the Akalis to disavow formally a 'Sikh Raj'. The Akalis refused to give Gandhi any such commitment. Master Tara Singh spent his life fusing the religious and political demands of the Sikhs, beginning by deliberately distancing the Akalis from the Congress, which wanted the Sikhs to keep religion out of politics, to give their gurdwaras to the Akalis and their vote to the Congress. Master Tara Singh was against any co-operation with the Congress in the 1937 elections, although the majority in the Akali Party decided in favour of an alliance. (The Unionists swept those polls, leaving the Akalis with just 10 seats.) He was finally able to break the Akali–Congress accord in the early 1940s, over an issue which the Sikhs have always considered essential to their interests – recruitment in the armed forces. While Gandhi and the Congress refused to join the British war effort, Master Tara Singh saw the Second World War as a 'golden chance' for the Sikhs to restore their old quota in the imperial army, brought down as punishment for their 'disloyal' Gurdwara Reform Movement.

But by 1942, the Akalis had also become convinced that they were being short-changed by the British. Despite their willingness to become fodder in European wars, they were getting no guarantees about a Sikh homeland in post-British India. The Shiromani Gurdwara Prabhandhak Committee (SGPC) handed over a memorandum to Sir Stafford Cripps on 31 March 1942, complaining that such treatment was hardly fair to the most loyal of Indians: 'The cause of the Sikh community has been lamentably betrayed. Ever since the British advent, our community has fought for England in every battlefield of the Empire, and this is our reward, that our position in the Punjab, which England promised to hold in trust, and in which we occupied a predominant position, has been finally liquidated.'

The Sikhs were terrified that 2 million of them would be left behind in a Muslim-majority country. They also began blaming the Congress for neglecting them; a curious accusation, considering that the Sikhs had been far more loyal to the British than to the Congress. On 20 August 1944, a huge Sikh meeting was held at Amritsar to condemn Mahatma Gandhi along with Jinnah. Giani Kartar Singh (quoted in the next day's edition of the *Civil and Military Gazette*) expressed the general sentiment when he said, 'If Pakistan is foisted upon the Sikhs with the help of British bayonets, we will tear it to shreds as Guru Gobind Singh tore up the Mughal empire.' Guru Gobind had not quite managed to tear up the Mughal empire; nor was Giani Kartar Singh able to prevent Pakistan. It was at this meeting that Master Tara Singh, realizing that Pakistan would after all be created, raised the formal demand for a sovereign Sikh nation. The idea was dismissed then as an 'impossible demand'. Despite all the scepticism of his colleagues, Master Tara Singh at least would spend the rest of his life trying to make the impossible possible, in one guise or another.

The problem of the 4 million Sikhs and Hindus in Pakistani Punjab, and the equivalent number of 4 million Muslims in Indian Punjab, was settled,

in the end, by the thugs and criminals employed by politicians to indulge
in one of the worst crimes in the history of the world (which, considering
the history of this world, is saying a good deal). The Muslim League had
been advocating the idea of an exchange of populations for a long time –
but no one was listening, not even the Muslims. The President of the
Punjab Muslim League, Iftikhar Hussain, the Nawab of Mamdot, was
quoted in *Dawn*, the party newspaper, on 3 December 1946 as saying that
an 'exchange of populations offered a most practical solution of the
multifarious problems of the Muslims. The exchange of population will
wipe out the most important argument against Pakistan which has been
persistently fired from the Congress armoury.' The interesting thing to
note is that even a few months before the creation of Pakistan, the Muslims
of East Punjab (clearly the most vulnerable Muslims in the country) had
not begun moving to the homeland Jinnah was offering them. The Sikhs
and Hindus were similarly transfixed on their side of Punjab. It was as if
no one could actually believe that the villages they had inhabited for
centuries would suddenly become death-pits, that neighbour would kill
neighbour, that child after child would be hacked, that mother and sister
would be raped and speared to death – all for the greed of a handful of
politicians. History has few parallels for the organized butchery of 1947.

One of the biggest mysteries of the partition of Punjab is why the mass
of the people started the journeys to their new countries only after India
had been divided, not before, despite all the propaganda and provocation.
The only logical answer is that they did not want to abandon their land
till the politicians left them with no other choice. By March 1947, the
Muslim League had discovered that neither the 4 million Muslims nor the
4 million Hindus and Sikhs were leaving the villages of their birth. And so
in March the Muslim League initiated anti-Hindu and anti-Sikh riots in
what is today Pakistan. Three months later the Sikhs had managed to
organize *their* thugs to drive the Muslims out. In June, partition was
announced. Even then, the caravans of despair waited till after the middle
of August. Perhaps no one, Muslim, Hindu or Sikh, could quite understand
what partition would actually mean.

As V. P. Menon has written in *Transfer of Power in India* (p. 436), August
seems strangely linked with British fortunes in India. In August 1765, the
Emperor Shah Alam the Second granted to the East India Company the
dewani, or revenue authority, of Bengal, Bihar and Orissa; in August 1858,
the Crown took over the government of India from the East India Company
(he might have added that in August 1857 the fate of India for the next

ninety years was decided during the battle for Delhi with the sepoys); in August 1947, the British left. That last August saw blood colour the fields of Punjab. The refugees, only a trickle before 15 August, now crossed over in waves. There is little point in repeating the horrible details; suffice to say that those trains and caravans and truck convoys carried so much fresh poison in them that it seeped across the subcontinent and is still powerful enough to destroy life. The leaders have said enough and been repeated too often. This author would like to quote a jemadar (a non-commissioned officer in the army) writing from his village in Jullundur to his major in the Eastern Command on 23 August 1947 (taken from Sir Francis Tuker's autobiography, *While Memory Serves*): 'This country has become a battlefield since the 16th August. One village attacks another village and one community another community. Nobody could sleep for a week. Villages are being destroyed and thousands are being killed or wounded. Smoke-fires are seen everywhere all around my village. Every day too many casualties take place in this country.'

The jemadar was stark and accurate. On 15 August this had been one country. On 16 August it became a battlefield. The Sikh and Muslim villagers who had lived together till the 15th, despite all the provocations – from Jehangir to Abdali to Jinnah – suddenly became divided; and the price was something the jemadar could only watch in anguish mixed with the wonder that comes from seeing the unbelievable. Every day to this very day too many casualties take place in this country.

The thought arises: did any of the men who divided India ever feel any guilt after this trauma? Brigadier-General Dyer could not sleep peacefully after 1919, but then he had a conscience. Did those who sponsored the massacre of hundreds of thousands of men, women and children (estimates have been given which vary from 200,000 to 500,000) ever lose any sleep? There is no evidence, either from India or Pakistan, that they did. But then, who wants to remember the truth about oneself? It is so much easier to place a white man's name at the top of the roll-call of hate, and quietly ignore the brown subcontinental villains who were criminals of a far worse kind.

India got 13 of the 29 districts, and 38 per cent of the land area, of Punjab, and 2 million Sikhs came, less those killed on the way, leaving behind their land and 150 religious shrines. On Baisakhi Day (13 April) 1947, Master Tara Singh and 280 followers had taken an oath of war at the Golden Temple and shouted, 'Death to Pakistan.' That slogan, what-ever else it may or may not have achieved, prevented one thing in the next three decades – any surreptitious alliance between the Sikhs and Pakistanis against the Union of India. The Sikhs, in fact, became the most zealous guardians of India's borders. And that zeal, in the end, won them a home.

8
The Bargain Hunters

The great two-way migration in Punjab did not solve the basic problem of the Sikhs: there still were not enough of them. In the triangular algebra of pre-partition Punjab, the Sikhs believed that they held the balance between the Muslims and the Hindus; in the post-partition arithmetic, they were a simple minority – 35 per cent against 62.3 per cent Hindus in the whole of the Punjab, including the princely states, as per the count of the 1951 census. The economic relationship did not change either. The Sikh peasantry still occupied the rural hinterland around the Hindu urban concentrations. The Sikhs who came from the west did not spread evenly across Punjab, tending to settle in the north-west (the south-west already had a good Sikh percentage), leading to the first jibe that this was deliberate policy aimed at the creation of a Sikh majority in a specific area.

We have seen the effort of the Sikh leadership to try to get a separate deal from the British by distancing themselves from the Congress, and then by flirting with the Muslim League (there was, for instance, an Akali in the Muslim League minority government in the North-West Frontier Province on the eve of partition). When the Cabinet Mission Plan, announced on 16 May 1946, took no notice of the demand for a Sikhistan, the Sikhs were forced to try to work out a deal with the Congress, particularly in view of the crucial 1946 elections. Master Tara Singh did his best to prevent this, and in the end it was not much of an alliance. The Congress, loath to yield Sikh seats, refused to compromise, and there was an agreement only on 4 of the 33 Sikh constituencies. The politics of Punjab, which had been different from the rest of the north, now fell into line, and the vacuum left by the collapsing Unionist Party was filled on a religious basis. The Muslim League took an overwhelming 75 out of the 86 Muslim seats. The Congress took an equally good share of the Hindu reserved constituencies, winning 40 of them. But the Congress, which had got a total of 51 seats, was not a one-religion party, unlike the Muslim League or the Akalis. Despite the presence of a specific Sikh party in the Akalis, Congress won 10 Sikh seats against the 22 won by the Akalis. The Congress even managed to get 1 Muslim seat. The Unionist Party was, with the death of its two great mentors, Sir Sikandar Hayat Khan and Sir Chotu Ram, only a shadow of its past self, but still true to its ideals. Its support cut across religious lines; 1 of its 20 victorious candidates was a Christian.

These election results are important because they challenge the Akalis' contention that they, and only they, are the voice of Sikh opinion. Certainly the election results and voting patterns of free India expose such a claim. But even in the elections conducted by the British, when the constituencies were allotted on a religious basis, at a time when religious passions were assuming their rawest forms, the Akalis could not stop the Congress from winning 10 Sikh seats. Even, therefore, in the most favourable circumstances, the Akalis took only 60 per cent of the Sikh seats, with secular parties (either the Congress or the Communists) getting the rest of the Sikh vote. This has been a fundamental problem for the Akalis, particularly after independence. The only answer they have is to try to bring more Sikhs into the Akali fold by provoking religious sentiments. Their frustration drives them towards increasing militancy with every defeat. The problem with the Akalis is that they cannot accept that fortunes must fluctuate in a democracy; in their doctrine the Sikh must be in permanent bondage to the Akali bandwagon, as it is a bondage sanctioned by Guru Gobind and reinforced by faith.

But the world has changed, and the Akalis have not kept pace. A democracy can accept and respond to the politics of struggle, but not to confrontation. Delhi is not occupied by either feudals or colonizers. The Akali leaders have behaved as the protectors of Sikhism: *ergo*, he who refuses protection is less than a Sikh. But the Sikh masses have not necessarily equated their survival with the survival of Akalis. One of the important causes of crisis in the eighties was simply that the people would not allow the Akalis to win and the Akalis would not allow themselves to lose.

The Sikh vote is not uni-dimensional. The Sikhs are divided too, not in as fragmented a fashion as the Hindus, but mutually antagonistic just the same. There are three strong interest groups: the peasantry (Jats); the urban artisans, shopkeepers or businessmen (Khatris, Aroras and Ramgarhias); and the Sikh scheduled castes, the converts from un-touchables (Mazhabis). The Jats are believed by some to be descended from

Scythian tribes who, a little after the Aryans, followed the same route across the Hindu Kush and settled in the area between Afghanistan and Rajasthan. They can be found in substantial numbers in all the three major religions of the Punjab – Islam, Hinduism and Sikhism. They today constitute the dominant Sikh class, both in numbers and wealth. They were the earliest bulk converts; Guru Arjun himself is believed to have brought them into the fold. They became the spearhead of the early Sikh armies and came into their own with the kingdom of Maharaja Ranjit Singh when the Sikh Jats became a great landowning aristocracy. Recruitment to the British Indian army, and the rising price of land, brought prosperity to even the smaller peasant and established the Jat's control over the community. The urban artisans and traders were later converts to Sikhism and their relationship with Hindus remained much closer, with frequent intermarriage in the equivalent Hindu castes. And then, of course, there were the conversions from among the untouchables, those unfortunate Indians condemned to a degradation which might be unbelievable were it not true. They were attracted to the promise of equality in Sikhism. They soon discovered that while things were not as bad as in Hinduism, they were not as good as the promise either. The Jat now worshipped and ate with the Mazhabi at the common kitchen in the gurdwara, but that was the sum total of the acceptance. The social and economic status of the untouchables continued as before.

Akali politics has been powered by the Jats, and the Mazhabi Sikhs have always been anti-Akali, with no illusions about how the comparatively landless Mazhabis would be treated in a Sikh Jat dominated country. This is why the Mazhabis, who form more than one-fifth of the Sikh population, have always opposed a Sikh state in any form. They even sought to scuttle the Akali demand, which was granted in 1966, of a Sikh-majority state within the Indian Union. Mazhabis have consistently voted against the Akalis in elections. So the Akalis, in fact, begin their campaign for the Sikh vote with only 80 per cent as their maximum base. Then the urban–rural conflict creates its variations, with the urban Sikh showing, except on unusual occasions, a preference for the Congress. On top of this, there are strong pockets of Communist influence in the Sikh peasantry: irrespective of the number of seats they may get, the Communists have consistently polled around 10 per cent of the vote. Add to this the fact that even within the Jat peasantry there is a section which does not share the Akali dream of a theocratic state, and we begin to see how difficult it is for the Akalis to come to power through democracy even in a Sikh-majority Punjab. The crunch comes, of course, with the Hindus, who will never vote for a purely Sikh party like the Akalis.

However, such mathematics was far from the Akali mind in 1947. Dreams were returned to the safe-deposit vault of the collective memory, while the practical task of rehabilitation of refugees was taken up in earnest. Delhi stepped in with a magnificent effort. The redistribution of the land left behind by the Muslims at once brought in a small revolution in landholding; the rich absentee landowner disappeared and ownership went to the peasant cultivator. Compensation to the refugees was made in terms of the productivity of the land, by what was known as the 'standard acre' – a plot which could yield 10 to 11 *maunds* (1 *maund* is about 80 pounds) of wheat. For the first time, a percentage of the Mazhabi Sikhs also became landowners. The Akalis decided that the best way to squeeze benefits for the Sikhs out of the ruling Congress Party was by allying with it: some of the prominent Akali leaders formally joined the Congress on the theory that their work as Akalis was over and their utility as Congressmen had begun.

As the Akalis drew near the Congress, Master Tara Singh retired temporarily from politics, concentrating instead on religious reawakening. He had tried at the second conference of the Sikh Students' Federation on 24–25 April 1948 to persuade the Akalis to retain their separate status to ensure the 'independent' character of this purely Sikh political party, but the Akalis preferred the pro-Congress strategy finalized by the Working Committee meeting on 17 March to join the Congress. The first priority was survival, now that their demand for a separate nation had been ignored.

On 22 March 1946, with the Cabinet Mission due to arrive in two days, the Akali Dal had passed a formal resolution demanding 'Sikhistan' because 'the entity of the Sikhs is being threatened on account of the persistent demand of Pakistan by the Muslims on the one hand and of danger of absorption by the Hindus on the other'. On 24 March, Sir Stafford Cripps, Lord Pethick-Lawrence and A. V. Alexander arrived in Delhi to hear what the Indians wanted. Representatives of the Sikhs could not put up a cogent case for 'Sikhistan' before the Cripps Mission. Master Tara Singh ended up pleading for a united India with a coalition government of all communities at the Centre; failing that, a separate Sikh state with the right to federate with either India or Pakistan. Giani Kartar Singh asked for a province in which the Sikhs would be dominant – or 'almost dominant'. Harnam Singh was opposed to partition and wanted guarantees for the Sikhs. Baldev Singh delineated a possible boundary for Sikhistan but ended up asking only for special protection in whatever political framework was created. But soon the Sikhs discovered that no one was interested in any kind of bargain with them, not the Congress, not the Muslim League, not the British empire. They threatened to boycott the elections and the interim government. The hunt for a deal was becoming a shade desperate now. Jawaharlal Nehru, then President of the Congress, stepped in to offer what was, at best, a very weak reassurance to the Sikhs, but which Akali leaders keep repeating to this day as a promise of bigger things. Nehru was quoted in the *Statesman* of 7 July thus: 'The brave Sikhs of the Punjab are entitled to special consideration. I see nothing wrong in an area and a set-up in the north where the Sikhs can also freely experience the glow of freedom.' It sounded nice but, as the Sikhs discovered after August 1947, it was not much of a deal. Instead of the glow of freedom, there was only the shadow of a Hindu majority.

In 1948, as the long process to redraw the internal map of India began, Punjab was converted into two administrative units. The Sikh princely states were merged (along with Malerkotla and Nalagarh) into a separate unit, to form the Patiala and East Punjab States Union (PEPSU). The Sikhs and the Hindus were in equal numbers in PEPSU (49.3 against 48.8 per cent), but for the first time an area had a dominant – or 'nearly dominant' – Sikh population. The Sikh refugees began to settle in the districts contiguous to PEPSU. The Home and the Rehabilitation Ministries of the Punjab government were headed then by Sikhs who had been prominent Akalis before partition, and some Hindus immediately began to suspect a deliberate design in this. Tension between the two communities built up. The first Sikh–Hindu battle was fought through the familiar proxy of language.

Three 'G's are at the centre of the Sikh faith: the Guru, the Granth and Gurumukhi (the Master, the Book, and the Script). The Punjabi script is Gurumukhi. This script, in which the Sikh scriptures are written, was created for the purpose by Angad, the second Guru, and it has become inseparable from the religion. But soon after partition, the Hindus, who normally speak Punjabi, began to claim that Hindi was their mother tongue, in order to deny Punjabi the status of the official language of the state government. The Sikhs sounded the alarm: the reabsorption was coming, and the opening thrust was this 'conspiracy' to kill Punjabi. They raised the demand for a smaller Punjab in which Punjabi, with the Gurumukhi script, could be the official language.

The first riots between the Hindus and the Sikhs in more than a century and a half broke out during the census operations of 1951 over the language issue. (The last major incident of Hindu–Sikh violence had taken place in 1796 when the troops of Sahib Singh of Patiala and other Sikh chieftains attacked Hindu priests and pilgrims during the Kumbha Mela, the great pilgrimage festival, at the holy Hindu city of Hardwar.) In secular India, the Hindus of Punjab started chanting 'Hindi, Hindu, Hindustan' evoking the dangerous trinity of the Hindi language, the Hindu religion and a Hindu India. The Sikhs responded with 'Dhoti, topi, Jumna paar' ('Send the wearer of the dhoti and the cap [i.e. the Hindu] across the river Jumna'). Those Akalis whose voice had been subdued since 1947 now began to reassert themselves – once again, the fanatic element within the majority had resurrected the theocrats in the minority. The whisper went around: Sikhs would never be safe without their own state. The slogan was 'Punjabi Suba'.

Jawaharlal Nehru was hardly a fanatic; not even those who hated him could ever accuse him of such pettiness. There was one thing, though, that he had become fanatical about: the preservation of the territorial integrity of India. To him, yet another division of Punjab, and the control of a small state in the hands of an unpredictable minority, neighbouring Islamic Pakistan on the west and a Muslim-majority Kashmir in the north, seemed nothing short of suicide. And till he died, through all the agitation and the pressure tactics, Nehru stuck to his position: he did not allow the formation of a Sikh-majority Punjab. It was only after he died in 1964 that the Sikhs got their Punjab – thanks partly to Nehru's daughter, Mrs Indira Gandhi. The Akali press vilified Nehru, particularly after the States Reorganization Commission in 1955 gave other lingual groups separate states but turned down the Sikhs on flimsy grounds. Sardar Hukum Singh, who was, ironically, later to become a Congressman and Speaker of Parliament, called Jawaharlal Nehru 'the spearhead of militant Hindu chauvinism who glibly talks about nationalism, a tyrant who eulogizes democracy and a goblian [like Goebbels] liar – in short a political cheat, deceiver and doubledealer in the service of Indian reaction.' Such tough talk did not faze Nehru in the least. Instead of cutting Punjab up, as the Sikhs wanted, his government actually made the state bigger in 1956.

The Akali Dal had resolved that: 'The true test of democracy, in the opinion of the Shiromani Akali Dal, is that the minorities should feel that they are really free and equal partners in the destiny of this country ... The Shiromani Akali Dal is in favour of formation of provinces on a linguistic and cultural basis throughout India, but it holds it as a question of life and death for the Sikhs for a new Punjab to be created immediately ... It believes in a Punjabi-speaking province as an autonomous unit of India.' In theory the States Reorganization Commission agreed: 'The demand for linguistic States does not represent more cultural revivalism. It has a wider purpose in that it seeks to secure for different linguistic groups political and economic justice. In multilingual States political leadership and administrative authority remain the monopoly of the dominant language groups, and linguistic minorities are denied an effective voice in the governance of their States.' In practice, the same Commission argued that the Sikhs, despite being a separate linguistic group, did not deserve a state of their own. Punjab was asked to solve the language problem by using both Punjabi/Gurumukhi and Hindi, and to live happily ever after. And instead of granting the Sikhs their smaller linguistic state, it proposed the integration of PEPSU and Himachal Pradesh into Punjab.

Master Tara Singh now rose to answer: 'A decree of Sikh annihilation has been passed. We are face to face with a calamity greater than that of 1947. The catastrophe of 1947 finished thousands of Sikhs. The report of the States Reorganization Commission wipes us out from the face of the world' (the *Spokesman*, 19 October 1955; the Commission's report had been presented to the government of India on 30 September 1955). Master Tara Singh had never been afraid to exaggerate, and his successors have learnt from their Master. But behind this rhetoric was a genuine resentment that the Sikhs were not being trusted and would never get their due. The Akali aim was now to convince the Sikh masses that the Congress could not be relied upon and would have to be challenged.

So far, in the elections, the Sikhs by and large had been displaying an embarrassing tendency to prefer the Congress to the Akalis. This had just been demonstrated once again in the midterm elections of PEPSU in 1954. Despite a Sikh population of nearly 50 per cent, the Akalis got only 27.6 per cent of the vote in PEPSU and only 10 of the 33 seats they contested. The Congress, on the other hand, won 22 seats with 40.4 per cent of the vote. In Punjab the Akalis had an even bigger problem. A dynamic and brilliant Congress Sikh leader, Pratap Singh Kairon, a graduate in political science from the University of Michigan, was sweeping the rural vote by resurrecting the old Unionist slogan of power to the villages. Congress Sikh chief ministers have always been a problem for Akalis. Even leaders lesser than Kairon, like Giani Zail Singh in the seventies (later to become President of India), and Darbara Singh in the eighties, have been able to demonstrate their support among the Sikhs. But the Akalis were so afraid by a Kairon-led Congress of being soundly defeated in the 1957 general elections that despite the weeping and wailing over Nehru's policies, the Dal sought an electoral alliance with the Congress, and under terms which could only have been humiliating to men like Master Tara Singh. On 2 October 1956, the Akali Dal, under the chairmanship of Master Tara Singh, decided to 'repose confidence in the Congress and its leaders' and confine itself to 'religious, educational, cultural, social and economic betterment of the Sikhs'. Moreover, the Dal formally deleted from its Constitution those clauses which might even remotely hint at the idea of a separate Sikh nation.

This was the last straw for Master Tara Singh. He could not resist the temptation to try to sabotage this alliance. And so in the 1957 general elections he put up his own candidates, and campaigned against the Congress. He was wiped out. He could not win a single seat. The Congress polled 47.5 per cent of the total vote, while the Communists took a good share, 13.6 per cent, thanks to the Congress–Akali alliance which drove the anti-Jat Mazhabi Sikhs towards the red flag.

Just when Akali aspirations seemed to have been defused by Kairon, a fresh burst of Hindu fanaticism gave them a handle with which to pick themselves up. A 'Save Hindi' movement was launched, ostensibly to save Hindi, but in truth to promote the urban Punjabi Hindu who had not found any representation in the 1957 Kairon Cabinet, composed of Congressmen, Akalis and leaders of the Hindu peasantry. The movement was short-lived, but Master Tara Singh got his chance. Kairon had failed to safeguard the rights of Sikhs, he said; Sikhs must have their own Punjab. On 12 October 1958, the first Punjabi Suba conference was held at Amritsar. The man soon entrusted with the 'dictatorship' of the struggle' was a favourite lieutenant of Master Tara Singh, and senior Vice-President of the Akali Dal, Sant Fateh Singh. (All Sikh agitations are controlled by 'dictators'. Akalis like the martial connotations of dictatorship.)

In January 1960 Master Tara Singh won the Sikh religious elections to the SGPC on the Punjabi Suba platform, and with his 131 victorious supporters took an oath that they would sacrifice their bodies, souls and properties (in that order) to make the Punjabi Suba a reality. In April 1960, the agitation for the Punjabi Suba was launched; it was, according to the Akali Dal resolution, 'Now or Never'.

As far as Jawaharlal Nehru was concerned, it was never. Kairon, as much of a hardliner as Nehru, immediately arrested Tara Singh. Sant Fateh Singh took over. The call was sent out to the villages to offer passive resistance; according to the Akali Dal, 57,000 Sikhs went to jail, though the government's figure put the number at 26,000. To raise passions, Sant Fateh Singh announced a 'fast unto death' in November 1960 and began it on 18 December. By now the disciple was getting a bit too popular for the Master's comfort, and tension had developed between the two. Kairon, sensing this, released Master Tara Singh, who announced that he would be the next to 'fast unto death' after Sant Fateh Singh. Body and soul were again being offered to the cause. However, the spirit was less than willing and the flesh was decidedly weak; all the fasts ended not in the promised death but with a refreshing glass of orange juice. Each time a weak compromise was passed off as a triumph to rescue the fasting Akali leaders. And the government of India began to believe what many cynics already suspected: that the fasts used in fact to be laced with secret nourishment. Sant Fateh Singh is believed to have actually gained weight during one of his fasts, according to the medical reports kept by the government. (Dharma Vira, the civil servant entrusted with the task of overseeing the division of Punjab in 1966, also mentioned this to the author.) The Sant's December 1960 fast was called off on 9 January 1961 with nothing gained.

It was Master Tara Singh's turn now. His fast duly began with much fanfare on Independence Day, 15 August 1961. But the Master now faced a most curious problem: the government was perfectly willing to let him fast unto death. And just to ensure that this was going to be truly a fast, elaborate security arrangements were made, and a constant watch kept to prevent surreptitious nourishment. On 1 October, the Master decided that the Punjabi Suba was not worth his life, and resumed eating. No one suffers as much ridicule as a martyr who is discovered to be just another human being. 'If I have acted treacherously, punish me,' announced Master Tara Singh. The Sikhs did. Master Tara Singh was ordered to clean the shoes of every devotee who came to the Golden Temple over a period of five days. A little while later the discredited giant was removed from both the SGPC and the Akali Dal. His successor was Sant Fateh Singh. The Master's reaction was predictable; he hardened his line even further, increasing his distance from the official Akali Dal.

The Akali Dal, despite its efforts in the last four years, saw its share of the vote decrease in the 1962 general elections, which it fought alone. In 1952 the Akalis had 24 per cent of the vote in the Sikh areas, now they got only 20.7 per cent. The Congress, on the other hand, received an overwhelming 45.7 per cent of the votes in the Sikh areas, higher than the votes it got from the Hindus, since its average for Punjab was 43.7 per cent. The Akali vote had got honed down to a section of the rural Sikhs. The paradox of a well-publicized movement built on a minority vote was again evident.

Master Tara Singh announced his own Akali Dal in July 1962, articulating now an unambiguous demand for a separate Sikh nation. But once again the Sikh masses showed on which side, the extreme or the moderate, they stood. In a by-election to the Punjab Legislative Assembly from the constituency of Patti in March 1964, Tara Singh's candidate got only 2,745 votes against Fateh Singh's 18,747. Each time they have had the opportunity through a democratic vote, the Sikhs have shown that they support either the Congress or the Akali moderates, and never preachers of violence and secession. But it was the extremists who always got the headlines and created the erroneous impression that they were the true voice of the Sikhs.

In any case it was not the bravado of the religious leaders, all of whom died peacefully in bed, which got the Sikhs their own Punjab. It was, instead, their patriotism in the crucial wars of 1962 and 1965 that reassured the government of India that the Sikhs were nationalists. In both the wars, the Sikhs responded magnificently, giving their utmost in men, money and heroism to defend the nation. The biggest danger came in 1965. Sant Fateh Singh had renewed the agitation for a Punjabi Suba, and Radio Pakistan was, through a regular series of broadcasts, assuring him of support if he wanted an independent nation. Pakistan must have been expecting a strong fifth column in Punjab when its troops crossed the international border at Chamb Jaurian on 1 September 1965. Instead, Pakistan got a shock. The Sikhs spearheaded the Indian response in Punjab, both as civilians and as soldiers, and blunted the Pakistani armour and infantry. The Sikhs had passed the test at a critical hour. Within two days of the 1965 cease-fire, Prime Minister Lal Bahadur Shastri set up a Parliamentary committee, with twenty-two members under the old militant Akali, and now Speaker of Parliament, Sardar Hukum Singh, and a three-member Cabinet subcommittee under Mrs Indira Gandhi, to re-examine the demand for a Punjabi Suba. There were no more doubts.

On 10 March 1966, the Congress Working Committee passed a resolution asking that a 'State with Punjabi as the State language be formed'. The decision was implemented. Punjab was divided again, this time into three parts. A Hindu-majority state of Haryana, with 16,835 square miles and 7.53 million people (of whom just 5 per cent were Sikhs), was created. Another chunk, 10,215 square miles and with 1.2 million people (barely 2 per cent of them Sikh), became the state of Himachal Pradesh. Punjab was reduced to just 20,254 square miles over the districts of Jullundur, Amritsar, Hoshiarpur, Ludhiana, Ferozepur, Gurdaspur, Patiala, Bhatinda and Kapurthala, plus odds and ends. It had a population of 11.58 million, and at last the Sikhs were in a majority somewhere; they were 56 per cent. Chandigarh was made the common capital of Punjab and Haryana, pending the time when Haryana could complete its new capital. Sant Fateh Singh was delighted, saying, 'A handsome baby has been born into my household' (the Sant was a bachelor). 'The Punjabi Suba is our last demand,' he promised, categorically dismissing as 'useless' Master Tara Singh's call to continue the march towards an independent Sikh country. The Master was more cynical. The Sant, he said, was a religious man who did not understand politics. There was some hope expressed in Delhi that the Akalis would disband themselves now that their purpose had been achieved, but the Akalis immediately plunged into a new quest – to win elections and form the government of their own state.

The Prime Minister at the time of the creation of the Sikh Punjab was Mrs Indira Gandhi – who would, after dramatic turns in her political fortunes, have to confront the violence of Sikh extremists in the eighties, and pay the price. The one senior Congress leader who vehemently opposed, in 1966, the creation of a separate Sikh state, was the Deputy Prime Minister, Morarji Desai. It is strange how things turn out. After upheavals in his political fortunes which were even more dramatic than Indira Gandhi's, Morarji Desai became Prime Minister of India. And he accorded the same Akalis the highest acceptability they have got so far in India's politics, by giving them two seats in the Union government formed in 1977.

9
The Politics of Faith

After the festivities were over, the Sikhs found that their basic problem had not changed: there were still not enough of them. There are two ways of looking at a figure like 56 per cent: you can be content about its being a majority, or you can be worried sick that it is too vulnerable an advantage. Guru Gobind Singh, who told the Sikhs that they had been born to rule, left his disciples with an ambition much larger than their population.

For the Akalis, 56 per cent meant an insufficient guarantee of power through the ballot. In Tamil Nadu the DMK could convert itself from a secessionist movement into an elected ruling force since there was no demographic confusion. The Akalis could not achieve a similarly smooth transformation because their popular base was not large enough. The only way the Akalis could hope to defeat the Congress was by allying with a major Hindu opposition party. While that might be theoretically feasible, and indeed did happen, it could hardly be very palatable – there would have to be too many uncomfortable compromises, as the experience of the years between 1967 and 1971 showed. The frustration of the Akalis was understandable: they were in the absurd situation of being unable to win elections in a state which they had created.

So the Sikh extremists had no illusions about the meaning of the second partition. It was only a staging-post for the next round. They wanted their independent Sikh nation in which only the Khalsa would rule (*Raj karega Khalsa*, as they reminded themselves after every religious service), and a Hindu population of over 40 per cent was simply too large to swallow. A theocratic state was impossible with such a massive and prosperous minority, propped up by a sympathetic neighbourhood to the south-east. Nor did the secessionists want to lose any of the land area which had come to Punjab in 1966; if anything, they wanted to add to it. The contours of their dream had been established; the task was to convert Punjab into Khalistan. They planned out a course of action which Jinnah had advocated when he had a similar problem in pre-1947 Punjab – an exchange of populations. And exactly like the Muslim League, the Sikh extremists knew that there was only one way to get rid of the Hindus from Punjab, and bring Sikhs living in the rest of India back to the 'motherland': violence. It was a strategy which would take time to mature – more than a decade, in fact, while an armed cadre was nurtured.

Sikh–Hindu relations had, of course, deteriorated from the high point of the common front against the Muslims. But the sentiment had stayed alive through the fluctuations of the first half of this century. As Dharma Vira, Governor of Punjab in 1966, told this author during a conversation in 1984, 'When I got married fifty years ago in Lahore, the first thing my parents told me to do after the marriage was to go to the Golden Temple in Amritsar, to bow one's head before the Granth Sahib. In those days it was quite a normal thing for one son in a Hindu family to become a Sikh. This lasted till about thirty years ago, when Hindus began feeling that an increase in the Sikh population was a direct threat to their own interest.'

In other words, this change of heart happened after 1947 – when the Muslims of Punjab had gone to their Pakistan, when the need for Hindu–Sikh amity had diminished, and when the tensions of the new conflict began to weigh on everyone's mind. Now there were more cynical interpretations. The Hindus, said some Sikhs, had worked out a beautiful arrangement for themselves: the Sikhs were entrusted with the hard work of tilling the land, growing the food and defending Punjab from the marauders of Kabul or Delhi, while the urban Hindus sat in the cities, controlled the economy, grew fat on moneylending and took all the soft jobs in bureaucracy, law, education, etc. In return, the Sikhs got the dubious distinction of being called associated members of Hinduism. Post-independence politics not only sharpened the differences, but gave them a violent edge.

One of the most important strands in the Sikh psyche is the belief in a martial spirit, physical prowess and virility. The origins lie in the long fight for survival against Muslim rulers; in the sanction to war given by Guru Hargobind, who wore two swords, one to signify his spiritual power (*Peeri*) and the other to fight the battles of the world (*Meeri*); in the creation of the Khalsa; in the unceasing skirmishes and wars fought by Banda Bahadur; in the successful creation of a great empire under Ranjit Singh. And then the British came and added an intellectual superstructure to this notion, with the theory of 'martial races'. The British motive was uncomplicated; those who helped them preserve the empire in 1857 were to be praised, while the spirit of the others had to be first ridiculed, then broken. The Sikhs were at the very top of the 'martial' list.

One of the most revealing books about this British theory was written in 1932 by Lieutenant-General Sir George MacMunn, KCB, KCSI, DSO, Colonel Commandant of the Royal Artillery; called *The Martial Races of India*, it was reprinted by Mittal Publications, New Delhi, in 1979. A few quotations will be self-explanatory: 'India unlike almost any country has a vast mass of unwarlike people. Who and what are the martial races of India, how do they come, and in what crucible, on what anvils hot with pain, spring the soldiers of India, whom surely Baba Gandhi [Mahatma Gandhi, that is] never fathered? ... We do not speak of the martial races of Britain as distinct from the non-martial, nor of Germany nor of France. But in India we speak of the martial races as a thing apart because the mass of the people have neither martial aptitude nor physical courage, the courage that we should talk of colloquially as "guts" ... The gentle yet merciless race of hereditary moneylenders, from which Lala Gandhi springs, only kept within bounds by an occasional flaying and roasting, have never been able to or even tried to protect their own hoards ...' And so on. The reader is welcome to feel any degree of nausea he likes, but Sir George was only putting down accepted wisdom about 'the *Badshah* or *Padishah*, the Great White King' whose 'white officers would lead them [the martial races of India]' to international glory. The anger, if any, might be better reserved for those who agreed to be led in the great task of an 'occasional flaying and roasting' of Lala Gandhi.

However, the conviction that they are martial (and in this the Sikhs are the same as their Rajput and Jat brethren among Punjabi Muslims, who indulge themselves similarly) is among the reasons why the Akalis formally demand of the government of India that arms licences should be abolished or, at the very least, that they should be distributed freely. (The licence is required by Sikhs only for guns, not swords and sabres, since the Constitution of India, through Article 25, has given the Sikh the fundamental right to carry a kirpan: 'The wearing and carrying of kirpans shall be deemed to be included in the profession of the Sikh religion.')

Nobody says very much in India about the theory of martial races, perhaps out of a wise desire not to poke their fingers into the nests of hornets. But the theory has played its part in creating an extremist fringe to the Sikh mass movement. This is strengthened by religious legitimacy. Guru Gobind had preached that *dharma*, or faith, could not be protected without *raj*, or rule, and power was not possible without recourse to arms. The extremists, therefore, are proud of violence, calling it a part of both their faith and their tradition. However, the colour of the real revolution which took place in Sikh-majority Punjab in the 1960s was not red; it was green.

The most interesting phenomenon of the Sikh experience in independent India came in the late sixties and seventies. It was the impact of prosperity, and the dramatic changes it wrought on this tough community with such a short, but crowded, history. It was the wealth created by the agricultural revolution of the late 1960s that sent Punjab out of the Third World and on the way to the First. One of the men who managed this boom was C. Subramaniam, the Congressman from Tamil Nadu who became Food Minister in Lal Bahadur Shastri's Cabinet after Nehru's death. Subramaniam had been a senior minister for many years. Such were the misplaced priorities in those days that the Ministry of Agriculture was considered too low in the Cabinet's pecking order for a person of Subramaniam's seniority, which showed a strange sense of what was important in a food-deficit country. Prime Minister Shastri could not convince any of his senior ministers that he wanted to raise the importance of the Agriculture Ministry, rather than devalue one of his colleagues, by making one of them the Food Minister. In the end, only Subramaniam understood what the new Prime Minister wanted. He accepted the portfolio. What followed was extraordinary. Within five years famished India solved its food-production problem.

The resources of the second Five-Year Plan had been shifted to heavy industry, as new irrigation schemes had helped the government meet the First Five-Year Plan's targets in agriculture, for the period 1952–7. But a warning that this shift might have been a mistake was sounded early, when a severe drought came in the late fifties. A second severe famine in the mid sixties could not be averted. To this burden was added the cost of two resource-sapping wars. From 10 to 11 million tonnes of food had to be imported to cover the deficit in a normal year. On top of this, massive food aid was required to prevent mass starvation deaths. Only the USA could provide this. Instead of being generous, President Lyndon Johnson chose to bully India. C. Subramaniam recalled to this author that it was a choice between starvation and 'becoming a satellite of the USA'. Subramaniam, who is not known for any strong sympathy towards the Russians, sounded bitter when he described Johnson's behaviour. The food did come from the USA but instead of helping, soured relations even further, and made India determined to become self-sufficient in food as soon as possible.

C. Subramaniam took two decisions immediately upon becoming Food Minister. First, he asked Indian scientists to intensify their work to apply the latest technology in seeds and fertilizers to Indian conditions. A beginning had already been made in 1963, when Dr N. E. Borlaug had sent from his laboratories in Mexico about 150 strains of dwarf wheat for experiments on the fields of Punjab and western Uttar Pradesh. The Ludhiana Agricultural University had already done excellent work on this programme. But it was under Subramaniam that the new strains, backed with fertilizer supplies, were heavily promoted, with demonstrations and promises of compensation if the crop failed. The Sikh farmers showed the enterprise to experiment, and duly prospered.

The second decision was more controversial: he argued that unless the country's cheap grain policy was changed, food production could not go up. He wanted the government to assure the farmers that there would be a government-supported base price for their production which would meet their costs and ensure a profit. There was an uproar in the Cabinet, as the other ministers saw what this would lead to – higher food prices all over the country. T. T. Krishnamachari, another senior minister from the south, called Subramaniam's proposal a 'disaster' which would antagonize the cities. Subramaniam asked the government to choose between self-sufficiency in food, and urban unrest. The Cabinet accepted the Food Minister's proposal. An immediate increase of 15 per cent in food prices was granted and a one-man (L. K. Jha) commission was appointed to look into the whole structure of prices. The Agricultural Prices Commission was formed, and continues to fix a support price every year. Droughts keep coming, but India no longer goes to Washington to beg for food. In a bad year, when the reserve stocks dip, the country goes to international grain markets, pays cash and buys what it needs.

According to Food Minister Rao Birendra Singh's statement during the 1984 budget session of Parliament, the production of foodgrains in India had reached 140 million tonnes. In 1955–6, it was only 69.38 million tonnes; in 1960–1, 82.21 million tonnes. In 1965–6, drought conditions brought it down to 72.35 million tonnes. The next year, 1966–7, production was about the same, 74.23 million tonnes. By 1967–8 the efforts of the government, the scientist and the farmer, began to pay off in a dramatic manner. Production shot up to an unprecedented high: 95.05 million tonnes. By 1969–70 it was verging on the century (99.50 million tonnes) and the next year it crossed the hundred mark when production reached 108.42 million tonnes. R. H. Cassen (*India: Population, Economy,*

Society, Macmillan, 1978) describes this achievement with a quotation from the famous historian Ibn Khaldun: 'Famines are not the result of the land's incapacity to cope with the increasing demand, but of the political chaos and physical oppression which invade the state in its decline.' The curve of India's fortunes had now turned upward. The challenge of famine was being met.

India was not synonymous with pestilence and famine when the British first came in their trading ships. The Mughal empire had become legendary in contemporary Europe, and westerners came to trade with and earn from a prosperous upper class in India. The subcontinent was famous for its cotton, silks and spices, and the general level of prosperity was higher than in the contemporary empires of the Bourbons, the Tudors or the Tsars. But weak government, political chaos and physical oppression brought great disasters: the whims of nature can be understood and tackled, it is more difficult to combat the cruelty of oppressive rulers. Punjab, an endemic victim of political mayhem, was constantly besieged by famine and pestilence. Hari Ram Gupta (*History of the Sikhs*, vol. 4, Manoharlal Publishers, 1982) narrates a typical tragedy: 'In 1781, 1782 and 1783 the rains failed completely. The famine affected almost the whole of northern India, but it was extremely acute in the Punjab ... Cattle perished of hunger and thirst by thousands. Innumerable people died. According to a contemporary, Harcharan Das, thousands of people died in Delhi alone in five or six days. Children wandered about to feed on berries of the jungle and fell an easy prey to wild beasts who lurked in close neighbourhood of villages in broad daylight ... Stories are told of parents devouring their children; and it is beyond doubt that children were during this fatal year gladly sold to anyone who would offer a few handfuls of grain as their price.'

This same Punjab in the 1980s began to send, alone, 60 per cent of the grain to the national food basket. Its per capita income of Rs 2,768 (all figures are of 1980–1) was far above the Indian average of Rs 1,571, with only the states of Haryana and Maharashtra coming anywhere near Punjab. The production of crops in Punjab had risen by six times since 1951. Agriculture contributed 58.12 per cent of the state's income, while employing 59.1 per cent of the total work-force. The production of rice rose from 892 kilograms per hectare in 1950–1 to 2,957 kilograms thirty years later; and wheat from 901 kilograms per hectare to 2,932 kilograms. And prosperity brought other benefits.

The spurt in education was reflected both in figures and in quality. The number of primary schools shot up from 7,183 in 1967–8 to 12,384 in 1981; middle schools from 863 to 1,410; high schools from 789 to 2,158. The number of arts and science colleges rose from 71 in 1968 to 161 in 1981; there were no medical colleges in 1968, but 8 in 1981. A large number of farmers began sending their children to the better urban schools, while in Punjab itself private English-medium schools were springing up, creating a new, rural, educated middle class. Half of the 54,000 unemployed graduates (there were no unemployed illiterates) in the state in the mid 1980s were from the rural areas. Economists of the Left were still arguing whether this 'green revolution' had pauperized the small and marginal farmer while turning the medium and large farmer into a capitalist, but no economist denied that there had been overall prosperity, thanks to individual enterprise, an assured irrigation base and the wonders of modern agricultural science. The farmer of Punjab was also wise enough to invest his surplus in trade, transport and small industry.

But wealth also brought its problems. The biggest one was the oldest one: the percentage of the Sikh population. It had gone up to a record high of 61 per cent in the 1971 census, but had begun to come down again. The Sikh leadership did not need any verification from the 1981 census; they could see the decline for themselves. Prosperity was, paradoxically, pushing up migration as the Sikhs now had the wherewithal to finance travel to foreign countries where lucrative jobs were available. More than 200,000 Sikh youths have settled down permanently outside India in the three decades since independence, according to just the official figures. Many more went abroad for a few years to earn dollars.

The migration did not always have to be legal, though even small towns, like Rode in the heart of rural Punjab, boasted two or three travel agencies. It was not a question of rags-to-riches for the Sikhs going out; suit-to-fur-coat might be a more appropriate symbol. An excellent example of shifting ambitions could be found in the village of Sansarpur, near Jullundur cantonment. This village had the reputation of producing an unending stream of champion hockey players, as one hero coached starry-eyed kids into becoming his successors. More than twenty Olympians had come from this small village, as hockey became the gateway both to fame and to enough fortune to build a comfortable house, and get a good assured government job in the Border Security Force, the Punjab Police or the railways. One of the greats, Balbir Singh (Junior), wistfully told this author that nobody wanted to play hockey any more;

they all dreamt of a job in Europe – after which lay the big car, the luxury house and, of course, a white woman. One villager put it differently: the most expensive commodity being smuggled out of Punjab in the 1980s was the human male.

Against this, there was a great migration of Hindus into Punjab, drawn in by the state's prosperity. As the need for farm labour increased to extraordinary levels, and all the available Sikh or local Hindu (that is, largely untouchable) labour was absorbed, the vacuum was filled by mass arrivals from the truly poor parts of India, like eastern Uttar Pradesh, Bihar and Madhya Pradesh. By 1981, these outsiders had begun to constitute as much as 37.7 per cent of the labour working on the fields. While a substantial section of these seasonal hands went back to their villages after the sowing or the harvesting, many decided to make Punjab their new home. There was no motivation to go back to the old village, where not merely was there extreme poverty but also far greater social tension. The Sikh was less caste-conscious than the upper-caste Hindu; the relationship in Punjab was one of employer and employee, and most often warm, instead of the master–animal relationship that existed in caste-ridden Bihar. But once again the demographic balance, always such a volatile problem, was in danger of turning against the Sikhs. By the 1980s, Sikhs constituted only 52 per cent of the population in their own state. And this problem was compounded by another, resulting from the new prosperity and peace.

This other threat which the Sikhs began facing was one of identity melting in the cauldron of new influences. The Hindus or Muslims could not be blamed this time; education, transnational industry and the impact of modernity, whether beneficial or baleful, were the reasons. If the Sikh youths were turning, thanks to their new-found leisure and money, to drugs and liquor (the liquor from the booming legal industry in India, and hashish from the booming illegal trade in Pakistan), it was no one else's fault. The flowing beard was also seen less often; more and more Sikhs began taking the easy way out by clipping their hair. It was midway house, neither the clean shave nor the untouched growth, but the trend was obvious. Any visitor to Punjab could easily verify for himself that the clipped beard had become as common by the eighties as once it was rare. The change was taking place even in the villages. The alarm bells began ringing once again.

And the people who rang them loudest were, naturally, the Akalis, for whom the survival of the Khalsa identity was the rationale for existence.

After all, the Akalis were the political wing of a religious movement, and any slackening of faith, any hint of apostasy, could hurt them at a fundamental level. Even the Jat Sikh villagers, whose votes had always gone to the Akalis, were becoming affected by new currents.

Free India has brought Sikhs prosperity outside agriculture, too. Though just under 2 per cent of the population, Sikhs account for 8 per cent of the total number of Central government employees; 256 (or one in every sixteen) of the 4,000 directly recruited officers in the Indian Administrative Service (successor to the old ICS nobility – the imperial Indian Civil Service) are Sikhs, as are 81 of the 1,527 officers of the parallel group in the police, the Indian Police Service. More than 7.5 per cent of the army is still Sikh. At the moment of writing, the President of India, Zail Singh, the Chief of the Air Force, Dilbagh Singh, and the Governor of the Reserve Bank of India, Manmohan Singh, are Sikhs. The Sikhs have developed a major interest in trade and business with the rest of India, and one-fifth of them live and prosper outside Punjab. The other minorities in India would give an arm and a leg for such statistics. The Muslims get their nominee as President thanks to the policy of rotation that has become the norm for that ceremonial office, but nothing comparable to the Sikhs at the level of real power – in the bureaucracy, or industry, or trade. This, therefore, is an important and influential section with little interest in Sikh fanaticism. It accepts the existence of the Akali Dal only to the extent that the party can be useful as a pressure group, or become a rallying point in the case of any genuine crisis.

Then there is the moderate Akali: committed to the religion, the Khalsa identity and the geographical integrity of India, but uncertain how to achieve political power, given the travails and contradictions of democracy in a state like Punjab. Treading the slippery middle ground between a theocratic ideology and a democratic commitment often leads the Akalis into confusion, rashness and then despair, as the consequence of their rhetoric begins to demand its price. The last layer in the Sikh fold, of course, is the extremist one, which wants to take the Sikhs away from India and believes it can do so by the gun, with a little help from Pakistan. This section has the advantage of a confidence which comes from being simple, clear and committed; they do not think, therefore they are.

10
Searching for Khalistan

It was a Cambridge man, Chaudhury Rahmat Ali, who first proposed a Muslim nation on the subcontinent, to be called Pakistan. It was an Oxford alumnus, Kapur Singh, born in 1909, selected to the exalted Indian Civil Service (ICS) and asked to 'retire' amidst corruption charges, who in the 1960s began reminding the Sikhs about their proposed independent nation of Khalistan ('the country of the pure, the nation of the Khalsa'). In 1941, when the Premier of Punjab, Sir Sikandar Hayat Khan, launched his powerful attack on the concept of Pakistan in the Punjab Legislative Assembly, his sarcasm about Chaudhury Rahmat Ali's scheme raised laughter from most sections of the House. Through the sixties and seventies Kapur Singh aroused similar condescension. Those who preferred sarcasm to political combat punned about Khalistan: in Hindi *Khali* means 'empty', and *stan* means 'place', therefore the proposed Sikh nation was nothing more than an empty place. Those who wanted to be extra nasty would add that Khalistan was a symbol of the Sikh's intellectual capacities.

The Master Tara Singh Akali Dal passed resolutions in May 1965 and December 1966 seeking 'a self-determined status within the Republic of India'. Mentioning the Republic of India was only a very thin cover. In 1970 and 1971, when the subcontinent was going through a phase of high drama with the crisis in Pakistan coming to a boil, Islamabad, playing Delhi at political chess, attempted to counter the Indian queen's sweeping moves in the east by advancing a few pawns in Punjab. A former Akali Dal general secretary, and briefly the Finance Minister of Punjab, Dr Jagjit Singh Chauhan, who had become a militant voice of the Tara Singh faction (the Master himself had died in 1968; his students carried on the work) now left the country, sought a British passport and announced plans to set up a 'Rebel Sikh Government' at Nankana Sahib, the birthplace of Guru Nanak, which was in Pakistan. (Delhi in 1971 was, of course, supporting the rebel government of Bangladesh on Indian territory, after the army crackdown in East Pakistan in March.) On 13 October 1971, Dr Chauhan paid for a half-page advertisement in *The New York Times* explaining the reasons why he wanted Khalistan. One of them is easy to guess: army quotas. The Sikh leadership was most upset at the government of India's new recruitment policy, announced by Defence Minister Jagjivan Ram in 1974, fixing proportions by population percentages. Punjab was allotted a 2.5-per-cent share: democratic India had finally refused to allow the 'martial races' their hegemony over jobs in the army.

The post-1967 political turmoil in Punjab had proved a bruising experience for the Akalis, teaching them that power was not necessarily an inevitable reward for a successful political movement. To understand the Akali ambivalence of the eighties, it is necessary to appreciate the true cause of their frustration: the difficulty they have both in winning elections and in holding on to power if they have won.

The first defeat that Mrs Indira Gandhi suffered in the whole of North India, from Amritsar to Calcutta, was not, as is the common impression, in the post-Emergency elections of 1977, but precisely a decade earlier, in the fourth general elections of 1967. Dr Ram Manohar Lohia, that great Socialist theorist and leader, was the architect of that defeat. He asked all the opposition parties to accept that singly they could never defeat the Congress, which would always emerge ahead in a split vote: he proposed just one opposition candidate in each constituency. It worked. The Congress managed to scrape together a government at the Centre, largely through overwhelming victories in the southern states of Andhra Pradesh and Karnataka and the western state of Maharashtra. But in Chandigarh, Simla, Jaipur, Lucknow, Bhopal, Bhubaneswar, Patna and Calcutta, the numerous opposition parties hastily cooked up 'United Front' governments. It was a great chance for the opposition to prove itself. It blew the opportunity. The Congress spent the next few years, till it swept back to power in 1971 and 1972, playing merry hell with these opposition coalitions, successfully arranging defections and destroying the credibility of the non-Congress parties. The only place where the Congress could not play this game was in the southern state of Tamil Nadu, where the DMK alone crushed the Congress and emerged as the undisputed alternative.

Given the strong ideological antagonisms that existed between the Sikh Akali Dal, the Hindu Jana Sangh and the irreligious Communists, pre-election solidarity between these, the main opposition parties in Punjab, was difficult. On top of this was the bitterness generated by splits; the Akalis had divided into two factions (Fateh Singh and Tara Singh) and even the Communists had split, the Marxists breaking away from the parent party. The Akalis of Sant Fateh Singh managed a pre-poll seat adjustment only with the Communists. But even this proved sufficient to defeat the Congress. Despite getting the largest share of the vote, 37.6 per cent, the Congress won only 48 of the 104 seats. The Sikhs formed 56 per cent of the population, but both the Akali factions together managed only a little less than 25 per cent of the vote. As usual, the moderate Akalis got the substantial share, with 20.46 per cent of the vote, and 24 seats. The Master Tara Singh faction was reduced to just 2 seats. The Jana Sangh, representing the Hindu extremists, got 9.85 per cent of the vote. The Communist share came down to 9 per cent, and they got 8 seats between them, the parent CPI winning 5, and the other 3 going to the Marxist CPI.

Despite the divergence in their manifestos, the opposition parties formed a coalition, chose Gurnam Singh (a barrister who had retired as judge of the Punjab High Court in 1959) of the Sant Akali Dal as their Chief Minister, and formed a ministry on 8 March 1967.

The sophisticated Gurnam Singh proved quite incapable of controlling or understanding the rough-and-tumble of Indian coalition politics. Greed and personal pique played their part too. For instance, upset at not being made a minister, the Vice-President of the Akali Dal, Harcharan Singh Hudiara, resigned from the party. The Congress leader, Gian Singh Rarewala, easily sabotaged this mess. He persuaded the Tara Singh hardliners, led by Lachman Singh Gill, to defect and form a new government with help from the Congress in the Legislature. Master Tara Singh could not live to see the first government headed by a disciple. He died on 22 November 1967, three days before Gill was sworn in. The Gill government made Punjabi the official language; Gill boasted that even Maharaja Ranjit Singh had not been able to achieve this – the question, of course, was whether Ranjit Singh ever wanted to. But soon the Congress withdrew its support from the minority government it had helped establish. An obdurate Gill, however, refused to resign; there was violence in the Legislature, and Delhi eventually imposed Governor's Rule on 13 August 1968, pending a midterm poll. If the reader has become totally confused by all this, that is perfectly understandable; so were the people of Punjab.

The Akalis adopted a different strategy for the 1969 elections. They could compromise with the urban Hindus of the Jana Sangh, but wanted no truck with the Communists who were their competitors for support among the Sikh peasantry. The evolution of the Akali alliances is interesting: it began with the Congress in the fifties, the Communists came in 1967, and now they were joining hands with their most bitter enemies, the Jana Sangh. But the last was also a most logical alliance as there was no conflict in the support bases: the Akalis could never get the Hindu vote and the Jana Sangh could never hope for support from the Sikh peasantry. The two communal parties wanted to become the sole representatives of their communities. To achieve that, the Congress, which obtained support from both Hindus and Sikhs, had to be demolished. It was Gurnam Singh who once again became Chief Minister in 1969.

It was a dramatic year in Indian politics. Mrs Gandhi broke her ties with the official Congress party, set up her own candidate in the indirect elections for the President of India, and master-minded a brilliant campaign which ensured her candidate's victory by a thin margin. Mrs Gandhi received crucial – very crucial – help from Gurnam Singh; in return, the Akalis were awarded Chandigarh.

When Punjab had been divided in 1966, the transfer of the capital, the new city of Chandigarh (designed, among others, by Le Corbusier), had been kept pending until the new state, Haryana, could construct its own capital. The Akalis did not want to wait. As early as 27 December 1966, Sant Fateh Singh had threatened to burn himself to death if Chandigarh was not transferred immediately; he did not carry out the threat. But in 1969, an old Sikh freedom-fighter, Darshan Singh Pheruman, died on 27 October after fasting for seventy-four days for the transfer of Chandigarh, which put to shame all the Sants who had been crying martyrdom too often. Conscious of the public mood, Sant Fateh Singh began, on Republic Day, 26 January 1970, yet another 'fast unto death' to force Delhi to transfer Chandigarh to Punjab. Within three days Mrs Gandhi rescued the Sant by announcing an award: Punjab would get Chandigarh, and Haryana would be compensated by being given part of the districts of Fazilka and Abohar, plus Rs 10 crores to build itself a new capital. The award was to be implemented by January 1975. Chief Minister Gurnam Singh and Akali leader Sant Fateh Singh each began claiming that it was his individual effort which had won this victory. The former said that this was reward for Akali support to Mrs Gandhi, which he had organized, in the presidential elections of 1969; Sant Fateh Singh said that Mrs Gandhi had been frightened by his threat to die.

(It turned out to be a pyrrhic victory. January 1975 came and went, but Chandigarh was not transferred to Punjab.) Gurnam Singh had to pay for forcing a confrontation with the religious leaders. He was expelled from the party. On 27 March 1970, another coalition ministry of the Akalis and the Jana Sangh took office, headed by the chosen nominee of Sant Fateh Singh, Prakash Singh Badal. Badal intensified the efforts to woo the peasantry. The Akalis exempted all holdings of up to five acres from payment of land revenues; introduced a higher guaranteed procurement price for foodgrains; demanded the abolition of the middle man in the grain trade (to the consternation of their partners, the Jana Sangh, who got substantial support from moneylenders and traders). But the years in power kept the Akali temperature very moderate indeed. This was also evident during their third spell in power, between 1977 and 1980. When in February 1978 a Sikh leader, Mahant Sewa Das, began yet another fast for Chandigarh, the Akali leaders defused tensions on the plea that communal harmony would be threatened by the fast.

Despite Badal's pro-peasant economic policy, the Akalis were wiped out in the 1971 and 1972 elections. Mrs Gandhi's Congress, with its magnetic promise to end poverty, won 11 out of the 12 Lok Sabha (Lower House) seats, and 66 of the 104 Assembly seats, in Punjab. Back to square one. And back therefore to the old problem: whenever the knights of the Khalsa do not become ministers of the government, they begin dropping dark hints about a Sikh homeland where their ministerships cannot be threatened by electoral defeat. And thus came in October 1973 what has become the famous and controversial Anandpur Sahib resolution.

The first threat to the life of the ninth Guru, Tegh Bahadur, had not come from the Mughals and their most maligned emperor, Aurangzeb Alamgir; it came from the Sikhs themselves. There was confusion about whether the previous Guru, Hari Kishen, had actually nominated his grand-uncle (or 'Baba Bakale') as his successor when he died of smallpox in the Delhi residence of Mirza Raja Jai Singh, one of the most important generals in the army of Aurangzeb (the Gurdwara Bangla Sahib has been built on this spot). Among the claimants to the Guruship were relatives Dhirmal and Ram Rai. The former tried to have Guru Tegh Bahadur assassinated. The Guru escaped his murderous relatives but, unable to raise support in Amritsar or Kiratpur, the capital city built by his father, he bought a small hill five miles north of Kiratpur and established his own capital. He named it Anandpur ('the city of bliss').

But the internal strife forced Guru Tegh Bahadur to leave Anandpur,

and he travelled east, up to Assam. In the meantime, the bigot in Aurangzeb had become active, and all suffered who did not subscribe to his specific
creed (the Shiah sect of Islam, for instance, was also a target; Aurangzeb
spent more than twenty years of his life at war with the Muslim kingdoms
of the Deccan whose rulers were Shiahs). Guru Tegh Bahadur returned
to the Punjab and found an ally in a Muslim Sufi mendicant, Hafiz Adam,
belonging to the order of Shaikh Ahmed Sirhindi. The two organized
a mass uprising against the Mughal Emperor. Aurangzeb himself was
in the Deccan, but his troops quelled the revolt and arrested Guru Tegh
Bahadur at Agra. He was sentenced to death and decapitated on 11
November 1675, in Delhi, at the place where the Gurdwara Sis Ganj
now stands. The Guru's body was cremated where the Gurdwara Rikab
Ganj has since been built, behind Parliament House in Delhi. The severed
head was taken to Anandpur and cremated there by his son and successor
Guru Gobind.

Anandpur Sahib, in other words, is a city full of symbolism to the
Sikhs, particularly to those raising the cry of battle against Delhi. It was
here that Guru Gobind built his first string of fortresses. It was in
Anandpur that he started the new community of the Khalsa, and then
defended the growing Sikh power, first against the attack by the con-
sortium of Hindu Rajput chiefs led by the Raja of Bilaspur, and later
against the Mughal forces led by Wazir Khan of Sirhind (Sirhind, further
to the north, literally means the 'Head of India'). It was at Anandpur
that most of the Dasam Granth was compiled before Guru Gobind Singh
was forced to abandon the city in 1704; Anandpur also has one of the
five *takhts* from where *hukumnamas* can be issued.

Anandpur was chosen in 1973 by the Akalis for the announcement
of their new programme. All the strands of the interrelated political–
religious nexus were rewoven, but the foundation was built on the same
old fear. As the Akali President, Sant Harchand Singh Longowal, said
in an explanatory pamphlet (titled 'You Owe Us Justice') sent later to
Members of Parliament, the root cause was 'the genuine foreboding that,
like Buddhism and Jainism earlier, they [the Sikhs] may also lose their
identity in the vast ocean of overwhelming Hindu majority'. The Nanakpanthis were saying that without political power they too would suffer the
fate of the Kabirpanthis.

On 11 December 1972, the Working Committee of the Akali Dal had
formed a subcommittee of 'Sikh intellectuals and thinkers' to 'redraw
the aims and objectives of the Sikh Panth and thus live up to the ex-

pectations of the Sikhs'. The chairman of the subcommittee was Surjit Singh Barnala (later to become Minister for Food and Agriculture in the government of Morarji Desai); its other members were Gurcharan Singh Tohra, MP and President of the SGPC, Jiwan Singh Umramangal, Gurmit Singh, Dr Bhagat Singh, Balwant Singh, Gian Singh Rarewala, Prem Singh Lalpura, Jaswinder Singh Brar, Bhag Singh, Major-General Gurbux Singh Badhni and Amar Singh Ambalvi. It met for the first time on 23 December, and after ten more meetings ('held at Chandigarh for its peaceful and congenial atmosphere', in the words of Ajmer Singh, secretary of the Akali Dal in 1977), a draft was drawn up which was submitted to the Working Committee of the Shiromani Akali Dal at Shri Anandpur Sahib ('the sacred and historic seat of the Tenth Lord') on 16 October 1973. The Working Committee approved it the next day.

The 'basic postulate' was thus defined: 'The Shiromani Akali Dal is the very embodiment of the hopes and aspirations of the Sikh nation and as such is fully entitled to its representation.' The controversy begins here itself. What did the Akalis mean by the 'Sikh nation'? Old fears stirred; Jinnah had got his Pakistan by insisting that the Muslims were a separate nation. The Akalis, who have never once officially advocated secession or indeed violence, explained that 'nation' was only the nearest English equivalent of the word used in the master version in Punjabi, *qaum*, which denotes community rather than nation. But was this explanation the truth or just another cover-up? What actually happened is clear enough: the word *qaum* was deliberately used by the drafting committee, with everyone fully aware of the capacity for different interpretations. Its use was an implied threat – that if the demands of the Akalis were not met, they would openly begin to use the interpretation less palatable to Delhi.

The Anandpur Sahib resolution had, naturally, a substantial religious component but there were only two religious demands that had any bearing on their relationship with the government of India. The Akalis wanted an All-India Gurdwara Act (the British had legislated only for the Punjab gurdwaras after the movement in the 1920s) 'to reintegrate the traditional preaching sects of Sikhism without in any way encroaching on the properties of their respective individual *maths*'. Secondly, the Akalis wanted free access to 'all those holy Sikh shrines, including Nankana Sahib, from which the Sikh Panth has been separated, for pilgrimage and proper upkeep'. In other words, they asked for a policy of friendship with Pakistan (where the shrines were) which could ensure trouble-free travel between the two countries, and perhaps even an arrangement whereby the Akalis could take charge of these shrines, with the permission of the Pakistani government.

The other religious clauses reflected the urgent worry about apostasy. Preachers and missionaries would be sent out to village and city, in India and abroad. A programme of born-again baptism (*Amrit Prachar*) would be taken up, particularly in schools and colleges; and so on. Mention was made of the problem of alcoholism and its corrosive effect on the purity of the Khalsa – in recognition of one of the less wholesome consequences of Punjab's prosperity. But it was the political implications of the Anandpur Sahib resolution which were more worrying to Delhi.

Once again, the phrasing of the introduction was left deliberately ambiguous. 'The political goal of the Panth, without doubt, is enshrined in the commandments of the Tenth Lord, in the pages of Sikh history and in the very heart of the Khalsa Panth, the ultimate objective of which is the pre-eminence of the Khalsa. The fundamental policy of the Shiromani Akali Dal is to seek the realization of this birthright of the Khalsa through creation of congenial environment and a political set-up.' Which commandment of the Tenth Lord, Guru Gobind? That the Khalsa shall rule? Rule what? A separate Sikh country? Since democracy was not giving the Akalis permanent rule, would they now opt for a theocracy where, as in Pakistan, rule by a minority could be justified in the name of religion? Islam had been in 'danger' so the mullahs took over power to 'save' it; would Sikhism similarly always be in 'danger' until the Akalis got their Sikhistan or Khalistan? Was this the 'ultimate objective' which was mentioned but not clearly explained? What was the 'birthright' that the Akalis were talking about? What did they mean by the 'creation of congenial environment and a political set-up'?

The resolution chalked out the next phase of the struggle. The first thing the Akalis wanted was to add to the geography of Punjab 'all those Punjabi-speaking areas deliberately kept out of Punjab, such as Dalhousie in Gurdaspur district, Chandigarh, Pinjore-Kalka and Ambala Sadar, etc., in Ambala district, the "Desh" area of Nalagarh; Shahabad and Gulha blocks of Karnal district; Tohana sub-tehsil, Ratia block and Sirsa tehsil of Hissar district and six tehsils of Ganganagar district in Rajasthan; merged with Punjab to constitute a single administrative unit where the interests of Sikhs and Sikhism are specifically protected'. And presumably where the interests of Hindu citizens could take a back seat. As far as the territorial demands are concerned, who can place a moratorium on claims? The more fertile dreamers in the Muslim League, as we have seen, used to imagine a Pakistan twice its present size. What the Pakistanis who encourage the Khalistan idea might not know is that the proposed Akali Sikh nation includes a large chunk of what is currently in Pakistan – including the city of Lahore.

The most serious political issue raised by the Anandpur Sahib resolution was the demand for the restructuring of the Constitution to ensure 'real federal principles, with equal representation at the Centre for all the states'. It suggested that the proposal of the Cabinet Mission in 1946 be revived, with the Central government in Delhi in charge only of defence, foreign affairs, currency and general communications. And as far as its opinion of Mrs Gandhi's foreign policy was concerned, it had absolutely no hesitation in saying that the 'foreign policy of India framed by the Congress Party ... is worthless, hopeless and highly detrimental to the interests of the country, the nation and mankind at large'. Considering that Mrs Gandhi's foreign policy had two years before achieved success beyond anyone's wildest expectations with the creation of Bangladesh, it was an interesting position to take. 'Shiromani Akali Dal shall extend its support only to that foreign policy of India which is based on the principles of peace and national interests. It strongly advocates a policy of peace with all neighbouring countries especially those inhabited by the Sikhs and their sacred shrines.' Simply put, the Akalis were asking for a soft Indo-Pakistani border at a time when 90,000 Pakistani prisoners of war had just left Indian camps. Was the Akali foreign policy a genuine call to peace in the subcontinent, or the first step towards a deal with Pakistan by which the latter would help in eventual war against Delhi for Khalistan? After all, Sheikh Mujibur Rahman's Awami League had been friendly to India, even at the risk of being called treacherous, for many years before the need arose to seek the help of Indian troops for the creation of Bangladesh.

Predictably, the issue of Sikh recruitment in the army was raised. The Akalis also wanted the kirpan to become part of the uniform for the Sikh soldier, and they proposed to organize ex-servicemen (as later events proved, this, too, was not as innocent as it might sound on paper; extremists used ex-soldiers in their squads). And of course, in honour of Sikh 'martial' traditions, the Akalis demanded that everyone bar the proven criminal should be 'at liberty to possess all types of small arms, like revolvers, guns, pistols, rifles, carbines, etc., without any licence, the only obligation being their registration'. Guru Gobind Singh had only insisted on the sword; the Sants of 1973 wanted to raise the 'defence' capability of the Sikh to modern levels. But defence against whom? There was no reason assigned for this demand. Had it been the Akali experience that Sikhs were being murdered in large numbers by the armies of Delhi and therefore needed this weaponry? Obviously not. Then why? Was this once again surreptitious preparation for the day when the Sikh *qaum* would be asked by its theologian leaders to rise in revolt? But other developments interrupted the sequence of events: for instance, 1975 and the Emergency.

Within three days of the Emergency being imposed, a special meeting of the Akali Dal executive spurned Mrs Gandhi's effort to woo them, and called the Emergency 'fascist', a 'rape of democracy and a great step towards dictatorship'. The elections of 1977 brought a windfall. It was in a sense like the Akali–Congress alliance of the 1950s, the difference being that the Congress had been replaced by the Janata. The Janata received unprecedented, and possibly unrepeatable, support in the whole of the north, where the Congress could not manage to win even one single seat. The Akali–Janata also demolished the Congress in Punjab. The Akalis polled their highest-ever share of the vote, 31.41 per cent, in the 1977 Assembly elections, to capture 58 seats. But the Akalis still could not make any great dent in the urban Sikh vote; and even a demoralized Congress remained the largest single vote-getter, with 34.07 per cent. However it won only 17 seats. The Communists, with a consistency that seemed to leave all political developments in the shade, polled their regular 10 per cent. Janata–Akali coalition governments came into power not only in Punjab but also in Delhi. The Akalis got 2 seats in the Union government and had their own Chief Minister, Prakash Singh Badal, in Punjab. The nature of their support base was reflected in the character of their ministers; there was not one urban Sikh as an Akali minister either in Delhi or Chandigarh.

The Janata Party had leaders at its apex who were, if anything, far more hardline about the Akali demands than Mrs Gandhi. Two of the three Congress ministers who had opposed conceding the Punjabi Suba in 1966 were in the Janata Cabinet: the towering leader from Orissa, Biju Patnaik, was now Minister for Steel and Mines, and of course Morarji Desai had become Prime Minister. In addition, there was the new Home Minister Charan Singh, a Hindu Jat follower of the proselytizing Arya Samaj. Charan Singh could understand a political alliance with Sikhs and Muslims but did not necessarily approve of them, considering both betrayers of Hinduism. Charan Singh's core support came from the Hindu Jats of Haryana and the 'backward castes' of Uttar Pradesh, and while his politics were generally moderate, his personal prejudices were not. His tolerance of the Akalis in the Cabinet did not extend to handing over Chandigarh to them.

Now that they were in power, the Akalis found it a little difficult to start a movement against themselves. But they went through the process of endorsement of the Anandpur Sahib resolution at an All-India conference of the party. On 28 and 29 October 1978 in Ludhiana, the President of the SGPC, Gurcharan Singh Tohra, and Chief Minister Prakash Singh Badal moved the twelve resolutions listing the Akali demands. They simultaneously stressed that the need of the moment was moderation; even Jagdev Singh Talwandi, the Akali President who was to break away to form a more strident Akali Dal in another year, cautioned the militants who had begun urging the start of the next battle against Delhi.

A section of the Akalis, perhaps apprehensive about where the militants would take them, had quietly begun to try to loosen the grip of the religious leaders, and to turn the Akali Dal into a genuine regional party, on the lines of the DMK, rather than keep it constricted to a party of the Sikhs. This was the only way, they felt, that the Akalis could become the natural alternative to the Congress in Punjab, since the Sikh vote, as everyone knew, was simply not large enough to ensure an Akali victory. These politicians used the alliance with Janata to build bridges to other national opposition parties in their attempt to establish the organization firmly in the Indian political spectrum. The hardliners sensed what was happening; and they understood that any dilution in the fundamental character of the party would kill the goal of independence. They had to force the moderates to get back into line. The extremists set up their first pressure group, the Dal Khalsa. Half a dozen of its activists demonstrated in Chandigarh in 1978 in front of the SGPC office where the Working Committee of the Akali Dal was meeting, and presented bangles to the leaders (bangles are a sign of femininity, and in the 'virile' and 'martial' mind of the Khalsa nothing is more contemptible than men behaving like women, the latter being synonymous with weakness). The Dal Khalsa made no secret of the fact that it wanted Khalistan. In April 1979 the Dal Khalsa challenged the Akalis in the SGPC elections, setting up fifteen candidates of its own; it was badly defeated, despite help from some unusual quarters which we shall examine later. Punjab politics took a bad toss when the Janata government in Delhi committed suicide in July 1979. Charan Singh took away a chunk of MPs to form his short-lived and unregretted ministry. Akali leaders fell out over which of the Janata factions to support, and Talwandi broke away to start his own Akali Dal. Like all Akalis drifting away from the mainstream, he chose to woo support the wrong way – by being more strident. And, as usual, it did not work. Talwandi did not go to the extent of demanding independence for the Sikhs. But he, with some others, now began paying homage to a militant who was much younger, much clearer, much more simplistic and much, much more ruthless than any of them. The name of a man who would soon begin sending squads to murder Hindus and Sikh 'traitors' now began to be heard; first with indifference, then with ridicule, then with anger, then with horror, and then with terror. The name was Jarnail Singh Bhindranwale.

11
Jarnail Singh Bhindranwale

'I do not want to rule. I would like Sikhs to rule; rule Delhi, rule the world: *Raj karega Khalsa, baaqi rahe na koe* ... In the next ten years, the Sikhs will get their liberation. That will definitely happen. I do not know if I will be alive to see a new country or not ... I have not started a new country, but that does not mean that I am against it. I am neither for nor against Khalistan. We want to stay in India as equals; it is now for Delhi to decide whether they will force us to take Khalistan or not, whether they will allow us to live with honour or not ... After all, Pakistan *was* created ...'

Men who order the death of other men do not necessarily have guilt or questions in their eyes. Many do so proudly: the judge or the general or the revolutionary. Or the self-appointed prophet. Sant Jarnail Singh Bhindranwale's eyes were smiling. He was obviously basking in the thought of yet another journalist come to pay homage and broadcast his importance. His followers, sitting at his feet, were aglow in the reflected glory; the whole world was coming to their leader. Behind me there was something even more exotic than a print journalist. A large European film crew was waiting to interview this young Sikh leader.

It was a fascinating scene. We were on the roof of one of the numerous buildings that surround the Golden Temple and form the huge complex which was out of the reach of the law of India until the Indian army moved in. The Sikhs would not allow any police or security forces to enter the premises, and the police would not dare go in. It was an independent sanctuary, housing not only the highest of the Sikh clergy but also known criminals who had taken shelter in the name of religion. Arms were stocked in underground vaults, with or without the permission of the Akal Takht, the highest Sikh religious authority. We were sitting with Sant Bhindranwale in the warmth of a pleasant winter sun on a February afternoon, on the roof of the Langar Sri Guru Ram Das Sahib, where the Sant normally spent his daylight hours. On the patchy lawn in front of the building was a disused Indian army field-gun, and Nihangs in different stages of opium intoxication were sprawled on the green. Across the field was a most interesting hoarding. There were caricatures of three evil men torturing the valiant, oppressed Sikhs: the first was a Muslim with a sword, and below him were the dates 1526 (representing the victory of Babar at Panipat) to 1849 (when the Sikh empire fell). The second villain was a Britisher with a gun; the dates said 1849 to 1947. The third had a raised stick and was a Hindu; below the drawing was written 1947, while blank space was left for the second date. (If the hoarding survived the army action, the blank may have been filled in.)

At the four corners and other points on the roof where Sant Bhindranwale sat were gun-toting guards, armed with sophisticated semi-automatics. These extremists periodically exchanged gunfire with the Indian policemen on the roads outside the Golden Temple. Sandbags heightened the siege atmosphere. Bhindranwale himself was armed with a holstered revolver, and there was spare ammunition in the belt. Around him were old men and women either seeking advice in whispers or looking at him in awe. They were all peasants. Some of the old men had become residents of the gurdwara after being thrown out of their homes by sons too impatient to wait for their fathers to die before seizing the family property. Bhindranwale communicated with them easily, talking with hardly a pause, his mouth opening continually to show yellowing teeth. He had a ready answer to every question, an immediate solution to every problem, whether of domestic happiness or religious philosophy. It was a conversation interrupted only by the laughter which followed one of his witticisms – and Bhindranwale provided the cue for laughter by leading it. His face was cunning, and his hands remained hidden under the loose wrap except when they moved swiftly and silently to seize and pocket a monetary gift – a one, five or ten rupee note – from a newly arrived devotee. And this scene was being played out against one of the strangest skylines in the world. The buildings of the city of Amritsar are of an even two-storey height and literally piled against one another; on the roofs, at eye level, stretches an endless crowd of television antennae – a strange cluster against the sky. Here again was visual confirmation of the extraordinary prosperity of Punjab: this was a city of new leisure, new education and increased liquor sales. Those television sets were bringing in ideas along with new forms of entertainment. The pure Khalsa

had survived the Muslim sword and the Hindu banking system. Could
he now escape the Punjabi television programme?

That is not as facetious as it may sound. Sant Bhindranwale himself
had no doubts about what he would do in his theocratic state to the
Sikh who, out of embarrassment or conviction bred by modern learning,
left his sword in the cupboard or styled his hair at the barber's. 'A Sikh,'
he told this author, 'should be a true Sikh. The most important thing
for me is *Amrit Prachar* [the preaching of purity]. If a true Sikh drinks,
he should be burnt alive.' Sant Jarnail Singh Bhindranwale was only
being more honest than, for instance, Jinnah, who never warned the
Muslims that in a theocratic state women could be stoned to death on
suspicion of adultery, as happened in Pakistan in 1983 and 1984, or
that men would be publicly flogged for drinking alcohol. Bhindranwale
had no qualms about administering his kind of justice: 'Those who commit
evil should be brought to justice. And evil is not what is imagined by
the individual but as described by the Guru Granth Sahib.' With, of course,
Bhindranwale as the unchallenged interpreter.

Bhindranwale was clear about what the Sikh must be. The Sikh was
pure; purity was his biggest asset, and it had to be preserved at any cost.
How was the Sikh more pure than the Hindu or the Muslim? Simple.
The Sikh was the only human being who kept his form precisely as God
had created it. The Hindus cut their hair, thereby touching something
that had been intended by God to grow to its natural length. The Muslims
snipped off something a little more painful when they were circumcised.
The Sikhs were the only ones, therefore, who left everything in the way
nature had intended. One was tempted to suggest that, according to this
very interesting theory, the nine Gurus before Gobind Singh were impure,
since they were not Khalsa and had obviously cut their hair at some
point; it was only Guru Gobind, two hundred years after Nanak, who
created this 'pure' Khalsa identity. However, the sight of rapid-fire, semi-
automatic guns in the hands of religious fanatics guarding the person,
pride and ideology of Bhindranwale tended to dampen any enthusiasm
for debate.

It did not take very long to realize that Sant Bhindranwale's intellectual
qualities were a trifle limited; when he was not sounding foolish, he
sounded ludicrous. According to Bhindranwale, the Hindu and the Muslim
were only disfigured Sikhs. Every individual man, he said, was born a
Sikh; he might then become a Hindu by cutting his hair or a Muslim
by circumcision. Bhindranwale also had his own special brand of history

of religions: 'There have been 300 million gods [*devtas*], 90 million goddesses [*devis*], 125,000 prophets, 64 yogins, and ten Gurus. All of them had long hair.' In other words, they were all true Sikhs. However, he was willing to co-exist with the other religions of the twentieth century, but on one condition – that everyone else should stop smoking (tobacco is banned by Sikh tradition). 'My work,' said Bhindranwale, 'is Gurbani reading, preaching purity, and saving people from intoxicants. However, I believe that a Hindu should be a true Hindu. What are the characteristics of a true Hindu? *Choti* [tuft of hair on the head], *topi* [cap], *dhoti*, twelve *tilaks* [caste marks] on the forehead, nose, chin, chest, armpits, cheeks, neck and top of the skull; the Hindu should wear nine threads and be a worshipper of Shiva's phallus. And the Hindu should not use tobacco. That Hindu is our brother. The Muslim should be a true Mussalman. He should accept that Allah is great and the Prophet is His messenger [incidentally, Bhindranwale, in his efforts to impress by reciting verses from the Quran, spoke complete undiluted rubbish instead of Arabic, till it seemed to the author like an extract from a bad comic show]. If the Muslim can recite his verses, pray five times a day, believe in Muhammad and not use tobacco, he is my friend.'

This man, around thirty-five years old when this conversation took place, was the Ayatollah Khomeini cum Jinnah of the secessionist movement in Punjab. He was born in a Jat Sikh family in Rode, a fairly large village with a population of about 8,000. Jarnail Singh was the youngest of the seven sons of Joginder Singh (from two wives) One brother was in the army, another was a teacher in a government school; the others worked on the forty acres that the father left them. There was a gurdwara very near Jarnail Singh's house and he was attracted to religion from a very early age. After class six, he went to serve in the religious order of the Damdama Saheb Taksal, begun by Baba Deep Singh. The twelfth Sant of this order was Sundar Singh from the village of Bhindranwalan, and it was after him that the Sants began to be given the honorific 'Bhindranwale' (of Bhindran). The fourteenth Sant of the order was Sant Kartar Singh who obviously instilled in his disciples a strong commitment to the idea of an independent Sikh nation. Kartar Singh's son, Bhai Amrik Singh, became the President of the All-India Sikh Students' Federation, which was banned in 1984 for secessionist activities. Bhai Amrik Singh was, in fact, expecting to be nominated Sant of the order after his father's death, but that prized post was to go to a favoured disciple rather than the son. On 3 August 1977, Sant Kartar Singh met with an accident which led to a head injury. Rather than allow the doctors to cut his hair so that the necessary operation could be performed, Sant Kartar Singh preferred to die with his Khalsa purity intact, and passed away at Brown Hospital, Ludhiana, on 16 August 1977. The successor named was Jarnail Singh, then only in his late twenties. Sant Jarnail Singh Bhindranwale took over the headquarters of the order, the Gurdwara Gurudarshan Prakash, at Chowk Mehta, about forty kilometres from Amritsar.

In July of the same year, Dr Jagjit Singh Chauhan, who had launched his Khalistan movement abroad, returned to India. No one took him seriously. In October, Chauhan helped organize the Dal Khalsa with a person named Harsimran Singh as the President. It hardly mattered that no one knew who this Harsimran Singh was; it was still a 'crazy' idea. The Dal Khalsa announced a two-point programme: to create Khalistan, and to make the Sikhs more conscious of their faith (the same old fear). In 1979, the Dal Khalsa, with the help of Bhindranwale, contested the Sikh religious elections to the SGPC against the Akalis. Bhai Amrik Singh stood from the Beas constituency but was badly trounced by the Akali candidate, Jiwan Singh Umramangal. The Congress did not put up any candidates, but its leader in Punjab, Giani Zail Singh, tried to embarrass the Akalis by financing and propping up the extremists who had their own grievances against the Akalis. In fact, in the initial days, it was Mrs Gandhi's Congress (Indira) which promoted Bhindranwale. Both the leader and the country had to pay a heavy price for this.

On 12 November 1979 Jagjit Singh Chauhan installed a small toy transmitter in the Golden Temple; recitations of the Granth Sahib over this began on 2 March 1980. This gesture blossomed into the demand for a permanent radio station to broadcast religious hymns. Once again, it was a double-edged idea: who could prevent a call to independence from such a radio station once it had been installed? And the priests surely did not need a radio station simply for extra decibels; there was enough amplification through the microphones. In March 1980, Chauhan hoisted the flag of Khalistan at Gurdwara Kesgarh Sahib in the historic city of Anandpur. By now he had found another 'Khalistani'. Balbir Singh Sandhu, a failed schoolteacher and failed journalist, in bad financial straits, had been introduced to Chauhan at a coffee-house in Jullundur, and joined the Khalistan movement. He had first come to the notice of the authorities when he broadcast a message over the toy radio at the Golden Temple. Chauhan appointed Sandhu the Secretary-General of the National Council of Khalistan. On 12 April an eleven-member Council

was announced. The next day Sandhu released stamps and passports
in the name of Khalistan. It was all still fun. One of the first journalists
to break the story at the national level was a correspondent of *Sunday*,
Madhu Jain, who still preserves as a memento the Khalistani passport
issued in her name by Sandhu. (Printed in Canada, it is a good-looking
document.)

On 8 June 1980, Sandhu told the Press that by 16 June the government
of Khalistan would be proclaimed from the Akal Takht at the Golden
Temple, while Chauhan (who had discreetly left the country by then)
would announce his Cabinet from abroad. Sandhu appealed to all
'freedom-loving' countries to recognize the 'government of Khalistan',
and warned the government of India not to use force against 'Khalistan'
or the new nation would appeal to both the superpowers to come to
its aid. On 16 June Dr Chauhan, now in Britain, solemnly made himself
President of Khalistan. He told journalists that he would soon open con-
sulates in London and some other European capitals. He said he was
discussing with Washington the prospects of setting up a government
in exile in the USA, and had asked for US military training for a
10,000-strong army. In India, on 15 August, Independence Day, a procession was taken out by the Khalistanis in Amritsar. By May 1981
Chauhan began claiming that the demand for Khalistan had received
the undeclared support of the Akal Takht and the SGPC, and therefore
of the Akali Dal. This seemed a valid claim when on 12 July 1981
Gurcharan Singh Tohra, the President of the SGPC, chaired a meeting
of the Akali Dal in New York which passed the resolution that the Sikhs
were a separate *qaum* and that steps should be taken to acquire associate
status with the United Nations, on the model of the Palestine Liberation
Organization. But in interviews given separately to the media, Tohra
dissociated himself from the Khalistan idea, and till the moment of writing,
neither the Akali Dal nor the SGPC nor the Akal Takht has formally
supported secession.

On the other hand, a number of organizations have done so, including
the All-India Sikh Students' Federation, which claimed to be the student
wing of the Akali Dal. The Dal Khalsa had been formed in June 1978
by merging elements from the Youth Akali Dal, the Sikh Young Association, the Sikh Naujawan Sabha, the Naujawan Akali Dal, etc. At the
54th Sikh Education Conference, organized by the Chief Khalsa Dewan
on 13 March 1981, a formal resolution was proposed, lustily cheered
and passed, under the chairmanship of another Sikh US national, Ganga

Singh Dhillon, demanding United Nations membership for 'Khalistan'. (The organizers were a bit embarrassed by this.)

The Dal Khalsa brought the Khalistan demand dramatic national attention when it hijacked an Indian Airlines Boeing 737, with 107 passengers, on its flight from Delhi to Srinagar, and took it to Pakistan. The hijackers were arrested in Lahore and the passengers released, but the point had been made. In retaliation the Punjab police raided the Dal Khalsa office in Chandigarh. Some of the secessionists escaped to the Golden Temple to avoid arrest. Sandhu, for instance, went to stay in Room Number 25 of Guru Nanak Niwas. And the Sikh religious leaders would not allow the police to enter the Golden Temple on the excuse that it was too holy to be desecrated by the filthy boots of the forces of law and order, though the Golden Temple did not seem to lose any of its sanctity, in Akali eyes, when harbouring murderers and wanted criminals.

By the last quarter of 1981, the extremists had turned their violent attention to ordinary citizens as the programme to clear the non-Sikhs out of Punjab began. By now they had infiltrated the police force, and friendly Sikh policemen would often turn the other way while pre-planned murders were committed. On 20 September at Jullundur, on the next day at Taran Taran, and on 16 November at Kapurthala, extremists shot four people dead. According to a secret Home Ministry document, 'the clue to the identity of the culprits also came from this sensational crime ... it was found that [the bullets] bore the inscription "REM-UMC-38". This ammunition was not available in India [where] .38 revolvers were being used by police and Air Force only. Inquiries made revealed that this ammunition had never been imported by Air Force or police. Thus, the police came to the conclusion that this was smuggled ammunition ... interrogation of smugglers of arms and ammunition was held and ultimately it led to the disclosure of the identity of culprits in a statement in [the] second week of November 1981 ... Unfortunately, the culprits were found [to have been] assisted by three head constables of police: namely, Sewa Singh, Gurnam Singh and Amarjit Singh of district Faridkot. H.C. [Head Constable] Gurnam Singh is a cousin of Bhai Amrik Singh, president, All-India Sikh Students' Federation, and a close associate of Sant Jarnail Singh Bhindranwale.'

The network was spreading, and the leader was getting established: Sant Jarnail Singh Bhindranwale. The Sant with a gun in his hand and a sermon on his lips had simultaneously launched his religious inquisition.

His first target was neither Hindus nor the government of India, but the 'deviant' Sikhs, the 'betrayers'. At the top of the list were the 'false' Nirankaris (as opposed to the 'true' Nirankaris).

God, preached Dyal Das in the middle of the nineteenth century, was formless (*nirankar*), and hence there could be no idol or image of God. He added that the veneration of saints was equally meaningless. Das, born in a Hindu merchant family from Peshawar, called himself 'the True Guru'. He died in 1855 and his sect of Nirankaris became the most prominent of the Hindu–Sikh midway orders. In the 1891 census, 38,907 persons said they were Hindu–Nirankaris and 11,817 said they were Sikh–Nirankaris. Understandably, the Nirankaris angered both the Hindu and the Sikh clergy. The Akalis respect Baba Dyal, because they believe that he was one of those reformers who helped save Sikhism from Hindus, even though Baba Dyal laid more stress on the Guru Granth Sahib than on the ten Gurus. According to *Genetics of the Sikh–Nirankari Tussle*, a pamphlet published by the SGPC and written by Bhai Hari Singh Shergill, editor of the *Punjabi Samachar*, 'Baba Dyal condemned and discarded Brahminic rituals ... [his] movement was aimed at restoring Sikh faith back to its original pristine form'. The Akali anger was directed against a deviant sect, begun a little before partition by Buta Singh, an employee of the Nirankar Darbar, who according to the booklet 'took to drinking and other allied social evils'.

The allied social evils were mentioned: 'He was a meat-eater cum wine addict and licentious freelancer in sex.' The booklet provides a few instances of alleged freelancing, and claims that Buta Singh died of syphilis in Murree, now in Pakistan, in 1943. His successor Avtar Singh apparently also specialized in 'allied social evils' including freelancing. These two claimed prophethood in direct succession to a most universal lineage: Adam, Noah, Rama, Moses, John the Baptist, Christ, Paul, Muhammad, Nanak, Gobind Singh, and Baba Dyal, up to Gurbachan Singh (the successor and son of Avtar Singh). Later, Gurbachan Singh denied any such claims to prophethood. Be that as it may, the Akalis saw sinister designs behind this deviant sect. According to the SGPC booklet, it was being deliberately encouraged by the government of India, which had begun in Sardar Patel's time as Home Minister to pollute the pure Khalsa by encouraging them to eat meat, drink liquor and be merry with women, 'thereby ... to demolish the image, capacity and competence of the Sikh Panth's mouthpiece, the Shiromani Akali Dal'. The SGPC booklet explained the true role of the Akali Dal: '*Having missed the bus in 1946–7* [author's italics] the Dal has continued to rightly clamour for restoring and rehabilitating the community's historic independent status in the aforesaid aspects.' The Akalis accuse the government in Delhi of spending 'crores' to support this Nirankari sect. They see the Nirankaris as yet another element in the 'Hindu conspiracy' to destroy the separate identity of Sikhism, and thereby prevent the emergence of a true Khalsa Raj.

A 'White Paper' issued by the SGPC reflects the Sikh anger: 'The main thrust and the real salience of this movement is anti-Sikhism, and its permissiveness and promiscuity is secondary. Its methodology is denigration and coarse ridicule of Sikh doctrines and practices and malicious outraging of Sikh religious sentiments and insulting Sikh religious beliefs. Its dynamism is politics, promoted and prompted by political power that aims at degrading and demoralizing the Sikh people permanently, to deprive them of the control of their own history and their spiritual potential and thus reducing them into secondary citizens and camp-followers, so as, eventually, to divest them of their living separateness, shrinking them into a footnote in history.'

Jarnail Singh Bhindranwale refused to become a footnote so easily. On 13 April 1978, on Baisakhi, sacred to the Sikhs because the Khalsa were ordained on that day, he led a demonstration against a conference of the Nirankaris which was taking place at Amritsar. The Nirankaris were prepared: in the resulting clash, thirteen pro-Bhindranwale Sikhs were killed, along with three Nirankaris and two passers-by. It made Bhindranwale's reputation. He now launched a series of vituperative public attacks on the Nirankaris and their 'protectors', the Hindus. On 24 April 1980, the chief of the Nirankaris, Baba Gurbachan Singh, was murdered in Delhi: and suddenly Bhindranwale was in every national headline when the Central Bureau of Investigation (CBI) put his name in the First Information Report, charging him with 'hatching the conspiracy for the murder'. But strangely, although Bhindranwale was moving around freely, he was never arrested in that case. Giani Zail Singh, incidentally, was the Home Minister of India.

Bhindranwale used his unspoken immunity to quickly build up his following. He toured the villages and set up cells. On 31 May 1981, he led a procession in Amritsar, demanding a ban, in this 'holy city of the Sikhs', on the sale of tobacco and cigarettes. The processionists showed their Khalsa fervour by burning a few cigarette shops. Sabotage of rail tracks also started; in September 1981, four such incidents were reported. On the other side, the Hindu reaction to this rising Sikh militancy had begun. Once again, Hindus told the census-takers of 1981 that Hindi, not Punjabi, was their mother tongue. One of the most important Hindu leaders was an Arya Samaji politician and newspaper owner cum editor, Lala Jagat Narain. On 9 September 1981, while the Lala was travelling in his Ambassador car on the Grand Trunk Road (now renamed the Sher Shah Suri Marg), Sikh extremists shot him dead. Among the accused, once again, was Bhindranwale. The police could not afford a repetition of their past leniency; Bhindranwale was asked to give himself up. He turned his surrender into a mammoth public show, doing it in front of an organized crowd of more than 200,000 Sikhs. The police, once again, chose not to find any evidence against him. Bhindranwale returned from jail a bigger hero.

In neighbouring Haryana, angry at the murder of Lala Jagat Narain, some Hindus desecrated the Granth Sahib. Bhindranwale's faction publicly threatened to destroy the Indian Constitution if this was ever repeated. And now young leaders like Harminder Singh Sandhu, general secretary of the All-India Sikh Students' Federation, threatened that Sikhs would not hesitate to shed blood if anything happened to Bhindranwale. Manjit Singh, brother of Bhai Amrik Singh, threatened to kill the children of the Punjab Chief Minister Darbara Singh and the BJP leader Atal Behari Vajpayee if Bhindranwale was touched. (Vajpayee, incidentally, is a bachelor.) And the president of the Punjab Policemen's Union, Karnail Singh, promised full support to Bhindranwale. The Sant's network was spreading.

The tempo of the violence kept rising. On 18 July 1982, the authorities finally arrested two leaders of the Bhindranwale faction, Bhai Amrik Singh and Baba Thara Singh, the manager of Bhindranwale's headquarters at Chowk Mehta. Bhindranwale now decided that discretion was the better part of valour. He ran away to hide in the Golden Temple – safe from the reach of policemen. Jarnail Singh Bhindranwale did not leave the sanctuary again – until the army brought out his corpse.

The Akalis had become bystanders in all this drama. They did not want to associate with the secessionist cry and the violence of Bhindranwale, but they were terrified of being left behind. If anyone else ever managed to lead a successful Sikh movement, their utility to the community would be destroyed. Nor could they rule out the possibility that the Congress (Indira) leaders were playing a double game. Supposing the Congress government negotiated with Bhindranwale and 'conceded' a few of his demands: where would the Akalis be then? It was, as events have proved, a tragic case of weak governance and mischievous response which stoked a fire that soon went out of control.

The extremists had stolen a march by starting an agitation without asking the Akalis for permission or even co-operation. However, the Akalis refused to take the option of grand gestures like demanding secession. When on 12 and 15 August 1981, a general secretary and MLA of the Akali Dal, Sukhjinder Singh, asked for a referendum in Punjab on the Khalistan issue, the party forced him to resign. The Akalis had three options open to them. The first was to work closely with the extremists; this was advocated by SGPC President, Gurcharan Singh Tohra. On the other hand, the former Chief Minister, Prakash Singh Badal, continued his silent efforts to take the party gradually away from the militant theocrats, completely rejecting Bhindranwale and his ilk. And the President of the Akali Dal, Sant Harchand Singh Longowal, tried to steer a middle course, depending on the issue involved and the political environment in which a decision had to be taken. However, all the leaders were agreed that the party would have to do something if it was not to be totally isolated. They began talking of a 'holy war' to win realization of the demands listed in the Anandpur Sahib resolution.

What were they, specifically? First, Chandigarh must come to Punjab, without any territorial compensation to Haryana. Second, Punjabi-speaking areas (parts of the districts of Fazilka and Abohar) left outside Punjab should be brought into the state. Third, the control of the Punjab irrigation headworks should be in the hands of the Punjab government, as should be the management of the Bhakra–Nangal dam. Fourth, Punjab, being a riparian state, must be allowed much more than the 24-per-cent share of the waters it gets (the rest went to non-riparian states like Haryana and Rajasthan). Fifth, there should be greater industrialization through a larger investment of central funds in Punjab. Sixth, the Centre, accepting the principle of genuine federalism, must surrender some of the power it had usurped from the states. Seventh, army recruitment should be on merit, not population percentage. Eighth, Sikh farmers in the Terai region of Uttar Pradesh should not face any harassment. Then there were the religious demands: the installation of a radio station to relay hymns from the Golden Temple; election to the managements of all gurdwaras in the country; and a ban on the sale of tobacco and liquor around the Golden Temple area – that is, in the precincts of the walled part of Amritsar. These demands were presented in 1981.

In the autumn of 1982, the government of India staged, at a prohibitive cost, the Asian Games. Such was the paranoia of a frightened Delhi that special security measures were mounted to prevent any sabotage by Sikh extremists. These measures included arbitrary body searches of Sikhs. Not even senior ex-servicemen (including generals) were exempt. Calling this the ultimate humiliation, the Akalis started a 'holy war' to achieve their demands. It was quite a while later, more than a year in fact, that the Akalis got a brainwave and added one more demand to their list.

Article 25 of the Constitution of India guarantees the fundamental right of every Indian to freedom of religion: 'Subject to public order, morality and health and to the other provisions of this Part, all persons are equally entitled to freedom of conscience and the right freely to profess, practise and propagate religion.' A second clause said: 'Nothing in this article shall affect the operation of any existing law or prevent the State from making any law (a) regulating or restricting any economic, financial, political or other secular activity which may be associated with religious practice; (b) providing for social welfare and reform or throwing open of Hindu religious institutions of a public character to all classes and sections of Hindus.' Two explanations followed. First, 'The wearing and carrying of kirpans shall be deemed to be included in the profession of the Sikh religion.' Second, 'In sub-clause (b) of clause (2), the reference to Hindus shall be construed as including a reference to persons professing the Sikh, Jaina or Buddhist religion, and the reference to Hindu religious institutions shall be construed accordingly.'

Red rag. To the Akali Dal, which was formed in 1920 precisely to rescue the Sikh faith and identity, the inclusion of the Sikh in the 'classes and sections of Hindus' was nothing short of sacrilege. The 'holy war' was intensified, and senior Akali leaders publicly burnt Article 25 of the Constitution and went to jail in March 1984. But the surprise was not that the Akalis were raising demands, but that there had not as yet been any solution to the Akali–Delhi confrontation. What the moderate Akalis really wanted was a 'victory' over Delhi which would enable them to take the initiative away from the extremists by restoring their credibility as 'champions of the Sikhs'. Even a blind government in Delhi could have seen that and offered a way out, as Nehru did so often when dealing with Master Tara Singh and Sant Fateh Singh. But instead of healing the wound, the government allowed it to become septic.

The truth was that, at one time or another, a solution had been worked out to each one of the Akali demands. And the moderate Akalis, eager to make matters easier for Delhi, were only too willing to leave the unresolved issues to the discretion of either the Supreme Court or an acceptable third party. The Akalis were as anxious to get off the back of the tiger as anyone else. Whatever may have been their contradictions, whatever their political ploys, they understood that this time around there was a dangerous element to the confrontation, over which they had no control: the violent, well-armed, well-financed secessionists, who were not responsible to majority Sikh opinion or to reason, and were fanatic about their dream.

The government had indicated that it was willing to concede the religious demands. There remained the political side. The biggest issue was Chandigarh. But Mrs Gandhi herself, as early as 1970, had categorically awarded Chandigarh to Punjab. As far as Fazilka and Abohar were concerned, to transfer them to Haryana a corridor ten miles long and four miles wide would have to be created, since the areas were not even contiguous to Haryana. They could easily be left in Punjab. The Akalis proposed a way out of the boundaries, headworks and water-distribution impasses by suggesting third-party arbitration. As for Centre–State relations, Delhi had appointed a commission to examine the matter. Army recruitment and the problems of the Terai region were not important enough to become stumbling-blocks. As for Article 25, the government was willing to let a panel of judges consider the proposed amendment. Then why was there no settlement? The answer did not lie only in intransigence, of which, of course, we had ample evidence. It also lay in a new, and very untypical, policy that influenced Congress (Indira) decision-making in the post-1980 spell of Mrs Indira Gandhi's rule.

A feeling had begun to grow, towards the end of the seventies, that since independence the minorities had been pampered at the cost of the Hindu majority. The charge of appeasement for electoral gain was brought particularly against the Congress, which had always sought and got the vote of the minorities. Nehru, of course, was the arch villain of this 'plot', but his daughter was held no less guilty. The highly publicized conversions to Islam of a few hundred untouchables in the Tamil Nadu village of Meenakshipuram in 1981 was propagated as the final straw. Hindu revivalists began saying that in Hindu-majority India it was Hinduism, not Islam, that was now in danger. Organizations like the Vishwa Hindu Parishad and Virat Hindu Sammelan (headed by the descendant of Gulab Singh Dogra, Karan Singh) doubled and redoubled their efforts to 'save Hinduism'. And such was the impact that even Mrs Gandhi began to believe that there was bound to be a 'Hindu backlash' against any further 'pampering' of the minorities. Far from challenging such revivalism, she decided to ride it as far as it would take her. And so, there was not even the minor consolation of words of sympathy from Mrs Gandhi after Moradabad saw in 1981 one of the worst instances of violence against Muslims in independent India. The Hindu revivalists reached their high point when in 1983 they organized cross-country marches to 'Save Hinduism'.

Mrs Gandhi often displayed an anti-minority stance. She kept hinting that the Muslims in India had still not given up their destructive games; there was always talk of a 'foreign conspiracy' behind any problem related to Muslims. The same suspicions were continually aroused about the Sikhs, and with the latter it became, to an extent, a self-fulfilling prophecy. Mrs Gandhi did not, therefore, have a Punjab policy; she had a minorities policy which she extended to the two minority states: Punjab, and Jammu and Kashmir. The Sikhs, and particularly the Akalis, were painted in the speeches made by her and her son, Rajiv Gandhi, as potential secessionists. And the Muslims of Jammu and Kashmir, along with their leader Dr Farooq Abdullah, also had to face blatant accusations of treachery, and worse. It was a radical departure from traditional Congress behaviour. In the past, if and when a section of the Sikhs or the Muslims tended to make anti-patriotic noises, it used to be deliberately played down by the Centre, while those Sikh and Muslim leaders who showed faith in the Constitution of India were given prominence. Now we had just the opposite scenario. While it was the National Conference leader Dr Farooq Abdullah who kept insisting every minute that he was an Indian first and last, and that Kashmir was an integral part of India, it was Indira and Rajiv Gandhi who kept making references, some snide, some open, to the quality of Farooq Abdullah's patriotism. It was a disastrous exercise in a centrifugal internal policy, born out of a misinterpretation of the popular Hindu mood of North India.

And so in Punjab, instead of co-operating with the Akalis to isolate the Sikh extremists, Delhi wittingly or unwittingly played into their hands. Fanatic Hindu organizations were encouraged to 'teach the Sikhs a lesson'. A Hindu Frankenstein, who would not listen when Delhi eventually began seeking peace, was encouraged: the Hindu Suraksha Samiti, or Hindu Safety Organization, led by Pawan Sharma, rose to the 'defence' of Hindus. The price which this Frankenstein extracted became evident in February 1984, when after successful private negotiations the government was ready to sign a settlement with the Akalis at a formal tripartite meeting

JARNAIL SINGH BHINDRANWALE

which included the opposition parties. On the very day of this meeting the chance of peace was sabotaged by the Samiti, which had become nervous about what the Akali–Congress deal might mean for it. While the talks were in progress, the Hindu Suraksha Samiti indulged in day-long violence against the Sikhs in Haryana, humiliating, terrorizing, injuring and killing innocent isolated Sikhs. The talks collapsed. And Bhindranwale, sitting in the comfort of the Golden Temple, was particularly delighted. Not only had Hindus destroyed the chance of a settlement, but he had more fodder for his anti-Hindu communalism.

But the most unique thing about the long tale of terror in the Punjab from 1981 to June 1984 was that, despite all this provocation and opportunity, despite all the engineered tension and suspicion, there was no outbreak of mass mayhem and rioting on the 1947 pattern. It is the age of the semi-automatic now, not the sword, and any such riots would have led to massacres. The Sikh masses did not respond to Bhindranwale's efforts to create anti-Hindu riots. The Akalis, caught in a cleft stick remained unsure about when to break publicly and openly with Bhindranwale. By May 1984 they were edging in that direction. The Akal Takht, the highest authority of the Sikh faith, began to prepare charges against Bhindranwale. The secessionist Sant responded by saying that he would not listen to the Akal Takht; the Akal Takht warned that never in the history of Sikhism had it been disobeyed, and it would not tolerate disobedience now.

Bhindranwale's problem was not only an uncertain Akali leadership, but also the fact that a large majority of the Sikhs were simply not interested in breaking India's unity. It was not only the urban or the Mazhabi Sikhs who felt this way, but also the Khalsa Jats, including most of Bhindranwale's neighbours in Rode, his birthplace. When I visited the village in February 1984, the young man I spoke to reacted sharply when I suggested that perhaps Rode should get ready to enjoy celebrity status as the new spiritual capital of Khalistan. 'Where do you stay?' he asked me. 'In Calcutta,' I replied. 'Could you rent me a room in Calcutta?' he asked. I asked why. 'To live in, if Khalistan ever becomes a reality,' he said. 'Who,' he asked, 'would want to live in a country ruled by this mad Sant?' How many people changed such views after the army action in the Golden Temple three months later? How many of those who spurned the living Bhindranwale have become followers of the dead secessionist? The question is unanswered.

A sharp man sitting on a roof, dreaming of becoming the preacher/

warrior/king, talking already as a head of state, saying that if the government of India, or its Prime Minister Mrs Gandhi, wanted to talk to him,
they could come to the Golden Temple, he would not go to Delhi: was
his death a victory?

Was he afraid of anything? I had asked. Anything, including death?
'I am not afraid of death,' he had answered. 'A Sikh cannot be afraid
of death; if he is afraid, he is not a Sikh.' There was the glow of adulation
on the surrounding faces, while the Sant looked most pleased with his
impromptu proverb.

The many threads of conviction, emotion, honour, identity, fear,
growth, prosperity, dependence, opportunism, chicanery, greed, nobility,
helplessness, fanaticism, ambition, these will knot and purl as Punjab goes
through yet another upheaval. The quadrangular war between a volatile,
if divided, Sikh majority, a determined secessionist, a hardened Hindu
and an elected government influenced by many variables, will test secular,
democratic India as never before. If India proves larger than the petty
ambitions of passing leaders, Sant Jarnail Singh Bhindranwale will lose.

12
Punjab: Death of a General

Sikh parents, like other Indians, name their children after their ambitions. Jarnail Singh's parents obviously wanted him to grow up to lead an army: 'Jarnail' is the Punjabi corruption of 'General'. Jarnail Singh had a martial bent, but he decided to use it in the service of religion. In fact, it was his brother who joined the Indian army as a jawan and by 1984 had become a subahdar (a non-commissioned officer). In the first week of June the brothers were on opposite sides of a vital war. After its murderous battle with the extremists inside the Golden Temple, when the Indian army pulled out the corpses of the extremists to burn them on a pyre, the body of Sant Jarnail Singh Bhindranwale was identified by his brother.

All through April, May and June of that year the violence in Punjab had been escalating. Journalists on night duty used to talk cynically about the Vietnam syndrome: you could always depend on a few casualties in Punjab to make up your lead story on a dull day. A mood of helplessness began to take hold of the country as minority fascism not only intensified but seemed to be achieving results. The secessionists began to imagine that dreams were in fact coming true. From London Dr Jagjit Singh Chauhan, self-styled President of Khalistan, sent word to Bhindranwale that the time had come to announce a provisional government of Khalistan; the response was positive. Dr Chauhan revealed this himself in an interview to Seema Mustafa which was published in *The Telegraph* on 19 June. The idea was to nominate a Parliament which would assemble in the Golden Temple, and form a government which would ask the Sikhs to give it both their loyalty and their taxes. In the meanwhile, Chauhan would open a Khalistan House in London and appeal to the nations of the world to 'recognize' Khalistan (government circles in New Delhi believed that a handful of countries was, in fact, ready to do that).

The Akalis, eager as usual to hang on to the coat-tails of any euphoric leader, decided to take their 'holy war' a notch higher. For more than a year they had been secretly meeting with Mrs Gandhi's government in an effort to work out a compromise, but distrust more than anything else killed the chances of success. Both sides accused each other of ambivalence and dishonesty. The hope of a negotiated settlement seemed lost. The Akalis declared that from 3 June, the birthday of Guru Arjun, they would prevent any transfer of foodgrains from Punjab to the rest of India, and ask the Sikhs to stop payment of all taxes.

The drama was clearly heading for some kind of denouement. A flashpoint was reached on 1 June when an exchange of gunfire between Bhindranwale's heavily armed men, from their vantage on the roofs of the buildings on the periphery of the Golden Temple complex, and the police forces stationed outside, left eleven people dead. The level of violence did not ease the next day: in cities across Punjab, terrorism killed twelve people. In a typical case, in Hoshiarpur, Om Prakash Bagga, a former MLA, aged forty-nine was gunned down by three terrorists riding a scooter. That evening a sudden announcement was made that the Prime Minister, Mrs Indira Gandhi, would make a special broadcast to the nation. It was at this point, for the first time, that the realization came: the unthinkable might happen – the army might be told to storm the Golden Temple complex.

The last time an army had entered the sanctum sanctorum of the Sikhs was when Ahmed Shah Abdali, angered by repeated raids on his loot-laden caravans returning to Afghanistan, ordered his men to blow up the Golden Temple in revenge. But that was more than two hundred years ago. The Golden Temple and its adjacent buildings were the most sacred Sikh shrines. Any damage to places like the Golden Temple, whose foundation had been laid by Guru Arjun, or the Akal Takht, built by Guru Hari Kishen, was bound to anger every Sikh, including those who had no sympathy for extremists. On the other hand, the secessionists were, basically, taking full advantage of the decency of others. Bhindranwale and his men had, with total impunity, turned the shrines into a fort. The law of India did not run here. Each day arms and instructions would be sent out from the Golden Temple to terrorists, to kill a few more Hindus. And the 'moderate' Akali leaders, like Tohra or Longowal or Badal, knew precisely what was going on but did not challenge it. Everyone knew that the situation had reached a point where only the army could take the extremists on. And Bhindranwale was confident that Mrs Gandhi would never dare send in the army. Mrs Gandhi did dare, as she had always done in her life.

On Saturday evening, 2 June, Mrs Gandhi came on national television to talk about Punjab. Her speech was preceded by two songs: the moving lyric written by Sir Muhammad Iqbal in the second decade of this century, when he still believed in a secular united India, *'Saare jahan se acha Hindustan hamara'* ('Hindustan is the most beautiful country in the world') and the *Saraswati Vandana* (the prayer to the Goddess Saraswati). Mrs Gandhi told the nation that the government had accepted most of the Akalis' demands and that agreement had not been possible only because they kept raising fresh ones. She charged that extremists seemed to be taking the Akali decisions now, and as an example she cited the non-co-operation movement scheduled to start the next day. Mrs Gandhi did not say that she had ordered the army to move into the Golden Temple, but this was now obvious. The man put in operational charge of the troops who would storm the Golden Temple was himself a Sikh, a war hero of 1965 and 1971, Lieutenant-General Ranjit Singh Dayal, Chief of Staff of the Western Command. On that very day he was also made adviser (security) to the Governor of Punjab, B. D. Pande.

The army had been preparing for such an eventuality: troops had already been placed in sensitive areas of Punjab on the thin excuse that, with the Border Security Force occupied against the Sikh extremists, the army would have to take on the anti-smuggling and security role usually performed by the BSF. Two infantry divisions from Meerut and Secunderabad moved into Amritsar. By the time the Prime Minister had finished her speech, they were taking positions around the Golden Temple. As Sunday dawned, everyone knew that the real battle had begun. Bhindranwale, normally ebullient and extrovert, was in a sombre mood that day. Journalists who had gathered in Amritsar to cover the beginning of the Akali non-co-operation movement went, as usual, to meet Bhindranwale. Sondeep Shankar, photographer for *The Telegraph*, who was one of the last outsiders to meet Bhindranwale, recalls: 'He was personally loading rifles and handing them to his followers. He said to us that if the army came in they would take them on.' That night at 9.00 p.m. a thirty-six-hour curfew was imposed all over Punjab. That was the time given to the army to finish those who wanted Khalistan.

All communications to and from Punjab by land, road and air were cut off. Journalists, both local and foreign, were politely told to give their typewriters a rest, and escorted out of Punjab. Generals Dayal and K. Sunderji, with their division and brigade commanders, set up operational headquarters within fifty metres of the main entrance to the Golden

Temple complex. The extremists had built a three-ring defence. On the outer periphery they took control of seventeen civilian houses outside the Temple area, from which to try to prevent the advance of the army. The second line of defence was created on the boundary buildings of the Temple complex: the roof-tops, the clock-tower and watch-towers, and the buildings from which they could control, with gunfire, the large central courtyard which the army would have to cross in order to seize the secessionist control room. Thirdly there was the control room itself, the sacred building of the Akal Takht, where the top leadership and the hard core waited. This was where Bhindranwale, Bhai Amrik Singh and their master strategist, Shahbeg Singh, were. Shahbeg Singh, like Lieutenant-General Dayal, was a war hero. He had retired as a major-general, and had been the brains behind the guerrilla war in Bangladesh in 1971, but had been 'released' from the army on corruption charges, and had now become a devoted Khalistani. (The last straw which made him lose faith in India, he told journalist Tavleen Singh a little before he died, came when he was humiliated on his way to Delhi at the time of the Asian Games in 1982.)

The battle began at 4.45 a.m. on the morning of 4 June; the first exchange of fire lasted five hours. A lull followed. On 5 June, the extremists opened fire first. The army was now beginning to get an idea of how well-armed the extremists were: there was no shortage of ammunition or weaponry. The two sides kept up their fire. At 7.00 p.m. the army decided to end the stalemate by bringing in bigger guns. A 3.7-inch mountain gun was used to blow off the minaret and the water-tank, from where the extremists had been successfully holding up the army. As the Khalistanis fell back in confusion, the soldiers moved quickly to establish a foothold inside the Temple. The task was now to cross the courtyard and take the Akal Takht. There were two problems which made this extremely dangerous: first, the murderous cross-fire which made any soldier a sitting duck, and second, the fact that the army had been given strict instructions that on no condition was it to damage the Golden Temple itself, which was situated in the middle of a pool in the centre of the courtyard. In other words, the army could not return fire freely, or use its heavy guns to blast through. The Indian army, in another display of spectacular discipline and valour, gave up more than two hundred lives but did not disobey orders.

The generals also discovered that the extremists had far more light and medium machine-guns than they had bargained for, and these were being used expertly, with deadly effect. At 10.30 p.m. that night, after having shut off the power, the army's main assault started. The terrorists lit two huge fires by which they could track army movement. The generals then brought up six Vijayanta tanks with blinding lights under whose cover the guards and the commandos began to advance. The soldiers took heavy casualties; they kept asking for fire support, but none came as the generals did not, under any circumstances, want to hit the Golden Temple. One unit of the army took one of the buildings in the periphery and a group of nearly four hundred people who had been trapped in the Temple surrendered – including the two senior Akali leaders, Sant Harchand Singh Longowal and Gurcharan Singh Tohra, and the lady who was in charge of the Babbar Khalsa, Bibi Amarjit Kaur. The surprise surrender was that of the young Harminder Singh Sandhu, secretary of the All-India Sikh Students' Federation.

By the next morning, after continuous battle, the army still had not reached the Akal Takht. It now brought in an armoured personnel carrier; the terrorists replied with anti-tank rockets! No one had imagined that Bhindranwale's men had arms of this level. In the end the army was forced to bring in tanks. It was dawn before the army entered the Akal Takht. Room-to-room fighting continued till noon, while isolated snipers kept up their attack till the next day. On the morning of 7 June, the troops finally managed to penetrate the basement of the Akal Takht. There, along with thirty-five other corpses (including those of Shahbeg Singh and Amrik Singh), was the body of Jarnail Singh Bhindranwale.

There was a sudden lull in the Punjab. All sections of Sikh opinion, however, from the urban sophisticates sipping their expensive Scotch in the bungalows of Delhi to the peasants in the fields, were horrified at what had happened. Even those who had never condoned secession could not get themselves to justify the army action. Sikhs mourned all over the world; Bhindranwale overnight became the hero he had never been when alive. The Hindu reaction was one of satisfaction, if not jubilation. For a week or two it seemed as if Mrs Gandhi had restored the popularity she had enjoyed after the Bangladesh war. Then the mood began cooling on both sides. The government, using all the resources at its command, rebuilt the Akal Takht. There was a foolish attempt to sidetrack the SGPC and put a Nihang leader of substantial girth and lean intelligence, Baba Santa Singh, in charge of the Golden Temple, but luckily wisdom prevailed and eventually the army returned the Temple to the High Priests.

President Zail Singh, who had earned the wrath of the Sikhs because he was the formal head of the government which had ordered the assault on the Golden Temple, rebuilt his bridges and saved himself from excommunication by apologizing to the High Priests for any mistakes he might have committed.

The terrorist violence in Punjab was not completely curbed, but it was no longer on the old scale. By the end of October India had begun to worry about other things. Mrs Gandhi's stock had dipped sharply after the fiasco in Andhra Pradesh where a legitimate government had been dismissed by a partisan governor acting on instructions from Delhi. The country reacted with impressive anger; democracy was obviously safe if people were willing to go on to the streets, face police bullets and die for the restoration of a popular government.

The excitement of elections was now in the air. They were scheduled for the first week of January, 1985. The insatiable opposition parties began their traditional round of pre-election wrangling; then settled on the idea that the best they could offer was a coalition government, and they should prepare the nation for such an eventuality.

If Punjab was mentioned at all, it was only in terms of whether elections were possible in the state or not. By the last week of October, Home Minister Narasimha Rao had begun saying that he saw no reason why elections should not be held in Punjab along with the rest of the country. Mrs Gandhi, however, was a little less optimistic. Addressing a press conference in Orissa on 30 October, at the end of what was clearly an electioneering tour, she said that she was not yet certain if the violence of the Sikh extremists had been controlled sufficiently to permit free and safe polling.

The next day Sikh extremists struck where it hurt the country most.

It is common knowledge that whenever she appeared in public, Mrs Indira Gandhi used to wear a bulletproof vest specially made for her. Her day in Delhi normally began with some time spent with ordinary people who were allowed to enter the compound of her prime-ministerial office-cum-residence, composed of two adjoining bungalows at the corner of Akbar Road and Safdarjang Road. Naturally, all visitors were thoroughly screened and searched for weapons; after Operation Bluestar, security had been further tightened.

On the morning of Wednesday, 31 October, this daily *darshan* was cancelled. The night before, her grandchildren had been involved in a minor accident, and an upset Mrs Gandhi was in no mood for smiles and pleasantries. The extra security force detailed to surround her for this public appearance was consequently withdrawn. That morning Mrs

Gandhi also decided to spend some time in her residential office, and therefore did not think it necessary to wear her bulletproof vest. She had left her living-quarters and was walking towards her office through the compound when two of her security guards, posted in her house for her protection, betrayed that trust and, from point-blank range, using a sten gun and a revolver, put seven bullets into her body before they themselves were shot by other security personnel.

Sub-Inspector Beant Singh and Constable Satwant Singh had taken revenge.

Obviously, the success of this conspiracy also amounted to a total failure of the intelligence services. The two Sikhs were certainly not alone in planning the assassination; that they remained without suspicion in the force deputed to guard the security of the Prime Minister's person indicates both their ability and the negligence of the government.

But that was not the question uppermost in the Indian mind when the news of this crime seeped through the country.

According to some reliable reports, Mrs Gandhi did not survive for very long, although she was operated on at the All-India Institute of Medical Sciences. The most crucial question of course was: who next? The senior leadership of the Congress (Indira) sat down to debate the problem. Rajiv Gandhi, Mrs Gandhi's surviving son and heir apparent, was an obvious claimant. He was not in Delhi that day, but campaigning in the Marxist stronghold of West Bengal where he was drawing substantial crowds. A policeman, receiving the news over the wireless, took a message on a slip of paper to Rajiv Gandhi at Kolaghat in rural Bengal. Mrs Gandhi had met with an accident, the paper read. Rajiv Gandhi must return to Delhi at once.

Her son surely must have suspected the worst, but he took the news calmly. He came back by a special plane. If there was a question mark against his name, it was only on account of his inexperience. Till his younger brother Sanjay had died in an air crash in 1980, Rajiv Gandhi had shown little inclination to heed the siren voice of political power. He was content to earn a comfortable living as an airline pilot. It was only after 1980 that his grooming began. He was only forty. Could he be entrusted with the responsibility of being Prime Minister of this nation of 700 million people?

While the debate went on, the official media of the government of India continued the fiction that Mrs Gandhi was still alive and fighting for her life in the hospital. The news agencies put out that she had passed away.

The newspapers prepared and published special editions. President Ronald Reagan sent his condolence message a full four hours before the government of India acknowledged that the Prime Minister had died. India was playing a one-day cricket match against Pakistan in the neighbouring country that day; a little after lunch the manager of the Indian team, Raj Singh of Dungarpur, tearfully announced that the team could not continue since the Prime Minister had passed away. But for All-India Radio Mrs Gandhi was still alive. By the evening the decision was finally made. Indira Gandhi was dead. Rajiv Gandhi was the next Prime Minister.

Perhaps the senior leaders had no choice. After the shock of the news had been absorbed, the whole country reacted with an anger and outrage rarely seen. *The Telegraph* headline perhaps summed it up most aptly: 'Mrs Gandhi shot dead, Nation wounded'.

From every part of the country there were reports of angry citizens closing down cities to mourn the death of a woman who had clearly become a martyr and could possibly become a goddess. Gradually, the anger began to take a dangerous form. It turned into violence against the Sikhs.

On the day Mrs Gandhi died, the violence was comparatively muted. But the next day, reports began coming of Sikhs celebrating Mrs Gandhi's assassination all over the world. In Britain and the USA, champagne corks had popped in front of television cameras. In Amritsar itself, Sikhs had been seen distributing sweets (just as some Hindus had distributed sweets when the Golden Temple was stormed). And the High Priests did their own bit to insult the Hindus by first condemning the assassins and then withdrawing their condemnation.

The Sikhs who gloried in the death of Mrs Gandhi had forgotten a very simple and very old fact about their existence.

There were not enough of them, and of their small number one-fifth lived outside Punjab. This 20 per cent were scattered in the cities of North India: in Delhi, in particular, but also in Patna, Calcutta, Bhopal, Kanpur, Dehra Dun, and a hundred other places. In addition, they were prosperous. They owned shops and cars. What started as widespread hostility to Sikhs was soon, inevitably, converted into something else. The urban lumpen, the poor, suddenly discovered that they had been given a licence to attack and loot.

When they tasted loot, they began searching for blood. A nightmare descended in Delhi. For the first time since partition, Sikhs became the target of the kind of horrible, unbelievable communal violence that this subcontinent had witnessed in 1947. Sikhs were sought out and burned to death. Children were killed, shops looted, cars burnt, markets destroyed, houses gutted. Trains were stopped, and Sikhs were picked out and murdered by mobs cheering wildly as they indulged in murder and mayhem.

The lumpenproletariat had taken over. The police were either spectators, or in fact participants. There was massacre in East Delhi. Trains kept coming to Delhi railway station, each conveying not passengers but horror stories. It was all here again: 1947. The same sequence: years of provocation by a minority's clergy beginning with little support from its own ranks. A gradual intensifying of the crisis. A nervous majority. Patience being stretched. And suddenly, one day, an event which sparked off majority fascism. If there was one difference between 1984 and 1947, it was that India was not under British rule. There was no third party to make any gifts.

Khalistan would not be as easily achieved as Pakistan, but on 31 October 1984, India witnessed the first battle of the second war for Khalistan. The first war had been fought between Jarnail Singh Bhindranwale and Mrs Indira Gandhi. On 31 October the conflict was handed over to the next generation.

Another chapter in the history of Punjab had come to an end. But the question was, what twist would the story now take? The relationship between the Sikhs and the Hindus had been fundamentally altered; the brotherhood was over. The Sikhs had now become, in every sense, particularly the psychological, a minority in India. The country had a Sikh as its President, Giani Zail Singh; but it would take more than such symbolic gestures to restore the commitment which had made the Sikhs the most valiant defenders of India in 1962, 1965 and 1971. Would a dead Bhindranwale be more powerful than a living one? The dominant section of the Akalis so far had always thought it wiser to reject secessionism; would they now change? Or would the broad majority of the Sikhs accept – as Lieutenant-General Dayal did – that theocratic forces which encouraged violence and secession had to be dealt with in this fashion? Would democracy and secularism still retain their powerful attraction for the Sikh majority? Would the values which had created this unique nation prove more powerful than the strain of a human tragedy? Short questions. Long answers.

PART III

KASHMIR

1
Democracy in Paradise

There are many advertisements for Paradise in the travel brochures of this world. One place which goes a long way towards living up to such a claim is a lovely lake-dotted valley west of the great Himalayas. Five thousand feet above the sea, the vale of Kashmir on the crown of India is surrounded by mountains on all sides: the Himalayas, the north Kashmir range, and the Pir Panjal in the south. While the total area of Kashmir state is much larger, the population is mainly concentrated in this valley, and 90 per cent of it is Muslim. Much prose and poetry, some of it inevitably turgid, has been lavished on this exquisite fairyland, but few have been as evocative as the most famous of all Kashmiris, Jawaharlal Nehru, in his *Autobiography*: 'Like some supremely beautiful woman, whose beauty is almost impersonal and above human desire, such was Kashmir in all its feminine beauty of river and valley and lake and graceful trees. And then another aspect of its magic beauty would come into view, a masculine one, of hard mountains and precipices, and snow-capped peaks and glaciers, and cruel and fierce torrents rushing down to the valleys below. It had a hundred faces and innumerable aspects, ever-changing, sometimes smiling, sometimes sad and full of sorrow ... It was like the face of the beloved that one sees in a dream and that fades away on awakening ...'

Once, the rough and difficult mountain passes provided the only entrance and exit to this valley. Its isolation did not necessarily leave it untouched by the great empires that surrounded it: Delhi to the south, the central Asian kingdoms to the north, the Afghans in the west and the Tibetans and Chinese in the east. But the mountains were good friends and loyal protectors. When one of the terrible line of Tartars, Zulfi Khan, also known as Dulchu, came with his horsemen in the early fourteenth century, he burnt Srinagar and took away enormous booty and 50,000 slaves (as the story goes), only to perish with his cavalry on his way back, in a snowstorm at the Devasar Pass.

In 1846, Kashmir's fortunes became linked to the province across the southern range of Pir Panjal, Jammu. The Dogra kings of Jammu bought Kashmir from the British for Rs 75 lakhs. It was hardly a purchase, more a gift from the British for services rendered by the Dogras in the wars against the Sikhs of Punjab. The kingdom of Jammu and Kashmir remained in Dogra hands for a hundred years, till October 1947. Srinagar in Kashmir became the summer capital, while the city of Jammu was the winter capital. The Dogras opened up the valley by building the Banihal Cart Road and the Jhelum Valley Road.

There was a Hindu majority in Jammu in the south, but overall the Muslims of the kingdom outnumbered the Hindus by three to one. By all the logic of partition, therefore, Kashmir should have gone to Pakistan, a country created in the name of India's Muslims. It did not. Jinnah tried whatever he could. First he tried wooing, both the Hindu Maharaja and the Muslim mass leaders. That failed. Then he sent in raiders to seize Kashmir by force within eight weeks of freedom, and after them regular Pakistani troops. They almost captured Srinagar at one point, but then were pushed back till they were left with a thin slice of the valley in the west and a large tract of the mountainous wasteland in the north, on the borders of Afghanistan and China. Kashmir remains divided today at about the line where the troops stood when the cease-fire in the first Indo-Pakistani war took effect on the last day of 1948. The overwhelming bulk of Kashmiris live in India; Srinagar is their capital. The Pakistani-controlled Kashmir is ruled from the city of Muzaffarabad by a government which labels its territory 'Azad Kashmir' (or 'Free Kashmir').

Two men kept Kashmir within India: two Kashmiris descended from Brahmin families. One, of course, was Jawaharlal Nehru, Prime Minister of India from 15 August 1947 till the day he died, 27 May 1964. The other was Sheikh Mohammad Abdullah, whose family was converted to Islam from Brahminism late in the eighteenth century. Sheikh Abdullah, fondly called *Baba-e-Qaum* ('Father of the Nation') and *Sher-e-Kashmir* ('The Lion of Kashmir'), gave his people self-confidence and an ideology that rescued them from the burden of an enslaved past and brought, for the first time in generations, hope to the land. He often used a line from his favourite poet, Iqbal, to describe his mission: '*Auron ka hai payam, mera payam aur hai*' (in the author's poor translation, this would become: 'Others have their message, my message is different'). In an achievement which the world still finds difficult to comprehend, given the fixed mirrors through which India is constantly viewed, Sheikh Abdullah and the

Kashmiris stayed with India rather than go with Pakistan in 1947. As Sheikh Abdullah said over and over again, he had a religion in common with Jinnah, but a dream in common with Nehru.

These two families, the Nehrus and the Abdullahs, have dominated the politics of India and Kashmir in a way which perhaps cannot be paralleled. The families have been the best of personal friends, and sometimes the worst of political enemies. When they have co-operated, there has been peace; when they have fought, Srinagar has erupted. Both have expressed strong commitment to Indian nationalism, secularism and democracy; and both have fallen prey to prejudices and weaknesses which when translated into the logic of power equations have rocked the nation. Kashmir, said both Sheikh Abdullah and Jawaharlal Nehru in one voice in 1947, had to remain in India because it was the ultimate laboratory in which all the ideas of humanism, democracy and friendship could be tested in the most difficult of conditions. If Muslim Kashmir could live and prosper in secular, socialist India, then there could be no finer argument against the theory which divided this country and created Pakistan.

Jinnah, despite being rebuffed so often by Sheikh Abdullah before partition, never imagined that there would be any problem about Kashmir's accession to Pakistan. After all, the British were sponsoring the division of India solely on the basis of religion. Kashmir was overwhelmingly Muslim; *ergo*, it was a part of Pakistan. Mountbatten, in fact, did his very best to force the Maharaja of Kashmir to accede to Pakistan. The first Home Minister of India, the steel-willed Sardar Patel, was also perfectly willing to grant Kashmir to Pakistan. Nor was there any question of geographical confusion. Not only did Kashmir have a substantial land border with the new country, but most of its essential supplies and services depended on the provinces which would go to Pakistan. There was only one hitch in this seemingly logical scenario.

The Kashmiris did not want to go to Pakistan. They refused to believe in the two-nation theory. Even while Hindus and Muslims were butchering each other on the borders of Kashmir, in Punjab and in the North-West Frontier Province in that extraordinary decade of the 1940s, there was not one case of bigoted murder in the valley of Kashmir. Instead, the Muslims of Kashmir died fighting against the Pakistanis who sent in both their army and their surrogates in a 'holy war' to 'liberate' their Muslim brethren in Kashmir. That is why Sheikh Abdullah could, with some pride, tell an audience of Muslims in Delhi on 20 October 1947, when the refugee camps were full and hearts were empty, 'I do not want that you should follow me or even Maulana Abbul Kalam Azad. But I ask you to follow the lead given by the Holy Prophet which was given to us 1300 years ago. Prophet Muhammad was a benefactor of all, and not Muslims alone . . . You fell a prey to the two-nation theory and hatred preached by some of your leaders. We, the people of Kashmir, resisted this, with the result that we are living in peace and you and thousands of your brethren are undergoing untold misery. My advice to you is, "Live peacefully, and do not be misled by propaganda." '

The Sheikh went with Gandhi and Nehru because of a common vision. But what if the guiding vision in Delhi ever changed? What if nationalism and democracy began to weaken, and reactionary religious forces began to assert themselves? What if the Indian Constitution was destroyed by its protectors? The Union of India was built on a certain ideology which allowed individual freedom while demanding a common commitment to the social philosophy of Mahatma Gandhi. The survival of the Union would also therefore depend on the preservation and strengthening of such values. In other words, the danger to India's unity was as much internal as external. If those in power in Delhi strayed away from the moorings on one excuse or the other, it could be as dangerous as a Pakistani army grabbing a chunk of land and declaring it free from the control of Delhi.

Sheikh Abdullah ruled Kashmir for only six years after independence. In 1953 he was sent to jail while his best friend was Prime Minister in Delhi. Sheikh Abdullah, still committed to the same goal, would return to rule Kashmir for the last seven years of his life, and when he died in 1982 the Indian flag was draped around his body. His son Dr Farooq Abdullah would succeed him, and then win a smashing victory in the elections of 1983 to prove that he had inherited, along with the belief, the votes. In July 1984 Dr Farooq Abdullah would be removed from office by a series of decisions which crushed the spirit of democracy, but were approved by the daughter of Nehru, Mrs Indira Gandhi. Just as in 1953, the people of Kashmir would come out on the streets to protest and die in police firing. Had nothing changed? Or, despite the aberrations of human behaviour, was there yet some hope of the dream of 1947 some day coming true?

2
Kings and Peasants

Hindu belief, expectedly, provides the most exquisite imagery for the origins of Kashmir. The valley was once a beautiful lake, the Sati Sar, inhabited by the snake people, the Nagas, who lived in terror of the demon Jaladeo. In desperation the Nagas went to their guardian, the Nila Naga, who prayed to his father, the sage Kashyap (born from the mind of Brahma, the creator of the universe). The sage went into a long penance for the deliverance of the Nagas. The gods took mercy. The Lord Shiva, his body smeared with ashes, and wearing only a loincloth, came down from his abode on the heights of Mount Kailash and threw his mighty trident into the side of the mountains, ripping open a hole through which the waters of the lake gushed out, draining the land. Shiva's consort Lakshmi then assumed the form of a myna bird and from a great height dropped a pebble on the demon which became embedded in his flesh and then, in a trice, grew to the size of a hill which became known as Hari Parbat. The Hari Parbat is now crowned by a fort built by the Emperor Akbar, and its slopes are strewn with Hindu, Muslim and Sikh shrines.

The land was called, in gratitude to the sage, Kashyapamar, which became gradually corrupted to Kashmir. Kashyap invited the people from the plains in the south to settle in this valley. Science can provide a convenient explanation for all this: an Ice Age lake, an earthquake bursting open a pass in the mountains, a geological upheaval throwing up a hill, etc. However, the mythology is not only more beautiful but the people believe it. Kashmir was one of the great centres of early Hinduism. Situated as it is, it could not but be on the crossroads of the travel of ideas. If Kashmir had been an independent country today, it would have had common borders with India on the south, China in the east, Afghanistan on the north-west, and Pakistan on the south-west, with the USSR hardly a slingshot away. Kashmir is, in a geo-political sense, a bulwark for whoever manages to control it. The first great emperor to do so was none other than Ashoka: the capital, Srinagar, was built by this man who turned Buddhism into an international faith.

For all that, the Kashmiris have always been poor. There is not much wealth in agriculture. Kashmir's only sustaining industry is rooted in the traditional skill of its craftworkers who produce the brilliantly patterned and intricately woven Kashmiri shawl. But here again the real money was made by the ruler and the trader, not the craftsman. Napoleon is believed to have sent a Kashmiri shawl to Josephine, who made it the fashionable rage of Paris, creating unprecedented demand and increasing the profits of the traders. The Kashmiris remained poor despite such markets. The poverty reached extraordinary levels at the beginning of this century. Nehru commented in his *Autobiography* (published in 1936): 'Kashmir, even more than the rest of India, is a land of contrasts. In this land, overladen with natural beauty and rich nature's gifts, stark poverty reigns and humanity is continually struggling for the barest of subsistences. The men and women of Kashmir are good to look at and pleasant to talk to. They are intelligent and clever with their hands. They have a rich and lovely country to live in. Why then should they be so terribly poor?' The answer lay in the feudalism and oppression which had been their fate.

The earliest known chronicler of this land, with a scape as serene as its politics were turbulent, is Kalhana, who wrote his *Rajtaringini* in the twelfth century. Kalhana described his people thus: 'Kashmir may be conquered by the force of spiritual merit but never by the force of soldiers.' This is something that the Kashmiris believe about themselves. It was Buddhism which first conquered the Kashmiris, before, in its decay, Hindu belief returned.

The armies of Mahmud of Ghazna in the eleventh century brought the first hint of Islam to Kashmir. But Islam itself came with the Sufi missionary Bulbul Shah, whose most important convert was Renchana, a Tibetan prince who had taken refuge in the court of Suhadeva, the Hindu king (1301–20). In 1320, a descendant of Changez Khan, Zulfi Khan (also called Dulchu), sacked Kashmir in well-known Tartar style. Suhadeva, instead of putting up a defence, ran away. When the havoc created by Dulchu had subsided, Renchana took the throne. He became a Muslim and took the name of Sadruddin. A little after him started a long line of Muslim kings, called the Saladins, who ruled for two hundred years, beginning with Shahmir in 1343. The greatest of them was

Zainulabidin, and till today innumerable places in the valley bear his name – Zaina Kadal, Zainapur, Zainagir, Zainadub. In 1585 Kashmir fell to the Mughal emperor, Akbar. His son Jehangir is remembered with affection in Kashmir, if nowhere else, for building the beautiful gardens of Shalimar and Chashme Shahi, Naseem and Verinag. When asked on his death-bed what his last wish was, Jehangir replied that he wanted to die in Kashmir. Barring the reign of Aurangzeb, Kashmir's Hindus had reason to welcome Mughal rule when punitive taxes, like the hated *jaziya*, were removed. In 1753 came the resurgent Afghans under the brilliant tyrant Ahmad Shah Durrani; local commanders, paying uncertain fealty to Kabul, terrorized the land. But the modern period starts with the absorption of Kashmir into Maharaja Ranjit Singh's growing empire, and the rise of an intelligent disciple of Machiavelli, Gulab Singh Dogra. By this time, 90 per cent of Kashmir's population was Muslim. Only the Kashmiri pandit, with patience, wile, administrative capacity and great pride, lived in the vale of Kashmir; the other Hindus of the kingdom lived on the plains of Jammu, which had once been dominated by the Rajputs before Muhammad Ghori destroyed their power in the twelfth century. They restored themselves only after the decline of the Mughal empire.

Rajput literally means 'son of a king'. Of mixed Aryan and Scythian blood, the clan claims descent from the ancient solar and lunar dynasties. Belief held that the first king of mankind was Manu Swayambhu, born of the creator Brahma; Manu was both male and female. The eldest of Manu's nine sons was also a hermaphrodite, and known, therefore, both by a male and a female name, Ila and Ilaa. From this arose the ruling clans of Suryavansha (solar, and therefore male) and Chandravansha (lunar, and female). The Dogras of Gulab Singh's family believed that they belonged to the solar dynasty. It was a long time since they had ruled, though.

Gulab Singh Dogra joined the Sikh army of Maharaja Ranjit Singh as a trooper in 1809, at the pay of Rs 3 a month. Born in 1792, Gulab Singh had no education, but he knew how to ride and fight, and his valour in the siege of Multan in 1819 brought him rewards. The next year Ranjit Singh gave him the *jagir*, or estate, of Jammu, and in 1822 the hereditary title of Raja 'provided that the Rajas be loyal to the State henceforward as they have been till now, that they receive our descendants with no less honour and submission ...' Gulab Singh had absolutely no intention of showing any honour or submission to the descendants. On 27 June 1839, Ranjit Singh died. Gulab Singh opened a dialogue with the British who were searching for an agent in the court of an empire they envied and sought to conquer.

The first important favour that Gulab Singh did the British was to allow their expeditionary force secure passage through Jammu on its way to fight the first Afghan war in 1841 (the Sikhs would not assure the British safe passage). The British were trounced at the Khyber Pass in January 1842, but they were grateful for the help and sent Gulab Singh a letter of thanks. The crucial moment came in the decisive battle of Sobraon, during the first Anglo-Sikh war, on 10 February 1846, which the British called 'the Waterloo of India'. As a member of the Lahore court, Gulab Singh should have fought alongside the Sikhs. Instead he kept away from a battle which the Sikhs lost only narrowly. In a letter written on 4 March 1846, Governor-General Lord Hardinge pointed out to Lord Ellenborough that the treachery had been planned: 'It was always intended that Gulab Singh whose troops had not fired a shot should have his case and position fully considered. His forbearance was in accordance with an intended policy.'

The game had started in 1845 when Gulab Singh's agent, Sheo Dutt, told Major Broadfoot, the British representative at Lahore, that he could gather '40,000 troops from the hills and attack the Sikhs'. In January 1846, a Bengali physician delivered a letter from Gulab Singh to Lieutenant E. Lake (assistant agent to the Governor-General) saying, 'He who wishes to climb the summit of a lofty mountain, must start at day-break; should he delay night may close over him ere he has gained the desire of his heart.' Gulab Singh had indeed begun early and the desire of his heart was realized on 16 March 1846 when the British paid their thirty pieces of silver through the Treaty of Amritsar. For a token sum of Rs 75 lakhs (called *Nanakshahi*), the British handed over Jammu and Kashmir to Gulab Singh. Of course, Gulab Singh was told to be careful and never forget who gave him Kashmir. Article 10 of the Treaty of Amritsar said, 'Maharaja Gulab Singh acknowledges the supremacy of the British government and will in token of such supremacy present annually to the British government one horse, twelve goats (six male and six female) and three pairs of Kashmiri shawls.'

One hundred years later, in August 1947, when Gandhi visited Kashmir, he still heard slogans denouncing this purchase of Kashmir for Rs 75 lakhs. The sheer humiliation of the idea of being bought and sold inflamed the Kashmiris as nothing else and was mainly responsible for the bitter anti-feudal mood which played such a considerable part in the confusion over Kashmir during partition.

For the British it was a reasonable bargain. They now had a loyal agent in the buffer state of Kashmir (they helped Gulab Singh take the valley on 9 November 1846), and the Dogras always lived up to British expectations, protesting their loyalty and helping with men and money whenever the empire needed it. In 1848, Gulab Singh refused to join an alliance of Dost Mohammad Khan of Afghanistan and the Sikhs under Maharaja Dalip Singh in what was the last major stand against the British. During the 1857 mutiny, Gulab Singh sent his son Ranbir Singh with 2,000 infantry, 200 cavalry and 6 heavy guns to help the British in the siege of Delhi. In August 1858 Gulab Singh died, but his heirs showed no dilution of loyalty. In the Anglo-Afghan war of 1878–80 Kashmir again joined the British cause with troops and artillery; in the First World War, the Second Kashmir Rifles with 1,200 troops went to help the British in 1914 and another detachment of 1,070 soldiers went in 1917; similar help was given in the Second World War. The British obliged with medals and a 21-gun salute (the other states so honoured were Hyderabad, Gwalior, Mysore and Baroda). Accepting the 'gift' of Jammu and Kashmir, Gulab Singh had described himself as *zar kharid*, or 'the slave bought with gold'. It was an accurate description.

Gulab Singh died of dropsy. If the first of the Dogra princes was to acquire a less than wholesome fame, the fourth and last, Hari Singh, achieved a different sort of reputation when in the year of his accession, 1925, he became the victim of a gang of blackmailers who caught him in the nude at the Savoy Hotel in London with a girl they had planted. The amount they siphoned off him before the police caught them is believed to be as much as £3,000,000. The London penny press had a good time covering the case of 'Mr A' as the Maharaja was discreetly described. Unfortunately, precise details were lost when the British government files on the personal habits of the princely order of India were destroyed by Sir Conrad Corfield, who was unnaturally protective towards royalty, before the British left in 1947. Weak, consumed by self-interest, Hari Singh symbolized all that was unacceptable about feudalism. While the Maharaja drained the state's revenues to live in luxury (or to pay blackmail), the people sank into utter despair and the anti-Muslim prejudice of the administration acquired its harshest tones. The journalist Gwasha Nath Kaul, who first published his *Kashmir Then and Now* in 1924, before Hari Singh's accession, notes in the eighth edition (published in 1967) that Srinagar city in the early twenties 'presented a grim picture – two prostitution centres at Zaina Kadal and Gow Kadal, thefts day and night, begging so common that a huge crowd pounced upon a *dumri* [one-sixteenth of an anna, which was one-sixteenth of a rupee], labour so cheap that a *khirwar* [about 80 pounds] of *shali* could be husked at annas four, unasked-for house to house service by women, illiteracy so glaring that only a few of God's anointed could read or write, unemployment so acute that hardly one was an earning member in a family of ten or twelve, birth rate low and death rate high due to diseases for which no treatment was available, recreations and amusements were unknown. Dirty clothes were a common feature, soap being both scarce and costly. The plight of Sikhs was equally frightful. Pandits as a class looked a little better off to the extent of a difference of up to 5 per cent ... 90 per cent of Muslim houses in Srinagar were mortgaged to Hindu *sahukars* [moneylenders].'

The anger of the Kashmiri Muslim had to find an outlet; that it had not erupted before is largely due to the extreme backwardness of the community, combined with an instinctive abhorrence of violence. The civil servant Walter Lawrence noted this at the turn of the century: 'Briefly, the Kashmiri cultivators have hitherto been treated as serfs, and have literally been forced to cultivate. They had no interest in their land, and were liable at any moment to be called away to work for officials or men of influence ... [But] crime is almost unknown in the villages. Property is absolutely safe, and I have never heard of such a thing as the theft of crops. Offences against the person are extremely rare; and when Kashmiris quarrel they call one another by bad names, and will occasionally go so far as to knock off a turban or seize an adversary by his effeminate gown. The sight of blood is abhorrent to them.'

The first time the oppressed revolted was in the summer of 1924 when there was an uprising by the labourers of the Srinagar Silk Factory. The next day they occupied a plot of land belonging to the government. The army came out, and the Maharaja took action against the leaders. Saaduddin Shawal was expelled, while the *jagir* of another leader, Noor Shah Naqshband, was confiscated. But this was only the prelude. The starved peasantry wanted to own the land on which it had been enslaved for centuries. The people wanted an end to their miserable poverty, and an end to the maharajas who had kept them on the edge of the starvation. The masses were ready. The time had come for a leader to show the way.

3
The Lion of Kashmir

To the north of the legendary Hari Parbat, on the shores of the lake Anchar Sar, lies the village of Sorah. Here lived a Brahmin family who survived by the manufacture of shawls and *dushalas*. According to family tradition, they were converted to Islam in 1766 by a Sufi, Mir Abdur Rashid Bayhaqi. Never very rich, their fortunes declined further with the heavy taxation on shawl manufacturers by the Dogras. Into this family, in 1905, was born a child who was given the name Sheikh Mohammad Abdullah. Abdullah was a posthumous child, born to the third wife, Khairun Nisa, of Sheikh Mohammad Ibrahim, fifteen days after the father died. The other two wives had also died, and Khairun Nisa had to look after the family alone, with help from her growing stepsons. Khairun Nisa had one ambition: to see her children escape this cycle of poverty, through education. She first sent Abdullah to the Sufi Akhun Mubarak Shah, from whom the child not only learnt the formal virtues of reading and writing Persian and Arabic, but also imbibed that quintessential Sufi doctrine, tolerance. It was during his childhood that Abdullah learnt to recite the Quran in a manner which would entrance the people (and irritate the mullahs who discovered that he was beating them at their own game).

But what Abdullah truly wanted to be was a doctor. He could not become one (later, two of his sons became doctors), but with some help he got admission into the famous Aligarh Muslim University and graduated with a Master's degree in science. Despite possessing such a rare qualification in that era, Sheikh Abdullah could not get a better job than that of a science teacher in the State High School of Srinagar: prejudice came in the way. It was a Kashmir simmering with anger to which Abdullah had returned. He was determined to bring about change, and he took to political work. A near-contemporary, D. N. Kaul, who rose to become Inspector-General of Police when Sheikh Abdullah was

Chief Minister towards the end of his life, described those days: 'My elder brother whom he [Sheikh Abdullah] taught science used to recall how the tall, slenderly built, fez-capped master in science would render many a scientific term into everyday Kashmiri so as to ensure quick and easy comprehension by the young, captive audience before him. He exuded awe among the students, not only by his censorious and rigorous sense of discipline, but also by his stature, physical and academic, not only vis-à-vis the students but even in comparison to other members of the teaching establishment. Soon after, through the narrow lanes of Srinagar I used to see him lead processions of arm-swinging, vociferously gesticulating and slogan-shouting men. I can still recall his sonorous, mellifluous voice in his public speeches which invariably began with recitations from the Quran or Iqbal's verses.' With his audience totally Muslim, and the influence of the university still dominant, Sheikh Abdullah organized the Muslim Conference to take up the cause of his community. But the strains of the future were visible even then: the true fight, he said, was against feudalism, and for self-rule and land reform.

The first spark came in July 1931. Muslim anger burst open when word spread that the Holy Quran had been desecrated by a constable in a Jammu jail. All the long-controlled anger against the Maharaja poured through this breach. Sheikh Abdullah took over the leadership of the movement, and added the demands for political rights and civic reforms, while articulating the problems of the peasants, workers and artisans. He launched a civil disobedience movement, and led the first batch of volunteers who were arrested and jailed in the Hari Parbat fort. On 13 July, a violent mob attacked the Central Jail at Srinagar and nine people died in police firing. Sheikh Abdullah never allowed Kashmir to forget that day, which he named 'Martyrs Day'. Each year, when he could, he used to remind Kashmir of the price paid by those who had died. The Maharaja's government was forced to appoint an inquiry commission under a Britisher, Sir Bertrand Glancy, which led to the first reforms Kashmir had seen as a consequence of a mass movement.

Sheikh Abdullah was now beginning to find himself. He discovered that he had no taste for an ideology which restricted itself to just one religion. As early as in 1932, he told the session of the Muslim Conference, 'We stand for the rights of all communities. Our country's progress is impossible so long as we do not establish amicable relations between the different communities.' But the name 'Muslim Conference' and such a message were in obvious contradiction. One or the other had to change.

The name went. Sheikh Abdullah later established just how committed he was to his economic programme: almost the first thing he did when he came to power in 1947 was to abolish the large landholdings of the *jagirdari* system. And on Martyrs Day 1949, he gave the peasants (83 per cent of the population) who tilled the land for the absentee landlords (13 per cent) the plots on which they worked. Sheikh Abdullah's Big Landed Estates Abolition Act became famous throughout India and embarrassed many a Socialist who had promised the same thing but been unable to deliver. For the Kashmiri peasant this was true freedom.

In 1933, Sheikh Abdullah married Begum Akbar Jehan (whose father was a Christian before converting to Islam). Their eldest child was a daughter, Khalida (who later married Ghulam Mohammad Shah); then came Farooq, Tariq, another daughter Suraiya, and Mustafa Kamal. Begum Abdullah did not end up behind any purdah; she participated fully in the stormy political career of her husband. Even by the early thirties, Sheikh Abdullah's reputation was spreading in the rest of India. In the commemoration volume published by the Kashmir University on the second anniversary of the Sheikh's death, Mrs Indira Gandhi says, 'I first saw Sheikh Sahib in 1934, leading a procession. Not long after, he came to be recognized as a prominent figure in our freedom movement. Like other popular leaders of the old princely states, he fought against the double yoke of feudalism and colonialism. He stoutly opposed the politics of the Muslim League and was a fine example of the secular ideal of our nation.'

And he remained such an example through the very worst period, the late thirties and the forties when Jinnah had begun making such dangerous waves in the name of religion. In 1939 he formally converted the 'Muslim Conference' into the 'National Conference'; the new name was carefully chosen to depict the difference between the ideas of the Muslim League and the ideas of the nationalist movement. Sheikh Abdullah had also begun to profess admiration for the experiment taking place in the northern neighbour, the USSR. The National Conference flag was kept a deliberate red, much to the alarm of the British. In the centre was a white plough, and the slogan given to the peasantry was: '*Alyaban hallakari, dushmanan challakari*' ('When the plough moves, it tears apart the enemy').

Sheikh Abdullah, along with Maulana Azad, became the doyen of the 'nationalist' Muslims. Kashmir was an obvious target for the Muslim League. Sheikh Abdullah actively challenged their philosophy and politics, saying that the two-nation theory was a poison which would cause devastation wherever it spread. If one appreciates the context in which the Sheikh was advocating unity, his achievement becomes all the more remarkable. The only thing the Kashmiri Muslims had before freedom was their number; both political and economic power were concentrated in the hands of Hindus. The Muslim had every reason in the world to be angry with the Hindu and to seek revenge. The peace of 1947 between Hindu and Muslim in Kashmir, which was largely due to Sheikh Abdullah's leadership, must rank as one of the extraordinary achievements of a remarkable life. Even Khan Abdul Ghaffar Khan, 'the Frontier Gandhi', had failed to prevent the Pathans of the North-West Frontier Province, adjoining Kashmir, from falling into the communal trap. The League tried its best. Jinnah offered Sheikh Abdullah power and prestige in Pakistan. When that failed, the League tried to foment trouble in the valley with the help of its old ally, the clergy, and the Jamaat-e-Islami (the Kashmiri unit of this organization has, till the moment of writing, not accepted the accession of Kashmir to India; it owes allegiance to the Pakistani Jamaat-e-Islami). But Sheikh Abdullah kept Kashmir safe from them. His message to the peasants was simple: there is no difference between the good Hindu and the good Muslim; not only do bad Hindus and Muslims create quarrels but often they unite against those trying to do some good.

In 1944 Sheikh Abdullah announced his blueprint for the Kashmir of the future, the New Kashmir. According to Pyare Lal Handoo, Law Minister under the Sheikh's son Farooq: 'The battle for political freedom [had to] mean the battle for economic emancipation ... once he got this programme adopted as the charter for political and economic emancipation of our state a swift wind of change swept the countryside till it culminated in the historic slogan of "Quit Kashmir" in 1946. It was in that period that the foundation of the Jammu and Kashmir of Sheikh Sahib's dreams was laid brick by brick.'

Anti-feudalism was, as we have seen, the other vital part of the Sheikh's programme. He would never accept the legitimacy of Maharaja Hari Singh – and could never conceive of giving the Maharaja the right to decide what the future of Kashmir should be. The controversial question of the plebiscite is often misinterpreted because it is thought to have originated from the desire of the Kashmiris to opt for Pakistan, which was later believed to have been thwarted by India. Nothing could be further from the truth. Since there was no legal way in which a representative government of Kashmir could join India in 1947, Sheikh Abdullah suggested (and Nehru readily agreed) that the Maharaja (who was an illegitimate representative of Kashmir, in the eyes of the Sheikh) could sign the accession for the time being, but that moral legitimacy should be given to the accession by referring it to the people. The Sheikh did not, in fact, suggest a specific plebiscite on the issue; a government elected by adult franchise under a popular Constitution, for instance, would have the right to confirm the accession to India. There was no doubt in anyone's mind that Kashmir should go to India; the question was what mode should be followed. As a lifelong enemy of feudalism, the Sheikh was not going to give a Maharaja the technical privilege of signing away the destiny of Kashmiris. The origins of the plebiscite lie, therefore, in Sheikh Abdullah's battle against kings, not in any fascination with the ideas of Jinnah, whom he held in contempt.

In its memorandum to the Cabinet Mission of 1946, headed by Sir Stafford Cripps, the National Conference had made its goal very clear: 'The national demand of the people of Kashmir is not merely the demand for a responsible government but their right to absolute freedom from the autocratic rule of the Dogra house.' The 'Quit Kashmir' movement of 1946 was launched against this ruling family by Sheikh Abdullah with the full support of Gandhi and Nehru. The Congress, being purely a freedom movement against foreign rule, restricted its existence to British India. But its counterpart in the states ruled by Indian princes was the All-India States Peoples Conference, under which head came the various liberation movements in the princely states. Nehru was President of this Conference in 1946, and Sheikh Abdullah the Vice-President. The Sheikh had carried his popular agitation against the Dogras to a high pitch by May of that year. On 15 May at Srinagar, he made a speech which had the feudal government trembling with rage. A few quotations will indicate the flavour: 'The demand that the princely order should quit the states is a logical extension of the policy of "Quit India" [launched by Gandhi in 1942 against the British; the Indian princes were allies by treaty and protectorates of the British]. When the freedom movement demands complete withdrawal of British power, logically enough the stooges of British imperialism should also go and restore sovereignty to its real owners, the people ... The rulers of Indian states have always played traitor to the cause of Indian freedom. A revolution upturned the mighty Tsars and the French Revolution made short work of the ruling class of France. The time has come to tear up the Treaty of Amritsar, and Quit Kashmir. Sovereignty is not the birthright of Maharaja Hari Singh. "Quit Kashmir" is not a question of revolt. It is a matter of right.'

Although extremely busy with the work of the Cripps Mission, Nehru could not resist the excitement of what was going on in Kashmir. He asked his vice-president to come to Delhi and brief him. Sheikh Abdullah left Srinagar almost as soon as he got the message, heading for Rawalpindi where he could catch a flight to Delhi. When he reached Ghari, about a hundred miles from Srinagar, Hari Singh's government arrested him on charges of sedition, the speech of 15 May being cited as evidence. Nehru learnt of the arrest of his friend through a telegram. He issued an angry statement wondering whether the princes of feudal India thought they would get away with 'minor changes in the façade' after independence. He added a caveat: the Sheikh had been arrested at the instigation of the British. 'We know very well that in such matters it is the [British] Resident [in the court of the princes] who plays a dominant role,' he said.

Nehru had reason to suggest that the British were keen to protect Hari Singh at that particular moment, thanks to their anxiety about Russian expansionism. Hari Singh, as head of the buffer state of Kashmir, played an important role in that policy. Perhaps this is why he was made a member of Churchill's War Cabinet – 'one of those elaborate farces at which the imperial British excelled, aimed at giving members of the British empire some sort of symbolic say in the affairs of state without any real power to influence decisions', according to Hari Singh's son, Karan Singh. In the fluid post-war world, the superpowers were eager to expand their areas of 'influence' (the respectable term for domination), and obviously Moscow looked keenly at its southern borders, Iran, Afghanistan, British India and Kashmir. The Communist Party of India was, of course, one of the instruments used to promote Soviet interests. The CPI not only backed the British war effort when the Congress refused co-operation, but also gave loud support to the idea of Pakistan after the Muslim League came over to the side of the British. Many Communists even joined the Muslim League (much to the chagrin of some of the fundamentalists, who could think of nothing more sacrilegious than a godless Communist). There was awareness of this in India, and a report in the *Hindusthan Standard* of 21 May 1946, datelined from Lahore, said, 'It was revealed in some political circles that the Communist Party of India had established a very strong "underground" office somewhere in Kashmir in order to be able to assist Russia in extending her influence in India. Russia, it is well known, has failed to achieve its object through Iran and for very good reasons does not want to manoeuvre it through Afghanistan. Muslims of the Punjab, who have already sensed the danger of the spread of Communism and influence of Russia, are very seriously considering the question of purifying the League of pro-Communist elements.'

Nehru was enraged at the behaviour of Hari Singh's government, and the 'reign of terror' it had let loose: deaths by police firing, bodies being soaked in petrol and burnt, the wounded being thrown into jails instead of being sent to hospital. He called Srinagar a 'city of the dead' and said conditions were reminiscent of Punjab under General Dyer – with people being made to crawl on the streets or to shout at the point of the bayonet, *Maharaja ki jai*' ('Victory to the Maharaja'). And he had fulsome praise for the Sheikh: 'Everyone who knows Kashmir also knows the position of Sheikh Abdullah there. He is the *Sher-e-Kashmir* [the lion of Kashmir] beloved by the people in the remotest valleys. Numerous legends and popular songs have grown around his personality. He has been and is one of my most valued colleagues in the States Peoples movement whose advice has been sought in all important matters. Does anybody think we are going to desert him?' Sham Lal, secretary of the National Conference Publicity Committee, told newsmen, 'The entire Kashmiri police force refused to lathi-charge their own brothers and sisters, as a result of which forty of these Kashmiri policemen have been taken into custody by the Dogra militarymen and the Kashmiri police force has been disarmed.' An acid Nehru said, 'The Blimps have ceased to rule in most countries. It is the unfortunate fate of Kashmir today to be in charge of Blimps.' He decided that he would personally lead a team of lawyers to defend Sheikh Abdullah at his trial. There could be no peace in Kashmir, he said, until Sheikh Abdullah was released.

Lord Wavell tried to persuade Nehru not to go to Kashmir, but he would not be deterred. Congress leaders pointed out that he was needed for the Cabinet Mission discussions, but Nehru went. On 15 June he sent a telegram to Hari Singh's government informing them that he was coming. Srinagar sent a cold reply: he would not be allowed to enter the province. At one o'clock on the afternoon of 19 June, Nehru, along with Asaf Ali, Dewan Chaman Lal, Tilak Raj Chadha and others, reached the Kohala bridge by car, about a hundred and forty miles from Srinagar on the Srinagar–Rawalpindi road. After lunch, they began walking across the bridge. The district magistrate served an order prohibiting Nehru from entering; he and his party continued walking. Nehru told the district magistrate that he had not obeyed any order of the British government for two decades, and he was hardly likely to obey the orders of Hari Singh and his disliked Prime Minister, Rai Bahadur Pandit Ram Chandra Kak. A military cordon was placed in Nehru's way. 'Perhaps,' Nehru told his companions, 'the Kashmir state authorities do not know that they are dealing with the President-elect of the Indian National Congress. I do not know what is going back.' And with that he simply walked through the unnerved cordon.

He and his followers were not stopped for three and a half miles, until the police confronted them again at seven-thirty in the evening. The car which had brought Nehru up to Kohala now arrived, and the party was driven to Domal for the night. Nehru was taken the next day to a dak bungalow at Uri, ninety-six miles from Srinagar, under arrest.

There was an uproar all over the country when news of Nehru's arrest spread. Congress workers prepared to enter Kashmir to offer themselves for arrest. Hari Singh's government allowed the counsel arranged for Sheikh Abdullah by Nehru, Baldev Sahay, ex-Advocate-General of Bihar, and Avdesh Narayan, to come to Srinagar, but would not allow Nehru to move freely. And Nehru would not leave without meeting Sheikh Abdullah. In Delhi, the Congress Working Committee was getting frantic; vital matters relating to the Cabinet Mission were awaiting a final decision, and Nehru – expected to lead any interim government forming the bridge between colonial rule and full independence – was sitting in a jail in Kashmir. Finally, the Congress President, Maulana Azad, ordered Nehru, as a disciplined Congressman, to return to Delhi. Gandhi sent word that Nehru's presence in Delhi was most essential. Nehru at first refused, requesting the 'Working Committee to proceed without me'. Azad replied, 'Remember you are under an organization which you have adorned for so long. Its needs must be paramount to you and me ...' Nehru relented: 'Received your message at one p.m. after lunch. In obedience to the direction of the Working Committee I am prepared to return immediately on the understanding that I will come back to Kashmir later.' Nehru left Kashmir, but by his gesture in coming he had perhaps won the heart of Kashmir. The Kashmiris, an emotional people, could never forget what Nehru did for them in such a dark hour, how he took their case and forced the government of Hari Singh to control its excesses. It was out of such common commitment that Kashmir's bonds with democratic India were forged.

The trial of Sheikh Abdullah began on 22 July 1946. Nehru came to watch the proceedings on 25 July, stayed for four days and met his friend four times. The Sheikh's defence was now in the hands of lawyers Shanti Swarup Dhawan and Asaf Ali, while Jai Gopal Seth from Lahore led the prosecution. Sheikh Abdullah himself perhaps settled the issue when, in a 3,000-word statement pleading not guilty, he said, 'I stand by whatever I have said or written in regard to the fundamental rights of the people of Jammu and Kashmir. My trial for sedition is something more than a personal charge against me. It is, in effect, the trial of the entire population of Jammu and Kashmir.' The sessions judge of Badambagh cantonment duly sentenced Sheikh Abdullah to three years' simple imprisonment and a fine of Rs 1,500 on the charge of sedition.

From jail, Sheikh Abdullah smuggled out a letter which summed up his thinking: 'Dear comrades-in-arms, this is a fight to the finish. Either we win our objective or we perish forever. I have said, and I still maintain, that Maharaja Hari Singh has no moral right to rule us, and as for his legal right to do so we will contest it whenever possible. With the disappearance of British imperialism from India, paramountcy automatically vests in the people, and it is for the Maharaja to seek a new relationship with the people. This new relationship can be possible on the basis of acceptance by the Maharaja of the people's demands, and on no other basis. He should read this writing on the wall or fight the people to a finish. He has to choose between the people and the present Premier Ram Chandra Kak. As long as the latter remains in the *gaddi* [chair] of the Prime Minister, there can be no peace in Kashmir. So, comrades, prepare yourselves for the last and final onslaught on this citadel of reaction and barbarism and rest assured that in the end victory will be ours. In this righteous struggle, individual sufferings do not matter. It is our noble objectives which should remain uppermost always in your heart. *Inquilab Zindabad* [Long Live the Revolution]! *Bainama Amritsar ko toro* [Destroy the Treaty of Amritsar]!'

Events were now moving fast in Delhi, and by June 1947 Pakistan had been conceded. Nehru kept complaining to Gandhi that while India was on the way to freedom, Sheikh Abdullah was still in jail, and the Congress had done nothing to get him out. He wanted to visit Kashmir. Gandhi advised against this, and said that he himself would go. Those were extraordinary times. Religious bigotry was at its height; there was bloodshed in every city. The panic had begun in Punjab. The nation was tense, wondering which state would opt for which country, and how it would all happen. Gandhi knew that a visit to Kashmir at that stage could be misinterpreted. He explained very clearly that he was not going to Kashmir to persuade Kashmiris to join India: it was completely up to the Kashmiris to decide whether they wanted to be in India or Pakistan. Gandhi was going to honour a commitment which had been delayed by the pressures of this unusual year: he was only going to meet Begum Abdullah to say that the Congress had not forgotten their cause. If Nehru went now, it might be misconstrued that the future Prime Minister of India had gone to coerce the Kashmiris. Gandhi left on 30 July 1947.

Gandhi got an immediate taste of Kashmiri emotions on his arrival; the unprecedented welcome was the first indication. Crowds lined the streets and shouted, *'Baghi Abdullah ki jai!'* ['Victory to rebel Abdullah!'] while Begum Abdullah garlanded him. He told the people that he had not come to meet the Maharaja but to see Begum Abdullah and National Conference workers. Hari Singh's government expected Gandhi to request a meeting with the Maharaja; Gandhi simply ignored the government. Hari Singh offered to host Gandhi in his palace; Gandhi refused, and stayed as a guest of the National Conference (who put him up at the house of Seth Kishorilal). Finally Prime Minister Kak went to call on Gandhi. Gandhi agreed to meet Hari Singh, but only to tell him, 'Your people are angry with you. I will not accept anything from you so long as they do not accept you. Please your people, and I will come and live with you in your palace for ten days.'

When Gandhi went to Mujahid Manzil (then, as now, the headquarters of the National Conference) to address the party workers there was uncontrollable enthusiasm, screams of *'Gandhiji ki jai'* ('Victory to Gandhi') filling the air, and crackers bursting in joy: more than 20,000 people had gathered. Gandhi had been given an unbelievable welcome by Muslim-majority Kashmir just two weeks before Pakistan was born.

Sheikh Abdullah was eventually removed to a comfortable place in Srinagar in September 1947 under pressure from the government of independent India, led by his friend, Jawaharlal Nehru, and released by the end of the month.

Kashmir, of course, was in raptures. The crowd at the Sheikh's first public speech was believed to number more than 100,000, an extraordinary figure given the small population of that mountainous state. Once again, on 4 October, at Hazooribagh, Sheikh Abdullah told the people what he had always believed. So much had happened since he had been sent to jail sixteen months back. Crucially, the country of Pakistan had been created. A choice had opened up for Kashmir; Maharaja Hari Singh had still not announced which country he would accede to. Sheikh Abdullah made it clear that the Maharaja did not have any right to represent the Kashmiris; the people must be allowed to decide, not their feudal ruler. This was the same principle on which India's Home Minister Sardar Patel had challenged the Muslim princes of Junagadh and Hyderabad who, despite having strong Hindu majorities, were threatening to announce either independence or accession to the theocratic state of Pakistan. Sheikh Abdullah asked that the same principle be extended to Kashmir.

The question now came as to what would be in the interests of the people. Should they join Pakistan, a Muslim country, or India, a secular country? Sheikh Abdullah answered the question in that speech. 'Pandit Jawaharlal Nehru is my friend and I hold Gandhiji in real reverence ... we shall not believe the two-nation theory which has spread so much poison. Kashmir showed the light at this juncture. When brother kills brother in the whole of Hindustan, Kashmir raised its voice of Hindu–Muslim unity. I can assure the Hindu and Sikh minorities here that as long as I am alive their life and honour will be quite safe.' We must remember what was happening in India and Pakistan even while Sheikh Abdullah was giving that speech: on that very day, in that very month, the Hindu–Muslim rioting was at its most ugly, its most brutal. And in the valley of Kashmir the National Conference was fighting every effort of the Muslim League with its own slogan, *'Hindu–Muslim ittehad ki jai!'* ('Victory to Hindu–Muslim friendship!').

Some idea of the state of the nation during that period can be obtained from speeches being made elsewhere. On 4 October, at his daily prayer meeting, a despairing Gandhi said that he used to ask God to let him live up to a hundred and twenty-five so that he could see *Ramrajya*, the 'Rule of Rama', in free India, but now life did not seem worth the effort. 'Hindus and Muslims,' said the man who had spent his life in this country trying to keep them friendly, 'today seemed to vie with each other in cruelty; men, women and children and the aged were not spared.' Nehru was angry at the kind of India he had inherited. In a speech to Congress workers at Delhi, he lashed out. Just four days before at a public meeting he had said that as long as he was alive India would not become a Hindu state. This meeting of Congress workers was held in the Subzi Mandi locality of Delhi, one of the worst-hit by communal violence. Fascism, he said, was gripping India; there were demands for a Hindu state. But he, the new Prime Minister, would not be party to such reactionary views. He believed in Congress values, and if such values were not acceptable to the people now, they should elect another Prime Minister. He would not change his beliefs for any number of votes.

In his 4 October speech, Sheikh Abdullah explained to his vast audience how the Muslim League had won its Pakistan. Nobody could have been more categorical: 'I never believed in the Pakistan slogan. It has been my firm conviction that this slogan will bring misery for all. I did not believe in the two-nation theory but in spite of it Pakistan is a reality ... What have the four and half crore [45 million] Muslims in India gained through it? I sympathize with them in their plight. Pro-Pakistan elements started their Direct Action [on 16 August] from Noakhali and inflicted untold sufferings on non-Muslims there. This was followed by revenge in Bihar. Later Hindus and Sikhs were killed in the Frontier Province and West Punjab which was followed by killings of Muslims in East Punjab and Delhi. This has been the result of the two-nation theory ... We want people's *raj* [rule] in Kashmir. It will not be a government of any particular community but of all – Hindus, Muslims and Sikhs.' That was Sheikh Abdullah at a moment in history when a word from him would have easily taken Kashmir into Pakistan, when Sardar Patel would have gladly allowed Kashmir to go if that would ensure easy assimilation of Hyderabad and Junagadh into India.

Sheikh Abdullah had been on his way to Delhi to meet Jawaharlal Nehru when the troops of Hari Singh arrested him in 1946. Now the Sheikh was the undisputed hero of Kashmir and Nehru was Prime Minister of India. Nehru invited him to come to Delhi to relax. Obviously, there was only one place where the guest could stay: 16 York Place, the makeshift residence of the new Prime Minister of India. The only problem that Nehru foresaw was how to handle his friend's fondness for good food (Sheikh Abdullah's appetite and taste in food were legendary). Nehru's daughter Indira came to Delhi on a visit from Allahabad and took charge. There would come another time, many storms later, when such a gesture would be repeated and the first thing that the Sheikh would do after being released from a long term in jail would be to make a quick visit to Kashmir, and then come to stay at the house of this 'dearest friend'. It would be in 1964, and the Sheikh would be emerging from imprisonment ordered not by Hari Singh, but by Nehru's government. But that was an extraordinary friendship, unclouded by the harshness of politics, possible only in a generation which had been taught never to hate and never to fear. B. K. Nehru in an essay in the commemoration volume recalls the quality of that relationship: 'Once in 1947 Jawaharlal Nehru and Sheikh dined with my wife and myself at our house, No. 1 Safdarjang Road. We had not till then begun to regard the observance of decorum in manners and dress as incompatible with democracy: security in those days had not made the lives of people in power as utterly impossible as it has made them now; and after dinner the four of us went to see a film, *The Razor's Edge*, based on Somerset Maugham's book, at the Regal cinema in Connaught Place, sitting in the balcony as ordinary people along with everybody else. This I should imagine was the last time that Jawaharlal Nehru ever saw a film privately in a public place.'

The storms were coming. And the friendship and faith of Nehru and Abdullah would be tested as nothing before during a crisis that not only shook the young countries of the subcontinent but demanded a price which is still being paid by later generations who had nothing to do with the original sin.

4
Raiders of the Lost Cause

There was a large public meeting in Peshawar in the North-West Frontier Province of Pakistan on 22 October 1947. The man addressing it should rightly have been living in India. All his life, he had fought for the creation of a secular nation and believed in non-violence, and was known as 'the Frontier Gandhi'. He was called Badshah Khan. In the current orgy of violence he saw his life's work disappearing, but he still tried to turn the tide. He told the gathered Pathans: 'One of the fundamental teachings of Islam is the spirit of toleration. The very word "Islam" signifies love and goodwill, which is also the hallmark of the Pathanic code. Hence anyone who harms any weak, unprotected or helpless person not only blots the fair name of Islam but commits an absolutely unPathanic act.' Those words were particularly ironic that day. On the border of the Frontier Province and Kashmir a different interpretation of Islam was being enacted.

Jinnah had done his best to ensure the accession of Kashmir to Pakistan; Sheikh Abdullah had always dismissed the idea as suicidal. When after partition neither the National Conference nor the Maharaja's government seemed willing to push Kashmir into Pakistan, Jinnah decided to use force. Maharaja Hari Singh by now had become entangled in disastrous daydreams, entertaining visions of an independent kingdom. There were even sycophantic suggestions from his courtiers that he might be able to recreate the empire of Maharaja Ranjit Singh. Despite the substantial nudge given by Lord Mountbatten during a visit to Kashmir in July, that the best thing to do would be to accede to Pakistan, the Maharaja had signed nothing by 15 August. Instead, Kashmir worked out a Standstill Agreement with both India and Pakistan. While India, torn apart by religious riots, worried about Hyderabad and Junagadh and refugees, Pakistan worked out a plan to seize Kashmir.

On 24 August Jinnah had asked his military secretary to arrange a two-week holiday in Kashmir in mid September, and was shocked to learn that Hari Singh would not allow him to set foot in the valley. Contemporaries say that this insult made Jinnah even more determined to have his holiday. Be that as it may, by mid September the plan to send the Pathan tribesmen from the Frontier Province to seize Kashmir was set in motion. For Pakistan, this would solve three problems at one stroke: first, it would divert the Pathans away from Kabul's overtures (when on 30 September 1947 Pakistan was admitted into the United Nations, Afghanistan was the only country to protest); second, it would bring Kashmir into Pakistan without the use of the Pakistani army, whose presence on Kashmiri soil would be legally untenable; and lastly it would provide the Pathans with a long-overdue opportunity to indulge in their favourite pastime – loot. The tribal leaders were told that not only was this a holy war to liberate their Muslim brethren from the clutches of a Hindu king, but that there was also plunder at the end of the rainbow. The raiders entered Kashmir on the night of 22–23 October across the Jhelum river. The border post was taken easily. Srinagar was about a hundred and forty miles away along a motorable road, and the summer capital of Jammu and Kashmir could have technically fallen within twenty-four hours. But when the leaders of the raiders decided to go straight ahead to Srinagar, they got an enormous shock. They discovered they did not have any followers. The Pathans had simply disappeared in the darkness of the night to the nearby town of Muzaffarabad – to loot. Between liberation and loot, they knew which was first priority. The march to Srinagar would be stalled by greed for a few crucial days in which the history of the subcontinent would be rewritten.

The victory of the goddess Durga over the demon Maheshasura was celebrated each year with great fanfare in the Kashmiri palace; Durga was a deity particularly revered by the Dogras. At the climax of the festival, it was the custom of the nobles to hand a piece of gold wrapped in silk to Hari Singh as a ritual pledge of allegiance. On the evening of 24 October 1947, the nobles were thus displaying their loyalty when the lights went off. They did not know why, but it was because the powerhouse of Mahura, which supplied electricity to the whole of the valley, had been seized by the raiders and blown up. The tribals were now within fifty miles of Srinagar. The noble ruler of Jammu and Kashmir did the first thing he could think of. He began packing his very large number of bags and, within twenty-four hours, fled, leaving his people to the mercy of the marauding tribals.

Nehru learnt about the crisis on the night of 24 October, and turned livid. The Sheikh was staying with him and they discussed the options. Sheikh Abdullah put his weight behind the decision to send Indian troops to rescue Kashmir. But Nehru wanted the legality of the action confirmed first. The next morning, 25 October, an extraordinary meeting of the Cabinet was held. That afternoon, a DC-3 of the Royal Indian Air Force landed at Srinagar: on board was the Secretary to the Government of India in the Ministry of States, V. P. Menon. His mission was to get the Maharaja to sign the papers ensuring the accession of Kashmir to India; Indian troops would not enter Kashmir until they had the legal right to do so. Preliminary discussions over, Menon flew back to Delhi. The next day he got into another aircraft and now headed for Jammu. (During the night, the Maharaja had fled Srinagar in a caravan of trucks and cars carrying his money and treasures to the safer city of Jammu.) The Maharaja gladly signed the papers. Kashmir became a part of India.

But there was a catch. It was only a provisional accession. On one principle Sheikh Abdullah would not submit: the family which had 'bought' Kashmir from the British for Rs 75 lakhs could not be allowed to decide the fate of Kashmir. Only the people of Kashmir had the right to do that, and they must be given the right to confirm this accession later. No one was yet very sure about the methodology of this ratification; it was Mountbatten who suggested a plebiscite, according to Nehru's biographer S. Gopal. At that time neither the provisional aspect of the accession nor the concept of a plebiscite were considered to be any problem. Sheikh Abdullah's commitment to India was beyond question. It was not Jinnah but Nehru himself who made public that there was a deliberate rider to the accession.

In a broadcast whose words have been repeated each time Kashmir has been debated, Nehru said on 2 November over All-India Radio: 'I want to speak to you tonight about Kashmir, not about the beauty of that famous valley but about the horror it has had to face recently ... It was on the night of October 24 that for the first time a request was made to us on behalf of Kashmir state for accession and military help ... The fate of Srinagar and the whole of Kashmir hung in the balance. We received urgent messages for aid not only from the Maharaja's government but from representatives of the people, notably the great leader of Kashmir, Sheikh Mohammad Abdullah, the president of the National Conference. Both the Kashmir government and the National Conference pressed us to accept the accession of Kashmir to the Indian

Union. We decided to accept this accession and to send troops by air, but we made a condition that the accession would have to be considered by the people of Kashmir later when peace and order were established. We were anxious not to finalize anything in a moment of crisis and without the fullest opportunity to the people of Kashmir to have their say. It was for them to ultimately decide. And let me make it clear that it has been our policy all along that where there is a dispute about the accession of a state to either dominion, the decision must be made by the people of that state. It was in accordance with this policy that we added a proviso to the instrument of accession of Kashmir.'

In fact, it was Jinnah who first rejected the idea of a plebiscite on the excuse that there could never be an honest vote as long as Indian troops were present in the state. Jinnah was sure that the Kashmiris under Sheikh Abdullah's leadership would vote for India.

In the same speech in which Nehru promised to confirm the accession by a 'referendum under international auspices like the United Nations' he also told the world why Kashmir was ideologically a part of India. 'Srinagar was in peril and the invader was almost at its doorstep. There was no administration left there, no troops, no police. Light and power had failed and there was a vast number of refugees there. And yet Srinagar functioned without obvious panic and the shops were open and people went about the streets. To what was this miracle due? Sheikh Abdullah and his colleagues of the National Conference and their unarmed volunteers, Muslim and Hindu and Sikh, took charge of the situation, kept order and prevented panic. It was a wonderful piece of work that they did at a moment when the nerves of most people might have failed them. They did so because of the strength of their organization, but even more so because they were determined to protect their country from the ruthless invader who was destroying their country and trying to compel them by terrorism to join Pakistan.'

Nehru was not exaggerating the role of Sheikh Abdullah at that vital hour when destinies were shifting in the balance. On Sunday 26 October, even while the accession was being signed by a scared Maharaja in Jammu, Sheikh Abdullah announced that a 10,000-strong Peace Brigade had been set up in Kashmir which would protect the people from the raiders. Some of the National Conference volunteers who fought the Pakistani tribals have become legendary, like Mir Maqbool Sherwani of Baramulla. When the Indian army finally entered Baramulla, they discovered that Maqbool Sherwani had been nailed to a pole and shot, and the only sign of life in that town was a whimpering dog crying over the dead bodies of the Mother Superior and the nuns at the Mission Hospital. When leaving for Kashmir on 27 October at the height of the peril (unlike his feudal predecessor Hari Singh, who had run in the opposite direction), Sheikh Abdullah said, 'I am going back to lead this resistance of the people to the invaders.'

According to the terms of the accession, Sheikh Abdullah was to head a new government, now that Hari Singh had vacated his responsibility. He was sworn in on 31 October, along with his close lieutenants, Mirza Afzal Beg, Bakshi Ghulam Mohammad, Sham Lal Saraf and G. M. Sadiq. Gandhi said at his prayer meeting that day that his heart went out to Sheikh Abdullah each time he heard the sound of the aeroplanes carrying troops and equipment to Kashmir (every spare plane in the country had been commandeered for the task). Those planes saved Kashmir. On 31 October, Nehru sent the first of two cables to Pakistan asking for peace. There was no reply. Pakistan obviously still thought it was going to win. But soon the tide of battle began to turn, and the raiders, although well equipped and in sufficient strength, began to be pushed back. By the time of the cease-fire fourteen months later, they would be left with just a wedge of ground in the west and desolate wasteland in the north. Indian commanders still think that they were stopped when they had almost solved the 'Kashmir problem' for their country; from the edge of Srinagar they had pushed the Pakistani army to west of Poonch, within sight of Pakistan, and were ready to attack Gilgit in the north. But Nehru accepted the cease-fire sponsored by the United Nations. However, the true problem in Kashmir was neither the attitude of Pakistan, which could not have been different, nor the quality of UN arbitration, which could not have been any more effective. The problem was that the two men who symbolized, in the India of 1947, those values which could keep the country united, began to have doubts.

Perhaps nowhere was the combination of emotion and faith that marked the bond of 1947 more visible than in Srinagar on 11 November, when Nehru came up from Delhi to visit Kashmir. By this time, the outskirts of Srinagar had been cleared and Brigadier L. P. Sen's troops had captured Baramulla. Sheikh Abdullah described the mood of the time when he said, 'The grave of Pakistan will be dug in the valley of Kashmir,' in an interview to the *Hindustan Times*, published on 5 November. On 11 November, in the company of Rafi Ahmed Kidwai, Achyut Patwardhan, and his daughter Indira Gandhi, Nehru reached Srinagar. There was another tumultuous welcome, the crowds lining the road from the airport to the city. At the public meeting that day, Nehru told the cheering mass, 'As in the past, so in the future, we shall stand together and face every enemy.' Then suddenly Nehru paused, turned and, emotionally, stretched out his hand towards the Sheikh sitting next to him. A surprised Sheikh immediately grasped Nehru's hand and the two friends, hands clasped in that universal gesture of love and loyalty, stood on the dais while the crowd roared.

Nehru, convinced of the legality of India's case, took the problem to the United Nations on 31 December 1947, much to its own regret later. Nehru wanted to put international pressure on Pakistan to withdraw the raiders. The President of the Security Council made the expected appeal to both sides for peace; the raiders, who had broken international law, behaved as if the Security Council did not exist. Pakistan's response to the UN efforts was to reinforce the raiders with regulars from their army when the Indian troops began their successful summer offensive. Pakistan now argued that India and Pakistan should withdraw troops simultaneously, under UN supervision, so that an 'honest' plebiscite could take place, ignoring the simple fact that it had no legal status in Kashmir, which India had. There was more than one catch to such an argument. Pakistan had the advantage of geography. It could always send back its surrogates, the tribals, and pretend once again that the attack on Kashmir was nothing but an 'internal' affair, as it had done in 1947 and was to do in 1965. Secondly, the Pakistani military concentrations were within easy striking distance of Kashmir: Abbotabad was only sixteen miles away, Rawalpindi thirty-one, Murree fifteen, Sialkot six and Jhelum just four. On the other hand, the difficulty in bringing in Indian forces in sufficient strength if a crisis occurred had become obvious the first time around. Such an effort could not be repeated.

Nor did Sheikh Abdullah, now Prime Minister of Kashmir, want the Indian army to withdraw. He went to New York and said that Kashmiris would never allow Pakistan to enslave them. 'There is no Hindu or Muslim question in Kashmir,' the Sheikh told a lunch meeting in New York in January 1948. 'We do not use this language in Kashmir ... The objective before the National Conference for the best part of seventeen years has been the attainment of a secular democracy.'

It would be pointless to get into the interminable proceedings of the United Nations on Kashmir, since its role, in the final analysis, has been only of formal significance. The battles that mattered were fought on the ground, or in bilateral talks between India and Pakistan. The Sheikh wanted Nehru to give Pakistan an ultimatum in 1947–8 and then declare war on the country, but Nehru turned down the idea. At the UN, the British and US delegations blatantly supported Pakistan's arguments on Kashmir. The British had accepted Jinnah's theory that Muslims and Hindus were separate nations; they could not believe that they were wrong, and that an area with as strong a Muslim majority as Kashmir might prefer to be with 'Hindu' India. Mountbatten had even gone to Kashmir in July 1947 to persuade Maharaja Hari Singh to accede to Pakistan. But Sheikh Abdullah insisted over and over again that he was on the side of India. After the cease-fire, exactly one year after the problem went to the UN, Pakistan sponsored the formation of the 'Azad Kashmir' government with its capital at Muzaffarabad (the first city looted by the raiders), on the territory under its control. But the cease-fire did end the fighting, and allowed the leaders to turn their minds to the promises they had to keep.

The Indian Constitution, recognizing the particular nature of a problem which had become internationalized, awarded Kashmir a 'special status' through Article 370. Now Sheikh Abdullah began the process of acquiring popular legitimacy for the accession. In October 1950 the general council of the National Conference formally demanded elections to create a Constituent Assembly; elections were held in September–October 1951. The National Conference won everything. Out of the 45 seats in the Valley and Ladakh, only in two constituencies was the party even opposed. Commenting on the victory, the general secretary of the National Conference, Maulana Masoodi, said that this was the unequivocal reply of Kashmir's Muslims to Pakistan's claims that they wanted to accede to Pakistan. Nehru went to Srinagar to celebrate the victory of his friend and was welcomed on 1 September with slogans like 'Nehru and India for ever' and 'Kashmir will go with Nehru, not warmongers'. Pakistan tried to destroy the credibility of these elections after it realized that pro-Pakistan candidates stood no chance of victory. Instructions were sent that these candidates should file their nominations and then try to get arrested so that Pakistan could claim that the elections were rigged. But Sheikh Abdullah's government, totally confident of victory, refused to arrest anyone. There was an outpouring of joy on the day the Constituent Assembly met, a feeling that at last, after so many centuries, the people of Kashmir were finally deciding their own fate. Addressing the Assembly, Maulana Masoodi said, 'Our future is now in our hands.

We have gained the right to mould our destiny after our own dreams.' At the public meeting on that day Sheikh Abdullah thanked the people of India and their leader Nehru for their help in Kashmir's 'darkest hour' – the Pakistani invasion. 'We have now regained the initiative and will take steps to mould the destiny of our country,' he said. On 5 November 1951, Sheikh Abdullah, in his first address to the Assembly, explained what the four principal tasks were: devising a Constitution for the future government of Kashmir; deciding the future of the royal dynasty; considering the problem of the former landowners who were demanding compensation for the land seized from them; and deciding on the accession to India. He said clearly that he considered accession to India the best option open to the Assembly.

However, soon a few doubts began to arise in his mind. The whole question of Kashmir's relations with India would have to be finally settled by the Constituent Assembly. What would that mean? Would it put an end to all leverage with Delhi? It is clear that Sheikh Abdullah now began to wonder if Kashmir should not opt for a degree of independence, even if limited, which would ensure that Kashmir did not become a 'slave' of India, after having just escaped the clutches of Pakistan. India was a secular state, true, but would it always remain so? There were enough communal Hindus ready to bare their fangs at the slightest opportunity. Part of the reason for the Sheikh's worry was that India might not always be ruled by a Nehru – indeed, the signs of Hindu bigotry were already visible in the government; partly it was the old ambition to remain independent; and partly such thoughts were helped along by the Americans and the British who could recognize the strategic importance of the extraordinary geographical situation of Kashmir, in the centre of five ambitious, substantial powers. A good monitoring base in Kashmir could keep a watch on a large part of the world. The Sheikh now began to talk about a withdrawal of Pakistani troops from Kashmir, Indian demilitarization and then the promised plebiscite conducted by the UN. Later, when he saw that neither India nor Pakistan showed any inclination to leave those parts of Kashmir where their troops were stationed, he began advocating a different future: a confederation of Pakistan, India and Kashmir, of the sort that had been suggested by the Cabinet Mission in 1946 for the whole subcontinent, with the Centre having limited powers and the states enjoying the fullest autonomy. Nehru and the Congress had rejected this idea, demanding instead the undiluted unity of India.

There was no shortage of *agents provocateurs* to carry reports to receptive ears in Delhi about any sign of a changing mood. The Sheikh had to be on his very best behaviour all the time or his enemies would pounce on him, shouting that he was a closet traitor. The feudal element may have lost its power, but it still retained its influence, particularly with the elite. The landowners whose property had been redistributed to the landless spread it about that the Sheikh's reforms were actually nothing but well-disguised anti-Hinduism, since it was the Hindu whose land had gone to the Muslim peasant and tiller of the soil.

In his marvellous book *Outside the Archives* (Sangam Books, 1984), Y. D. Gundevia, who began his career in the Indian Civil Service and retired after thirty-six years, which included serving as Nehru's last Foreign Secretary, records a conversation he had with Sheikh Abdullah in 1949. Gundevia was suggesting the possibility of an independent Kashmir with both India and Pakistan as guarantors of its defence and independence. Replied the Sheikh, 'No, no. This would never work. Pakistan has taught us a lesson. Kashmir is too small and too poor. Pakistan would swallow Kashmir at one gulp. They have tried this once; they would do it again.' Comments Gundevia: 'This, strangely enough, is not the record of any sinister conversation between some British or American dignitary and Sheikh Abdullah ... I was asking the question and it was Sheikh giving me the negative.'

It has to be stressed that in 1947, for Nehru and the Sheikh on one side and Jinnah on the other, the battle for Kashmir was an ideological one. Without Kashmir, Pakistan's whole theory of Hindu and Muslim being separate nations collapsed; if the Muslims of Kashmir did not want to be part of an Islamic state, then obviously Jinnah's whole campaign stood exposed. Similarly, for Nehru, the fact that a Muslim-majority state wanted to join a secular democracy, not a religious state, was the ultimate triumph of the nationalism that the Congress had preached. Both Nehru and the Sheikh kept hammering at this point. In an interview published in the *Journal of the Indo-Japanese Association* (July–November 1957), when this question was put to him for the thousandth time, Nehru explained: 'Pakistan has put forth [the justification] that the majority of the people in Kashmir are Muslims. Now, that is a very odd argument. Once we admit that states are formed on the basis of religion, we go back to the Middle Ages in Europe or elsewhere. It is an impossible argument. If we admit it, then within India, as it is today after partition, there are 40 million Muslims. Are they Pakistani citizens and do they owe their allegiance to Pakistan? Every village in India has Muslims. There are Christians. Is there Christian nationality or Muslim nationality or Buddhist nationality or Hindu nationality? It is an impossible proposition ... Kashmir is, undoubtedly, that is, legally speaking, historically speaking, constitutionally speaking, a part of India, a part of the Union of India.'

Not even in his most depressed days did Sheikh Abdullah ever reject this ideology. When Sheikh Abdullah visited Pakistan for the first time, in May 1964, after more than a decade in Indian jails, the Pakistanis thought that the Sheikh would now at last sound disillusioned with 'secular' India and accept that the Muslim could not live in peace, safety and honour in Hindu-majority India. Sheikh Abdullah disappointed his hosts by saying that he still believed in secularism and rejected the two-nation theory. The *Dawn* of Karachi tried to put a brave face on it by commenting in an editorial, 'Sheikh Abdullah's statement and his references to India's so-called secularism have caused a certain amount of disappointment among the public in general, and the intelligentsia in particular.' Others sounded more bitter that the Sheikh had attacked neither 'blackmailer' Nehru nor 'militaristic' India. However, bigots in India also did their best to destroy the Sheikh–Nehru relationship, and to a large extent succeeded by 1953.

In 1952, Nehru and Abdullah came to what is known as the Delhi agreement. Gundevia writes: 'I was talking to Sheikh Sahib somewhere in Old Delhi, where he was under 'house arrest' [in the 1960s]. This was one of those unnecessarily hush-hush, after-dark visits in a police jeep in the first years after Shastri's death. When I mentioned the Delhi agreement, Sheikh told me, with some emotion, that Jawaharlal had agreed to leave so many things to the Kashmir Constituent Assembly to decide, and Nehru's last words were: "Oh, we will bind you in chains of gold, don't worry" ... How did the chains of gold come to be exchanged for shackles on the wrists of one of them, only a year later? Sheikh's explanation to me, in the same conversation, was that it was the gradual victory of "right-wingers, reactionaries and petty men". In his view, he said to me, "The reactionary elements had ample access to Delhi" – not to Nehru's court, but certainly elsewhere. "Sardar Patel and several others," Sheikh went on, "had no faith in me. Nehru first resisted the campaign of vilification against me, but ultimately he succumbed."'

Having been smashed in the elections of 1951–2, the Indian religious bigots attacked Nehru by a different method. The one point at which they thought him to be vulnerable was in his faith in Sheikh Abdullah. Since they could not get Nehru, they would get the Sheikh. They were eminently successful. They were helped, of course, by Pakistan's continued intransigence and propaganda. Pakistan had already lost on every front. With the defeat of the raiders and then of the Pakistani army, they had lost the war on the battlefield. With the accession of Hari Singh to India, they had lost the struggle in legal terms. And with Sheikh Abdullah's unambiguous rejection of Pakistan, they had lost the moral battle too.

It will seem utterly paradoxical to those used to seeing Indian problems through the conventional Hindu–Muslim enmity syndrome, but it was Sheikh Abdullah who, in 1948, was worried that certain Hindu leaders in Delhi were deliberately trying to gift Kashmir away to Pakistan. Patel, in fact, protested against this, since Abdullah was obviously implying that it was Patel who was guilty of such intentions. But by 1952, the same communal Hindu lobby had begun making heavy play of Sheikh Abdullah's alleged ambivalence on the status of Kashmir. Differences which arose during the debates of the Kashmir Constituent Assembly, inevitable in the best of circumstances, were turned into matters of life and death. Towards the end of 1952, a group of organizations whose aims could hardly be in doubt joined hands to launch an anti-Sheikh agitation in Jammu. They were the newly formed Jana Sangh led by Syama Prasad Mookerjee, the Hindu Mahasabha, the Rashtriya Swayam-sevak Sangh, the Jammu Praja Parishad – all Hindu parties – and the Akali Dal of the Sikhs led by the virulent Master Tara Singh. For a man who had shown so much courage and initiative in much more serious situations, Nehru was strangely ineffective in this crisis. Had he lost his nerve or was his faith in his friend waning? S. Gopal, the most authoritative as well as sympathetic biographer of Nehru, writes in the second volume of his three-volume work, that this particular agitation could have returned the country to the havoc of the partition violence. 'Such potential danger called for quick and firm action at many levels; but nowhere was Nehru fully successful, and in consequence the crisis mounted beyond control. His orders that every attempt at disturbance within India should be suppressed were carried out only half-heartedly. The Home Ministry was at this time in the hands of Kailas Nath Katju, a loyal follower of Nehru but long past his prime; and his doddering ineptitude was accentuated by the tardiness of many officials whose communal sympathies were barely concealed. Nor did the effort of Nehru to isolate the agitation, so as to reveal its personal and communal tones, make much headway ... Above all, Nehru failed in his major thrust of seeking to isolate the communal nucleus of the agitation by establishing that Sheikh Abdullah's administration was secular, broad-minded and national.'

Mookerjee's agitation only served to resurrect fears in the National Conference about how sharp the edge of Hindu fanaticism could be. That was a dangerous time to have doubts, considering that the Constituent Assembly was preparing its final decisions. The temptation to keep the ultimate control of Kashmir's destiny in the hands of Kashmiris rather than surrender it to Delhi played its part. Sheikh Abdullah never asked for independence (he described the idea as 'trash') if for no other reason than that it was simply not viable. Kashmir was too weak to be independent. But he began talking about autonomy within the Indian Union. Nehru was also convinced that the Americans were encouraging such moves. According to S. Gopal, Nehru attempted 'to suppress firmly the activities of the Hindu communalists which were little short of treason, thereby giving Abdullah time to recover his nerve ... Nehru's hand, however, was weakened by the persistent inefficiency of the Home Ministry. Katju was unwilling to act on his Prime Minister's suggestion [to ban the Jana Sangh and arrest the agitators].'

The Home Minister of India was clearly under the influence of those who wanted to see Sheikh Abdullah removed. Among them (for understandable reasons, given the fact that he had just lost his little empire) was Dr Karan Singh, son of Maharaja Hari Singh, who had been made the constitutional head of state (a ceremonial post) in view of the family's place in Kashmir's history. Karan Singh urged that Sheikh Abdullah be forced to begin a dialogue with the agitators. Nehru dismissed such a compromise sharply, writing to Karan Singh, 'In my view what these people [the agitators] have done is little short of treason to the country and the people should realize it' (quoted by Karan Singh in his autobiography, *Heir Apparent*, Oxford University Press). In March 1953 the conspiracy to remove Sheikh Abdullah was set in motion. The man chosen to be Brutus was Bakshi Ghulam Mohammad, the deputy Prime Minister, whom Karan Singh describes as 'pragmatic'. In June, Mookerjee decided to cross into Jammu without obtaining the necessary permit to do so. Rather than stop him from going to Jammu at such a volatile time, officials of the Punjab government actually accompanied Mookerjee and helped him cross the border – such was the support that the man accused by Nehru of leading a treacherous agitation, got from the administration. Nehru protested angrily both to the Chief Minister of Punjab, Bhimsen Sachar, and to his own Home Minister, Katju, for allowing Mookerjee to enter Jammu and Kashmir; incredibly, the Prime Minister was ignored. Mookerjee was arrested by Abdullah's government and, as luck would have it, he died of a heart attack while in jail. This was just the kind of handle his enemies needed to call Sheikh Abdullah a villain.

On 10 July the Sheikh made a speech which was used to prove that he had now become a 'traitor' to India. At the Mujahid Manzil, the head-quarters of the National Conference, Sheikh Abdullah is quoted as having said that even Nehru could not control communal elements in India and the time might come when Kashmir would have to say 'goodbye' to secular India. In the party's Working Committee, the Sheikh's closest aide, Mirza Afzal Beg, suggested that the accession to India should not go beyond what had been agreed with Hari Singh in 1947, Delhi controlling only defence, foreign affairs and communications. Bakshi spoke up for wider co-operation. The showdown was coming, and a depressed Nehru could only watch events take their course. The Sheikh began to get vitriolic, particularly after he discovered that the colleagues whom he had trusted were turning against him, and that his ideological commitment was being held in doubt, 'The propaganda barrage unleashed in the press,' says Gundevia, 'said Sheikh Abdullah was a turncoat, he was pro-Pakistan, he was about to repudiate Kashmir's accession to India, he wanted an independent Kashmir ...' On 7 August, Sheikh Abdullah decided to move against his detractors in the Cabinet, and asked for the resignation of his Health Minister, Pandit Sham Lal Saraf. On 8 August, Karan Singh was sent a copy of a memorandum signed by Bakshi Ghulam Mohammad, Finance Minister G. L. Dogra, and Sham Lal Saraf, addressed to Sheikh Abdullah, accusing him of trying to 'precipitate a rupture in the relationship of the state with India', and informing the Prime Minister that in their view the Cabinet had 'lost the confidence of the people'. The same day the Sheikh left for Gulmarg to spend a quiet weekend with his wife and family.

Nehru is quoted by Gopal as having written to Girija Shankar Bajpai on 24 August 1953, 'For the last three months I have seen this coming, creeping up as some kind of invisible disaster, I did not of course know the exact shape it would take. To the last moment, I was not clear what exactly would happen.' What happened was that Karan Singh spent the afternoon of 8 August drafting a dismissal order: 'And whereas a stage has been reached in which the very process of honest and efficient administration has become impracticable; and whereas, finally, the functioning of the present Cabinet on the basis of joint responsibility has become impossible and the resultant conflicts have gravely jeopardized the unity, prosperity and stability of the state ... [I] do hereby dismiss Sheikh Mohammad Abdullah from the Prime Ministership of the state of Jammu and Kashmir and consequently the Council of Ministers headed by him is dissolved forthwith.'

The weather on the evening of 8 August was straight out of *Macbeth* when Karan Singh's ADC, Major B. S. Bajwa, along with a party of policemen, took the difficult road to Gulmarg via Tangmarg. There was thunder, lightning and rain. The Sheikh and his wife were asleep when Major Bajwa knocked on the door at eleven at night. Police had surrounded the house. The Sheikh was given two hours to pack and say his *namaz* (his prayers). In the early hours of the morning he was taken away to what would be the beginning of more than a decade of spells in jail, and two decades in the wilderness, which would test the faith and the courage of the Lion of Kashmir. His colleagues and supporters like Mirza Afzal Beg were also arrested. In the darkness of the same night, before dawn had broken, a new government, headed by Bakshi Ghulam Mohammad, had been sworn in. The only condition that Bakshi made before taking over was that Sheikh Abdullah be arrested; he would not be able to control Kashmir if the Sheikh was a free man. And propaganda was planted in the Press that India had been saved: Sheikh Abdullah had been arrested just before crossing over to Pakistan that stormy night!

Nehru was never told that his friend would be imprisoned. The politicians all over India were also strangely quiet; even those from the opposition. There was clearly a lack of confidence in the nation, a fear that perhaps this was the price necessary for survival and integrity. Even Ram Manohar Lohia, the Socialist leader who could be expected to criticize Nehru for just about everything, was muted in his assessment. Only later would some leaders, like Jayaprakash Narayan and Ashoka Mehta, begin arguing that the Sheikh's arrest was a disaster, and that he was not in fact a secessionist. (But perhaps the guilt at the silence of 1953 was washed away in 1984 when the government of Farooq Abdullah was removed in similar fashion on similar excuses. Opposition leaders from all over the country rallied to the support of Sheikh Abdullah's son, Farooq.) As Gundevia puts it when describing the Sheikh's arrest, 'This was a dual blow. Not only was Sheikh Abdullah defeated; Jawaharlal Nehru was also defeated.'

Long afterwards, in 1978, during a conversation with the author, Sheikh Abdullah said he had faced three major crises in his life. The first was when the mullahs of Kashmir tried to destroy him after he had converted the Muslim Conference into the National Conference. How had he tackled them, I asked. 'By becoming a mullah myself,' the Sheikh replied with a laugh. 'Another was in 1947 when the entire country was plunged in darkness. There were communal riots all around us. In the Punjab, a wave of RSS [Rashtriya Swayamsevak Sangh] killings, and on the other side the Muslim League killing all non-Muslims. We were caught between the two sides. From the north came the raiders bringing their fire of Muslim communalism and from the south the RSS with their fire of Hindu communalism.' But Kashmir was saved. The experience of jail in 1953 'was the third crisis, when our faith in secularism, democracy and socialism was put to a severe test. That time my colleagues in jail told me: "What is left now? Why should we go to India, if this is the result? We should go to Pakistan." But the fact is that the ideals we stood for were more important than Pakistan or India. We had joined India because of its ideals – secularism and socialism. India wanted to build a state where humanism would prevail. So long as India sticks to these ideals, our people have a place nowhere else but in India.'

5
Nothing Proved

In a political career extending more than fifty years, Sheikh Mohammad Abdullah was imprisoned nine times and spent a total of fifteen years, seven months and five days in detention. Life was hard in the jails of Maharaja Hari Singh; once, the Sheikh even went on a fast to protest the diet and the conditions. But imprisonment under Hari Singh he could accept. He found it more difficult to understand why a friend like Nehru should have lost faith in him, and why a democrat should have disregarded the common commitment to liberty. The propaganda barrage unleashed against him and his family could have only added salt to the wounds. Apart from the constant refrain that Sheikh Abdullah was working to take Kashmir to Pakistan, there were more sinister charges – that Begum Abdullah was getting large sums of money from Pakistan, for instance. With Bakshi Ghulam Mohammad determined to prove that he had acted in the national interest, and the intelligence agencies and the Home Ministry in Delhi crowded with people more than anxious to destroy Sheikh Abdullah, a tremendous effort was mounted to find evidence of treason. For four years the Intelligence Bureau kept claiming that it was on the verge of finding proof of the Sheikh's involvement in a pro-Pakistan conspiracy, but nothing could ever be found. A charge could not even be framed. And Sheikh Abdullah remained in jail.

Begum Akbar Jehan Abdullah, his wife, recounted a charming story about the first time she saw her husband, in an interview to Udayan Sharma (*Sunday*, 5 June 1983). She came from a wealthy and liberal background; her family owned the famous Nedous' hotel in Srinagar. Girls could not study in Kashmir in those days, so she used to live outside Kashmir. She was 'only a young girl of sixteen or seventeen' then, and had gone up to Srinagar for her holidays in 1932. The slim, tall, young man had come to the hotel to persuade her father to give a donation to their political cause, when the future Begum Abdullah saw him. She asked her mother who this man was. He was an 'angel' to the Kashmiris, said her mother, an angel who was helping them fight for their rights against the Maharaja. Clearly attracted, the girl wanted to take a better look, but the rules of modesty prevented her from going to where he was sitting with her father. However, soon negotiations were begun for their marriage. When her father, Harry Nedou, first heard about the idea, he threw his hands up in horror. 'Oh God!' he said, 'this man is going to spend his whole life in jail. What will happen to my little girl?' The indulgent father gave in to his little girl's wishes, but that was a prophetic comment. Sheikh Abdullah would stay in jail even when the world could charge him with nothing, as between 1953 and 1958.

Finally, some opposition parties launched a campaign in 1957 demanding the Sheikh's release. An exasperated Nehru ordered that the Sheikh be freed. On 8 January 1958, after nearly four and a half years, at five o'clock in the evening the orders of release reached the bungalow where the Sheikh was lodged, in the mountain resort of Kud, on the Jammu side of the Banihal range. The government told him that his monthly stipend of Rs 1,000 and his daily allowance were being stopped, and a car was present to take him to his family in Srinagar. Sheikh Abdullah sent the car back and decided to stay on in jail for just another day – at his own expense. He would not use the government car. Friends soon arranged transport he considered a bit less obnoxious.

Much had changed by then. The Kashmir Constituent Assembly had confirmed the accession to India and agreed on a Constitution which had come into effect on 26 January 1957. Bakshi Ghulam Mohammad, who had taken over the National Conference and the government, was still the Chief Minister, but some of his allies had fallen out by now, accusing him of being both inefficient and corrupt. Obviously feeling the absence of freedom under Bakshi, G. M. Sadiq and D. P. Dhar had launched the Democratic National Conference. The Sheikh's supporters had collected under the banner of the newly formed Plebiscite Front, led by Mirza Afzal Beg. It was a one-point party: democracy had been 'murdered' on 9 August 1953, with the Sheikh's arrest; the Constituent Assembly was no longer representative of the people's will and therefore all its decisions were null and void; it was imperative, consequently, that a fresh plebiscite be held to determine the people's will even in relation to accession.

For Sheikh Abdullah the political clock of Kashmir had stopped an hour before midnight on 8 August 1953, and he would accept no settlement with Delhi which did not restore the status quo. And what about his essential ideology? Had these four years of arbitrary imprisonment changed that?

He met the Press on 10 January 1958. Dressed in a black *sherwani* (the formal Indian long coat) and white *pyjamas*, he looked cheerful. The answer to the obvious first question was that in these four years his faith in Gandhi had only increased. Gandhi's life and experiences had been, in the difficult days, a 'beacon light'. 'I am the same Abdullah as in 1947,' he stressed. 'When people were massacred elsewhere, I tried to preserve the ideal of Gandhiji. I continue to do so. I have not changed. My views are firm. I am not the kind of politician who will hide facts from others. All know my views. Naturally, the people are the final arbiters; I am not the final arbiter ... I do not have the guns to coerce the people or the money to bribe them, but only persuasion.'

If Sheikh Abdullah was bitter it was about those he felt had betrayed him to get into power in 1953: 'I have not learnt to stab friends in the back, many of whom I brought up and regarded as members of my family. I have not learnt the art of intriguing or betraying friends.'

The anger of the Sheikh and the arguments offered by those who left him are best summed up in the correspondence between the Sheikh and G. M. Sadiq, which took place after August 1956, when the Sheikh learnt that the Constituent Assembly was about to ratify a Constitution. (The correspondence was made available to the author by the Sadiq family.) Sadiq was the President of the Constituent Assembly then, and the Sheikh warned him 'of the grave consequences likely to follow your contemplated action'. Sheikh Abdullah described what, in his opinion, Kashmir had now become – 'a veritable hell ... an iron curtain was thrown over the valley, suppressing all facts from the outside world'. The 'coup' of 9 August 1953 was 'the result of a deep conspiracy with communal and reactionary elements and other vested interests'. The Sheikh ended: 'I am confident that should you persist in your anti-people course of action and try and foist a Constitution on the people of Kashmir ... they will fight back your designs to the bitter end.'

In his reply, dated 11 September 1956, Sadiq reminded the Sheikh that in his first speech to the Assembly the Sheikh himself had advised 'that while safeguarding our autonomy to the fullest extent so as to enable us to have the liberty to build our country according to the past traditions and genius of our people, we may also, by suitable Constitutional arrangements with the [Indian] Union, establish our right to seek and compel federal co-operation and assistance in this great task, as well as

offer our fullest co-operation and assistance to the Union'. Sadiq argued
that it was the Sheikh whose commitment to India had begun wavering
after the Delhi agreement of August 1952. He accused the Sheikh of
starting the 'agonizing search for alternatives to our accession with India.
You will kindly recall that throughout the period you declared your
fascination for independence of a truncated state which would, more or
less, include only the valley of Kashmir. You clung to this idea in spite of
our solemn entreaties to you and irrespective of the weighty arguments
you had marshalled against it on earlier occasions.'

On 26 September, the Sheikh sent his reply. He first pointed out that
Sadiq had sidetracked the charge that the Constituent Assembly had lost
its representative character after the 'murder of democracy'. Then he
came to the allegation of conspiracy: 'Immediately after my arrest, you
were the first person to characterize the 9th August action as "appropriate
and opportune". You rushed to Delhi and Bombay soon after and accused
me of having conspired with some foreign powers in order to convert
Kashmir into a second Korea. You threatened that the government was
in possession of some unimpeachable evidence to establish the charge.
Though more than three years have passed by, the so-called evidence of
these wild charges has yet to see the light of day.' The Sheikh went on to
say that if the Bakshi group did believe that they were in a majority, then
the legitimate course would have been to bring a Motion of No Confidence
against the Sheikh and vote him out of power on the floor of the House.
It would be perfectly legitimate for them after that to shape the Constitution in the manner they wanted. 'If the motion were carried,' wrote the
Sheikh, 'I would have tendered my resignation.' But that chance was
never given, of course, and even Jawaharlal Nehru, despite his emotional
and intellectual commitment to democracy, let this aberration pass, on the
catch-all excuse of national interest. But never did the Sheikh publicly
blame his friend for this, though in private he may have raised the matter.

In fact, there can be no better tribute to the personality if not the politics
of Jawaharlal Nehru than that given by the man who had just spent more
than four years in jail: 'How can I forget all the love and affection he has
shown me all along, treating me as a member of his family? I can
understand [that] there were so many forces: when one is in the thick of
a struggle, one is subjected to so many pulls, vested interests, national and
international stresses. If one man can stand up to these pressures, it is
Panditji [Nehru]. Probably the forces of the situation were such [that]
to bring about a speedy solution he put me into prison.'

On 12 January 1958, Sheikh Abdullah reached Srinagar. The city rang with shouts of *'Sher-e-Kashmir Zindabad'* ('Long live the Lion of Kashmir'), and crowds surged to see their hero. The Abdullah oratory was at its most powerful at the public meeting on 13 January. In an impassioned speech, he attacked those who argued that the accession should be considered final now that the Constituent Assembly had approved it. The Assembly had lost its democratic character and the people now had to be given another chance to vote. 'Mr Nehru extended his hand to the Kashmiris in Lal Chowk in Srinagar [on that emotional day in November 1947] and assured the people that the ultimate decision on the question of Kashmir's accession would rest with the people. This assurance was confirmed by India later in the Security Council. I ask Mr Nehru, why is he silent now on this? Does he consider Kashmiris cows and goats now?' And India could not hope to win the 'affection' of the Kashmiris, he added, by the kind of behaviour it had shown in 1953. 'The only people who can decide [on the future of Kashmir] are the people of Kashmir, four million men, women and children, Muslims and Hindus who inhabit this land.'

In Delhi, Defence Minister V. K. Krishna Menon called such speeches 'treasonable', and of course Bakshi Ghulam Mohammad insisted each day that the accession to India was now beyond dispute. Once again, the intelligence agencies set to work. (It should be remembered, at this point, that the right to propagate secession from the Union was still guaranteed under the fundamental right of free speech through Article 19 of the Constitution. The DMK in the south, for instance, had secession as the basic platform of its manifesto. It was only when the 16th Amendment was passed by Parliament in 1963, that this freedom was withdrawn.)

The Prime Minister of Pakistan, Malik Feroz Khan Noon, had put the truth most bluntly when, on the day Sheikh Abdullah had been released, he remarked that the detention of the Sheikh had proved to be a good platform for Pakistani propaganda. 'I am sorry we have lost that platform now,' he added. As things transpired, all Noon had to do was wait for four months. On 30 April 1958, at 11.15 at night, Sheikh Abdullah was arrested once again, this time under the Preventive Detention Act. 'His remaining at large was hazardous to the security of the state,' intoned the Inspector-General of Police, D. W. Mehra. The story (easily lapped up) was spread that the Sheikh had given shelter to criminals wanted in connection with incidents of loot, arson and murder provoked by the Plebiscite Front. The usual propaganda offensive was mounted. Bakshi Ghulam Mohammad told the *Daily Telegraph* of London, in an interview published on 2 May, 'He preached Muslim fanaticism ... There is no doubt that Sheikh Abdullah was in league with Pakistan. It was from there that in all probability he was getting funds to raise his private army.' Nehru himself believed that the Sheikh was 'now following a policy which is narrow-minded, communal and very dangerous'. Sheikh Abdullah tried to correct this impression of Nehru's. A. M. Rosenthal, then Delhi correspondent of *The New York Times*, quoted the letter Sheikh Abdullah wrote to Nehru from jail: 'I am silently watching all this in order to know for myself how Indian democracy is functioning in that part of the state which is predominantly Muslim. There is no doubt that I do not agree with the policy the government of India is pursuing ... This ten-year-old dispute [can be resolved only] by conceding the right of self-determination to the people of Kashmir, which you once so ardently supported ... I still believe that the key of the solution lies in your hands, and I appeal to you not to be deceived by Bakshi and his other supporters, in pursuing a policy which in the end is bound to be disastrous for all ... I hope you are keeping well.'

In retrospect, the decision to rearrest the Sheikh seems more logical and more necessary than the decision to arrest him. Bakshi's reasons for the rearrest can be ignored as irresponsible; but Nehru cannot be defended for calling the Sheikh 'communal'. How often Pakistan must have wished in those two and a half decades that the Sheikh was truly what his critics accused him of being! But no one can yet trace a single statement made by the Sheikh advocating that Kashmir join Pakistan, or that Kashmiris vote for Pakistan in a plebiscite. But he was also single-minded about the right of the Kashmiris to determine their own future, with freedom and honour. He saw that as the basic contribution he could make to his people: restore to them that pride and self-confidence destroyed by a succession of rulers, Mughal or Sikh or Dogra. And in his own arbitrary dismissal he saw the return of colonization, the mischief of quasi-feudal forces, and a contempt for the will of the people. He could not accept this without surrendering everything he had fought for all his life. There is no doubt that if he had been left free in 1958 the government of India would have found it impossible to deal with the popular anger. The decision made in 1953 was a bad one, but once it had been made, Nehru had to go through with the logic of the bad decision; error could only be controlled by further error.

The problem over the plebiscite that the Sheikh wanted was very simple: the ruling elite in Delhi now felt sure that the Muslims of Kashmir would not vote to join India, particularly after the arrest of the Sheikh. If Nehru had been ardent about the plebiscite before, it was because he was certain – just as the Sheikh himself was certain – that the people would say an overwhelming yes to India. This was proved in the elections for the Constituent Assembly in 1951, when all pro-Pakistan elements were humiliated. Anger against the raiders sent by Pakistan was at a peak; slogans against Pakistani 'warmongers' were common. But by 1953, Delhi's confidence in the Kashmiri's commitment to secularism had ebbed drastically, just as the Kashmiri's faith in Delhi's commitment to democracy had become uncertain. By 1958, the government of India had announced that there was no longer any question of a plebiscite. The official explanation was that a plebiscite had been promised only after Pakistani troops left Kashmir. They still had not, so there could be no plebiscite. And of course, the Pakistani troops are still there and will not go unless the Indian army is strong enough to drive them out. Since neither the Indian nor the Pakistani army seems, at the moment of writing, in a position to drive the other out, Kashmir will remain divided until the day – if that ever comes – when the old country returns to unity and a genuine confederation. The last time that the idea of a confederation was canvassed was in 1964: that was the last thing that the two friends, Jawaharlal Nehru and Sheikh Abdullah, would attempt together, in that event-filled summer.

But six summers before 1964, Sheikh Abdullah went on trial on the charge of conspiracy to overthrow the Jammu and Kashmir government by 'means of criminal force'. On 21 May 1958, in a magistrate's court in Jammu, began what became notorious as the 'Kashmir Conspiracy Case', against twenty-five accused. On 23 October, J. P. Mitter, senior prosecution counsel, moved to include among the 'conspirators' the stars who had been missing so far, Sheikh Abdullah and Mirza Afzal Beg. The court was packed on 24 October. Dressed in a chocolate *kurta pyjama* and a jacket, Sheikh Abdullah greeted all those gathered, with a generous smile. The next day he told the court that he had gone through the complaint 'not without considerable amusement'. Then he defined what, in his view, this case was all about: 'There is a political design behind this prosecution, that is clear. The complaint is nothing but politics.' Instead of being called a conspirator, he should more correctly be described as a victim of a conspiracy, said the Sheikh. It would take six years for the government of India to admit that the Sheikh was right. With all the power of the state behind them, with all the determination in their hearts to malign him, the

Sheikh's detractors once again were able to prove nothing. Sheikh Abdullah would leave jail once again with his head high.

The government of Jammu and Kashmir, during the period of the Sheikh's jail terms, gave up even pretending to be democratic. Elections, of course, had to be held under the law, but they were blatantly fixed to prevent pro-Abdullah candidates from winning. In a letter which has acquired some fame, Nehru himself wrote to Bakshi Ghulam Mohammad after his National Conference had 'won' almost all the seats in the 1962 elections: 'In fact, it would strengthen your position much more if you lost a few seats to bona fide opponents.' Nehru made an attempt to get the Sheikh released in April 1962, according to S. Gopal, but the Home Minister and the Srinagar government thwarted Nehru.

The war with China in 1962 had a substantial impact on the Kashmir problem. The USA and Britain had helped to restrain Ayub Khan from opening up the Kashmir front while the Indian army was taking a beating in the Himalayas, but after the cease-fire and the unexpected Chinese withdrawal, there was Anglo-American pressure on Nehru to settle the Kashmir problem with Pakistan. Pakistan was gleeful about the Chinese victory, and Ayub Khan never lost an opportunity to taunt any Indian dignitary about the collapse of their 'great Indian army' which had performed so well in the two world wars. A long round of talks between India and Pakistan began in December 1962 in Rawalpindi, Delhi, Karachi and Calcutta, lasting till March the next year. India was willing to offer Pakistan 1,500 square miles more than she already held in Kashmir, provided Pakistan accepted the new line as an international boundary. But Ayub Khan and his rising protégé with a flair for dramatics, Zulfiqar Ali Bhutto, had other ideas. Pakistan made its intentions clear when, just a day before the talks with India were to open, it announced a provisional boundary agreement between Pakistan and China, to be replaced by a formal treaty after the Kashmir problem was solved. (The conditionality was important, since Pakistan was in effect handing over a huge, barren but strategic chunk of Kashmir to China.) This was hardly the proper gesture to make to India on the eve of discussions which were scheduled to lead to a 'historic' peace. Bhutto, confident he had the upper hand, said that Pakistan would be satisfied with nothing less than the whole of the Kashmir valley, barring a small portion adjoining Himachal Pradesh. As Bhutto told the Indian delegation (quoted by Gundevia, who was a participant), 'You are a defeated nation, don't you see?' But that was a time in India's history when a thirty-seven-year-old Pakistani politician on the make could get away with such statements. Pakistan and China had become new friends, and Bhutto could boast or threaten that in any future war with India the most powerful nation in Asia would be on the side of Pakistan – plus, of course, the fact that Pakistan's arms and ammunition had already come from the most powerful nation in the world. (When India asked the US and Britain for 500 million dollars' worth of arms after the 1962 war, and got in the end nothing more than 60 million dollars' worth, Pakistan had already received 800 million dollars' worth of arms from the West.) It was this Pakistani arrogance which pushed the country into the war of 1965, which Ayub Khan and Bhutto were convinced would be a walk-over. And it was this over-confidence which led Ayub Khan to contemptuously dismiss the Nehru–Abdullah proposal of 1964. Lost in their dreams of a military victory in Kashmir, the Pakistanis forgot the fire which had started in their own backyard – although Nehru tried to warn them about it.

Even before the 1962 talks with Pakistan, Nehru had begun to see wisdom in the idea that the only true solution to the India–Pakistan tangle was a confederation. Nehru felt it should be a quadrangular union: India–West Pakistan–Kashmir–East Bengal. A confederation, with a common defence, foreign and communications policy, would not only defuse the struggle for Kashmir, but also solve the distance gap between the two halves of Pakistan, and by granting more autonomy control the rising anger of East Bengal. As Nehru told the Delhi correspondent of the *Washington Post* (printed on 19 December 1962, and quoted also by S. Gopal): 'Confederation remains our ultimate goal. Look at Europe, at the Common Market. This is the urge everywhere. There are no two peoples anywhere nearer than those of India and Pakistan, though if we say it, they are alarmed and think we want to swallow them.'

Nehru had also begun to feel guilty about Sheikh Abdullah. He said that the country did not seem to have the courage to release the Sheikh. Then an incident occurred in Srinagar which showed how easily the volcano might erupt, without the co-operation of Sheikh Abdullah and his loyalists. In the beautiful mosque at Hazratbal, whose Friday-prayer congregations Sheikh Abdullah addressed so often, is enshrined a single strand of the hair of the Prophet Muhammad, placed there in the seventeenth century. On 12 December 1963, this holy relic was found to be missing. Srinagar erupted. For a week, the people were on the streets, and in the forefront of the agitation were the pro-Abdullah forces. A week later the relic mysteriously reappeared. Cynics questioned whether it was the genuine article or a fake placed there to calm passions. The Srinagar government fuelled such suspicions by preventing independent witnesses from examining the strand of hair to pronounce on its authenticity. Nehru intervened, and asked Lal Bahadur Shastri, then a minister without portfolio, to fly to Srinagar. Maulana Masoodi, an old comrade of Sheikh Abdullah, was among the group of religious men specially requested by Shastri to examine the holy relic. There was a huge sigh of relief when they declared the hair to be genuine.

Shastri, after this incident, joined the group urging Nehru to order the release of the Sheikh. Nehru asked Shastri to meet the Sheikh in jail. Shastri did so. But the Sheikh would not accept any conditions for release: had he been willing to do that, he would have been a free man long ago. For the Home Ministry, the Sheikh was still a great danger to the nation. One day, notes Gundevia (who was present during the incident), Nehru simply lost his temper at a bureaucrat conveying such doubts and said furiously, 'If a damned thing can't be proved in four years, in six years, there's obviously nothing to be proved.'

On 5 April 1964, acting on Nehru's direct instructions, bypassing the Home Ministry in Delhi, the Prime Minister of Kashmir, G. M. Sadiq, announced that the case against Sheikh Abdullah was being withdrawn immediately. The Sheikh was released on 8 April. And once again it was a triumphant journey from Jammu to Srinagar. If anything, Sheikh Abdullah sounded more philosophical about his years in jail this time than last. He was not bitter, he said. 'It is all part of the game and I have taken it in that spirit.'

On 2 April Nehru sent a personal letter to his old friend, inviting him to come to Delhi and stay with him on his release. The letter reached the Sheikh on 7 April, by which time plans for a road journey to Srinagar had already been made. The Sheikh was able to come to Delhi as Nehru's house guest only on 29 April. Now began a round of intense consultations, not only with Nehru, but also with other important national leaders, including those who had left the Congress, like Jayaprakash Narayan, C. Rajagopalachari and Acharya Kripalani. Sheikh Abdullah also went to discuss the situation with the venerable Acharya Vinoba Bhave, the Gandhian who had turned ascetic and now lived at his ashram in Wardha ('If you succeed in combining spiritualism with practical politics,' the Sheikh told a press conference, 'then you do not have to worry about anything').

The Sheikh's preconditions were still the same: any solution should be honourable to the Kashmiris, and Indian secularism must not be disturbed. But the stress had shifted in the era following the India–China war. During the war itself the Sheikh had written to Nehru saying that freedom had to be preserved jointly, and one important step towards creating the joint endeavour was a solution of the Kashmir problem. Now he argued that a large chunk of Pakistan-held Kashmir had been given away to China because of the bitterness between India and Pakistan. The vital task was not simply confirming the legality or otherwise of Kashmir's accession, but finding a solution which could restore to the subcontinent the peace and friendship which had been destroyed by the conflict over Kashmir. The only logical answer to the Sheikh's mind, was a confederation of India, Pakistan and Kashmir. Sheikh Abdullah was in an exhilarated mood at that period. After those long years in jail, participation in the nation's politics at the highest levels must have been adrenalin enough.

On 6 May came a further injection. Ayub Khan, feeling that Pakistan was being left behind in the excitement, sent a letter to Sheikh Abdullah, saying: 'You are obviously discussing the future of Kashmir with Indian leaders. Considering that we have given a solemn pledge to the people of Kashmir that the future of the state would be decided in accordance with their wishes as envisaged in the UN resolutions, and the fact that we have vital interests in Kashmir, you will understand our anxiety that no settlement is reached without due consultation and agreement with us. Therefore, if you think that the time is ripe now for such consultation, we would be very happy to receive you here and discuss this matter with you.'

Invitation accepted. Sheikh Abdullah was keen to test the confederation idea on the Pakistanis. Perhaps Nehru had seen too much, and become cynical. He was convinced that the Pakistanis would not buy it and that the idea would come to nothing; that Ayub Khan would describe it as a barely camouflaged attempt to merge Pakistan once again into India. Sheikh Abdullah was more confident about success. He replied to Ayub Khan that he would be delighted to avail himself of his 'kind invitation' as soon as a 'proposal takes concrete shape'. The Sheikh even proposed going to Pakistan by walking across the Kashmir cease-fire line in a gesture reminiscent of what Gandhi had wanted to do to the borders of India and Pakistan – to destroy them by not recognizing them. Gandhi was assassinated before he could do that. Nehru was horrified when he heard that something similar might happen to the Sheikh if he tried to do anything so foolhardy. Who could guarantee security? Sheikh Abdullah was outraged when he learnt that the plan to walk across the cease-fire line had been opposed. He blamed the bureaucrats. It took a lot of persuasion to make him change his mind. But when he reached Pakistan on 24 May, it was by a special Pakistan International Airways aircraft.

Pakistan, determined to make this as big a news-story as possible, gave Sheikh Abdullah a great welcome. At the airport to receive him were Zulfiqar Ali Bhutto, then Ayub Khan's Foreign Minister, and Habibullah Khan, Minister for Home and Kashmir Affairs. The Sheikh was accompanied by Mirza Afzal Beg and Maulana Masoodi, and by the son whom he was already grooming to be his heir, Farooq Abdullah. The 10,000 crowd broke through the police cordon to greet the Sheikh at the airport. But within two days, Sheikh Abdullah had disappointed his Pakistani hosts. He refused to criticize India; far from doing so, he kept praising India's secular ideals. Ayub Khan met the Sheikh within hours of the latter's arrival. As expected, he shot down the idea of a confederation, labelling it in his autobiography an 'absurd proposal' brought at the instance of Nehru (Abdullah wrote to Ayub Khan denying that he was set up by Nehru). And the Pakistani media, waiting to praise Abdullah, found it must denounce him. The Sheikh was warned not to become an agent who had come to ensure the sale of Kashmir to India in order to protect Indian Muslims! Most extraordinary logic, but then it was always such logic which created Pakistan. Be that as it may, the only concession that Sheikh Abdullah managed to extract from Ayub Khan was a promise to visit India. Abdullah asked Nehru to send an invitation to Ayub Khan. An ill, tired Nehru had left for Dehra Dun on a much-needed holiday, on the day that Sheikh Abdullah had left for Pakistan. But the invitation was quickly written, and it reached the Indian High Commissioner in Pakistan for onward delivery to Ayub Khan on 27 May 1964.

On that same day, 27 May 1964, Jawaharlal Nehru, one of the greatest men this subcontinent has been privileged to call a son, died.

On 27 May, Sheikh Abdullah was in the part of Kashmir he had not seen since 1947, in Muzaffarabad with K. H. Khurshid, the President of 'Azad Kashmir'. It was here that news reached him that Nehru had passed away. Sheikh Abdullah broke down and sobbed uncontrollably for a few minutes. He was asked for a comment and could not manage anything; all he could say was, 'He is dead ... I can't meet him ... I can't say anything ...' And then he broke down again. He cancelled the rest of his tour and returned home to India the next day.

It was the beginning of another decade in jail and exile.

6

To Die an Indian

'Since some time past we have been strongly feeling that time has come [sic] when we should take the public at large into our confidence as to how we feel about Kashmir's relationship with India, taking into consideration the actual conditions prevailing in the state and outside it. The people of this subcontinent, more particularly those of the state, full well know that we have striven hard during the past eleven years to give finality to the accession of the state with India, which took place in 1947. In season and out of it, we have spared no pains to declare it as complete and irrevocable, and have made all possible sacrifice to that end. Unfortunately our efforts have completely failed to bring about the desired result ... Within the state, the mass of people have not shown any change of heart. They have gone through sufferings and sacrifices, and have consistently demanded implementation of pledges given to them by India, Pakistan and the United Nations. The resultant uncertainty and insecurity has brought about, in addition to perpetual agony, political and economic collapse, and the people are going through perhaps the worst and the most miserable phase in the history of the state.'

One more example of Sheikh Abdullah letting off steam? No. That statement was issued by Bakshi Ghulam Mohammad in 1964, after he had been removed from the prime-ministership of Kashmir. In 1963, a suddenly zealous Nehru (said the sharp and acerbic leader Minoo Masani, 'Defeat has gone to his head') began a massive effort to restore to the Congress Party the principles that had rusted in the years of power. Senior Cabinet ministers, and Chief Ministers of the states, were asked to resign to devote their time to party work. It was a convenient euphemism to get rid of some corrupt men. In that mood, Bakshi Ghulam Mohammad was replaced by G. M. Sadiq. Politics in Kashmir had by then sunk to pretty low levels, starting with 1953 and going steeply down thereafter.

With no need to lie any more, Bakshi was now speaking the truth about

Kashmir. There was still only one man to whom the people would listen, there was still only one man whose word would ensure popular legitimacy to accession to India; and his name was Sheikh Mohammad Abdullah.

After Nehru's death, the Sheikh suddenly had to deal with a generation in Delhi with whom he had no personal rapport. Shastri and Swaran Singh were good men, but no peers of the Sheikh. Moreover, the communal Hindu element in the power structure, which had been kept under some control by Nehru, now revived. Prime Minister Shastri began, thanks to his own experience in the Hazratbal affair in 1963, with sympathy for the Sheikh. But once again there was no shortage of people who were determined to destroy any chance of amity. Sheikh Abdullah, too, was convinced that Shastri would not be able to take a stand against such forces. As he told *Le Monde* in April 1965: 'Mr Shastri has not the same strength as Mr Nehru. There has been a set-back in India since Mr Shastri came to power.' Typically, this only made the Sheikh more obstinate. There was a sharper edge to the statements he was never shy of making. He would not budge from the idea of self-determination for the Kashmiris, and each time he said anything of this sort there were loud cries from Delhi's patriots.

In February 1965, the Sheikh went on a long foreign tour preparatory to a pilgrimage to Mecca during the Haj. Pakistan–China relations were blossoming in that period, and China had openly supported the demand for a plebiscite in Kashmir. In an interview on 12 March 1965, given to the London correspondent of *Dawn*, the Karachi newspaper, Sheikh Abdullah welcomed the Chinese stand. On 28 March, Bhutto revealed at a dinner in honour of Chen-yi, the Chinese Foreign Minister, in Karachi, that China had invited Sheikh Abdullah. There was a predictable uproar in India, where the Sheikh was denounced as a traitor. There was, simultaneously, a concerted attack in the Indian Parliament on the Sheikh over the manner in which he had filled in the application form to obtain his passport, which had first been given to him by the government of Jawaharlal Nehru prior to his Pakistan visit in May 1964. On the application form, in answer to the question of nationality, Sheikh Abdullah had entered 'Kashmiri Muslim'. Nehru had ignored this, pointing out that if Sheikh Abdullah was willing to travel on an Indian passport, that was good enough for him. But in Shastri's time, this was treated as evidence of treachery, and Parliament heard nothing but member after member attacking the government for being party to this 'secessionism'. With memories of the genius still fresh, Nehru was not named, but there was derisive laughter when the Speaker, on 29 March, mentioned that the Sheikh's passport had been cleared at the 'highest level' by the Nehru government.

On 30 March, the Kashmir Assembly brought Kashmir, which had been granted the privilege of special nomenclatures, more into line with the rest of the country by changing the different designations which the equivalents of the Governor and the Chief Minister enjoyed. Instead of a Governor, Jammu and Kashmir had a *Sadr-i-Riyasat*, or President, and its Chief Minister was still called 'Prime Minister'. Moreover, the *Sadr* was not appointed by the President of India but was elected by the House. All this was changed.

On 31 March, Prime Minister Shastri reflected the mood of Parliament when he warned Sheikh Abdullah that 'drastic steps' would be taken if the latter visited China. The government also apologized for the earlier lapse on the passport issue, and promised that such a thing would not happen again. But that very day, the Sheikh was doing something that would provide an even bigger weapon to his tormentors. At a party in Algiers he met and spoke to Chou En-lai, the Prime Minister of China.

The next day Shastri told Parliament that the government had taken a 'serious view' of this meeting. On 2 April, Shastri explained to the Congress parliamentary party that the Sheikh–Chou conversation was deemed a hostile act, and the Sheikh's passport would either be impounded upon his return, or cancelled to compel him to return. And if he defied the government by travelling to hostile nations, he would be declared *persona non grata*. Bhutto, always waiting for his chance, immediately jumped into the fray and offered Sheikh Abdullah a Pakistani passport. Sheikh Abdullah ignored the generosity. On 5 April, Foreign Minister Swaran Singh informed a cheering Lok Sabha (the Lower House) that the endorsement for those countries not specifically on the itinerary of the Sheikh's pilgrimage would be cancelled immediately, and that the passport would be valid only till 30 April. When by 29 April the pilgrimage was still not over, the government provided the Sheikh with an emergency permit so that he might stay for another eight days. The passport was cancelled. When Sheikh and Begum Abdullah returned to India on 9 May, it was back to that familiar haunt predicted by the Sheikh's father-in-law: jail. The only difference was this time it was jail in the lovely southern hill resorts of Ooty and Kodaikanal.

Another thirty months of freedom were lost, but at least this time it was a gilded cage. Suraiya Ali, the Sheikh's daughter and youngest child, came down to stay with her parents during this period of detention. She recalls in the commemoration volume published by Kashmir University: 'My papa is [first] taken to Ooty along with his close confidant Mr Beg ... Papa is shifted to Kodaikanal as he is a tourist attraction: crowds of people question the wisdom of the action of the Indian government against him ... We are taken to a beautiful three-storeyed mansion known as Koh-i-noor Palace where papa is waiting at the entrance to greet us ... We are given the top storey while the security staff stay in the second storey and servants on the ground floor ... Not many may be aware about the culinary skills of papa. His morning hours are spent in cooking and he specializes in cooking *korma*, *roghan josh*, and a dish called *shub-daig* – a curry of meat and turnips cooked on simmering heat for many hours. The aroma of his cooking tickles even the nostrils of the security staff! I can vividly see a fat security officer standing and waiting at the stairs for the servants taking away the left-overs to share with him. One thing I learn from papa is not to idle away one's time. He engages a tutor, no doubt at government expense, to teach him Tamil ... Evenings are spent in long walks which enable us to visit the whole of Kodai. In all, we spent two and a half years in Kodai, two months at the AIIMS [hospital] and about a year at 3 Kotla Lane [in Delhi] before coming back to our native land. It was his grit and indomitable determination that carried him along, and indeed his unflinching confidence in people. People to him were the ultimate, the supreme power.'

It was just as well, perhaps, that Sheikh Abdullah was in detention in that year of the bitter war with Pakistan. Bhutto and Ayub Khan, unable to learn any lesson from history, tried the same tactics that Jinnah had attempted to snatch Kashmir. The tribal raiders came crying '*Jehad!*' ('Holy War!'), followed by the Pakistani armed forces, and once again the Kashmiri Muslim rejected them. Pakistan could never realize that Kashmiris may have been unhappy with Delhi, but they were not interested in Pakistan either; in fact, between the two India was always preferred. India not only turned back the initially successful Pakistani thrust but had her enemy on the defensive by the time of the cease-fire. Ayub Khan could not survive the consequences of the war he expected to win by the raider–soldier combination.

However, one of the Sheikh's sons went over to the side of Pakistan during this war. Both the sons who would later play a part in Kashmir's politics, the elder Farooq and the younger Tariq, were living in England then. Nehru had taken a personal interest in the well-being of his friend's children. He had Farooq admitted to the Jaipur Medical College, where he got his degree in medicine, and then went to live and practise in England. Tariq Abdullah also went to stay in London. Nehru helped him get a job in the Indian High Commission. But when the 1965 war came Tariq Abdullah switched sides, becoming an employee of the Pakistani High Commission. Pakistan was delighted; this was excellent propaganda material. Tariq Abdullah was made a member of the Pakistani delegation to the United Nations. (Tariq Abdullah has had a history of unstable behaviour, which often embarrassed Sheikh Abdullah later when he had become Chief Minister and given his son a job in government. Once in a fit of pique he sacked 326 employees, and typed out the dismissal order of each one himself. His Indian passport was restored on the eve of the Kashmir accord of 1975.)

The continued detention of Sheikh Abdullah had now begun to weigh heavily on the conscience of at least some of India's national leaders. One of them was the Socialist leader Jayaprakash Narayan. On 23 June 1966, he sent a 'strictly confidential' letter to Mrs Indira Gandhi (first published by Bhola Chatterjee in his book *Conflict in JP's Politics*, Ankur Publishing, Delhi). In this he examined the Kashmir problem with typical honesty, and deserves to be quoted at some length. Said Narayan: 'We profess democracy, but rule by force in Kashmir – unless we have auto-suggested ourselves into believing that the two general elections under Bakshi Sahib had expressed the will of the people, or that the Sadiq government [then in power] is based on popular support except for a small minority of pro-Pakistan traitors. We profess secularism, but let Hindu nationalism stampede us into trying to establish it by repression. Kashmir has distorted India's image for the world as nothing has done. There is no nation in the world, not even Russia, which appreciates our Kashmir policy, though some of them might, for their own reasons, give us their support … That problem exists not because Pakistan wants to grab Kashmir, but because there is deep and widespread political discontent among the people.

'Historical events, some without, some within, our control, have narrowed down greatly the room for manoeuvrability. For instance, any manner of de-accession of any part of the state is now impracticable – no matter how just or fair according to the principles of democracy and secularism. Whatever be the solution, it has to be found within the limitations of the accession. It is here that Sheikh [Abdullah's] role may become decisive … Nor do I think he is a traitor. Nobody can be held to be a traitor by the government of India unless it has been established in accordance to due process.

'I would like to close this chapter with one more quotation from the Sheikh. Before he left for his trip abroad this is what he had said at a farewell function at the Constitution Club on 10 February 1965: "We might have differences among ourselves. But after all India is the home-land of all of us. If, God forbid, India ceases to be India and goes down, how can others be saved?" ... Why do I plead for Sheikh [Abdullah's] release? Because that may give us the only chance we have of solving the Kashmir problem.'

The release did come, on 2 January 1968, but the solution still had to wait the outcome of another war with Pakistan, the division of the country created in the name of Islam, and a commitment by both countries that whether they said so formally or not, the cease-fire line in Kashmir would be treated for all practical purposes as the official boundary.

Everything had happened and nothing had changed in January 1968. The Sheikh told the BBC after his release that he now hoped to pick up the thread where it had snapped with Nehru's death in 1964. Addressing the Muslims after the prayers on the festival of Id, he told them that they must see India as their country; they must live and die here. At a press conference on 3 January, he narrated his side of the Chou En-lai story. He had met Chou at a party and asked about the portion of Kashmir which was now in China's possession, and about China's relations with India. The Sheikh said that he had later briefed the Indian ambassador at Algiers so that the Indian government could be informed.

The question before Mrs Gandhi, now Prime Minister, was how to resolve the Kashmir tangle, and find a place for the Sheikh in Srinagar, without undoing the legality of the accession. As Jayaprakash Narayan, who was now very close to the Sheikh, put it: 'While Sheikh Sahib's release is a vindication, though belated, of India's democratic way of life, that is the less important aspect of it. What is more important is utilization of this opportunity constructively and imaginatively for satisfying the aspirations of the people of Kashmir for a status that would give self-respect and self-government as a part of the larger Indian community.' The Sheikh met Mrs Gandhi twice in January 1968. A dialogue had obviously started. But it would take many more years to reach fruition.

The Sheikh now began to involve others, too, in the search for a solution, rather than restricting it to an individual crusade. In October 1968 he organized a six-day All-Kashmir State Peoples Convention. Most of the important parties were represented. Jayaprakash Narayan in-augurated the convention. A solution was suggested in the idea of greater autonomy for all the states of the Indian Union. This would satisfy Kashmir's desire for self-government without making the solution seem as if it was specially created only for Kashmir. Narayan made it clear that no one would accept the idea of Kashmir outside India but said: 'In a vast country like ours, national unity can only be fostered in an atmosphere of wise understanding of regional sentiments and interests and of a spirit of mutual tolerance.' Among those attending, interestingly, were men who had sent the Sheikh to jail in 1953 – Bakshi Ghulam Mohammad and Sham Lal Saraf. But the Sheikh still insisted that if the subcontinent did not want any more wars over Kashmir, then there had to be a round-table conference of the representatives of India, Pakistan and Kashmir, prefer-ably with the help of a mediator, and a solution thrashed out which would concede the 'substance' of the 'demand for self-determination' and remain honourable to both India and Pakistan. There was, obviously, still a squint in the Sheikh's eye. That would finally disappear with the collapse of the idea of Pakistan after the 1971 war.

The elections in Pakistan in 1970 became a plebiscite in East Pakistan. The message of Sheikh Mujibur Rahman's extraordinary victory was clear: Bengal wanted the very loosest of links with Punjab, and if Islamabad was not willing to grant such autonomy to Dhaka, the east would demand independence. Mrs Gandhi, of course, was wholehearted in her support for the autonomy/independence of East Pakistan. But it was a bit difficult to square such sympathy for the Bengalis with the situation in Kashmir. Sheikh Abdullah's Plebiscite Front was still alive. (One of its senior leaders was the Sheikh's son-in-law Ghulam Mohammad Shah, husband of his eldest daughter, Khalida.) With the attention of the world turned towards the subcontinent, and reporters tripping over each other to get out news-stories, Mrs Gandhi hardly savoured the prospect of Sheikh Abdullah doing a Mujib on her. On 9 January 1971, Sheikh Abdullah, the ever-faithful Mirza Afzal Beg and G. M. Shah were pro-hibited from entering Kashmir. About four hundred Plebiscite Front leaders were arrested. P. K. Dave, Chief Secretary to the Jammu and Kashmir government, said that such action was necessary to prevent mass-scale 'subversive activities'. The Plebiscite Front was soon banned. It was only on 5 June 1972, after the Indian army had won its famous victory in December 1971, that Sheikh Abdullah was allowed to return home. It would have been embarrassing to keep Sheikh Abdullah out of

Kashmir at that point: Bhutto was coming to India by the end of June for peace talks in Simla.

By now the Sheikh had finally become convinced that the only hope of a solution lay in a bilateral deal with Delhi. Pakistan had lost its moorings. On 23 June, speaking at the Hazratbal mosque, Sheikh Abdullah announced that he had given Mirza Afzal Beg 'full authority' to discuss with any representative of Mrs Gandhi a 'greater autonomy formula for Kashmir'. And he told his followers 'not to look towards Pakistan or any other power' to help them in 'their struggle to attain a respectable place in the world'. On 25 June, there were anti-Sheikh demonstrations (led, of course, by mullahs) in Pakistan-occupied Kashmir condemning his 'surrender' to India.

In the early hours of Monday 2 July 1972, Zulfiqar Ali Bhutto and Indira Gandhi agreed, through the document called the Simla pact, that 'in Jammu and Kashmir, the line of control resulting from the cease-fire of 17 December 1971, shall be respected by both sides without prejudice to the recognized position of either side. Neither side shall seek to alter it unilaterally, irrespective of mutual differences and legal interpretations; both sides further undertake to refrain from the threat of the use of force in violation of this line.' Even if they did not admit it, India and Pakistan had by this document partitioned Kashmir.

Sheikh Abdullah could not restrain a few murmurs, but he knew that the chance of any kind of independent status for Kashmir was over. From here to the Kashmir accord of 1975 was only a question of time. One of the men who played a key part in arranging the accord was the much-admired statesman D. P. Dhar who also played a vital role in the successful handling of the Bangladesh affair. On 28 December 1973, he sent a confidential note to Mrs Gandhi in which he outlined what the Sheikh really wanted before he would settle: 'I have been informed very reliably of the proposals in their broad sense, which Sheikh Sahib is likely to make to the PM when he meets her. He would like to have a midterm poll for the J and K Legislature ... The time which he has in mind would be roughly March 1975. He would like to utilize the interregnum for consolidating his own party, which is in a poor shape due to internal dissensions, so that he is in a position to face the combined onslaught of the pro-Pakistani elements [in the valley] ... About unresolved issues which relate to the whole gamut of the subjects at present ceded to the Centre under the Constitution, he feels that he would pose them for a decision in the Assembly after it was reconstituted after fresh elections.'

The Sheikh had now begun talking as a man whose fight with Delhi was over, and whose attention had shifted to the other problems afflicting Kashmir. On 29 December 1973, the Chief Minister of Kashmir, Syed Mir Qasim, sent D. P. Dhar details of a speech which the Sheikh made in front of a hundred and fifty prominent citizens at the Jammu guest-house on 19 December, now justifying the relationship with India. 'The Sheikh said he had "identity of outlook with Nehru and other Indian leaders and they had struggled together for secularism and justice for all, irrespective of caste and creed ... Unfortunately the country was partitioned in 1947. But in spite of this division we thought that we should make Kashmir a laboratory of secularism and even Gandhiji described it as a beacon of light when the entire subcontinent was engulfed in communal holocaust ... We wanted that Kashmir should remain a part of India with honour. In this connection I urged the people to achieve self-sufficiency in food and wanted the state not to become a burden on the Centre. But I was misunderstood and some people tried to ridicule my stand by saying that Sheikh Abdullah is advising people to eat potatoes and produce less children. As a result the state had to spend huge amounts on food subsidy. I shall want the state not to become a burden on India, but become self-reliant and self-sufficient. We should try to stand on our own legs and not to go to the country like beggars. At present the state is badly under the debt of the Centre and has not been able even to pay the interest on the loans."'

The man who was in charge of the final negotiations with Sheikh Abdullah was a brilliant and trusted bureaucrat in Mrs Gandhi's government, G. Parthasarathy. On 24 February 1975, the text of the six-point Kashmir accord was announced in Parliament: Jammu and Kashmir, a 'constituent unit of the Union of India', would continue to be governed by Article 370; the state would have the residuary powers of legislation, but Parliament would retain the power to legislate on any matter concerning the territorial integrity of the country. The sharing of powers was based on the premise that the Centre's responsibility would be the unity of the country while the state would be in charge of its welfare.

The Congress was in power in Srinagar then, with Syed Mir Qasim as the Chief Minister. Qasim had been against the Sheikh in 1953. Now he was willing, even eager, to make way for the Sheikh. On 25 February 1975, Sheikh Mohammad Abdullah was sworn-in as Leader of the House and Chief Minister of Jammu and Kashmir. The office that had been snatched away in 1953 had been returned to him after more than twenty-one years in which the Sheikh had suffered, with courage, honour and determination, more than is the lot of most heroes.

But perhaps a more difficult part of the journey had also begun that day. The DMK in Tamil Nadu gave up notions of independence in the 1960s; the National Conference did it in the 1970s. But in both states, the act of faith had to be confirmed by the successful practice of democracy. What the people wanted was not so much independence as the feel of self-rule, the satisfaction of having control over their own destinies. After centuries of feudalism and colonialism, this was only a natural aspiration. The fear in some regions of the subcontinent was that feudalism and colonialism would only be replaced by a new form of domination in a democracy. The Muslim League leaders said that a democratic India would be a pseudonym for an India ruled by Hindu chauvinists; Muslims could never feel the sense of participation which was an essential prerequisite of patriotism. The Tamil leaders of the DMK were convinced that – after the gloss of pretty statements had been wiped away – the Union of India would boil down to the domination of the Hindi states over the non-Hindi states in general, and over the South in particular. The National Conference under Sheikh Abdullah, despite its proven commitment to the fundamental values of the new India, secularism, socialism and democracy, began to wonder if this idealism could survive the onslaught of petty minds once the generation which gave India its freedom had passed away. The doubts were real, and had to be faced with maturity by an emerging nation being gradually moulded into shape. The quality and degree of tension differed. The idea of Tamil secession never provoked a bitter response because Tamil Nadu was never involved in the horrible strife during partition. But Muslim had fought Hindu in 1947, and though the Kashmiri Muslim had shown unique idealism in those years, he still had to face suspicions of being soft towards Pakistan.

Kashmir had seen two bogus elections conducted by Bakshi Ghulam Mohammad, and they had done nothing to convince the Kashmiri about the virtues of the system. Now the Sheikh had returned. If he could leave behind a memory of success, he would go a long way towards convincing Kashmir that the marriage with India was a fruitful decision. The Sheikh's first test would come sooner than he had bargained for.

Even by the standards of the seventies, an extraordinary decade, 1975 was a year of high drama. The Emergency came in June of that year. By March 1977, Mrs Gandhi had held and lost the elections, and the Janata Party came to power with Morarji Desai as the Prime Minister. The

Congress reacted in a most curious fashion in Kashmir after losing power in Delhi. Its leader in Kashmir, Mufti Mohammad Sayeed, informed the Governor, L. K. Jha, on 26 March (in the same week in which the Congress lost power) that the party was withdrawing the support it had extended to Sheikh Abdullah. By the terms of the 1975 accord, it was the Congress members who voted Sheikh Abdullah to the post of Chief Minister pending Assembly elections which the Sheikh's party could contest. The Sheikh was stunned. He had, despite his reservations about some aspects of the Emergency, been extremely careful to say or do nothing that could be construed as anti-Mrs Gandhi during the election campaign. But now, at a public meeting on 30 March, a very bitter Sheikh said that the Congress had always betrayed him. However, this time there was a government in Delhi which was committed to democracy. It agreed that the simplest way out was fresh elections. All the parties entered the fray, with varying degrees of optimism. The Janata also entered the ring, instead of using the opportunity to build an alliance with the Sheikh. The others seemed to have forgotten what the Sheikh meant to Kashmir. He showed them in the elections of July 1977. He won an overwhelming victory. The Congress of Mufti Sayeed could not win a single seat in the valley of Kashmir. On 9 July 1977 Sheikh Abdullah was sworn in as Chief Minister, and remained in the chair till the day he died, on 8 September 1982.

But power brought its own quota of problems. The history of suspicion between Srinagar and Delhi could not be erased, nor had the breed of *agents provocateurs* died. Though the Janata had indulged in a bitter fight against the Sheikh and the National Conference during the election campaign of 1977, it did have the decency to let the Sheikh remain in peace after he had won his convincing victory. In the 1980 general elections, the Sheikh openly supported Mrs Gandhi against the Janata. While he himself did not travel the campaign trail, his son Dr Farooq Abdullah did. And after she won, there was a great reception for her during her first visit to Kashmir in her new term as Prime Minister. But that honeymoon was one of the shortest even in a country where political marriages are notoriously fickle. It was not long, as we shall see, before Farooq Abdullah began to feel the familiar pangs of betrayal.

But what saddened the Sheikh more than anything else was the corruption that some of his relatives began to indulge in. Ashok Jaitley, one of those many bureaucrats who served under a man worthy of their hero-worship, recalls a case where one of the relatives of the Sheikh, angry at the honesty of an officer who would not co-operate in corruption, tried to put the officer into trouble. The Sheikh called the officer and said, 'My relative sometimes loses his balance. But he is my relative. Please accept my sincere apologies on his behalf.' At the end of the day one could not have much respect left for such relatives. Comparing the Sheikh's generation and their successors, B. K. Nehru said, 'Our leaders then were called politicians. Those who sit in the seats of power today are also called politicians. It is extremely ironical that these two entirely different kinds of human beings, who have virtually nothing in common, should be described by the same word ... [The former exercised power] with the honesty, the dedication and the selflessness which had ruled them throughout their lives. It was for these qualities, which the Sheikh had in plenty, and his willingness to suffer imprisonment and worse for his ideals and his principles, that he was a national hero.'

However, even national heroes have to leave behind successors. Given the propensities of democracy, family style, which is rampant in India, it was inevitable that the heir would come from the family. The choice was limited to two persons. The first claimant was the son-in-law, G. M. Shah, whose credentials as a political aide were perfect but whose credibility as a political leader left something to be desired. But perhaps it was simple love for his son Farooq which made the Sheikh opt for him. In any case, a war ensued between the two which had all the morality of Mughal succession politics. There would be a heavy price to be paid for this.

The Sheikh had suffered his first heart attack in June 1977. The second came at two o'clock in the afternoon of 5 September 1982. It was apparent that this time the Sheikh could not survive. As the news filtered through the streets and the villages of the valley, a vigil was started by the people outside his house, and the whole of Kashmir began to pray: 'La-e-la-ha-il-allah, Zinda thawaun Abdullah' ('There is only one God; may He keep Abdullah alive'), and 'Ya Rubba, asso dee balai Sher-e-Kashmirus' ('O God, take away our years and give them to the Lion of Kashmir'). The next day, Mrs Gandhi flew down from Delhi to see the Sheikh. He was conscious, and sipped a glass of orange juice in her presence. But his eyes said that the story was over. Around him, the tension of a future without the Sheikh had begun to gnaw at hearts and minds even as all present tried to lose themselves in the effort to keep the Sheikh alive. At about 6.40 p.m., in the evening of 8 September, the shopkeepers in Srinagar pulled down their shutters and the wail of mourning began to be heard across the valley. There had been no official announcement of the Sheikh's death. In fact,

Srinagar Radio broadcast an item saying that the Sheikh was still alive. That was untrue, of course. The people, as usual, knew better.

The government of India refused to take the slightest risk at an hour which must have been a policy-planner's nightmare. It was a question of giving practical shape to the principle, 'The king is dead; long live the king!' While the world was misinformed about the death of Sheikh Mohammad Abdullah, his son – then the most junior minister in the state Cabinet – was sworn in as successor. Good contingency planning had taken care both of the legality and the political nuances – it was G. M. Shah who was made to propose formally the name of the man he hated, Dr Farooq Abdullah, as the next Chief Minister. The news of the Sheikh's death was made known only at 12.30 a.m. that night (leading to the curious headline in the Delhi edition of one newspaper, 'Sheikh may have died'; however, most other newspapers were more certain).

'Az chu matam baja ... Asee roau bab' ('Mourn today for we have lost our father'). There is no statement, no tribute, which can better convey what the Sheikh meant to Kashmir than the reaction of the people. They swarmed to the Polo Grounds, where the body lay in state, and then walked the twelve kilometres to the burial site under the shade of a chinar tree near the mosque of Hazratbal. There was no Muslim, Hindu and Sikh that day: it was a visual display of the slogan Sheikh Abdullah had given in the forties, which was being chanted repeatedly at the funeral: 'Sher-e-Kashmir ka kya irshad? Hindu, Muslim, Sikh ittehad' ('What was the Sheikh's message? Friendship between Hindu, Muslim and Sikh'). Men and women, old and young, whoever had been touched by the magic of a great life, came that day to say goodbye.

And that body, upon which the eyes of the world rested, was draped in the Indian tricolour. Sheikh Abdullah had died an Indian.

The government of Pakistan had no comment to offer on the death of Sheikh Mohammad Abdullah.

7

The Second Trial

Sheikh Abdullah always said his Friday prayers at the Hazratbal mosque if he was in Srinagar. He often turned that occasion into a dialogue with the people. If he had a political statement to make then, he addressed the congregation; otherwise it was an opportunity for informal mingling which brought him both physically and emotionally close to the people he loved and trusted. One Friday in the early summer of 1981, he said to the crowd around him that he was feeling old and tired and wanted to gradually hand over his responsibilities to a younger man. Could they suggest anyone's name? They knew the answer which the old lion wanted to hear. Someone duly shouted out the name: 'Farooq Abdullah!' Others loyally took up the chant. The democratic monarch had heard the voice of the people. The coronation was set for 21 August 1981.

Royalty would have envied the show put up in Srinagar on that August day, when Farooq Abdullah was made the president of the National Conference, and heir apparent. The city was packed with people, a tide surging and ebbing and flowing through the streets. Word had gone out that the Sheikh wanted Srinagar to look red: red for the blood of martyrs, red for the colour of the National Conference flag, red to symbolize the emancipation of the peasants. Everyone waved a party flag, on every building the red banner fluttered. In the lovely summer sunlight of the afternoon, Farooq Abdullah, standing in an open jeep, led the procession from the party headquarters, Mujahid Manzil, towards Iqbal Park. It took five hours to cover the distance of about three kilometres. Dusk was falling when father anointed son: 'This crown that I am placing on your head is made of thorns. You are young, Farooq Abdullah, young enough to face the challenges of life, and I pray that God gives you the courage to fulfil your responsibility to these people whom I have nurtured with such pride, and to whom I have given the best years of my life.' Then the Sheikh broke down, and the crowd roared as one, 'Amen.' Father pinned the presidential badge on the son's chest. The torch had passed.

At around midnight on 8 September 1982, the power became *de jure* when Farooq Abdullah, with New Delhi's approval, took the oath of office. On 11 September all forty-six members of the National Conference legislature party, voting on a motion moved by G. M. Shah, approved the election of the new Chief Minister. The correct thing would have been, of course, to do it the other way round, but Delhi did not want any time-gap in the succession formalities. What most worried Delhi was that the small but well-organized and well-financed pro-Pakistan groups in Kashmir might try to exploit the opportunity provided by the confusion and emotion in the wake of the Sheikh's death. In turn, Pakistan might be tempted to intervene. It was not an idle fear. Tavleen Singh, reporting for *Sunday* (6 September 1981) had quoted Saifuddin Qari, second-in-command of the pro-Pakistan organization Jamaat-e-Islami, as saying that there would be a 'tremendous change' after the Sheikh's death. 'We have the Kashmiri intelligentsia on our side, because we are the only party with character and principles ... Once [the Sheikh] goes there will be a tremendous change.'

Farooq Abdullah had his work cut out for him. He had first to defuse the dreams of closet and open secessionists. Then there was the corruption which had spread under his indulgent father. And, of course, there was the continuing problem of relations with the Centre, exacerbated at this moment over the Resettlement Bill by which Sheikh Abdullah wanted to give those in Pakistan-occupied Kashmir the right to return to and settle in the parent country. Delhi thought this Bill would become a virtual invitation to Pakistani-trained spies and saboteurs, and refused to give its assent. The general expectation was that Farooq Abdullah, unsure and inexperienced, and without the benefit of his father's advice, would behave cautiously. The handsome, young, golf-playing, westernized son who had inherited a state as a legacy from a great father, surprised all those observers who had been standing on the sidelines, waiting for him to falter or slip. Farooq Abdullah quickly indicated the kind of Chief Minister he would be: dramatic, open, unafraid, and in constant communication with the people. Farooq Abdullah got out of the ivory tower – and, literally, on to a motor cycle. There was rarely if ever any security around him. Quite often he could be seen careering down a Srinagar street on his motor cycle, with one of his three children riding pillion, making for the Dal Lake for a swim. Or the Chief Minister might be driving his car and stop suddenly to prod a policeman to clear the traffic faster. He brought a sense of intimacy, even fun, to the exercise of power, without diluting the sense of responsibility. His critics, of course, started by condemning him as a wastrel or a playboy who could not be trusted with such an important legacy. But he showed his detractors very quickly that when he did make political decisions, he could not only be sharp, even ruthless, but also win acclaim.

The very first thing he did after coming to power was to dismiss, to their utter shock and horror, all those ministers who had acquired the reputation of being 'stalwarts' under the benign eye of the Sheikh. Farooq Abdullah replaced the entire Cabinet with one he could trust, with the result that an old war-horse like D. D. Thakur found himself without the familiar comfort of a ministerial chair. Those who had acquired a reputation of being corrupt were studiously kept out of office. Then there were pro-Pakistan organizations to tackle. Farooq Abdullah publicly warned them not to create trouble, and then suggested that if he could get the support of all the parties on the decision he would ban them. As far as relations with Delhi were concerned, the new Chief Minister already had an excellent personal rapport with the Nehrus. He called Mrs Gandhi 'Mummy' and was a good friend of Rajiv Gandhi. He tried to turn this personal equation into a political alliance. Not only, for instance, would he personally see Rajiv Gandhi off at Srinagar airport, but he took care to see that Delhi was informed about the decisions he was taking so that there was no ground for suspicion. And lastly, there was the family quarrel with his brother-in-law, G. M. Shah. Shah offered to stop sulking if he was made the deputy Chief Minister, but Farooq Abdullah decided that he could not trust him. As events proved, the Chief Minister was right.

There was more than just political animosity between the two men. Farooq Abdullah told this author in an interview: 'My father always felt that he had made the greatest mistake by having married [my sister] to Shah, and that he had to make it up to her somehow. I think the split [between Shah and me] came when I became the president of the party and was finally taken on as a minister. That is the time when Shah resigned from the Cabinet. My sister, however, continued to come to our house to see my father. Even after my father died she used to come and see my mother sometimes, but she never had much to do with me as she felt that I had taken the crown from her husband's head.' In the fascinating, personalized world of Indian democracy these things not only matter but, as we shall see, sometimes become arbiters of a state's destiny.

Mrs Gandhi's problem was how to find an acceptable equation between her responsibilities as Prime Minister with the nation's integrity and defence her primary duty, her personal relations with the Abdullahs, and her partisan interest as president of the party which was now in fact named after her – the 'Congress (Indira)'. A Farooq Abdullah government was, by any criterion, essential to Kashmir's security in 1982, but could this be considered the only option for the state? Could she – should she – give up her inherent right as a political leader to promote her party, and attempt, as was legitimate in any democracy, to win elections there too? Sheikh Abdullah had offered a solution to this quandary, when he said that the National Conference could become an affiliate of the Congress in Jammu and Kashmir. But Mrs Gandhi saw dangers in this, too. Supposing the affiliated party wandered away from the commitment to the national unity? Was it not essential that the Congress retain a presence in the state, to step in if such an eventuality arose? Mrs Gandhi would not, therefore, accept the position that the Congress leave Kashmir to the Conference. Even during the Sheikh's lifetime she came to the state on party-promotion tours. Nor was she above irritating the Sheikh by passing critical remarks about the quality of his secularism. In April 1981, for instance, she expressed her sympathy with the Hindus of Jammu who were facing the problem of 'insecurity' in a Muslim-majority state. Sheikh Abdullah, in an interview to the *Indian Express*, accepted that this jibe was part of a 'battle in party interests' but added: 'The war among parties should not harm our national interests ... My ancestors were Hindus. In Kashmir we have the same blood, all are brothers and continue to have the same culture. Such remarks, therefore, surprise us all and if the Prime Minister of the country makes such a charge, people outside the state will take it seriously.'

The Abdullahs were always conscious that, no matter how many times they protested otherwise, they would forever be vulnerable to the charge of being 'soft' towards Pakistan, and in quiet league with secessionists. They knew that each time Delhi wanted them to kneel, it would always resurrect this allegation and, if necessary, even use such an excuse to dismiss the government. Sheikh Abdullah had spent his life listening to accusations of treachery; his only answer lay in his personal faith and self-confidence, and in the end he was vindicated. Farooq Abdullah, also, knew that it was only a matter of time before the many hostile forces started such a smear campaign against him. Typically, he decided to meet the problem head-on. One of the mistakes which the Sheikh had made, in his son's view, was that he had kept himself confined, by and large, to his own state. Farooq Abdullah decided that he would build personal and political bridges across the country. He would convince India, and not just Mrs Gandhi, about his commitment to the country. If he could clear the minds of the people and the political parties in the rest of the country, he would be much less dependent on the goodwill of just one party, the Congress. If, therefore, he was ever called secessionist, he hoped that there would be more than one powerful voice in India saying that the accusation was a partisan fraud designed to cover up an unethical power game.

Farooq Abdullah began by asking for a ban on all communal organizations, whether Hindu or Muslim. Far from welcoming the thought, the Congress shrank away from the idea. Nikhil Chakravartty, editor of *Mainstream* and a journalist who has followed the Kashmir story with both personal interest and intellectual independence, commented: 'Parties claiming to be secular, the Congress as well as the Communist, are in office in different states of India. How is it that they have not yet extended enthusiastic support to Dr Farooq Abdullah's proposal to ban communal organizations? Still more surprising is the subdued, if not almost muffled, response of Congress (I) [Indira] leaders in Jammu and Kashmir to the Farooq proposal.' The Congress was 'muffled' because it had never been averse to using such communal organizations to create trouble for the National Conference government, and it did not want to foreclose this option. Elections, last held in 1977, were, after all, due by 1983.

The Congressmen of Kashmir had an additional problem. They had been kept out of power since 1975. Now that the Sheikh was dead, they faced the prospect of another long spell in the wilderness if the son was allowed to establish his sway. They were therefore keen not only to contest but to win enough seats to enable them to organize defections from the National Conference and form a government (the Congress could never hope for an outright victory). The only senior Congress leader to oppose this line of thinking was the man who had voluntarily left the Chief Minister's chair to make way for Sheikh Abdullah, Syed Mir Qasim. He argued that it was essential for the welfare of India and the prosperity of Kashmir to allow Farooq Abdullah an unhindered spell in power if the latter won the elections. In fact, he wanted a Conference–Congress alliance, even if it had to be at the expense of his own party. The Congress must make that much of a sacrifice, he argued, in the national interest. No one was listening.

On 18 June 1983, Qasim wrote to Mrs Gandhi: 'You are fully conversant with the persistent efforts made by me in my humble way to accelerate the process that culminated in the historic accord with Sheikh

Sahib [in 1975] which demonstrated to the world the inherent strength and capacity of Indian democracy to absorb voices of dissent and to evolve amicable solutions to the most difficult problems ... a section of the Congress (I) [Indira] found it difficult to reconcile to the new situation. This section wanted to cling to power and had, most probably, never visualized parting with power in the broader national interest.' They were the villains, in Qasim's eyes, who had sabotaged the chance of the alliance.

Mrs Gandhi replied, 'For me the [1975] accord was, and remains, a method of fruitful co-operation among all the secular and patriotic forces in the state. It certainly did not mean that the Congress should fade into oblivion. I did not and cannot accept this interpretation of the accord. But this seems to be your view. What was worse was that you succeeded in persuading Sheikh Sahib and later Dr Farooq Abdullah to accept your version. This is what lay behind the National Conference's arrogance of power.'

Well, at least the arrogance was based on the strength of the popular will. Farooq Abdullah and his mother, Begum Akbar Jehan, knew that they could win the elections without any help from the Congress; an alliance was only an insurance policy against later machinations. But the Congress asked for a price which was too high. Farooq Abdullah would not accept any agreement which did not ensure an overwhelming majority for the Conference in the Assembly; memories of betrayal were too strong. Talks with the Congress broke down. Both sides prepared for the showdown on 5 June 1983. Mercy was neither requested nor was it given. The Congress used all the power at its command – and it had a great deal of it both being the largest political party in the country and having the resources of the Central government at its call. Small parties, which could not win a seat on their own but could give vital help in a constituency or two, were avidly wooed. In the process, Farooq Abdullah received the support of a family which had been a bitter enemy of the Abdullahs for fifty years. Maulana Yusuf Shah, a religious leader, had disliked the Sheikh even in the thirties when both were in the Muslim Conference. After the Sheikh started the National Conference, the Maulana, a staunch fundamentalist, kept alive the rump of the Muslim Conference and later went over for a while to Pakistan-occupied Kashmir. But in the Kashmir of Sheikh Abdullah, Maulana Yusuf Shah was an object of ridicule: the Sheikh was labelled the lion, and Yusuf Shah was nicknamed the goat. Maulana's heir, Mirwaiz Farooq, for a long while took the position that Kashmir be given to Pakistan. But in 1977 he formally renounced this to join the Janata Party. Before the 1983 elections, because of his known antagonism to the Abdullahs, Mirwaiz was wooed by the Congress. But he decided to support Farooq Abdullah instead, much to everyone's surprise.

If Farooq Abdullah made a mistake it was when he succumbed to pressure from his mother, who did not want a split in the family, and accepted twelve names suggested by G. M. Shah for the list of candidates which he announced at a mammoth public meeting on 29 April. The crowd, shocked that Shah loyalists had not been eliminated, reacted, booing and throwing slippers at the dais when these names were mentioned. The mistake would prove to be very costly. Shah hardly made a secret of his future intentions. Not only did he refuse to campaign for the Conference, but he met Congress leaders in Srinagar at the very height of the electioneering. In Jammu, Mrs Gandhi conducted an aggressive campaign with a distinct pro-Hindu bias on the assumption (a correct one) that she had little chance of winning any Muslim votes in the valley and might as well concentrate on the Hindus of the plains. Farooq Abdullah campaigned as his father's heir, the protector both of the Kashmiri Muslim and of Indian secularism. His father's slogan of Muslim–Hindu–Sikh unity was a constant refrain. He reminded the people that Sheikh Abdullah in his will had appealed to Kashmiris always to defend the 'fort of the National Conference'. One of his election pamphlets equated the Congress with Maharaja Hari Singh – both had 'enslaved' Kashmiris. Said Farooq Abdullah, 'These forces should remember that Sheikh Abdullah had handed over his mission to me during his lifetime. They think if Farooq Abdullah is not stopped at this moment, he would become another Sheikh Abdullah tomorrow and would teach the people of the state the lessons of state autonomy, self-respect and a special identity.' Tavleen Singh reported in *The Telegraph* on the rather individual style of a Chief Minister who had lived in England: 'Dr Abdullah wears jeans, a T-shirt, an English raincoat and army boots. He gets the kind of response that almost no other politician gets in the rest of India. When he arrives they [the supporters] force him to get off [the van] and walk among the people. They practically carry him to the stage. If there is no stage he climbs on to the roof of his Matador [van] and speaks through a megaphone. He speaks to them in Kashmiri, cracks jokes, asks them to shout slogans, and tells them that it is vital that they go out early on June 5 and cast their votes.'

The results showed that the National Conference fort was well-protected. Farooq Abdullah won by a landslide, though the Congress did very well in Jammu. However, even in Jammu the National Conference won more seats than Sheikh Abdullah himself had done in 1977. It got 38 per cent of the votes in Jammu, a significant increase from 1977. The result was evidence, said the party, of its secular character, proof that it was not a party of Kashmiri Muslims alone.

The Jamaat-e-Islami put up thirty-five candidates. Its line was unambiguous: India was 'an occupation force' in Kashmir and the National Conference leaders were 'Indian dogs'. 'Hamaara leader Rasool-Allah [Our leader is the Prophet],' they said, and asked the people to vote for them so that they could ensure an Islami nizaam (Islamic government) in Kashmir. The Jamaat was wiped out.

But the Congress would not accept defeat. It had, with the help of its control of and influence over the media, spread the impression that it was going to win the elections. Now it began to claim that the National Conference had cheated, and won by rigging and violence. With the advantage of power in Delhi, the charge was bandied about for a while, until it died a natural death. But it was clear that the battle between the Congress and the Conference would continue.

Addressing the congregation at the Jama Masjid in Srinagar after the victory, Farooq Abdullah said that his fight with the Congress (Indira) was not over yet: 'I will fight them in the streets and all corners of the country. My test is over. But they have to face the electorate [in the rest of the country] soon and let us see how they fare.' He added that he would seek a closer relationship with the opposition parties who 'had come here to stand by us in our hour of need'. Senior opposition leaders like H. N. Bahuguna and Biju Patnaik had, in fact, campaigned for the National Conference.

The confrontation with Mrs Gandhi truly began on 28 May 1982. On that day in the southern city of Vijayawada, the charismatic N. T. Rama Rao, film star turned politician, had called a meeting of opposition leaders from all over the country. The purpose was ostensibly to initiate joint action on problems of Centre–State relations, but there was also the hope that such a meeting would lead to a united front against the Congress in the next general elections. On 28 May, despite the fact that electioneering in his state was at fever pitch, Farooq Abdullah was present in Vijayawada. Mrs Gandhi, on her election tour to Jammu and Kashmir, publicly protested that Farooq Abdullah was joining hands with 'my enemies'. She had genuine cause for surprise. Farooq Abdullah had, in fact, done something which even his father had not. No matter what the extent of his problems with them, Sheikh Abdullah had always maintained that the Nehru family should be supported in the rest of the country. In fact, all the Sheikh wanted was a bargain: the Nehrus could keep India if they gave the Abdullahs Kashmir. In both the 1977 and the 1980 general elections, the Sheikh supported Mrs Gandhi. But Farooq Abdullah wanted more than one basket for his eggs. And so he was among the three chief ministers and eleven senior party leaders who, at Vijayawada, charged the Congress (Indira) with ruining the nation. And he promised to host the third of this series of meetings, in Srinagar in October.

The Congress actively sought to break this budding unity among opposition parties. One of the chief ministers who had been present at Vijayawada, M. G. Ramachandran of Tamil Nadu, did a deal with the Congress and backed out. A great deal of pressure was put on Farooq Abdullah to cancel the October meeting. Farooq Abdullah decided that he could not let down his 'brothers'. And in the first week of October, the leaders of India opposed to Mrs Gandhi duly gathered in Srinagar, as much in a gesture of solidarity as in an effort to demand a shift in the balance of power between the Centre and the states.

The reaction was immediate. The plan to unseat Farooq Abdullah through defections was set in motion. G. M. Shah was asked to pull his rabbits out of the National Conference hat. It turned out that things were not going to be as easy as expected. Conscious of precisely such a possibility, Sheikh Abdullah had pushed through the Representation of the People Act aimed against defection. The only technicality through which the law could be circumvented was over the definition of 'defector', but here, too, one would need a governor with a very lax attitude towards the truth to replace a chief minister. The Governor of Jammu and Kashmir in October 1983 was the man with whom Sheikh Abdullah and Nehru had gone to see *The Razor's Edge* in 1947 in Delhi, B. K. Nehru. He would not be party to such questionable tactics. Aware of what was going on, Dr Abdullah, on his part, decided that he had had enough of his brother-in-law. On 4 October, the Working Committee of the National Conference expelled G. M. Shah from the party.

Frustrated, the Congress (Indira) now shifted the focus to a familiar charge: that Farooq Abdullah was in league with those determined to destroy India. Sikh extremists were being trained in armed warfare in Kashmir, said Congress leaders (including Mrs Gandhi and her son). There was never any evidence of this. Even the White Paper which the government published on Punjab in 1984, after the army action, could not prove that Farooq Abdullah had any links with Sikh extremists. But the massive government-controlled radio and television spread the propaganda to every corner of the country. An incident on 13 October 1983 during a one-day cricket match between India and the West Indies in Srinagar was blown up into a major scandal. A small group of pro-Pakistan students used the opportunity provided by live television coverage of the match to raise anti-India slogans from a corner of the stands. Dr Abdullah was livid: 'Our heads hang in shame over the incident,' he told a public meeting at Sopore. But rather than portray him as the man who could challenge and control such forces, the government media made it sound as if the Chief Minister himself was behind the demonstration. The fact that Dr Abdullah launched an angry tirade against the Jamaat-e-Islami after this was rarely mentioned. Nor could the official media find time to report Farooq Abdullah's repeated commitment to the integrity of India. Farooq Abdullah had to be given a bad name before he could be hanged. In the mean while, the Punjab crisis also reached a flashpoint. The army action in the Golden Temple led to nation-wide support for Mrs Gandhi. In such a glow, someone got the idea that another bird could be killed too. G. M. Shah was given the green signal once again. But this time better precautions had been taken. B. K. Nehru was transferred to Gujarat, and in his stead a pliable bureaucrat, Jagmohan, was installed as Governor in Srinagar.

The festival of Id is the happiest day in the Islamic calendar. Coming at the end of a month of penance, fasting and prayer, Ramazan, it is an occasion on which Muslims celebrate the brotherhood, peace and equality that constitute the ideological underpinnings of their faith. The day begins with a prayer of thanksgiving, after which all Muslims, irrespective of economic status or social position, embrace. People visit one another, and the festivities stretch well into the second day. The last thing on anyone's mind during Id is treachery.

Even then, Farooq Abdullah had no reason to be as complacent as he was on the Id of 1984, 30 June. The conspiracy against him was already under way, and a more observant chief minister would have had better intelligence of what was going on. But while the Chief Minister was lost in the Id embraces of friends and colleagues, his brother-in-law was sharpening the knife. Once again, it all happened in the darkness of the night. On Sunday, 1 July, Shafi Shaiza, a well-known orator and Conference supporter, hosted an Id dinner. Tariq Abdullah, the younger brother who allied himself with Shah, could not resist telling the guests that very soon the friends of Farooq Abdullah would learn a lesson. Nobody took Tariq seriously; with a known history of rashness, he often made such threats. At a quarter to eleven that night, twelve National Conference members of the Jammu and Kashmir Legislative Assembly, along with one independent, met at the house of a businessman known to be close to the Abdullahs. A little after eleven at night, they telephoned the Governor, Jagmohan, that they were ready. The Governor told them to come to his official residence, the Raj Bhavan, only at dawn. He had other things to set up. The most important of them was to bring in paramilitary forces which could suppress the anger of the people when they came out on the streets after Farooq Abdullah had been dismissed.

With an elected Chief Minister still legally in power, the Governor had no authority to take such administrative decisions. But law was at a premium that night; the only objective was to preserve order after the knife had been placed in the back. Jagmohan had the help of two important bureaucrats: Chief Secretary Noor Mohammad, and Director-General of Police Pir Ghulam Hassan Shah. These government officers were also doing something totally illegal by taking their instructions from the Governor, with a Chief Minister still in office. Shah, in fact, had been due to retire from service on 30 June but Farooq Abdullah had given him a special two-year extension. It seemed a strange way of saying thank you.

Early on the morning of 2 July, senior officials were woken and told to report for duty at Srinagar airport at once as special flights would land soon. At 6.45 a.m. the first Boeing 737 requisitioned from Indian Airlines touched down at Srinagar airport. Its passengers were men from the Madhya Pradesh Special Armed Police, a constabulary specially trained in anti-dacoity operations. Once again, their arrival was totally illegal since there had been no approval from the elected government. In fact, the only man who could have sanctioned the presence of these policemen, Farooq Abdullah, had no idea that they were in Srinagar till long after they arrived.

At around five-thirty in the morning, while Farooq Abdullah was still asleep, four cars drove past his house on Gupkar Road carrying the defectors and a Congress leader, Iftikhar Ansari, to meet the Governor. They submitted a handwritten letter saying that they were withdrawing support from Abdullah. The Governor telephoned the Chief Minister at seven-thirty in the morning. Farooq Abdullah was shocked. He demanded that his majority be tested where the law required it to be tested – on the floor of the Assembly. In 1953, his father had asked for the same privilege.

The son, too, was refused. Abdullah then demanded fresh elections. That, of course, was out of the question. That evening G. M. Shah (who was not even a member of the properly elected Assembly) was sworn-in as the Chief Minister of Jammu and Kashmir.

Each of the thirteen men and women who had switched sides was made a Cabinet minister. The Governor announced that the new Chief Minister would have to prove his majority in the Assembly on 31 July. But that, of course, was not the question. What was in doubt was whether, according to the anti-defection law, the members who had deserted Farooq Abdullah retained the right to vote in the Assembly at all. The Governor argued that this was not defection, but a 'split'. It was the kind of argument which democracy, since it lives as much by spirit as by law, cannot bear to hear too often.

The people showed on whose side they were. All those extra policemen were very necessary. Srinagar was in turmoil, and only continuous curfew and police firing could bring temporary peace. Once again, the Kashmiri's faith in democracy, in the right of his elected leaders to exercise power, was being severely tested. But this time Kashmir was not alone. From every corner of the nation there were protests, and when Parliament convened later in the month there were days of uproar as opposition leaders demanded an explanation from the government for such behaviour. From across the country leaders of all political shades came to Srinagar to march with Kashmiris against the new government. There was the academic Marxist Finance Minister from West Bengal, Dr Ashok Mitra, and the Socialist orator representing a Bihar constituency in Parliament, George Fernandes. From Maharashtra, Sharad Pawar raised his voice, and from the south both the sophisticated R. K. Hegde and the saffron-clad N. T. Rama Rao called this a crime against democracy. Chandra Shekhar, leader of the Janata Party and an MP from Uttar Pradesh, promised that his party would take up Farooq Abdullah's fight; other UP leaders, like H. N. Bahuguna and Chandrajit Yadav, showed similar commitment. On 12 July, four non-Congress chief ministers decided to express their anger by walking out of the annual National Development Council meeting between the Prime Minister and the heads of the state governments; there had never been a walk-out from this non-partisan forum before. There might have been many things in common between 1953 and 1984, but at least there was one great difference: the country was not silent this time. And it was because India was a democracy, despite the aberrations of some of its democrats, that

Farooq Abdullah could say, to the cheers of the crowds, that he would take his fight against Mrs Gandhi to every corner of India. And, of course, if he could take his fight to every corner of India, there was no need to take it to any corner of Pakistan.

If what happened in Kashmir had been only another instance of Tammany Hall politics, it would not have been of any exceptional significance. But crucial to the Kashmir problem is the question of trust, and the Hindu's doubts about the quality and extent of the Muslim's patriotism. Jammu and Kashmir, being a Muslim-majority state and adjacent to Pakistan, is obviously at the centre of the storm of suspicion. The non-Muslim ruling elite can be divided into two rough groups: one has a deep-seated hatred of Muslims as a community, and would like to subjugate and hurt this community in every way in order to settle what it perceives to be the scores of history; and the other is the secular nationalist element. The first, being small, might be easily controlled, were it not for the fact that even the second has reasons for doubt after being defeated by Jinnah and the Muslim League in 1947. It is difficult, therefore, to know when a political decision is taken, with what motive it is being done. After all, an extremist does not often make the mistake of an obvious display of fangs; in any case, it is always the rational argument which is used to justify even a blatantly communal decision. For the Muslim at the receiving end, it can become enormously difficult to define the dividing line. In the long run, the decision whether to trust the system or not is possible only through an examination of the record, rather than the merits of a particular decision.

The Kashmiri asks a good question these days. He does not deny that he joined India in 1947. All he wants to know is if this is the same India that he joined in 1947. He wants to know whether the values of Mahatma Gandhi – who was cheered by the Muslims of Srinagar less than a fortnight before Pakistan was born – still mean anything to the men and women who exercise power in Delhi. The Union of India was built on the rock called the Constitution of India: 'We, the people of India, having solemnly resolved to constitute India into a sovereign socialist secular democratic Republic and to secure to all its citizens: Justice, social, economic and political; Liberty of thought, expression, belief, faith and worship; Equality of status and of opportunity; and to promote among them all Fraternity assuring the dignity of the individual and the unity and integrity of the nation.' The Kashmiri could be expected to fight the fundamentalist raider from Pakistan in defence of such a promise, but not to exchange the raider for a Delhi in which the secular faith had died.

Kashmir, as Sheikh Abdullah and Jawaharlal Nehru promised, remains the laboratory of secular and democratic India. The idea of India will succeed or fail in this Muslim-majority state. On Sunday, 12 August 1984, when news reached the subcontinent that Pakistan had won the Olympic gold medal in hockey, small groups of young men, waving green flags, took out processions and burst crackers to celebrate. The momentum of public opinion in Kashmir will either veer towards such pro-Pakistan gestures or stay, as it has done, with India, depending largely on the unwinding of the democratic process in the eighties. If those who win elections are not allowed to rule, then Pakistan could yet win the war it lost in 1947. But if Kashmir has self-rule, then *Islamabad dur ast* (Islamabad is too far).

8
Guilty till Proved Innocent?

On 14 August 1947 Mahomed Ali Jinnah sold the birthright of the Indian Muslim for a bowl of soup. Insisting that religion and nationhood were inseparable, he demanded and got a country whose two wings were flung a thousand miles apart; it was Jinnah's conceit that his theory of religion being equivalent to nation could bridge the geographical and cultural distance. The evidence that Islam was not sufficient to glue together a modern nation was available all over the world, and nowhere more than in the Arab world itself: one religion, one language, and yet a dozen nations. But Jinnah convinced enough Muslims of this subcontinent that they could not survive as equal citizens in the land of Gandhi, that they must have their own home, even though the cost of building it would be heavy. The many contradictions in his thesis started tumbling out almost as soon as Pakistan was accepted. Going through the record of the comments made by the Muslim League leaders themselves after they got Pakistan, it seems that they, too, began to have doubts about what they had done. Certainly, they were in no mood to sound those doubts too loudly; they had to maintain the euphoria of victory. But there was a growing list of unanswered and unanswerable questions.

The most crucial, of course, was simply this: if Jinnah was right, how could he leave this enormous number of 40 million Muslims behind in 'Hindu' India? Perhaps the ultimate paradox was that Pakistan was formed in those areas where the Muslims least needed protection from Hindus, since these were Muslim-majority regions. If anything, it was Hindus who needed protection from Muslims in West Punjab, Sind, East Bengal and the Frontier. Jinnah tried to answer this problematical question when addressing the Pakistani army officers on 11 October 1947: 'My advice to Muslim brethren in India is to give unflinching loyalty to the state in which they happen to be.' After ten years of his insisting that loyalty to a Hindu-majority state was simply unacceptable to the Indian Muslim, that bit of advice on 11 October was rather gratuitous.

But Jinnah, as we have seen earlier, became a sudden convert to the idea of a secular state after Pakistan was accepted. It was the very concept that he used to ridicule each time Gandhi or Nehru mentioned it as the foundation of a new and united India. At that famous press conference on 13 July 1947 Jinnah said, 'The minorities will be safe-guarded [in Pakistan]. Their religion or their faith or belief will be protected in every way possible. There will be no interference of any kind with their freedom of worship.' Today, of course, not even the Ahmadiyas are equal citizens of Jinnah's Pakistan. But it was not Jinnah alone who could not conceive of the kind of state Pakistan would become. On 12 August Shahid Suhrawardy said, before laying down office as the last Prime Minister of United Bengal: 'I shall hold it always as a calamity that Bengal has been partitioned. East and West are far too inter-mingled with each other not to feel a wrench at a division, and not to hope that some time or other we shall be united once more. But we have to make the best of what has been thrown out of the political whirlpool ... A time is bound to come when the problem of majority and minority will be wiped out and the Hindus and Muslims of each area will work with each other as nationals of that area for the progress and prosperity of their area, and will co-operate with each other on common economic and political principles ... May God grant that peace once more descend upon this country, the peace born not by imposition of power but of the willing hearts of men.'

There was now talk of peace by the men who were witnessing an awful civil war they had helped launch. A. K. Fazlul Haq said on 14 August: 'My first appeal will be to my brother Muslims. I humbly beseech them to remember that our holy religion Islam is pre-eminently the religion of peace. "Peace" is the greeting of one Muslim to another ... "The goal to which Islam leads is the abode of Peace" [the Holy Quran, chapter ten, verse 25] ... Dear brethren, pause and reflect. Those who have been exciting your passions to break the peace and even to commit the murders of innocents have been proved to be political swindlers, who have shame-fully deserted you at the time of trial and left you to your fate. The political movements for which you have been utilized have benefited only those swindlers who are getting fat jobs, but the poor and destitute have been completely deserted and their condition is now far worse than before.'

Peace. For more than two decades, one man had been consistent in his search for this peace, without compromise, without surrender. 'Hindu–Muslim unity is not less important than the spinning-wheel. It is the breath of our life ... [But] I know some Hindus and some Mussalmans who prefer the present condition of dependence on Great Britain if they cannot have either wholly Hindu or wholly Mussalman India. Happily their number is small.' That was Gandhi at the 39th session of the Congress, in Belgaum, in 1924. Their number was small, yes, but effective. And they created such a divide between the Indian Hindu and the Indian Muslim that they tore apart the country in 1947.

And perhaps nothing symbolized both the absurdity and the venom of their hate better than the fact that Jinnah's house in Delhi was bought for Rs 3 lakhs on 8 August by a rich businessman, Rama Krishna Dalmia, who converted it into the headquarters of the Anti-Cow-Slaughter League. The flag of the cow was flown on the house of the father of Pakistan. It is impossible for any sane person to know whether to laugh or to cry.

Who is the Indian Muslim? The classic work on the subject has been done by the extraordinary Professor M. Mujeeb (*The Indian Muslims*, George Allen and Unwin, 1967). His answer is: 'The principle of the census, that anyone who is an Indian and calls himself a Muslim is an Indian Muslim, obviously gives no indication of what it is to be an Indian Muslim ... The only unifying factor among Indian Muslims was common allegiance to Islam. This allegiance created the sentiment of belonging to a community, and this sentiment has been the point at which religion, the instinct for self-preservation, political interest and social traditions can be said to meet. This sentiment can be latent or dormant for generations, but it can also be roused to fever pitch within an incredibly short time ... But this does not mean that the Indian Muslims have been amorphous as a community ... Because of the latent desire for unity it was all too easy to confuse the identity of the Indian Muslims as believers in Islam with their identity as a distinct body politic, as a nation, which they never were and never wanted to be.'

But the Hindu fundamentalists, who came into their own in this century and still command the allegiance of a section of the urban middle class, refused to accept that there was anything called the *Indian* Muslim. In their view, the Muslim, by definition, was a foreigner and not an immigrant. India was, and could only be, a Hindu nation; and Indian culture could only be Hindu culture in its Sanskritic form. A composite culture was a corruption which had to be cleansed. Only those religions could be called Indian which had their birth in this land: so while Buddhism and Sikhism were acceptable as quasi-Hindu faiths, Islam, Christianity, Judaism and Zoroastrianism were foreign systems of belief. The Hindus were the natural owners of the holy land of India, had always been sons of this soil; the rest were foreign invaders. The ancient Hindu civilization had been a glorious period in history; society was stable, thanks to the cohesion provided by the caste system; it was a golden age of great empires and extraordinary scientific achievement. The fall came with the arrival of the plundering tyrannous Muslim who converted by force of the sword, and introduced political and social conflict into India. Thus evolved, in the words of Bipin Chandra (*Communalism in Modern India*, Vikas Publishing House, 1984), 'the communal stereotype of Muslims being inherently cruel, sexually debauched and aggressive. It was used by the Hindu communalists to create a feeling and even a psychosis of fear which normally a majority would not have felt, to demand the denial of equal citizenship rights to Muslims ... and to deny the possibility of Hindu–Muslim unity in the present because of the historical memories of tyranny. The more rabid communal elements even promoted the theory that Hindus should seek revenge, or at least compensation, for the wrongs done to them in the medieval period. It was essential to the claim that India was solely the Hindus' "hereditary territory" or possession, and to thus emphasize the "foreignness" of Muslims and to deny that long residence in India could give them the right to become Indians.'

But there was an obvious catch to this thesis: the Hindus were themselves technically foreigners, the Aryans having migrated to the subcontinent around 1500 BC from the Russian steppes. Moreover, one of the heroes of modern India who could not be accused of being an agent of the Muslims, Lokmanya Tilak, had accepted in print that the Aryans indeed had come from the Arctic. Well, there was only one way to square the circle: if the Hindus could not go up to the Arctic, then the Arctic must come down to India! And so one of the major intellectuals of the Hindu fundamentalist movement, M. S. Golwalkar, wrote in his book *We*: 'The Arctic home in the Vedas was verily in Hindusthan itself and it was not the Hindus who migrated to that land but the Arctic zone which emigrated and left the Hindus in Hindusthan.' One would not waste space over such nonsense except that Golwalkar's disciples are a powerful influence in Indian politics today, and remain one of the prime causes of the continuing violence between Hindu and Muslim which threatens to rip this country apart.

History was and is presented as a story of centuries of Muslim tyranny. Muslims were 'rapists' and 'murdering hordes', 'our old and bitter enemies', and much else. It is not difficult to see how passions could be roused by such rhetoric, particularly during times of tension. Muslim communalists only helped encourage this view of history. Sir Feroz Khan Noon, who would one day become Prime Minister of Pakistan, used to threaten the Hindus in his speeches during the critical years of 1946 and 1947 that they would be massacred just as Changez Khan had massacred them. Sir Feroz did not know that Changez Khan was not a Muslim at all but a Mongol, whose god was Tengiri, and who killed Muslims in equally large numbers whenever an Islamic kingdom was his target. In an article written in prison in August 1934, Nehru commented: 'There is a common belief among the Hindus that Islam is an intolerant religion and that it has spread by means of the sword. Most of them would mention the names of Changez Khan and Timur and Mahmud of Ghazni [or Ghazna] as examples of Muslim tyrants. I wonder how many know that Changez Khan was not even a Mohammedan or that Timur was as fond of erecting his favourite pyramid of heads in western Asia where Islam flourished, as in India? Or that Mahmud of Ghazni threatened the Khalifa of Baghdad with dire penalties?'

Since half-truths and myths play such an important part in the Hindu–Muslim relation in India, it is necessary to examine the historical record. All the details of fact used below can be found in the standard work, *An Advanced History of India* by R. C. Majumdar, H. C. Raychaudhury and Kalikinkar Datta. I have deliberately used their history since the bias of their interpretation and adjectives is in favour of Hindu fundamentalism. But even by their own narration of facts, it is quite clear that the battles fought in the last thousand years were between kings, not religions. It was the interplay of feudal ambitions, abilities and weaknesses that led to the fall of one dynasty and the rise of another. Religious fervour, if it entered the picture, was only used to the extent that even a modern army uses race to bind together a regiment. There have been hardly any battles, ever since the Muslims came, which can be called purely Hindu–Muslim affairs. There was always a mix in the line-up of the opposing troops.

The first Muslim to come with an army was a young Arab (according to some accounts, he was only seventeen). Nephew and son-in-law of the Governor of Iraq, Muhammad Bin Qasim was sent to punish the Brahmin King of Sind, Dahir, for encouraging pirates to seize Arab ships.

Qasim defeated Dahir in 712, but even in this first encounter between the 'foreign' Arab Muslim and the indigenous Brahmin, Qasim had on his side a number of Buddhist priests and local chiefs who were against Dahir. Of course, this is labelled 'treachery', but the simple truth is that the chiefs saw this merely as the battle between one feudal king and another. The Arabs and their local allies conquered all the area that is now southern Pakistan till they were stopped by the Karakotas in the north, the Chalukyas in the south and the Pratiharas in the east. Soon the Arabs broke from the caliphate and established the independent kingdom of Sind which remained largely untouched by the great tremors in the north.

The great villain in Hindu eyes, an epitome of the evil-Muslim syndrome, is Mahmud of Ghazna, whom Nehru referred to in the article quoted above, and who is still hated for the destruction and loot of the famous temple of Somnath. He came seventeen times to steal the 'wealth of Ind' and each time he took away as much as he could carry. He brought Punjab into the Afghan empire, but his main purpose in life was to keep an insatiable treasury full enough to finance both his frequent campaigns and his patronage of arts and literature. Majumdar, Raychaudhury and Datta describe him thus: 'Sultan Mahmud was undoubtedly one of the greatest military leaders the world has seen. His cool courage, prudence, resourcefulness and other qualities make him one of the most interesting personalities in Asiatic history. In addition to his victorious expeditions in India he had to his credit two memorable campaigns against hostile Turks in the course of which he routed the hosts of Ilak Khan and the Seljuqs. Great as a warrior, the Sultan was no less eminent as a patron of the arts and letters ..., He was neither a missionary for the propagation of his religion in this country nor an architect of empire.' But it is as a violent proselytizer that he is remembered at the mass level, thanks both to the Hindus who were angry at the looting of the Somnath temple, and the Muslims (like Sir Feroz Khan Noon) who called him a great sword of Islam. Mahmud's sword was used only for the greater good of Mahmud, and in that he was no different from other feudal rulers.

The man who first established in Delhi a kingdom ruled by Muslims was an Afghan called Muhammad, from Ghur, a small principality in the south-east of Herat. He was an empire-builder, and whoever stood in his way had to match arms with him. His first success was against the Muslim rulers of Multan in 1175. By 1181, Peshawar and Sialkot had fallen. He then entered into an alliance with a Hindu king, Vijaya

Dev of Jammu, to defeat the Muslim ruler of Lahore, Khusrau Malik. It was only after this that Muhammad Ghori came into conflict with the man who has inspired so much hero-worship, Prithviraj Chauhan, the Rajput ruler of the territory between Delhi and Ajmer.

The two battles between Ghori and Chauhan in 1191 and 1192 are the source of much mythology, thanks partly to the fanciful writing of the British historian, Colonel James Tod. The most powerful northern king at the time was Jaychandra, or Jaichand, who ruled from Kannauj. The handsome Prithviraj is said to have carried away the beautiful daughter of Jaichand, and the bitter father is considered a 'traitor' to Mother India because he is alleged to have invited Ghori to attack Prithviraj Chauhan and take over Delhi. Thus is built the myth that the Indian hero was defeated by the 'marauding Muslim foreigner' only by treachery. Let us dip into our *Advanced History*: 'There is no reason, however, to believe that Jaichand invited Muhammad of Ghur to invade India. The invasion of this country was an almost inevitable corollary to Muhammad's complete victory over the Ghaznavids in the Punjab.' But this is not what schoolchildren are told.

The first encounter between Ghori and Chauhan took place at Tarain, eighty-four miles north of Delhi. Prithviraj, at the head of the Rajput confederacy, had 200,000 horse and 3,000 elephants at his command. Ghori, himself leading the centre, with a wing on either side, was outnumbered and outfought. The wings were driven back from the field, and the centre collapsed when Muhammad was injured after a personal clash with Govind Rai, Prithviraj's brother. The Afghans were pursued for forty miles, but their horses were faster, and they lived to fight the next year. This time Ghori came with 120,000 troops and a different battle plan. Four divisions of 10,000 each were deputed to avoid the elephants and attack the left, the right, the centre and, through a flanking movement, the rear. The battle began at nine in the morning. By the afternoon. Ghori was ready for the *coup de grâce*: he charged with his choicest, and still fresh, cavalry of 12,000 at the centre, and the Rajput edifice collapsed. Prithviraj was caught while escaping, near the river Saraswati, and killed. Thus began Muslim rule in Delhi.

The image of the Muslim as the rapist, as the sex-hungry fiend lusting after Hindu queens who preferred to commit suicide rather than submit to the evil conqueror, begins with the story about that great expansionist who wanted to be a second Alexander, Alauddin Khilji (1296–1316). He was the best of the generals of Jalaluddin Firuz (the man who brought the Ashoka pillar to Delhi). Buoyed by his military victories in the Deccan, Khilji seized power in Delhi through the effective use of the knife, on 19 July 1296. He quickly expanded his empire; by 1297 the Baghela Rajput prince of Gujarat, Rai Karnadeva II, was defeated and his wife Kamala Devi later became the favourite wife of Khilji. Khilji's next target was the fort of Ranthambor, a symbol of Rajput power. It was held by Hamir Deva, who had angered Khilji by giving shelter to the rebels called the 'New Mussalmans'. The fort, defended both by Rajputs and the Muslim rebels, held out, and in the end Khilji himself had to march to secure Ranthambor in July 1301. The Muslims were caught and executed. The Rajputs, in a typical display of their well-known valour, died fighting, while their women committed suicide through sati. A plain enough story. But the folklore is circulated that Khilji lusted after the Rajput princess Padmini and reduced Ranthambor only to seize her. In defeat, says the legend, Padmini preferred to die in sati rather than enter Khilji's harem. What do our historians say? 'If tradition is to be believed, its [the Ranthambor expedition's] immediate cause was his [Khilji's] infatuation for Rana Ratan Singh's queen, Padmini, of exquisite beauty. But this fact is not explicitly mentioned in any contemporary chronicle or inscription.'

It does not matter to the propagandist what the truth about the past is, as long as the present can be poisoned by propaganda. Sometimes the outright lie will do, as in the Khilji story; sometimes selectivity is sufficient. Take the first and third battles of Panipat, at each of which an army came from beyond the Khyber Pass to challenge and defeat Delhi. But who fought whom in these battles? Where was it ever a question of the Muslim invader faced by a Hindu Indian saving the pride of India? Not at all. Or examine the much-trumpeted battle of Haldighati, about which there is the most extraordinary distortion. Let us take a brief look at some of the famous battles whose stories are embedded in the Indian consciousness.

The Chugtai descendant of Changez Khan and Timur, Babar, had only 12,000 men when he entered India through the Khyber Pass and crossed the Indus at Attock – less troops than were under the command of Alexander of Macedon. Babar crossed the river Beas, the last natural barrier before Delhi, on 2 January 1526. Delhi was under the Afghan Ibrahim Lodi, heir of a line which had seized power in 1451 with the accession of Bahlul Khan. (Ibrahim Khan had obviously become an Indian in his habits by now; he is said to have consulted astrologers who predicted victory but removed themselves to a safe place in case their advance information turned out to be wrong.) Babar reached the field of Panipat on 1 April and set up his defences, his key weapon being a park of artillery. Ibrahim Khan, who had allowed Babar to travel four hundred miles without a serious challenge, now brought up 100,000 men, and the battle was joined on 21 April. The Afghans were brave, the Mughals had the skill: planning and artillery won the day. Ibrahim Lodi died fighting. On Friday, 27 April, for the first time a prayer in the name of a great Mughal was offered in the mosques of Delhi. But the Afghans were not totally beaten yet. Ibrahim's brother Mahmud Lodi went to the Rajputs and sought their support. Rana Sangha of Mewar, blind in one eye, crippled in one leg, without one arm, and carrying the scars of eighty-odd wounds acquired in a lifetime of fighting, declared that he would support the claim of Mahmud as the Sultan of Delhi. He organized a great alliance of Rajputs to challenge the usurper Babar. In 1527 Rana Sangha marched with an army including the rulers of Marwar, Amber, Gwalior, Ajmer, Chanderi and 120 lesser Rajput chiefs with 80,000 horse and 500 war elephants. With them were Mahmud Lodi with 10,000 horse, Hasan Khan Mewati with 12,000 horse, and Salahuddin of Raisin with 30,000 horse. Babar's generals panicked when this great host assembled at Kanwaha, a village west of Agra. It was yet another hour in which the future of India rested on the quality of one man's leadership. Using all the oratory and spirit he could summon, Babar persuaded his generals that Delhi could not be surrendered without battle. On 16 March 1527, Babar scattered this army of Rajputs and Afghans, and established what was to blossom into the greatest empire Delhi had known.

These are matters of historical fact. But how do they measure up to the theory of foreign Muslim invader being challenged by patriotic Hindu Indian? They do not. True, Babar was in 1526 both a foreigner and a Muslim, but in the armies ranged against him were Muslims, thousands of whom died fighting him; they or their ancestors had once come from another country but had now settled down. The Chugtais removed the Afghans from power but, unlike the British in 1947, the Afghans did not go 'home'. This country had become their home. Their descendants are still living across the north of India, speaking Bhojpuri or other local dialects. They would be extremely surprised to be called foreigners. As for the battle of Kanwaha, there are people who try to portray it as a war which 'nationalist' Rajput Hindus fought and lost against the foreign Muslim Mughals. But then it is impossible to explain why Muslim Afghans should shed their blood alongside Rajputs in defence of a Hindu India. Since such questions cannot be answered, the facts are often selectively suppressed. This is evident in the work of even a great historian like Jadunath Sarkar. In 1930–40 Sir Jadunath wrote, on commission from Maharaja Sawai Man Singh II, the last ruler of Jaipur state, *A History of Jaipur*; the manuscript was published by Orient Longman for a mass audience in 1984. In his narration of the famous battle of Haldighati, between the forces of the Emperor Akbar and the Maharana of Mewar, Pratap Singh, Sir Jadunath deliberately avoids mentioning that there were Muslim Afghans on the side of Maharana Pratap Singh too. The reason: if he admits that Muslims fought by the side of the Maharana, then he cannot come to the kind of conclusion he does: 'It is the losing side [of Rana Pratap] who have made that yellow defile a haunted holy ground for pilgrims of Indian patriotism.' Haldighati has long been a favourite 'example' of 'Hindu–Indian patriotism' versus 'foreign–Muslim invaders'. The truth completely explodes such a categorization, and proves that it was nothing more than a regional challenge to imperial power.

The battle of Haldighati was fought on 18 June 1576 when the Emperor Akbar asked his famous general Raja Man Singh (a Rajput prince himself) to bring Mewar, which still refused to accept the overlordship of Delhi, to terms. Rana Pratap met the Mughal force, commanded personally by Raja Man Singh, at the end of the narrow, three-mile-long pass through the hills, called Haldighati. Describing the array of the Mewar forces, Sir Jadunath Sarkar writes: 'The Maharana himself led the centre, as was the invariable rule with the commander-in-chief. His right and left wings were respectively commanded by Ram Sah Tonwar and Bida, the Jhala chieftain. The post of the greatest danger at the head of the vanguard, was fittingly taken by Ramdas Rathor, the seventh son of Jaimal, the martyred defender of Chitor.' There is no mention whatsoever that with Rana Pratap was also a body of cavalry under the Afghan Hakim Khan Sur who led the charge that scattered the imperial troops at the beginning of the battle. In fact, while Rana Pratap escaped and survived, Hakim Khan died at Haldighati. R. C. Majumdar in *The Mughal Empire* (Bharatiya Vidya Bhavan, 1974) does, however, deign to admit: 'The Mewar army at the battle of Haldighati was quite formidable and in every way a match for the Mughal army. Evidently a long time must have been spent to raise and equip this army, and get the support of Afghans like Hakim Sur Pathan, who fought for Mewar at Haldighati.' The chapter in which this point is admitted is, however, headlined 'Hindu Resistance

to Muslim Domination'. In such a fashion did historians contribute to
Hindu–Muslim enmity by concealing or misinterpreting the truth. What
really happened at Haldighati?

Three hours after sunrise the battle was joined. With Man Singh at
the head of the imperial force were two other Rajput commanders, Rai
Lon Karan and Raja Jagannath, along with the Barha Sayyids, Ghiyasud-
din and Ali Asaf Khan; the strength of the imperial army was around
10,000. Rana Pratap had 3,000 horse, 2,000 infantry, 100 elephants
and 400 bowmen. Man Singh placed his forces in the classic Mughal
formation: vanguard, centre, right, left, rearguard, and an *iltmish*, or
advance reserve, which could move to help wherever required. Since the
Rana's troops had to come through the narrow pass on to the battlefield, they could not make a proper formation. The first round of the
battle, however, went to Rana Pratap. A charge by Hakim Khan Sur,
the Afghan, put Lon Karan's Rajputs to flight. The imperial army drew
back from the heights to a spot where they could fight on their terms,
a place now known as the Rakta Talao, which means the 'pool of blood'.
Man Singh's tactical sense won the day, the rout being complete after
he was able to hold off the final charge of the Rana's elephants. According to Badayuni, an eyewitness, the Mewar army lost 500 dead, and the
imperialists about 150 killed and 350 wounded. But the popular stories
about Haldighati say that 80,000 of the finest flower of Rajput chivalry
died to protect the honour of Hindu India against the evil Muslim. Apart
from the figures being considerably smaller, there were as many Rajputs
in Akbar's army as there were in Rana Pratap's. But normal political
struggles, whether for regional independence or based on economic
demands, have been converted into religious–national wars. As the
historian Dr Satish Chandra points out in an essay, 'The roots of Hindu
communalism', bigotry 'is carried a stage further by depicting all movements opposed to the government irrespective of their own objective and
social content as Hindu resistance to Muslim tyranny. Thus leaders such
as Rana Pratap and Shivaji who fought for regional independence and
represented certain social classes, are regarded as national heroes fighting
against oppressive foreign rule. From this it is a short distance to argue
that the entire period of Muslim rule in India was foreign rule and that
even an Akbar or a Dara [Shikoh] could not change its basic character.'

Shivaji is an important figure in the pantheon, since it is put out that
it was under this Maratha chieftain that the martial revival of Hinduism
truly began. The great advantage that Shivaji has over Rana Pratap,

his rival for the messiahdom of Hindu resurgence, is that the man Shivaji challenged, Aurangzeb, can easily fit the label of Muslim oppressor. Rana Pratap's foe, on the other hand, was the great and liberal Emperor Akbar. V. D. Savarkar summed up Shivaji's place in what might be called the 'communal history of India' in his address to the Hindu Mahasabha in the late thirties: 'Thousands upon thousands, princes and peasants alike, revolted and rose as Hindus under Hindu flags and fought and fell in fighting against their non-Hindu foes. Till at last Shivaji was born, the hour of Hindu triumph was struck, the day of Moslem supremacy set.' It is perfectly true that Shivaji announced the *Hindu Padshahi* ('the Hindu Empire') and was crowned *Chhatrapati* ('Lord of the Umbrella', or 'King of Kings') on 16 June 1674, but there is no evidence to suggest that he wanted to drive all the Muslims out of India because he felt they were foreign oppressors. A few decades later, Ranjit Singh built a Khalsa Sikh kingdom, but it was not anti-Hindu or anti-Muslim for that. Shivaji was a true genius who inspired the Marathas to become the dominant power of the eighteenth century, but to convert his war against the Mughals into a war against the Muslims is the work of mischievous interpreters. In fact, very often he fought in alliance with a Muslim feudal. Towards the end of his life, the Sultan of neighbouring Golcunda was his greatest ally in their common cause against Aurangzeb – an emperor who, in fact, expended far more of his time, energy and money in wars against the Muslim rulers of Bijapur and Golcunda than he did against the Marathas. Neither can we say that the Marathas considered the Mughals untouchable. When Aurangzeb's son Prince Akbar revolted, his chief ally was Shambhuji, Shivaji's son. And for a while, Shivaji was even an accepted noble in Aurangzeb's court.

Shahji, Shivaji's father, began as a trooper in the army of the Sultan of Ahmadnagar. His abilities led to high office. In 1636, he entered the service of Bijapur state. Shivaji had been born by then, but Shahji had left his wife Jija Bai and gone to his *jagir* – his estate – in Bijapur with a second wife. Jija Bai was descended from the Yadava rulers of Devagiri; from his father's side Shivaji could claim descent from the famous Sisodia Rajputs of Mewar. It was good fighting tradition that Shivaji inherited, and very early he showed that he was more than a cut above the ordinary. In 1646 he captured the fortress of Torna, and then built the fort of Rajgarh nearby to create a base for expansion. He strung a chain of forts from which he harassed Bijapur and constructed an empire. By January 1656 he had annexed Javli (which doubled his revenue) by having its ruler Chandra Rao murdered. He now could think of taking on the Mughals, and his first skirmish with them came in 1657.

In 1659 came the event which is still controversial. The Sultan of Bijapur sent his general, Afzal Khan, against Shivaji. At a peace conference between them, arranged by a Brahmin mediator, Shivaji killed Afzal Khan with hidden steel claws. Shivaji's protagonists say that he was only acting in self-defence; others, that he had behaved treacherously. The more important point perhaps is that despite all this turmoil and war, Shivaji's father remained a senior officer in the Bijapur court. And it was he who helped organize a truce between Bijapur and Shivaji when the Mughal army under Shaista Khan was sent by Aurangzeb to check this rising Maratha power. Quite clearly Shivaji did not consider the Sultan of Bijapur to be a 'foreigner' who was enslaving the Hindus of India; no, he was just another piece of middling strength on the complicated political chessboard of India. Shaista Khan, despite his early successes, failed to subdue Shivaji.

Now Aurangzeb sent his best general to bring the Marathas to heel. And this man was not a vicious Muslim bigot, but a Rajput, in the best traditions. Mirza Raja Jai Singh, of Amber, led a successful expeditionary force against Shivaji in 1665. On 22 June the Mughals were given 23 of Shivaji's 35 forts, and a promise of 5,000 cavalry for the Mughal army – in fact, Shivaji himself supported the Mughals in their next war with Bijapur. Shivaji was made a Raja by Aurangzeb and given a *jagir* in Berar and the rank of a noble commanding 5,000 horse. However, Shivaji felt that this rank was an insult to his true status; he should have been given higher honours. Suspecting that he might be nothing more than a glorified prisoner in Delhi, he escaped to his forts.

For three years there was peace with the Mughals, but by 1670 Shivaji was back on the victory trail. By 1674 he had acquired the political strength to declare himself *Chhatrapati*, and by the time he died on 14 April 1680 he had left behind a strong empire. It is an irony that a man of Shivaji's personal commitment to equality and friendship with other communities (a trait which his Maratha successors did not necessarily share) should become a symbol of Hindu militancy. Shivaji was a brilliant commander who established a regional power, to do which he had to challenge Delhi, irrespective of who sat on the throne there. There were Muslims among his senior army officers. (At the crucial third battle of Panipat, against the Afghan Ahmed Shah Abdali, the Maratha artillery and left flank were under Ibrahim Khan Gardi; the tradition had not broken.)

The misinterpretation of Shivaji's success is largely because Shivaji was the first Hindu ruler able to hold his own against, and then to defeat, the near-invincible joint Muslim–Rajput imperial Mughal armies, which were a product of the great alliance. Shivaji did this by creating a camaraderie, a sense of unity and equality, which was rarely evident in the Hindu armies of the past. One of the many troublesome questions of Indian history is how, time after time, could the smaller armies, led by Muslims, which had travelled hundreds of miles from their base in difficult campaigns, with almost contemptuous ease smash the much larger armies they faced, either along the way or at Delhi. Vincent Smith offers an answer in *The Oxford History of India*: 'The Hindu strategy and tactics were old-fashioned, based on ancient textbooks which took no account of foreign methods, and the unity of command on the Indian side was always more or less hampered by tribal, sectarian and caste divisions.'

9
'Glory to Mother Bharat'

That the Indian caste system crucially affected military efficiency against foreign foes is an unverified viewpoint, but an interesting and logical one. Hindu society was certainly vulnerable because of its caste system, which left it prone not only to military conquest but also to proselytization. The rigid structure of the army was only a mirror of the rigidity of the social structure. It was the inherent weakness of Hinduism, and not any great sabre-rattling, that made one-third of India Muslim. While there was undoubtedly an element of forced conversion, or the simple lure of the religion of the dominant ruling class, this cannot adequately explain the extent and the strength of the conversions to Islam. The men who came to conquer became in fact immigrants, settling on the land and bringing their belief and life-style with them. They mingled with the people to a degree which simply could not be a part of political control. Example, and persuasion by the Sufis, attracted those at the lower end of the social scale, in particular. There is recognition of this reality today; when a present-day leader like Charan Singh (who became Prime Minister for a brief while at the fag-end of the Janata phase) advocates that those who consciously stretch across the caste barriers (for instance, through marriage) must be rewarded by government jobs, it is essentially an effort to protect Hindu society from further collapse. Sheikh Abdullah used repeatedly to say that if there had been no caste system in India, there might have been no conversions in India either.

It is simple enough to see how there can be no unity among Hindus as long as there continues to be faith in the caste system. One of the reasons why Hindu fundamentalist organizations cannot make much headway in terms of the popular vote is precisely because the 82.72 per cent of the country who accept the denomination are only census Hindus. The untouchables and the tribals are antagonistic to caste Hindu society, and not only because of economic exploitation. The social humiliation is such that they are made to live at a deliberate distance in rural India.

The differences and subdifferences within the range of the caste system, from the nobility of the Brahmin and the Thakur to the fringes of the barely touchable lower castes, are the nightmare of a politician attempting to build a coalition broad enough to vote him or her into power. The fascination of the 'golden ancient Hindu society' is really restricted to the few castes on the top of the heap. It is not in the least surprising, therefore, that the leadership of the most powerful Hindu organization in the country, which fantasizes about creating a Hindu kingdom from Afghanistan to Burma, and whose leaders were men like Golwalkar and Savarkar, is a virtual monopoly of Brahmins. This is the Rashtriya Swayamsevak Sangh, popularly called the RSS.

'The RSS line is very clear. It is a *supra*-party, paramilitary organization which wants to take over the state and the nation and establish an authoritarian regime in the manner of the Nazi leaders,' wrote the ideologue and leader of the Janata Party, Madhu Limaye, in an article in *Sunday* on 10 June 1979 – just before the Janata government in Delhi fell because it would not formally sever connections with the RSS. Limaye was only echoing something which Gandhi had said long ago. According to his secretary Pyarelal, Gandhi had described the RSS as a 'communal body with a totalitarian outlook' and compared them to the Nazis and Fascists. And it all began when in the 1920s Gandhi took the Congress firmly towards secularism.

Keshav Hedgewar was born on 1 April 1889, the third son of a Brahmin priest, Baliram Hedgewar, from the village of Kundkurti in the Deccan. His parents died by 1902, and his elder brother Mahadev began to look after the family. It was not a happy childhood; the elder brother constantly beat up the younger. Determined to be a doctor, Keshav joined the Calcutta Medical College. His interest in politics was encouraged by the Maharashtrian leader Dr B. S. Moonje who had also helped him financially during his student days. Men like Moonje were deeply upset at the ideological turn that Gandhi was giving to the Congress in the 1920s. Unable in the end to challenge Gandhi on the Congress platform, they began thinking of setting up organizations which would more correctly reflect their dream of a free India primarily serving the interests of the Hindus. They were angered at the thought that after all these centuries of Muslim rule, Gandhi was once again going to 'surrender' to the Muslims and treat them as equal citizens of this Hindu land.

Explaining why the RSS was started, Hedgewar's biographer C. P. Bhishikar writes: 'Doctorji [Hedgewar] thought deeply over a long period

on the question of national identity ... Why should there be any confusion about nationhood in Hindustan? ... Why have strange expressions
like nationalist Mussalman and nationalist Christian come into currency?'
The RSS anger was well-focused: the greatest danger to Hindu nationalism came from the 'snakes', Hedgewar's term for the Muslims. An official
publication of the RSS, *Sri Guruji, The Man and his Mission*, explains:
'It became evident that Hindus were the nation in Bharat and that
Hindutva was *Rashtriyatva* [that is, 'Hinduism' was 'nationalism'; incidentally Jinnah agreed that Hindus were a separate nation] ... The agony of
the great soul [of Hedgewar] expressed itself in the formation of the
Rashtriya Swayamsevak Sangh. With four friends he started the day-to-
day programme of the RSS. The great day was the auspicious Vijay
Dashami day of 1925.'

The five friends who started the RSS were Dr B. S. Moonje, Dr L. V.
Paranjpe, Dr Tholkar, Babarao Savarkar and Dr Hedgewar himself. There
was an initial hitch about the name. In 1921 the Congress had begun
an organization by a similar name; it had become defunct, but the idea
of any shadow of the hated Congress falling on this new, pure effort was
anathema. 'Hindu Swayamsevak Sangh' was suggested as an alternative,
but Hedgewar insisted on the concept of nationalism being included in
the title, and so the RSS it was. Inevitably the RSS first acquired a
public reputation as the 'saviour' of the Hindus after its role in the Hindu–
Muslim riots in Nagpur, in September 1927.

The RSS kept away from the independence struggle because it had
only contempt and hatred for the man leading it: Gandhi. In fact, some
people have suspected the RSS of helping the British against Gandhi.
But the RSS came into its own during the communal riots. By 1945
it had 10,000 cadres and was rich enough to build its headquarters,
the Hedgewar Bhawan, in less than a year. In the madness of the pre-
partition phase there was even an RSS wing within the highest echelons
of government, in the Imperial Civil Service, most of whose Indian recruits
were Oxbridge graduates. The RSS actually believed that power was
within its grasp, not through conventional democracy, but through its
control of the ruling system. Levers, not numbers, were its target. And
the RSS could not believe that the British would actually surrender power
to the khadi-clad Congressmen. Des Raj Goyal, an ex-RSS man, recalls
in his informative book *RSS* (Radha Krishna Prakashan, New Delhi) that
he was present at a cadre meeting addressed by Hedgewar's successor,
Guru Golwalkar. When asked what would be the RSS role after the British

left India, Golwalkar replied with an ironic laugh, 'Do you believe that the British will quit? The nincompoops into whose hands they are giving the reins of government will not be able to hold on even for two months.'

In 1939 the RSS formally introduced a Sanskrit prayer for its members:

O affectionate Motherland I bow to you eternally
O land of the Hindus you have reared in comfort
O sacred, good land, I dedicate my being to you
I bow before you again and again.
Mighty God, we the integral members of the Hindu Rashtra salute you reverently.

Before a member is admitted to the sacred fold of the RSS, he must take this oath: 'In the name of the omnipotent God and my forefathers I solemnly swear that I am becoming a member of the RSS to promote the Hindu religion, Hindu society and Hindu culture and thereby achieve the true greatness of the country of Bharat. I shall do the work of the Sangh honestly, without thought of gain, with my body, mind and soul, and never break this oath all my life. Glory to Mother Bharat.'

The RSS suffered a set-back in 1948; even Sardar Patel could not over-look a crime it had inspired – the assassination of the Mahatma. Home Minister Sardar Patel banned the RSS as 'in practice members of the RSS have not adhered to their professed ideals. The objectionable and even harmful activities of the Sangh have, however, continued unabated and the cult of violence sponsored and inspired by the activities of the Sangh has claimed many victims. The latest and most precious to fall was Gandhiji himself.' The ban was lifted in July 1949 when the RSS argued that nothing had been legally proved against it. But now it agreed to function 'under a written and published Constitution, restricting its activities to the cultural sphere, abjuring violence and secrecy, professing loyalty to the Constitution of India and the national flag, and providing for a democratic organization'. When the Constitution was published, Article 5 said: 'While recognizing the duty of every citizen to be loyal to and to respect the state flag, the Sangh has, as its flag, the Bhagwadhwaj, the age-old symbol of Hindu culture.' And Article 6 (a) said that only a 'male Hindu of eighteen years or more' could become a member of the RSS.

The next time that the RSS was banned was when, after the declaration of the Emergency, Mrs Indira Gandhi banned all communal organizations, including the RSS and the Jamaat-e-Islami. Later, after the Emergency had been lifted, the RSS would pretend to have played a very brave role during this crucial period. But the truth was different.

10
A Phenomenon of Democracy

The then chief of the RSS, Madhukar Dattatraya Deoras, was under arrest when the RSS was banned on 4 July 1975. From jail, the RSS chief began pleading for a compromise; the evidence came tumbling out later when letters sent by the RSS chief to the government during the Emergency were leaked. He sent the first letter to Mrs Gandhi under the thin pretext of wanting to comment on her Independence Day broadcast to the nation. 'I listened,' wrote Deoras, 'with rapt attention to your well-balanced speech to the nation relayed from All-India Radio, so I took the opportunity to write to you.' After a long sermon on how the RSS was a pure, cultural outfit with no interest in politics and nothing but the best of intentions towards Muslims and Christians, the letter ended with the comment that it would be a source of immense pleasure for Deoras to meet Mrs Gandhi. Another letter congratulated Mrs Gandhi on her victory in the Supreme Court absolving her of any wrongdoing in the 1971 elections, and there was an offer to put 100,000 RSS volunteers at the command of Mrs Gandhi so that the nation could prosper. RSS periodicals began to praise Mrs Gandhi and her son Sanjay Gandhi. Later, of course, when the Janata won the 1977 elections, the RSS went about claiming that it was the true hero of the Emergency struggle. It used the Janata rule very effectively to try to place its sympathizers in key positions. Conscious of the role of false history, pro-RSS politicians put pressure on the Janata government to remove books by honest historians, like Romila Thapar, from the approved list for educational institutions. They failed, but not for lack of trying. Eventually, the pressures they created, including their aggressive role in the riots against Muslims, literally blew the government apart.

But the reason why the RSS surrendered so meekly during the Emergency was the nature of its support base. While the Brahmins and the Thakurs might extend their sympathy for the ambitions of the RSS, the politics of these two castes remain by and large linked to national parties with a plural base. The RSS gets its hard core and its soft core alike from the urban middle class, and in particular the petty bourgeoisie: in fact, in many areas the RSS is known as the 'Bania, or traders', party'. It was these traders who got frightened of government repression, and particularly of tax raids. The 'trader' image does not help the RSS since it drives away the peasantry. But the RSS cannot escape this image because it is directly related to the pattern of Muslim life in India.

Muslims form over 11 per cent of India's population, but nowhere, apart from Jammu and Kashmir, and the territorially insignificant island of Lakshadweep, are they in a majority. In Kashmir, 6 districts contain most of the state's 66 per cent Muslims. But out of the 356 other districts of India only 2 more, Murshidabad in West Bengal and the newly created Malappuram in Kerala, have Muslim majorities. In 234 districts Muslims are less than 10 per cent of the population. In only 30 districts are they more than 20 per cent; nearly half the Muslim population lives in the three huge states of Uttar Pradesh, Bihar and Bengal. While the reasons are historical, the thin spread tends to produce greater insecurity and to make the community less self-confident than it might have been.

Moreover, Muslim economic power has traditionally been limited to land. The landed classes of Uttar Pradesh and their companion bureaucrats went to Pakistan in 1947. The Muslims who were left behind were the smaller peasantry, the landless labourers, the artisans in the villages, and the lower middle class in the cities. Muslims have never had a capitalist class, although they lived in much higher numbers in the urban areas. According to the 1971 census, 16.21 per cent of the urban population of India was Muslim, whereas the community formed only 9.96 per cent of the rural population. Partition was a hard blow to the Muslim in democratic India. In the villages the protection of the landlord disappeared, while the artisan simply could not match the competition of the new factories – he had neither the entrepreneurial ability nor the advantage of finance. In the urban areas, the Muslim had to face severe discrimination in an already overcrowded job market controlled by either Bania capital or an unsympathetic bureaucracy. While peaceful survival, even if bleak, was possible in the rural areas, life was ruthless and competitive in the urban areas, particularly in the small town. And the Muslim had no option but to create his own employment through craft or trade. Competition with the Hindu petty bourgeoisie inevitably took a communal and violent turn in towns of small or medium size, like Aligarh,

Jamshedpur, Jabalpur, Ahmadabad, Moradabad or Bhiwandi, which became chronically prone to religious violence. In the larger port cities, particularly in Calcutta and Bombay, the Muslim youth had a second opportunity: they became employees in the flourishing business of smuggling, under the protection of Muslim underworld leaders who were the front men of an extensive black economy. For the Hindu petty bourgeoisie in the inland towns the RSS became a convenient protection force, where economic interest could be disguised behind a larger purpose which would and did attract the support both of the youth committed to a Hindu India and of the simple lumpenproletariat. The Muslims had no real answer to this, since they could not expect the quiet patronage of the authorities for parallel organizations.

As far as powerful jobs were concerned, Muslims simply did not have them for one reason or another, including their inhibitions about the kind of education required in this society nudged along by a sluggish mixed economy and dominated by conservative interests. While statistics never convey the whole truth, they do often show the way to the truth. Syed Shahabuddin, a foreign service officer who gave up a brilliant career to join politics and is now general secretary of the Janata Party, often publishes indicative statistics in a 'monthly journal of reference, research and documentation' which he brings out, *Muslim India*. As of the beginning of 1981, there were only 116 Muslims out of the total of 3,883 Indian Administrative Service officers in the country. The proportion in the Indian Police Service was similar: 50 out of 1,753. There were just 2,479 Muslims among the 113,772 officers of nationalized banks. The proportion in Central government offices and state government offices was 4.41 and 6.01 per cent. In the judicial services the community had 303 officers out of 4,898. The only place where the Muslims had a share proportionate to their population was in the huge public-sector under-takings of both the state and Central governments, where there were 51,755 Muslim officers out of a total of 476,972. A random survey of senior Muslim employees in the private sector did not sound very en-couraging either: Pond's India Ltd, 1 out of 115; DCM, 2 out of 987; Brooke Bond, 14 out of 673; ITC, 17 out of 966; J. K. Synthetics, 5 out of 536; Ambalal Sarabhai, 5 out of 628 (the figures were obtained from the annual general reports of the companies, which have to list the salaries of senior employees).

The economic problems of Muslims have been caused both by default and neglect – default on the part of the Muslims, and neglect by the country. The post-independence Muslim leadership in India was in either confusion or depression. Congressmen were depressed, while those Muslim League leaders who found themselves left behind began to rant in despair. A typical example is the statement made by Latifur Rahman, leader of the Muslim League in the Orissa Assembly, on 25 September 1947: 'The Mussalmans of the Indian Union now realize that they have committed a blunder in supporting the movement for Pakistan ... Let us now forget the two-nation theory and owe allegiance to the Indian Union inasmuch as in spite of the platitudes of the Pakistanis they cannot do anything for our safety and it would be futile for us to look up to them for protection.' At the very top of the list of priorities was safety, allied to protection from the extreme but understandable anger of the refugees and the local Hindus. Gandhi had said too often that he would rather die than see his India in the grip of such violence; on 30 January 1948 he paid the price. But that death did bring about what he had spent his life trying to achieve: it ended the madness. There was a pause long enough for Muslims to begin to pick up the pieces. But the important nationalist Muslim leaders could not find the energy or time to map out the future. The three who could have led the revival of the community were Maulana Azad, Rafi Kidwai and Sheikh Abdullah. The Sheikh remained in Kashmir; Rafi Ahmed Kidwai died too soon, and the Maulana followed a little after. The ruling party tended to promote those Muslims who could find a balance between its need for their vote and the Muslim's need for help. The simplest way of doing so was to ignore the difficult business of economic needs and concentrate on the protection of identity and religious rights. The stress, therefore, was on organizing the community to withstand attacks on its person, on its religious law, the Muslim Personal Law, and on its institutions, like schools and *wakf* foundations. Protection of Urdu became a matter of life and death, even as in reaction the extremist Hindus made its destruction their ambition. (In the process, of course, a beautiful language was injured.) The small number of educated and financially confident Muslims still had half an eye on Pakistan; the most famous instance is perhaps Asif Iqbal, the cricketer who went on to captain Pakistan. He started his career as a member of the Hyderabad state cricket team and played up to Ranji Trophy level before migrating to Pakistan in the mid sixties. Educationally, the mass of Muslims could not get out of the Urdu-school syndrome. Maulana Azad urged them not to treat Hindi as a hostile language but to get to terms with it, as it would only be in their own interest to do so. The advice was not heeded. And English was beyond the means of this economically depressed community, even if it might have been within the range of its ambition.

If perhaps a date has to be given for the change in attitudes it is 1971, the year Pakistan died. By this time, the post-1947 generation ('Midnight's Children') was also coming of age. There was no shortage of problems that it had to face, but it started off with one advantage: it did not have to feel any guilt about partitioning the country. And it soon made it clear that it was not going meekly to accept bullying either. It knew that it would have to live and toil in the place where it was born: both the dream and the nightmare were over. Only the hard business of ensuring the survival of a minority with honour and a full stomach remained. But how was the full stomach going to come about, particularly when the economy could not fully sustain the aspirations of the majority? The only way was self-help, and this involved greater participation in the democratic process, the election to power of those people who might be able to respond to the real needs of the Muslims. Obviously this could not happen overnight; this has to be a long process. But one crucial thing that happened was that the Muslim vote was no longer tucked in the pocket of the Congress. The vote for the Congress had been the protection money Muslims paid in return for the promise of security. The moment they began to switch their vote according to their needs they also became a more integral part of the only process which could rescue them from their plight.

In 1968, the Congress leader Humayun Kabir, delivering the Azad Memorial lecture at Osmania University, said: 'As industrialization develops, as economic prosperity grows, cases of unfairness and discrimination will we hope gradually be eliminated.' And then he made what was the essential point: 'Where there is no democracy, the question of minorities as such cannot arise. If the state is totalitarian, or autocratic, or monarchic, the voice of the dominant authority will be supreme. But in a democracy each element has a claim and, what is more important, the right to preserve its identity ... Minorities are thus essentially a phenomenon of democracy.' Assimilation, participation, trust, confidence, and then the growth and development of Indian Muslims will once again take the same course that Indian democracy takes.

*

On 15 August 1947 India's existence was threatened in many ways. But there were five points at which the map could yet have been altered. There was the small state of Junagadh, with its Hindu majority and a quirky Muslim ruler who wanted to go to Pakistan; within weeks of independence he left for Pakistan with his dogs (leaving his wives behind). There was the large state of Hyderabad, with its Hindu majority and its obstinate Muslim ruler who wanted independence and had warplanes stationed in Pakistan ready to fight India; within some months he, too, gave up his ambitions. In the south, next door to Hyderabad, there grew a secessionist movement in Tamil Nadu. In the north, the Sikhs began demanding self-rule and a home of their own. And to the north of Punjab, the promise of a secular Kashmir soured as doubt and ill will combined to put Sheikh Abdullah in jail.

In 1963, the Tamils abandoned their secessionist ideas, and by 1967 took over power in their state with such a firm grasp that at the time of writing they have not yet surrendered it. In 1966, the Sikh leaders announced jubilantly that their problems had been solved with the formation of the Sikh-majority Punjab. In 1975, Sheikh Abdullah accepted that the accession of Kashmir to India was final, and he died in 1982 as an elected leader of a state of India, with the Indian tricolour draped across his body.

But by the 1980s, questions are stirring again. In Kashmir, the concept of self-rule has again received a jolt. In Punjab, drift and mischief allowed a dangerous extremist, Jarnail Singh Bhindranwale, to hurt not only the country but also the Sikhs he wanted to free. Where now? The answer will lie in the way democracy unwinds, in the experience of the people, and in whether their anger can be absorbed (as it once was in the fifties and sixties) and their passion converted into productive participation. India cannot be controlled by the forces of law and order until the people themselves vote for the law and the people themselves contribute to the order. The success so far quite outweighs the *quantum* of failure. As for the future, there are always two ways of looking at the same evidence, two paths that can be traced with the same material.

In 1949 Maulana Abul Kalam Azad went to deliver the convocation address at Aligarh Muslim University, the institution which could have justly claimed that it did as much as Jinnah to create Pakistan. Said the Maulana who refused to bargain with his birthright as an Indian: 'I am not aware what the state of your minds is today, nor in what colours the future appears to you. Does it bring to you the message of closing doors or of opening gates that introduce you to new vistas of experience? I do not know what visions are before you, but I will tell you what visions I see. In the words of the Persian poet,

'*Tafawut ast main-i-shanidan-i-man-o-to*
Tu bastan-i-dar, o, man fatahe-bab me shanwam

'What you and I hear are different:
You hear the sound of closing doors,
But I of doors that open.'

Index

MORE ABOUT PENGUINS, PELICANS
AND PUFFINS

For further information about books available from Penguins please write to Dept EP, Penguin Books Ltd, Harmondsworth, Middlesex UB7 0DA.

In the U.S.A.: For a complete list of books available from Penguins in the United States write to Dept DG, Penguin Books, 299 Murray Hill Parkway, East Rutherford, New Jersey 07073.

In Canada: For a complete list of books available from Penguins in Canada write to Penguin Books Canada Ltd, 2801 John Street, Markham, Ontario L3R 1B4.

In Australia: For a complete list of books available from Penguins in Australia write to the Marketing Department, Penguin Books Australia Ltd, P.O. Box 257, Ringwood, Victoria 3134.

In New Zealand: For a complete list of books available from Penguins in New Zealand write to the Marketing Department, Penguin Books (N.Z.) Ltd, Private Bag, Takapuna, Auckland 9.

In India: For a complete list of books available from Penguins in India write to Penguin Overseas Ltd, 706 Eros Apartments, 56 Nehru Place, New Delhi 110019.

Published in Penguins

AN AUTOBIOGRAPHY
or The Story of My Experiments with Truth
M. K. Gandhi

'I have nothing new to teach the world. Truth and non-violence are as old as hills.'

Mahatma Gandhi's aim in writing this autobiography was to give an account of his spiritual progress towards truth. Absolute Truth is his sovereign principle and non-violence the method of pursuing it. In politics it meant freedom from foreign domination, within Hindu society it was the breaking down of barriers raised by caste and custom, in society it was living close to nature.

Written in 1925 under the title *The Story of My Experiments with Truth*, his work describes the practical application of his beliefs. The implementation of his doctrine, Gandhi believed, would result in a loose federation of village republics, freed forever from British control and influence.

Gandhi succeeded in uniting India in a national movement and did as much in the first half of the twentieth century as any other single individual to change the course of history.

'His early life described vividly and meticulously' – Percival Spear in *A History of India*

Published in Pelicans

A HISTORY OF INDIA

VOLUME ONE

Romila Thapar

The first volume of this history traces the evolution of India before contact with modern Europe was established in the sixteenth century. Romila Thapar is the Reader in History at the University of Delhi: her account of the development of India's social and economic structure is arranged within a framework of the principal political and dynastic events. Her narrative covers some 2,500 years of India's history, from the establishment of Aryan culture in about 1000 B.C. to the coming of the Mughuls in A.D. 1526 and the first appearance of European trading companies. In particular she deals interestingly with the many manifestations of Indian culture, as seen in religion, art, and literature, in ideas and institutions.

Published in Pelicans

A HISTORY OF INDIA

VOLUME TWO

Percival Spear

It is the aim of this book to relate the history of the Indian people as a whole, and to make plain the unity of texture in the development of Indian society from the Mughal period to the reign of Nehru.

Dr Spear, a specialist in Indian history, takes the unusual and illuminating approach of dealing with the Mughal and British periods together in one volume, on the principle of continuity. He views the Mughal rule as a preparation and a precondition for the modern age ushered in by the British Raj as a harbinger to India of western civilization, which precipitated the transformation of India that is still in progress.

Published in Penguin Classics

THE BHAGAVAD GITA

Translated by Juan Mascaró

The eighteen chapters of the Bhagavad Gita (*c.* 500 B.C.), the glory of Sanskrit literature, encompass the whole spiritual struggle of a human soul, and the three central themes of this immortal poem – Love, Light and Life – arise from the symphonic vision of God in all things and of all things in God.

'The task of truly translating such a work is indeed formidable. To hope for success in it the translator must at least possess three qualities. He must be an artist in words as well as a Sanskrit scholar, and above all, perhaps, he must be deeply sympathetic with the spirit of the original. Mr Mascaró has succeeded so well because he possesses all these qualifications' – *The Times Literary Supplement*

Published in Penguins

ACT OF DARKNESS
Francis King

Only murder a young throat slit in peculiarly horrific circumstances could have detonated the atmosphere of langour and profound sexual unease in the Thompson household.

Francis King's glittering thriller opens in India during the 1930s, at the lush summer villa of the Thompson family. Father, stepmother, daughter, governess, ayah – the whole shocked family are under suspicion. A 'confession' is made.

But in Francis King's hands the spiciest of evil motives are merely decoys, and the truth seems to wink and slither forever out of reach . . .

'So beautifully written that one is reluctant to reveal who is murdered, let alone who dunnit . . . brilliantly successful' Auberon Waugh in the *Daily Mail*

'Dark, lurid and shattering . . . he is a master novelist' Melvyn Bragg in *Punch*

'There is no denying its compulsive, convulsive grip' Christopher Wordsworth in the *Guardian*

'Unputdownable' Paul Bailey in the *Standard*

Published in Penguins

THE KINGDOM BY THE SEA
Paul Theroux

Paul Theroux's round-Britain travelogue is funny, perceptive and, said the *Sunday Times*, 'best avoided by patriots with high blood pressure ...'

After eleven years living as an American in London, Theroux set out to travel clockwise round the coast and find out what Britain and the British are really like. It was 1982, the summer of the Falklands War and the Royal Baby, and the ideal time, he found, to surprise the British into talking about themselves. The result is vivid, and – as you'd expect from the author of *The Great Railway Bazaar* – absolutely riveting reading.

'Theroux is appalled and he admires ... he describes it all brilliantly and honestly' – Anthony Burgess in the *Observer*

'Fascinating ... Paul Theroux is perhaps the best travel writer around' – *Newsweek*

A PASSAGE TO INDIA

E. M. Forster

'That Marabar Case' was an event which threw the city of Chandrapore into a fever of racial feeling. Miss Quested, on a visit from England to the man she expected to marry, showed an interest in Indian ways of life which was frowned upon by the sun-baked British community. And the prejudice which most of them felt and expressed against any social contacts between the British and the Indians appeared, at first, to be justified when she returned, alone and distressed, from an excursion to the caves in the company of a young Indian doctor. He was arrested on a charge of attempted assault, but when the case came to trial Miss Quested withdrew her accusation and the doctor was set free. Was she the victim of an hallucination, a complex, an unidentified intruder, or what? In this dramatic story E. M. Forster depicts, with sympathy and discernment, the complicated Oriental reaction to British rule in India, and reveals the conflict of temperament and tradition involved in that relationship.